Java Performance and Scalability

A Quantitative Approach

Henry H. Liu

PerfMath

ISBN-13: 978-1482348019
ISBN-10: 1482348012

10 9 8 7 6 5 4 3 2 1

20151012

To My Family

Contents

LIST OF PROGRAMS AND SCRIPTS .... **XI**

TABLE OF FIGURES .... **XIV**

PREFACE .... **XXIII**

WHY THIS BOOK XXIII

WHOM THIS BOOK IS FOR XXIV

HOW THIS BOOK IS ORGANIZED XXIV

SOFTWARE AND HARDWARE XXV

HOW TO USE THIS BOOK XXV

TYPOGRAPHIC CONVENTIONS XXV

HOW TO REACH THE AUTHOR XXVI

THE BOOK'S WEB SITE XXVI

ACKNOWLEDGEMENTS .... **XXVII**

PART I JAVA PERFORMANCE AND SCALABILITY: BASICS **1**

1 SOFTWARE PERFORMANCE AND SCALABILITY **3**

1.1 PERFORMANCE AND SCALABILITY METRICS 3

1.1.1 An Analogy between Electrical Circuits and Computer Systems *4*

1.1.2 Ohm's Law versus Little's Law *5*

1.2 A PRIMER ON QUEUING THEORY 5

1.2.1 Response Time Performance Laws *6*

1.2.2 The Throughput Performance Law *8*

1.2.3 Jackson's Theorem *8*

1.3 A REAL WORLD CASE STUDY 10

1.3.1 Test Environment *10*

1.3.2 CPU as a Critical Performance Factor *11*

1.3.3 Hyper-Threaded or Non-Hyper-Threaded *14*

1.4 PERFORMANCE VERSUS SCALABILITY 15

1.5 LINEAR SCALABILITY? 18

1.6 SYSTEM PERFORMANCE COUNTERS 19

1.6.1 Windows *19*

1.6.2 Linux *22*

1.7 SUMMARY 24

EXERCISES 25

REFERENCES 25

2 COMPUTER HARDWARE ARCHITECTURE 27

2.1 HISTORY OF INTEL PROCESSORS 28

2.1.1 4-bit to 32-bit computing *29*

2.1.2 CPU GHz racing *30*

2.1.3 Multicore processors *31*

2.2 INTERNALS OF THE INTEL 80386 MICROPROCESSORS 32

2.3 PERFORMANCE FEATURES OF THE INTEL CORE I7 PROCESSORS 35

2.3.1 Intel's New Microarchitecture *35*

2.3.2 Intel's QuickPath Interconnect Technology *36*

2.3.3 Intel's Turbo Boost Technology *37*

2.3.4 Smart L3 Cache ... *38*

2.3.5 Hyper-Threading Re-Introduced ... *38*

2.4 CPU BENCHMARKING ... 39

2.5 SUMMARY ... 41

EXERCISES ... 41

REFERENCES ... 41

3 JAVA VIRTUAL MACHINE FUNDAMENTALS ... 43

3.1 JAVA VIRTUAL MACHINES (JVMS) ... 45

3.1.1 Overview ... *45*

3.1.2 Java Program Execution ... *46*

3.1.3 JVM Runtime Data Areas ... *47*

3.1.4 JVM Instruction Set ... *48*

3.1.5 The HotSpot JVM ... *51*

3.2 JAVA MEMORY MANAGEMENT ... 51

3.3 A SCALAR GARBAGE COLLECTION ALGORITHM ... 52

3.3.1 Reference Counting ... *52*

3.3.2 Cyclic Reference Structures ... *53*

3.4 VECTORIAL GARBAGE COLLECTION ALGORITHMS ... 54

3.4.1 Simple Mark-and-Sweep ... *55*

3.4.2 Tri-Colour Marking ... *56*

3.5 IMPLEMENTATION STRATEGIES ... 58

3.5.1 Serial versus Parallel ... *59*

3.5.2 Non-Compacting versus Compacting versus Copying ... *59*

3.5.3 Stop-and-Copy (or Two Space Collection) versus Concurrent ... *61*

3.5.4 Generational Strategy ... *62*

3.5.5 Incremental strategy ... *62*

3.6 SUMMARY ... 63

EXERCISES ... 63

REFERENCES 64

4 HOTSPOT JVMS 65

4.1 ORACLE JDK PERFORMANCE FEATURES 65

4.1.1 Oracle JDK Version History 65

4.1.2 JIT Compilation 66

4.1.3 Adaptive Optimization 66

4.1.4 New Input/Output (NIO) 66

4.1.5 Concurrent Utilities 67

4.1.6 Java Quick Starter 67

4.1.7 Cold Start versus Warm Start 67

4.2 GARBAGE COLLECTORS IN HOTSPOT JVMS 68

4.2.1 Generations 68

4.2.2 GC Performance Metrics 69

4.2.3 Garbage Collectors with the HotSpot JVMs 69

4.2.4 Concurrent Mark and Sweep (CMS) 70

4.2.5 Garbage First (G1) GC 73

4.3 HELPING GARBAGE COLLECTORS 73

4.4 GARBAGE COLLECTION TUNING 74

4.4.1 HotSpot JVM Command Line Options 74

4.4.2 Sizing a Heap 74

4.4.3 Tuning a Throughput Garbage Collector 75

4.4.4 Adaptive Heap Sizing 75

4.4.5 Tuning a CMS Garbage Collector 76

4.4.6 Dealing With OutOfMemoryErrors 76

4.5 GARBAGE COLLECTION MONITORING 77

4.5.1 Java Ergonomic Defaults 77

4.5.2 JConsole 78

4.5.3 VisualVM 82

4.5.4 Enabling Remote Access for VisualVM *91*
4.5.5 Overhead of VisualVM *92*
4.5.6 Sampling Snapshots *93*
4.5.7 Application Snapshots *93*
4.5.8 Reading GC Logs *95*
4.6 SUMMARY 100
EXERCISES 101
REFERENCES 101
PART II JAVA PERFORMANCE AND SCALABILITY: PRACTICE 103
5 64-BIT ENTERPRISE JAVA COMPUTING 105
5.1 THE BITS 105
5.2 MEMORY BLOAT FROM 32-BIT TO 64-BIT 107
5.3 64-BIT JVMS 108
5.4 COMPRESSING ORDINARY OBJECT POINTERS WITH USECOMPRESSEDOOPS FLAG 109
5.5 CASE STUDY: USECOMPRESSEDOOPS 110
5.5.1 The 64-bit System Under Test: AMD64 Opteron *110*
5.5.2 The Principle of "Comparable Workloads, One Single Variable" *110*
5.5.3 The Measurements and Comparisons *111*
5.6 SUMMARY 123
EXERCISES 123
REFERENCES 123
6 TUNING JAVA FOR BEST POSSIBLE PERFORMANCE AND SCALABILITY 125
6.1 QUANTIFYING PERFORMANCE AND SCALABILITY ISSUES 126
6.1.1 Application Architecture *126*
6.1.2 Test Environment *126*
6.1.3 Hardware Specs *127*
6.1.4 Load Testing *127*
6.1.5 Performance and Scalability Issues *127*

6.2 APPLICATION PROFILING 130
6.2.1 Profiling the 400 Concurrent User Run with VisualVM 130
6.2.2 Profiling in Single Threaded Mode 133
6.3 RESOLUTION 136
6.3.1 Newer JDKs 137
6.3.2 Faster Hardware 138
6.4 JVM TUNING 143
6.4.1 Quantifying the Performance and Scalability Issues 144
6.4.2 Baseline with the Throughput GC 144
6.4.3 Switching to the CMS GC 148
6.4.4 Verifying the Parameters Used In Conjunction with -XX:+UseConcMarkSweepGC 151
6.5 SYSTEMATICAL TUNINGS FOR BEST POSSIBLE PERFORMANCE AND SCALABILITY 153
6.5.1 Establishing a Solid Baseline 153
6.5.2 Quantifying the Baseline 154
6.5.3 JDBC Tunings 157
6.5.4 Sizing Thread Pools with PSI-Probe and VisualVM 159
6.5.5 JVM Statistics 161
6.6 SCALABILITY TESTING 161
6.6.1 Average Response Times 162
6.6.2 System Resource Utilizations 163
6.6.3 JVM Activity Analysis 164
6.6.4 Thread Pool Analysis 165
6.6.5 Database Activity Analysis 166
6.6.6 Fine-Tuning JDBC Connection Pool 167
6.6.7 Further Tuning with JVM options -XX:+AggressiveOpts and -XX:+DoEscapeAnalysis 170
6.6.8 Scaling Beyond 174
6.6.9 Trials with G1 GC 175

6.7 SUMMARY ... 178
EXERCISES ... 179
REFERENCES ... 179
7 JAVA PERFORMANCE AND SCALABILITY BY DESIGN ... 181
7.1 THE CPUCHECK PROGRAM ... 181
7.1.1 The Admin Server ... 182
7.1.2 The Client ... 189
7.2 THE SERVICEDIRECTORY PROGRAM ... 191
7.2.1 The Static Algorithm ... 192
7.2.2 The Recursive Algorithm ... 193
7.2.3 The Dynamic Algorithm ... 193
7.3 TEST RESULTS ... 193
7.3.1 Performance Gaps with the Static, Recursive and Dynamic Algorithms ... 193
7.3.2 Part versus Whole in Evaluating Performance ... 194
7.4 BOTTLENECK ANALYSIS ... 195
7.5 ARRAY PROCESSING TO BOAST PERFORMANCE AND SCALABILITY SIGNIFICANTLY ... 197
7.6 PERFORMANCE AND SCALABILITY ANTI-PATTERNS ... 198
7.7 SUMMARY ... 199
EXERCISES ... 199
REFERENCES ... 200
8 JAVA PERFORMANCE AND SCALABILITY ON LINUX ... 201
8.1 THE EVOLUTION OF UNIX ... 201
8.2 LINUX AND ITS VARIANTS ... 202
8.2.1 Linux Kernel Features ... 202
8.2.2 Debian/Ubuntu ... 205
8.2.3 Fedora ... 205
8.2.4 Red Hat Enterprise Linux (RHEL) ... 205
8.2.5 OpenSUSE/SUSE Linux Enterprise ... 205

8.2.6 CentOS ... *206*
8.2.7 Installing CentsOS 7 as a VM on VMware Fusion 7 ... *207*
8.2.8 Configuring CentOS 7 ... *208*
8.3 LINUX ARCHITECTURE ... 210
8.3.1 The Standard C Library ... *210*
8.3.2 System Calls ... *211*
8.3.3 Responsibilities of the Kernel ... *212*
8.3.4 Virtual Memory ... *212*
8.3.5 Virtual and Physical Address Spaces ... *213*
8.3.6 Page Tables ... *214*
8.3.7 Swapping and Page Reclaiming ... *215*
8.3.8 UMA versus NUMA ... *215*
8.3.9 Processes ... *217*
8.3.10 Threads ... *218*
8.4 KNOWING ABOUT YOUR LINUX SYSTEMS ... 218
8.4.1 Version of a Linux System ... *218*
8.4.2 CPU model ... *219*
8.4.3 Memory ... *222*
8.4.4 Disk ... *224*
8.4.5 Network ... *225*
8.4.6 Checking and Configuring Kernel Parameters ... *226*
8.4.7 Configuring Shell Limits for a User ... *228*
8.4.8 Linux Performance Diagnostic Utilities ... *230*
8.5 CASE STUDY: JAVA PERFORMANCE AND SCALABILITY ON LINUX ... 237
8.5.1 The Linux System Activity Monitoring Procedure ... *237*
8.5.2 Test Results ... *238*
8.5.3 Post-Analysis ... *240*
8.5.4 Linux versus Windows ... *248*

8.6 SUMMARY 251
EXERCISES 252
REFERENCES 252
APPENDIX A A CASE STUDY WITH THE INTEL TURBO BOOST TECHNOLOGY ON LINUX 253
A.1 INTRODUCTION 253
A.2 INTEL CORE I7/XEON DYNAMIC POWER MANAGEMENT 254
A.3 CPU OVERCLOCKING 256
A.4 A CASE STUDY WITH INTEL'S TURBO BOOST TECHNOLOGY 257
A.4 RECOMMENDATIONS 261
APPENDIX B CPUCHECK: AN CLIENT/SERVER JAVA PROGRAM FOR BENCHMARKING CPUS 265
B.1 HOW TO RUN CPUCHECK 265
B.2 MORE ABOUT CPUCHECK 267
APPENDIX C THE DISKCHECK PROGRAM FOR BENCHMARKING IO 291
APPENDIX D SETTING UP X11 FOR LINUX 295
APPENDIX E LINUX SYSTEM AND PERFORMANCE UTILITIES 297
E.1 LINUX SYSTEM UTILITIES 297
E.3 THE SAR UTILITY 298
APPENDIX F THE HARP UTILITY FOR OPTIMIZING UI PERFORMANCE 301
F.1 SETTING UP A JDK FOR RUNNING THE HARP TOOL 302
F.2 HOW TO SAVE NETWORK TRAFFIC CAPTURED WITH CDT IN HAR FORMAT 303
F.3 HOW TO RUN THE HARP TOOL 305
F.4 FEEDBACK 306
F.5 BEST PRACTICES WITH USING THE HARP TOOL 306
INDEX 307

List of Programs and Scripts

Listing 1.1 Mirabeau-perfLog.txt 20

Listing 4.1 GC logs from -Xloggc:sd-0.log 96

Listing 4.2 GC logs from -Xloggc:sd-1.log -XX:+PrintGCDetails 97

Listing 4.3 GC logs from -Xloggc:sd-2.log -XX:+PrintGCDetails -XX:+PrintGCDateStamps -XX:+PrintGCTimeStamps 98

Listing 4.4 GC logs from -Xloggc:sd-3.log -XX:+PrintGCDetails --XX:+UseConcMarkSweepGC -XX:MaxGCPauseMillis=200 99

Listing 4.5 GC output from the jstat utility 99

Listing 6.1 Global Transaction Datasource Defined in oracle-xa-ds.xml 158

Listing 6.2 Additional Tunable JDBC Pool Parameters 158

Listing 7.1 AdminInterface.java 183

Listing 7.2 AdminServer.java 183

Listing 7.3 AdminConsole.java 185

Listing 7.4 AdminProxy.java 190

Listing 7.5 AdminClient.java 191

Listing 8.1 Output from the command of "lscpu" on a Linux VM (pf01) 220

Listing 8.2 Output from the command of "lscpu" on a Linux system (physical) (icmn) 221

Listing 8.3 Output from the command of "lscpu" on a Linux desktop system (physical) (w9ms) 221

Listing 8.4 Output of the "cat /proc/meminfo" command obtained on a Xeon X5550 Linux system ...222

Listing 8.5 Output of the "dmidecode --type memory" command obtained on the same Xeon X5550 Linux system 223

Listing 8.6 Output of the "free –m" command from the same Xeon X5550 Linux system 224

Listing 8.7 Output of the "df –m" command on Linux 225

Listing 8.8 Output of the netstat command executed on a Linux machine named "icmn" 225

Listing 8.9 Setting kernel parameters on a Linux machine used as an Oracle 11g database server (portion of the /etc/sysctl.conf file) 228

Listing 8.10 Shell limits set for the oracle user on the Oracle server (mitwo) in /etc/security/limits.conf 229

Listing 8.11 Shell limits set for the root user on the Java application server (icmn) in /etc/security/limits.conf 229

Listing 8.12 output of the command "ulimit –a" executed on the Oracle server (mitwo).......................230

Listing 8.13 output of the command "ulimit –a" executed on the Java application server (icmn)..........230

Listing 8.14 A bash script (ps_mon.sh) for monitoring a process on a Linux system 236

Listing 8.15 Portion of the vmstat data gathered during the 500 concurrent user run............................242

Listing 8.16 (a) Output from the "sar –u –s 11:11:01" command.......................243

Listing 8.16 (b) Output from the "sar –r –s 11:11:01" command 244

Listing 8.16 (c) Output from the "sar –q 5 10" command.......................244

Listing 8.16 (d) Output from the "sar –w 5 10" command 244

Listing 8.17 Data collected using the ps_mon.sh script during the 500 concurrent user run. 245

Listing A.1 Output of the command *cpupower idle-info* executed on a Red Hat Linux system with Intel(R) Xeon(R) CPU E5-4650 @ 2.70GHz 255

Listing A.2 Frequencies after carrying out step 3 263

Listing B.1 compileServer.bat.......................268

Listing B.2 copyBinary.bat 268

Listing B.3 runServer.bat 269

Listing B.4 compileClient.bat 269

Listing B.5 services.properties 270

Listing B.6 runClient.bat 270
Listing B.7 ServiceDirectory.java 270
Listing C.1 The services.properties file used with CPUCheck for generating the ioTest1.txt file 292
Listing C.2 DiskCheck.java 293

Table of Figures

Figure 1.1 Current, voltage and resistance in an electrical circuit 4

Figure 1.2 A computer system accessed by users 4

Figure 1.3 Single queue, multi-server (SQMS) and multi-queue, multi-server (MQMS) models 7

Figure 1.4 A queuing system with feedback 9

Figure 1.5 Performance and scalability test environment for a JEE-based enterprise Web application 11

Figure 1.6 Average CPU usage (%) associated with the test results listed in Table 1.2 14

Figure 1.7 Task Manager (upper) and Computer Management (lower) views showing 8 CPUs on a Core™ i7-based system 15

Figure 1.8 Measured average response times versus the number of concurrent users 17

Figure 1.9 Average response times for a subset of actions versus the number of concurrent users 17

Figure 1.10 Scalability: linear versus measured 18

Figure 1.11 CPU utilizations on the E5620-based JEE application server corresponding to Test C listed in Table 1.2 21

Figure 1.12 CPU utilizations on the i7-based JEE application server corresponding to Test D listed in Table 1.2 21

Figure 1.13 CPU usage of an Oracle database server collected with the `vmstat` tool on RedHat Linux corresponding to Test C listed in Table 1.2 23

Figure 1.14 CPU usage of an Oracle database server collected with the `vmstat` tool on RedHat Linux corresponding to Test D listed in Table 1.2 23

Figure 2.1 Intel 80386 microprocessor architecture 34

Figure 2.2 Internal functional units of an 80386 microprocessor 34

Figure 2.3 Microarchitecture comparison between previous generation and new Nehalem for Intel single-CPU based systems 36

Figure 2.4 Microarchitecture comparison between previous generation and new Nehalem for Intel multi-core based systems 37

Figure 2.5 Quad core i7 local caches and inclusive shared L3 cache 38

Figure 2.6 Hyper-threading re-introduced with Core i7-based systems 39

Figure 2.7 Xeon E5620 versus Core i7-2600 40

Figure 3.1 The complete stack of a Java application 44

Figure 3.2 Changes of reference count with object allocation (a) and de-allocation (b) 53

Figure 3.3 A cyclic reference structure in (a) becomes unreachable after the head node is de-referenced (b) 54

Figure 3.4 Mark-and-sweep GC: (a) initial state, (b) after marking, and (c) after sweeping 56

Figure 3.5 Tri-color mark-and-sweep GC algorithm 58

Figure 3.6 Serial (left) versus parallel (right) GC strategy 59

Figure 3.7 Non-compacting versus compacting versus copying GC strategy 61

Figure 3.8 Stop-the-world versus concurrent GC strategy 62

Figure 3.9 One time versus incremental GC strategy 63

Figure 4.1 Heap structure for generational GC strategy with the HotSpot JVMs 69

Figure 4.2 one-time, stop-the-world versus CMS GC 71

Figure 4.3 The CMS collector sweeps but does not compact the tenured generation, resulting in fragmented tenured region 72

Figure 4.4 JConsole startup page after the CPUCheck sample is started up 79

Figure 4.5 JConsole Memory Tab showing total GC times and algorithms 80

Figure 4.6 JConsole display with the *ParNew* and *CMS* collectors for the young and old generations, respectively 81

Figure 4.7 JConsole Overview page.. 82

Figure 4.8 VisualVM start-up page.. 83

Figure 4.9 VisualVM *Overview* tab 84

Figure 4.10 VisualVM *Monitor* tab 84

Figure 4.11 VisualVM Threads tab 85

Figure 4.12 VisualVM Sampler tab / CPU sampling 86

Figure 4.13 VisualVM Sampler tab / Memory sampling 87

Figure 4.14 VisualVM CPU profiling 87

Figure 4.15 VisualVM memory profiling 88

Figure 4.16 VisualVM/Visual GC plugin in action with the Service Admin sample 90

Figure 4.17 CPU profiling snapshot showing a Call Tree and Hot Spots 94

Figure 4.18 Sampler | CPU | Snapshot taken with the default CPU settings 95

Figure 5.1 Three test runs for investigating the effects of compressing ordinary object pointers. The second run failed. The 1st and 3rd runs demonstrated comparable workloads 111

Figure 5.2 AppServer: The effects of oops compression on (a) heap usage, (b) Eden space, and (c) tenured space 113

Figure 5.3 AppServer: (a) average size of each heap region without oops compression, (b) with oops compression and (c) comparison between without and with oops compression 114

Figure 5.4 Analytical Engine: The effects of oops compression on (a) heap usage, (b) Eden region and (c) tenured region (upper – oops uncompressed; lower: oopscompressed) 116

Figure 5.5 Analytical Engine: (a) average size of each heap region without oops compression, (b) with oops compression and (c) comparison between without and with oops compression 117

Figure 5.6 Working set comparison. In each chart, the upper curve corresponds to oops uncompressed, and the lower curve to oops compressed 119

Figure 5.7 Comparison of the average total CPU usage for the entire system 120

Figure 5.8 Comparison of the average process CPU usage for the AppServer........................ 121

Figure 5.9 Comparison of the average process CPU usage for the AnalyticalEngine.............. 122

Figure 6.1 Application UI average response times measured with 200 and 400 concurrent users with two different versions of JEAS... 128

Figure 6.2 Application UI performance degradation caused by upgrading the application from JEAS 4 to JEAS 5.. 129

Figure 6.3 Average CPU utilizations with 200 (left) and 400 (right) concurrent user runs on JEAS 4 129

Figure 6.4 Average CPU utilizations with 200 (left) and 400 (right) concurrent user runs on JEAS 5 130

Figure 6.5 VisualVM calibration.. 131

Figure 6.6 VisualVM Monitor page with the application at the end of the run 132

Figure 6.7 VisualGC page at the end of the run.. 133

Figure 6.8 VisualVM Sampler did not work with 200 – 400 concurrent user runs................. 133

Figure 6.9 HotSpots methods sorted by Self Time (CPU) from the JEAS 4 profile 135

Figure 6.10 HotSpots methods sorted by Self Time (CPU) from the JEAS 5 profile 135

Figure 6.11 Back traces in *method view* for the hot method of `java.security.AccessController.doPrivileged` from the JEAS 4 profile 136

Figure 6.12 Back traces in method view for the hot method of `java.security.AccessController.doPrivileged` from the JEAS 5 profile 136

Figure 6.13 Average CPU utilizations with JEAS 4 (left) and JEAS 5 (right) runs for 400 concurrent users with JDK 1.6.0 update 31 in place of 1.6.0 update 21................................ 138

Figure 6.14 Average response time comparison between Xeon E5620 and X5550 based JEE servers (400 concurrent users and JDK 1.6.0 update 31 were used for both cases)............... 139

Figure 6.15 HotSpots methods sorted by Self Time (CPU) from the JEAS 4 profile obtained on the Xeon X5550 based JEE application server 141

Figure 6.16 HotSpots methods sorted by Self Time (CPU) from the JEAS 5 profile obtained on the Xeon X5550 based JEE application server 142

Figure 6.17 Back traces for `java.security.AccessController` from the JEAS 4 profile obtained on the Xeon X5550 based JEE application server 142

Figure 6.18 Back traces for `java.security.AccessController` from the JEAS 5 profile obtained on the Xeon X5550 based JEE application server 143

Figure 6.19 *CPU*, *Heap*, *Classes* and *Threads* statistics prior to the run 146

Figure 6.20 *Visual GC* statistics prior to the run........ 147

Figure 6.21 *CPU*, *Heap*, *Classes* and *Threads* statistics at the end of the run........ 147

Figure 6.22 *Visual GC* statistics at the end of the run 148

Figure 6.23 *CPU*, *Heap*, *Classes* and *Threads* statistics at the end of the run using the CMS garbage collector (........ 150

Figure 6.24 *VisualGC* statistics at the end of the run with........ 150

Figure 6.25 *CPU*, *Heap*, *Classes* and *Threads* statistics at the end of the run........ 152

Figure 6.26 *VisualGC* statistics at the end of the run with........ 152

Figure 6.27 Oracle AWR report statistics collected during the baseline run 156

Figure 6.28 VisualVM Monitor view taken at the end of the baseline run........ 157

Figure 6.29 Thread pools monitored with PSI-Probe at the beginning, mid-point, and the end of the run........ 160

Figure 6.30 CPU and Heap GC patterns with 300, 500, and 700 concurrent users from top to bottom........ 164

Figure 6.31 Top five events for 300 concurrent user run 167

Figure 6.32 Top five events for 500 concurrent user run 167

Figure 6.33 Top five events for 700 concurrent user run 167

Figure 6.34 CPU and GC patterns versus JDBC connection pool sizes, corresponding to those two runs shown in Table 6.23 (other conditions: 700 concurrent users with CMS GC) 169

Figure 6.35 Top five wait events corresponding to those two runs shown in Table 6.23 170

Figure 6.36 CPU and GC patterns corresponding to runs #1 – 3 shown in Table 6.25 from top to bottom. 173

Figure 6.37 Top five wait events corresponding to runs 174

Figure 6.38 CPU & GC patterns with the 800 concurrent user run 174

Figure 6.39 Top five wait events on the database with the 800 concurrent user run 175

Figure 6.40 Performance and scalability comparison between the G1 (upper) and CMS (lower) garbage collectors with a real enterprise Java application 176

Figure 6.41 CPU pattern comparison between CMS and G1... 177

Figure 6.42 Top 5 wait event comparison between the G1 run (upper) and CMS run (lower) with the 700 concurrent users.. 178

Figure 7.1 CPUCheck program structure 182

Figure 7.2 Elapsed times associated with creating a service directory tree structure of 33,479 nodes with three different algorithms 194

Figure 7.3 Total wall-clock times associated with creating a service directory tree structure of 33,479 nodes using three different algorithms and sending it to the service admin console 195

Figure 7.4 A computing task consisting of two sequential stages 196

Figure 7.5 Total execution time versus ARRAY_SIZE with array processing applied to the recursive algorithm (tree size: 6 levels x 8 child nodes / per parent node = 299,592 nodes total).. 198

Figure 7.6 Total execution time versus ARRAY_SIZE with array processing applied to the dynamic algorithm for the same tree size of 6x8. 198

Figure 8.1 The architecture of a typical Linux system 211

Figure 8.2 Division of a virtual address space between the kernel and a user program on a 32-bit system... 213

Figure 8.3 Memory mapping from virtual to physical address space 213

Figure 8.4 Three-level multilevel paging 214

Figure 8.5 Schematic illustrations of UMA (upper) versus NUMA (lower) CPU-RAM paths (note that each CPU-RAM unit is called a *node*) 216

Figure 8.6 A typical top session 232

Figure 8.7 Select options when top is running (taken from a CentOS 7 Linux)....................... 232

Figure 8.8 The *vmstat* utility output showing all metrics it collects....................................... 234

Figure 8.9 Performance and scalability of a real enterprise Java application on Linux 240

Figure 8.10 Three "top" screenshots taken at the intervals of 24 minutes, 28 minutes, and 55 minutes since the 500 concurrent user run started.......... 242

Figure 8.11 Resident size evolution of the enterprise Java application under test with 500 concurrent users.......... 246

Figure 8.12 CPU utilizations with 500 (lower curve), 700 (middle curve), and 800 (upper curve) concurrent users (this chart was made by importing *vmstat* data into Excel, which required replacing the first space at the beginning of each line of the *vmstat* data files by applying ":1,$s/^ //g" in the *vi* editor).......... 247

Figure 8.13 Performance comparison between Windows and Linux using a same enterprise Java application with 700 concurrent users.......... 248

Figure 8.14 User CPU trace comparison between Windows (lighter, dotted curve) and Linux (darker, solid curve).......... 249

Figure 8.15 VisualVM CPU and GC activity screenshot for the Linux run.......... 250

Figure 8.16 VisualVM CPU and GC activity screenshot for the Windows run.......... 251

Figure A.1 Performance comparison between Windows (lower) and Linux (upper) when the Turbo Boost feature was not configured properly on Linux.......... 258

Figure A.2 Output of the "lscpu" command on the Linux box.......... 259

Figure A.3 Initial setting of *the cpufreq scaling_governor* on the Linux box (the first command shows the effective scaling governor out of the two available settings of *userspace* and *performance* as shown by the second command).......... 259

Figure A.4 Output of the command "cpupower –c 0-3 monitor" on that Linux box (in case you cannot see clearly the upper most screenshot, I have chopped it into two segments as shown by the middle and bottom screenshots).......... 260

Figure A.5 (a) Left: Core running frequencies after setting power management to "OS-Control" at the BIOS level when the system was being rebooted; (b) Right: Core running frequencies after increasing the base CPU frequency from 1200 MHz to the marked base frequency of 2700 MHz. 260

Figure A.6 Effects of the Turbo Boost settings on the average elapsed time in milliseconds of the application tested with 30 threads.......... 261

Figure A.7 The contents of the /sys/devices/systems/cpu folder.......... 262

Figure A.8 The scaling governor for cpu0 after carrying out step 2.......... 262

Figure B.1 An example output of running CPUCheck on the client console 266

Figure B.2 A service directory tree structure of 6 levels deep with 8 sub-nodes per node 267

Figure B.3 Initial empty service admin console 269

Figure C.1 An example DiskCheck run output on an i7-2600 based Windows PC 291

Figure D.1 Status of the Xming server on Windows 296

Figure D.2 The *xclock* program for verifying that X11 has been set up properly between Linux and Windows 296

Figure F.1 An HTTP request/response displayed on CDT 302

Figure F.2 Explanations on resource network timing 303

Figure F.3 CDT with Chrome 304

Figure F.4 Save As HAR with content option with CDT 305

Preface

Why This Book

Since its introduction in early 1990's along with the dawn of the Internet age, Java has become one of the most widely used programming languages for building software products. Java-based software ranges from games to appliances, from client software to server software, from personal computing to enterprise applications - almost in every category. It is estimated that there are millions of Java developers worldwide today.

Obviously, for standalone and personal software built in Java, *performance* is one of the key non-functional requirements. For enterprise software built in Java, one also needs to add *scalability* in addition to *performance*. Although books and other types of loosely presented materials are available about Java application performance and scalability, they are not necessarily delivered in a data-driven, fact-based, quantitative approach that includes both theory and practice. This text attempts to fill in all those gaps so that developers can count on it as a reliable source for building as much performance and scalability as possible into their Java-based software.

Performance tuning is both science and art. It's *science* as we can measure quantitatively. Sometimes we can even predict based on queuing theory what we would get after applying a tuning. However, it's also *art* as it takes a lot of practice and patience to master it. I feel obligated to share the *science* and *art* aspects of software performance engineering through my practices, especially in context of Java applications.

WHOM THIS BOOK IS FOR

Obviously, this book is for those who are interested in learning about Java application performance and scalability. No matter what role you play on your team, a developer, an architect or a manager, this text will help you gain truly applicable skills in a most efficient and relevant manner so that your Java-based software will be high performing and scalable.

HOW THIS BOOK IS ORGANIZED

This book consists of the following two main parts:

- **Part I Java Performance and Scalability: Basics**. The purpose of this part is to help a reader acquire a basic set of knowledge to get ready for meeting actual Java performance and scalability issues in reality. It includes the following four chapters:
    - Chapter 1 *Software Performance and Scalability* presents a primer on queuing theory, and then explains the concepts of performance and scalability using a real-product based case study.
    - Chapter 2 *Computer Hardware Architecture* helps a reader acquire some basic knowledge about computer hardware architecture as one of the most important factors in determining the performance and scalability of a Java application.
    - Chapter 3 *Java Virtual Machine Fundamentals* helps a reader understand how a JVM works, especially in garbage collections.
    - Chapter 4 *HotSpot JVMs* gets specific with real JVMs like HotSpot JVMs as an extension to Chapter 3 to close the gap between theory and reality.
- **Part II Java Performance and Scalability: Practice**. This part focuses more on the practical aspects of Java performance and scalability. It consists of the following three chapters:
    - Chapter *5 64-Bit Enterprise Java Computing* introduces the trend from 32-bit to 64-bit computing. It is augmented with a real product based case study with quantitative data about ordinary object points (oops) that most Java developers are concerned about.
    - Chapter 6 *Tuning Java for Best Possible Performance and Scalability* introduces methodologies, procedures, and proper tools for tuning Java applications for best possible performance and scalability. A case study is used throughout the chapter to show how to use VisualVM and other tools to help analyze performance and scalability issues with a real product. A comparison between the G1 GC and CMS GC is also presented at the end of this chapter using that real product.
    - Chapter 7 *Java Performance and Scalability by Design* uses my CPUCheck program to demonstrate how different algorithmic design and implementation choices can have profound impacts on a product. It also covers how to perform bottleneck analysis. An effective performance and scalability technique of array processing is illustrated quantitatively. This

chapter is wrapped up with a section to help raise developers awareness of performance and scalability ant-patterns.

- Chapter 8 *Java Performance and Scalability on Linux* focuses on optimizing Java performance and scalability on Linux. It introduces not only the core Linux kernel concepts but also the utilities for monitoring Linux system activities. It teaches how to get to know about your Linux machine quickly from the system performance and scalability perspectives, how to check and configure Linux kernel parameters from the application performance and scalability perspectives, and how to check and configure user shell limits for the user who launches the application. Finally, it uses a case study based on a real product to help illustrate the above concepts and procedures. It also compares the Java performance and scalability between Windows and Linux with the same enterprise application on the same hardware, with some interesting observations shared.

This book also includes two appendices about my CPUCheck and DiskCheck programs that I have been using to check out quickly if the systems I use are properly sized. They are not as elaborate as many formal CPU and IO benchmarking suites, but simple and useful enough for software developers to learn quickly about the power of the systems they use.

SOFTWARE AND HARDWARE

Since Java runs on every major computing platform, you can try some of the examples in this book even on a latest Windows PC or Linux system. My recommendation would be a latest, Intel i7-based, 64-bit Windows 7 PC with 4–8 GB RAM (for your reference, my system is an 8 GB RAM, Intel Core i7-2600, quad-core/hyper-threading desktop. It runs on the 64-bit Windows 7 Professional at a clock rate of 3.4 GHz. This is a very fast and high-capacity machine that I can install the entire stack of an enterprise application on it, including the servers for Web, application, and database.

HOW TO USE THIS BOOK

There are three ways to use this book:

1 Follow the structure laid out logically in the text and learn progressively from simple to complicated concepts and case studies.
2 Use the samples as your learning base for trying out various best performance and scalability practices that are pertinent to your interests.
3 Take a cursory look just for a general understanding about Java application performance and scalability.

TYPOGRAPHIC CONVENTIONS

Times New Roman indicates normal text blocks.

Italic indicates *emphasis*, *definitions*, *email addresses*, and *URLs* in general.

Calibri font indicates code listings, scripts, and all other types of programming segments.

`Courier` indicates programming elements outside a program or script as well as everything related to executing a program or script such as commands, file names, directoy paths, entries on an HTML form, etc.

How To Reach The Author

All errors in the text are the author's responsibility. You are welcome to email your questions and comments to me at *henry_h_liu@perfmath.com.* Your valuable feedback will be greatly appreciated.

The Book's Web Site

This book has a companion website at http://www.perfmath.com. For downloads and updates, please visit the book's website.

Henry H. Liu, Ph. D.

California

Summer, 2012

Acknowledgements

First, I would really like to thank the self-publishing vendor I have chosen for making this book available to my audience. This is the most cost-effective and efficient approach for both my audience and myself. Computer and software technologies evolve so fast that a more timely publishing approach is beneficial for all of us.

I would also like to thank many excellent engineers I have worked with, from whom I have learnt so much about Java application performance and scalability. Many excellent texts have helped me build my careers at different stages as well. I am really fortunate to have had a physicist career and then a software engineer career at present so that I can apply many valuable things I learnt in doing physics research to computers. A data-driven, objective mind and trying to be rigorous in reasoning perhaps are the most valuable traits I inherited from my previous physics research career to my current computer career.

Of course, as always, my gratitude extends to my wife Sarah and our son William, as I could have not been able to complete this book without their support and patience.

At last, I'd like to acknowledge NASA's permission for using the Spirit illustration on the cover design to express the theme of this book in an indirect context. I have been deeply impressed by the splendid endeavor of NASA's launching of rover Spirit to Mars. It's the best annotation of what *performance* and *scalability* mean – how *fast* and how *far* one can go.

Part I Java Performance and Scalability: Basics

We could have dived into Java application performance and scalability directly right from this moment. However, based on my experience, developers typically are too immersed in writing code to have a basic understanding on the following few important aspects related to Java performance and scalability in general:

- **Concepts of software performance and scalability in general.** Concepts of software performance and scalability are intuitive and easy to understand. However, it's beneficial to have a deeper and more complete understanding on these concepts in order to be able to design and implement performance and scalability into a product and meet such non-functional requirements on schedule. A very minimum understanding on queuing theory is also beneficial.
- **The system performance counters**. All computer systems provide a large collection of system performance counters to help quantify the usage of the system resources that all computing tasks rely on. However, in general, only a very small subset of the entire collection is more relevant in trouble-shooting the performance and scalability issue or bottleneck of an application in question. Among all those counters, CPU usage counter is usually the # 1 object to look into.
- **The underlying computer hardware architecture as a critical software performance and scalability factor**. The computer hardware architecture is one of the few most critical factors in determining the performance and scalability of an enterprise application. This is true whether an application is built in Java or any other programing languages. Furthermore, with a given computer hardware system, the CPU architecture is one of the most critical factors along with other specs such as memory, I/O (network and disk), etc., in determining the performance and scalability of an enterprise application.
- **JVM internals and HotSpot JVMs**. In order to be able to cope with Java application performance and scalability issues effectively and efficiently, it is necessary to have a minimum understanding on JVM internals, in particular how garbage collection works. It's also important to understand all

major performance and scalability features built into each release of HotSpot JVMs, because most likely your Java application would run on a HotSpot JVM.

This first part of the text is designed around the above concerns. Specifically, it consists of the following four chapters:

- Chapter 1: *Software Performance and Scalability*. This chapter first presents a primer on queuing theory as an entry to the Java application performance and scalability field. It then uses a real world case study out of my real experience to demonstrate how a same product exhibited drastically different performance and scalability characteristics on different server systems with different CPU models and configurations. This case study is also used for reviewing some of the performance and scalability terminologies so that all of us will be on the same page before we delve into Java application performance and scalability throughout this book. How to set up system counters to monitor and analyze performance and scalability issues on Windows and Linux systems is covered in this chapter as well.
- Chapter 2: *Computer Hardware Architecture*. This chapter explores various generations of Intel processor architecture to help you get refreshed and updated on some of the most critical performance and scalability features designed into those most widely used Intel-architecture based systems that constitute a large bulk of today's IT production environment. We particularly introduce Intel's core i7 based systems, which deliver outstanding performance for both single-threaded and multi-thread applications.
- Chapter 3: *Java Virtual Machine Fundamentals*. This chapter helps you understand how a JVM works behind the scene in general, especially how various types of garbage collection schemes work in general.
- *Chapter 4: HotSpot JVMs*. Since most likely you run your Java application on a HotSpot JVM, it's critical to be able to understand all critical HotSpot specific JVM options so that you would be able to configure your HotSpot JVM optimally to condition your JVM environment for best possible performance and scalability for your application.

Next, let us start with a primer on queuing theory and then a Java-based, real world case study to help illustrate the concepts of software performance and scalability in general.

1 Software Performance and Scalability

This chapter starts off with explaining the concepts of software performance and scalability with an analogy between electrical circuits and computer systems. As we will see, there is a remarkable resemblance between the two, although at very different scales and contexts.

Then it uses a case study out of my real experience with a real enterprise Web application based on JEE (Java Enterprise Edition) to help further solidify our understanding on what the concepts of performance and scalability are really about and why they are important for enterprise applications. This case study also helps define the concrete artifacts expected out of your performance and scalability testing efforts as deliverables either internally to your organization or externally to customers. It proves convincingly what a critical role the computer CPU architecture plays in determining the performance and scalability of an enterprise application built either with Java or with any other software technologies.

In addition, we introduce system performance counters on Windows and Linux upfront in this chapter, which will be used throughout this text whenever we need to characterize or diagnose a performance and scalability issue of a Java-based enterprise application. Such a foundation is necessary before we embark on Java application performance and scalability throughout this text.

1.1 Performance and Scalability Metrics

Many things in the universe seemingly are unrelated to each other, but in the end, it turns out that all things are related. For a very long time, I felt that the concepts of software performance and scalability did not seem to be too distant to me even when I learnt these concepts in context of software. Finally, I realized that it's the electrical circuit theory I was taught in college that brought me to my fresh memory of the concepts of software performance and scalability. So what does electrical circuit theory have to do with the concepts of software performance and scalability? Let's make this analogy clear next.

1.1.1 An Analogy between Electrical Circuits and Computer Systems

Figure 1.1 shows how the concepts of voltage, current and resistance are expressed in a circuit. There are three basic concepts with an electrical circuit: voltage (V), current (I), and resistance (R). Each of them is reviewed as follows:

- Voltage (V) – The electrical force that causes current to flow in a circuit. It's measured in Volts.
- Current (I) - The movement of electrical charge through the circuit. Since electrons are negatively charged, the direction of current flow and electron movement are opposite. It's measured in Amperes.
- Resistance (R) – Causes an opposition to the flow of electricity in a circuit. It is used to control the amount of voltage and/or amperage in a circuit. It's measured in Ohms.

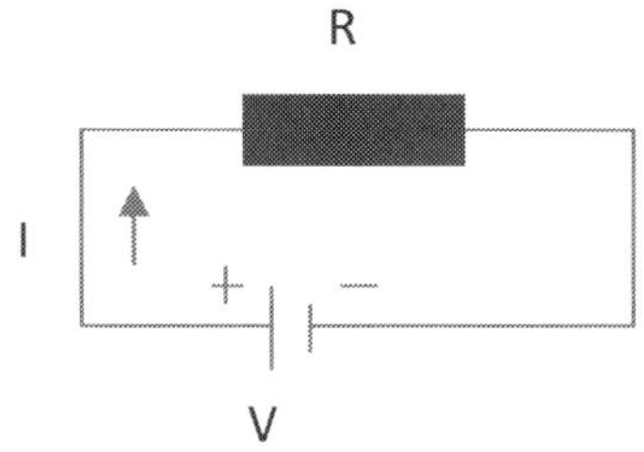

Figure 1.1 Current, voltage and resistance in an electrical circuit

So why do we bother to bring this up? Here is the analogy between an electrical circuit and a computer system. Refer to Figure 1.2, it is seen that a computer system is characterized with three major metrics as well:

- The number of users accessing the system, measured by the number of *concurrent users* (N).
- The number of tasks the system is processing over a given period, measured in terms of *throughput* (X).
- And how fast users can get their responses back from the system, measured by the amount of time taken from end to end in terms of *response times* (T).

Next, let's review the laws relevant to our analogy between electrical circuits and computer systems we briefed above.

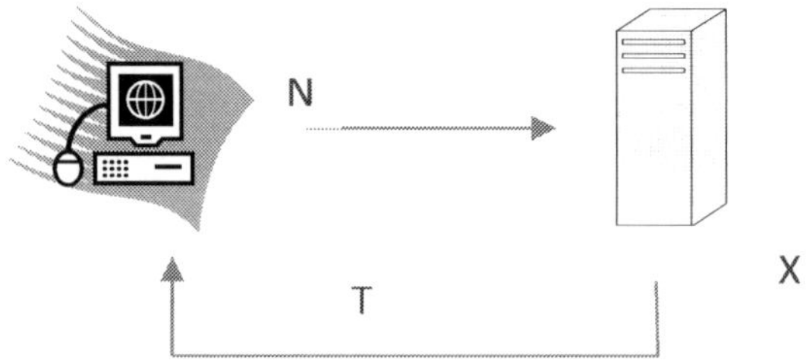

Figure 1.2 A computer system accessed by users

1.1.2 Ohm's Law versus Little's Law

It's well known that Ohm's law governs the relationship among current, voltage and resistance as follows in three equivalent forms:

$$I = V/R \text{ or } V = IR \text{ or } R = V/I \qquad (1.1)$$

Throughout this text, the terms of concurrent users (N), throughput (X) and response times (T) appear a lot. Similar to Ohm's law, there is a Little's law stating that the average number of users (n) stressing the system is statistically equal to the product of throughput (X) and average response time (R) in the following form:

$$n = X \times R \qquad (1.2)$$

Note that I have switched to using n for average number of concurrent users and R for average response time to be consistent with conventions in queuing theory, which is the theoretical framework for studying system performance. Notice the similarities between Eq. (1.1) for electrical circuits and (1.2) for computer systems. Conceptually, the two are analogous in the following ways:

- The concept of response time in computer systems is analogous to that of voltage in electrical circuits.
- The concept of throughput in computer systems is analogous to that of current in electrical circuits.
- The concept of concurrent users in computer systems is analogous to that of resistance in electrical circuits.

And there is even a more remarkable resemblance between the two, considering that in electrical circuits, resistance represents the force resisting the flowing of electrical charge, whereas in computer systems, concurrent users cause system resource contention often in the form of lock contentions, which tends to be a negative force to system performance and scalability. Electronic scientists research on how to reduce resistance so that currents can flow faster, and we computer engineers also research (and practice more importantly) on how to reduce resource utilizations and lock contentions so that a computer system can perform and scale better with more users or heavier computing tasks. This is what we are set out to do throughout this text. But before taking off, let us have a brief review on some important concepts in queuing theory next.

1.2 A PRIMER ON QUEUING THEORY

If you are interested in a more thorough coverage on queuing theory, you may want to check out my other book *Software Performance and Scalability: A Quantitative Approach* [Liu, 2009]. Otherwise, let us have a brief but sufficient coverage on queuing theory in this section.

Queuing theory essentially is a discipline about how to maximize system performance with a given set of participating resources. Little's law we introduced in the preceding section is a special but very common case, which requires an equilibrium condition, under which the incoming user arrival rate is statistically equal to the outgoing system throughput. Little's law is very helpful in helping analyze the operational performance of a system. However, we need to extend beyond Little's law for more insightful analysis on the performance and scalability issues of a computer system. For example, there are a few limitations with Little's law:

- Little's law does not tell why a system is fast or slow.
- Little's law does not tell what we can do to improve system performance.

We need to decompose the two terms on the right-hand-side of Eq. (1.2) (one is *throughput* X and the other is *response time* R) and introduce new performance laws to answer the questions as described above. First, let us introduce the response time performance laws.

In addition to the concepts of concurrent users, throughput, and response time, we need to introduce two more metrics as described as follows:

- **Resource Utilization** (U). The concept of *resource utilization* is intuitive and easy to define: It measures the portion of time a component or system is busy over a given period. It is represented in letter U in queuing theory. Resource utilization is one of the key metrics looked at when diagnosing a system performance and scalability issue, because too many users accessing a system would drive up system utilizations and cause more resistance or contention to the system, thus impacting the system performance. A well-built system would consume less and do more, which is the ultimate goal of system performance and scalability engineering.
- **Service Time** (S). This is another very important metric in queuing theory. The concept *of service time* describes the amount of time required for processing a computing task when the system is essentially idle with no contention at all. This is important because it sets a best case limit to the performance of a system. For example, if the service time of a system is 2 seconds, there is no way for any user to see a better than 2 second response time.

1.2.1 Response Time Performance Laws

Now we have enough metrics defined for presenting response time performance laws. We start with the simplest queuing model of a single queue in front of a single server. In this case, the response time is expressed in the form of:

$$R = S/(1-U) \qquad (1.3)$$

Two observations can be made immediately:

- If the system is nearly idle or U is close to zero, then the response time R is essentially equal to the service time S.
- The response time increases rapidly as the system becomes busier and busier, namely, $U\uparrow\rightarrow R\uparrow$ (you can read this as "*U goes up would drive R up*."). This is why when we feel a system is slow, we first check out how busy the system is. A special point to remember according to Eq. (1.3) is that the response time would triple when the system utilization approaches to about 67%. This is why for online transaction processing (OLTP) type of applications, it's desirable to keep system utilization level not to exceed about 70% (it's important to understand that the above equation was derived based an open-model and it becomes less accurate with U > 70%). However, batch job type of applications allows system utilizations to go higher than 70%.

The above equation applies to a single queue, single server system, as we pointed out. Now, we can ask how we can improve system performance according to Eq. (1.3) as our theoretical guide. We have a few options:

- Reducing service time *S* as much as possible. This would require hardware vendors to deliver faster and faster hardware, which has been the trend for decades. Because this is so important, the next chapter is dedicated to computer hardware architecture.
- Reducing service time *S* as much as possible *again.* This time, the responsibility is not with hardware vendors but with us. We need to design better algorithms and implement more efficiently so that valuable computing resources are not consumed to process wastes. This would be a resounding metaphor throughout this text.
- Keeping system utilization as low as possible. Of course, asking users not use the system too much would certainly help, but that's not the answer we are looking for. In addition to having leaner, more efficient designs and implementations for an application to help keep system utilization low, tuning system and application configurations often helps drastically beyond what one can do with faster hardware or retrofitting the application. I have plenty of such examples in my other performance books, and some new case studies are presented later in this book.

In fact, Eq. (1.3) is not what we have to say about response time performance laws. Beyond single queue, single server systems (SQSS), we can also have single queue, multi-server (SQMS) systems and multi-queue, multi-server (MQMS) systems, as shown in Figure 1.3 where beans represent incoming requests, boxes represent queues and circles represent servers. A SQMS system is equivalent to a multi-CPU system, whereas an MQMS system is equivalent to a clustered system with load balancing across multiple servers in the cluster. The former is called *scaling-up* or *vertical scaling*, while the latter is called *scaling-out* or *horizontal scale*.

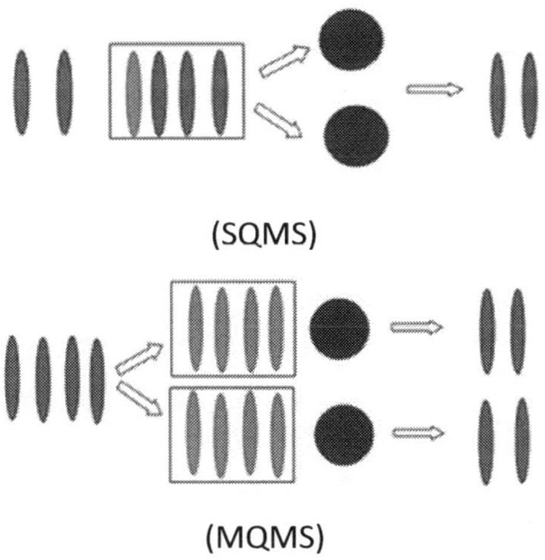

Figure 1.3 Single queue, multi-server (SQMS) and multi-queue, multi-server (MQMS) models

No matter how we call it, SQMS and MQMS are commonly used techniques for scaling software applications in order to be able to support more users. To be complete, the response time laws for SQMS and MQMS systems are presented as follows, with *m* representing the number of servers:

$$R \approx \frac{S}{1-\rho^m} \qquad \text{(SQMS)} \quad (1.4)$$

$$R = \frac{S}{1-\rho} \qquad \text{(MQMS)} \quad (1.5)$$

where the system utilization has been normalized from U for SQSS systems to $\rho = U/m$ with $0 \leq \rho \leq 1$ for SQMS and MQMS systems. Since for large values of m, $\rho^m << \rho$, an SQMS system is generally considered a more efficient choice than an MQMS system performance wise. However, scaling-up is ultimately limited by insurmountable contentions and the only way to improve scalability is to *scale out*.

1.2.2 The Throughput Performance Law

Several years ago, while working on a real enterprise product, I came up with a formula to help myself and others optimize the throughput of the system. Later, I posted this formula as an exercise in my other book *Software Performance and Scalability: A Quantitative Approach (Wiley, 2009)* to help college/graduate CS students and performance engineers learn about software performance and scalability. It states that if a system has N objects to process through two consecutive stages, the system throughput (X_0) can be expressed as

$$X_0 = \frac{X_1 \times X_2}{X_1 + X_2} \qquad (1.6)$$

where $X_1 = N/\Delta T_1$ (stage 1) is the stage 1throughput and $X_2 = N/\Delta T_2$ is the stage 2 throughput. This is a very representative case where a system has two or more tasks to process sequentially. For example, with an enterprise application, a user request has to go through a full chain from a Web server, through an application server and a database server, and then backwards to the user with a response to complete the loop. In such cases, Eq. (1.6) is particularly useful, which clearly states that one should focus on the slower stage as under the condition of, for example, $X_1 >> X_2$, namely, stage 1 is much faster than stage 2, $X_0 \cong X_2$ or we can say that the system throughput is essentially limited by the slower stage 2 throughput. This tells that one should focus more on improving the throughput of stage 2 rather than that of stage 1. Therefore, the above throughput performance law can be used to help guide on which part a team should spend its effort in optimizing the performance of its product. It is discussed more in Chapter 7 in context of bottleneck analysis.

1.2.3 Jackson's Theorem

Jackson's theorem is an important milestone in the development history of queuing theory. His research was about queuing systems with feedback [Jackson, 1963]. Figure 1.5 shows what a queuing system with feedback looks like. In context of customer-server setups, the concept of feedback means that a customer may come back and be served more than once by the server, while in context of computer systems, it means that a resource may be visited multiple times in order to complete a transaction. Either way, the model remains the same as illustrated in Figure 1.4. The symbols labeled in Figure 1.4 represent the following variables:

- External arrival rate λ. This is the average arrival rate of external, new incoming customers or requests.

- Internal arrival rate λ_1. This is the average arrival rate to the system that includes both new and returning customers or requests.
- Probability *p*. This is the probability that a customer or request may revisit the system. Note that when $p = 0$, the model is termed an *open model* with no revisiting customers or requests, and when $p = 1$, the model is termed a *closed model* with no customers or requests leaving the system permanently.

Jackson's theorem typically is applied to analyzing a system with multiple components or subsystems. Each component or subsystem is also called a *queuing node*. It states that although the total incoming arrivals may not follow a Poisson distribution, if each node maintains an equilibrium condition under which no entities are created or lost in the node, then each node still follows the Poisson distribution, and the system's temporal property can be obtained by linearly superimpose the temporal property of each individual node. Not surprisingly, the concept of *service time S* we introduced earlier is now superseded with the concept of *service demand* D_i, which is defined as follows:

$$D_i = V_i \times S_i \qquad (1.7)$$

where the subscript *i* represents the ith queuing node, V_i and S_i are the number of visits to the queuing node and average service time required per visit at the node, respectively.

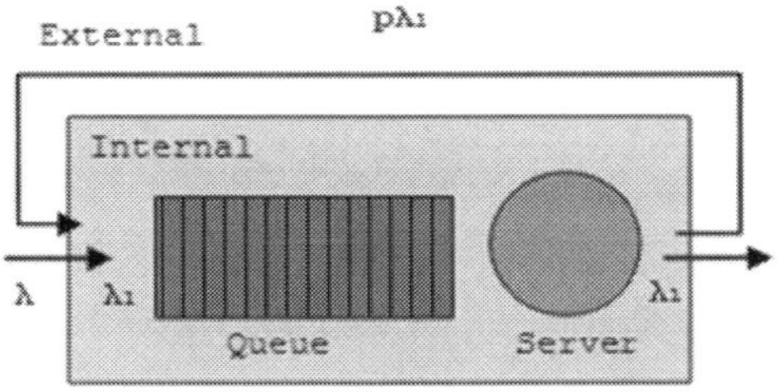

Figure 1.4 A queuing system with feedback

Jackson's theorem appears to be very abstract, but it has very practical implications. It helps us understand the behavior of a system based on what we know about the behavior of each individual component or node. To make it simple and relevant to computer system performance, let's assume that we have a system that consists of multiple components and user requests are processed sequentially through these components. Let's also assume that the system throughput X_0 is known and resource utilization U_i of each component is known (these assumptions are satisfied easily in reality). Then we can arrive at the system response time by following the below procedure:

- The service demand at each node can be calculated according to:

$$D_i = X_0 / U_i \qquad (1.8)$$

- With the service demand D_i and utilization U_i known, we can then calculate the average residence time R_i' of a request at queue node *i* as follows

$$R_i' = V_i \times R_i = D_i / (1 - U_i) \qquad (1.9)$$

- The total average system response time R_0 is the sum of residence times over all queue nodes from i =1 through $i = K$ where K is the total number of nodes constituting the entire system, namely,

$$R_0 = \sum_{i=1}^{K} R_i' \qquad (1.10)$$

Although the essence of Jackson's theorem is what is implied in Eq. (1.10), to understand the most relevant and important part of Jackson's theorem to computer system performance, we need to look at it backwards as follows:

- Eq. (1.10). In order to minimize system response time R_0, we need to minimize residence time at each node R_i'.
- Eq. (1.9). In order to minimize residence time at each node R_i', we need to minimize service demand D_i and resource utilization U_i at the node.
- Eq. (1.7). In order to minimize service demand D_i at a node, one option is to minimize the number of visits a node is revisited. In fact, this is the foundation of array processing performance optimization technique as is discussed in Chapter 7 later. It also explains why most profilers provide statistical numbers of CPU time and # of invocations for a method. You can consider these two quantities as service time S_i and the number of visits V_i in Eq. (1.7). The product of these two quantities would be service demand D_i - the left-hand-side of Eq. (1.7). Therefore, we are essentially applying Jackson's theorem unconsciously every time when we profile and optimize the performance of an application by looking at the CPU time and # of invocations for a hot method.

We wrap up our primer on queuing theory with Jackson's theorem. Next, we use a real world case study to help solidify the theoretical concepts and performance laws based on queuing theory we introduced in this section.

1.3 A REAL WORLD CASE STUDY

In addition to helping solidify the theoretical concepts and performance laws we introduced in the previous section, another purpose with this case study is to help present a complete and consistent view on the performance and scalability aspects associated with an enterprise application. It's important to understand that Java is a great technology for building enterprise software, but not all Java-based software products are guaranteed to perform and scale. Especially, understanding what hardware resources are required for running a Java-based enterprise application in order to deliver the expected application performance and scalability to customers is as equally important as coding it.

I have to mention that throughout presenting this case study, the actual application context is less important, since we are most interested in the performance and scalability aspects of the application rather than what it actually does. Next, let us jump to the test environment used for this case study directly.

1.3.1 Test Environment

Figure 1.5 shows the deployment architecture of the JEE-based enterprise Web application. It adopts a standard multi-tier architecture. It runs on a JEE *Application Server* with a built-in Web Server, which depends on an Authentication Server to authenticate users. Both the JEE Application Server and the

Authentication Server interact with a common backend database, which supports multiple database platforms, but it runs on Oracle 11g R2 with this case study. Both the JEE Application Server and the Authentication Server run on 64-bit Windows 2008 R2 Enterprise Server, while the database server runs on a RedHat Enterprise Linux Server Release 6.0 (Santiago).

One of the customer requirements was that the application should provide adequate performance for up to hundreds of concurrent users. Here the term '*concurrent*' means that users are logged into the system and are actually using the application, namely, driving the system busy while performing their normal functions. I used one of the commercial load test tools named Silk Performer to simulate that kind of concurrency with projected, representative workloads.

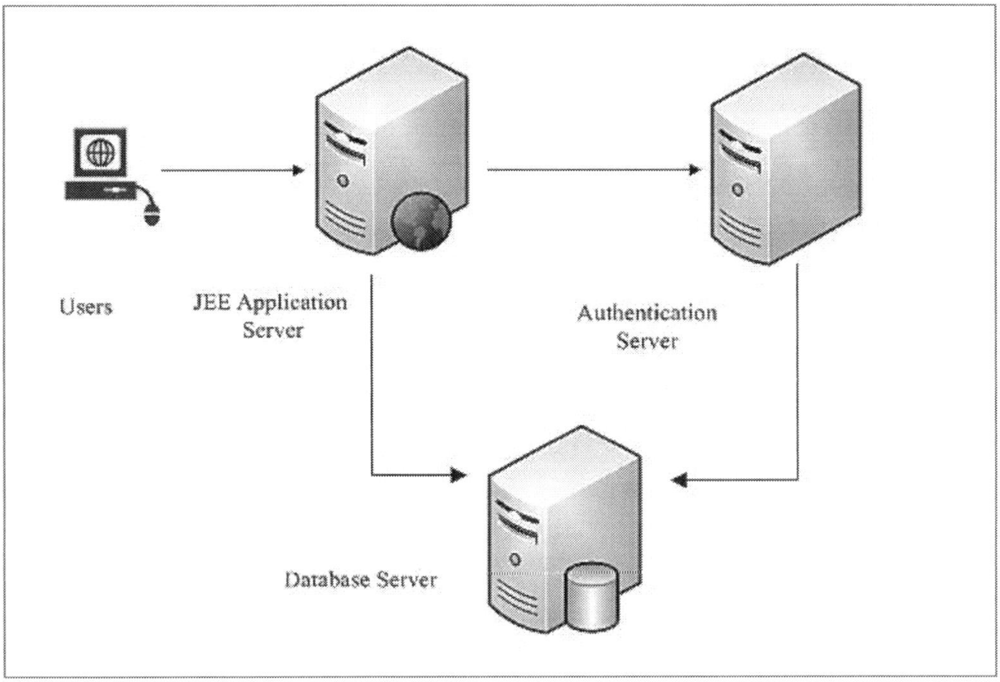

Figure 1.5 Performance and scalability test environment for a JEE-based enterprise Web application

As it turned out, the performance and scalability of this enterprise Web application were largely pegged down on the JEE application server. The hardware requirements for the authentication server and the database server could be easily met, while the JEE application server must be equipped with high-end Intel processors in order to achieve the best possible performance and scalability for supporting a large number of concurrent users. This peculiarity has made it an idea case study to show how *newer, faster* CPUs could help resolve application performance and scalability issues decisively, as discussed next.

1.3.2 CPU as a Critical Performance Factor

The performance and scalability of this enterprise Web application was tested with four different hardware configurations for the JEE application server as listed in Table 1.1. All other test conditions remained the same for all these runs, for example:

- The same use scenarios were used with the same workload model and the same number of 300 concurrent users.
- The same database server and same authentication server were used without altering any configuration parameters.
- The same version of JVM (64-bit Java 1.6.0 update 21) was used for the JEE application server on each of the four different hardware systems with different CPU configurations.

Table 1.1 Four Different Hardware Systems with Different CPU Capacities for the JEE Application Server (E7330, E5320, E5620 are all Intel Xeon based CPUs, while i7 is the Newest Intel Core i7 CPU)

CPU Model	# of cores	# of Processors	CPU GHz
VM: E7330 for ESX server	8 vCPUs	8 (not hyper-threaded)	2.4 GHz
E5320	8 cores	8 (not hyper-threaded)	1.86 GHz
E5620	8 cores	16 (hyper-threaded)	2.4 GHz
i7-2600	4 cores	8 (hyper-threaded)	3.4 GHz

Table 1.2 shows the average response times in seconds for 14 representative user actions out of about 50 in total, measured on JEE application server configuration arranged from the least powerful to the most powerful CPUs for Test A through D, respectively. The following observations can be made:

- The use of a VM slice for the JEE application server resulted in large response times of up to 123 seconds. The average response time was 28.7 seconds as shown at the end of the table, which was reduced to 7.48, 2.78, and 0.95 seconds, respectively, when the JEE application server was moved to and tested on each of the three physical systems powered by Intel's Xeon E5320, E5620 and latest i7 CPUs, respectively.
- If we use the normalized average response time as the base for comparison, it is seen that with this application:
    - The two quad-core E5320 based server performed 4 times better than the 8-vCPU VM slice out of a 16-core physical ESX server.
    - The two quad-core E5620 based server performed 10 times better than the 8-vCPU VM slice.
    - The single quad core, hyper-threaded, i7-based server performed 30 times better than the 8-vCPU VM slice.
- With all three physical systems, it is seen that the two quad-core E5620 based server and the single quad-core i7-based server performed 3 and 8 times better than the 8-core E5320-based server, respectively.
- The best performer is the i7-based system, which performed 3 times better than the E5620-based server.

From this real-product based case study, we see that CPUs of a hardware system can make a huge impact on the performance and scalability of a CPU-intensive enterprise application. This is obvious but often overlooked by developers that whenever a performance issue occurs it's always considered an application or database issue rather than a significantly under-sized hardware issue. If the issue were with the hardware, it would be much less costly and much easier to move to a newer, more powerful hardware system than to optimize the application at the code level to make it work on a virtualized slice or low-end physical systems.

Table 1.2 UI Average Response Times (Seconds) Obtained with the JEE Application Server Deployed and Tested on Each of the Four Different Hardware Systems with Different CPU Configurations

Test Case/action	**Test A** (VM)	**Test B** (E5320)	**Test C** (E5620)	**Test D** (i7-2600)
a00_login	78.66	3.22	1.78	1.35
a01_save	31.92	7.11	2.40	1.15
a02_load	28.48	7.16	2.30	0.92
a03_search	22.01	4.39	1.73	0.54
a04_save	29.77	5.64	2.13	0.74
a05_save	30.43	4.73	1.84	0.58
a06_save	123.06	20.87	4.10	1.49
a07_load	10.82	6.74	1.91	0.75
a08_view	6.66	4.32	1.25	0.51
a09_save	19.71	6.48	2.50	1.19
a10_save	7.44	12.02	4.40	1.21
a11_search	3.21	4.81	0.93	0.38
a12_analyzing	6.17	10.79	8.96	1.55
a13_statistics	3.52	6.45	2.77	0.97
average	**28.70**	**7.48**	**2.78**	**0.95**
Ratio (base: VM)	1	4	10	30
Ratio (base: E5320)		1	3	8
Ratio (base: E5620)			1	3

Figure 1.6 shows the total CPU usage averaged over all CPUs associated with each test case listed in Table 1.2, which was 64%, 72%, 37% and 21% for the 8vCPU VM, Xeon E5320, Xeon E5620, and Core i7 CPU configurations for the JEE application server, respectively. It is seen that the best case was with the Core i7 CPU configuration, which resulted in the best average response time of slightly less than one second with the lowest average CPU utilization of 21% only, which in turn implies that even more users can be supported.

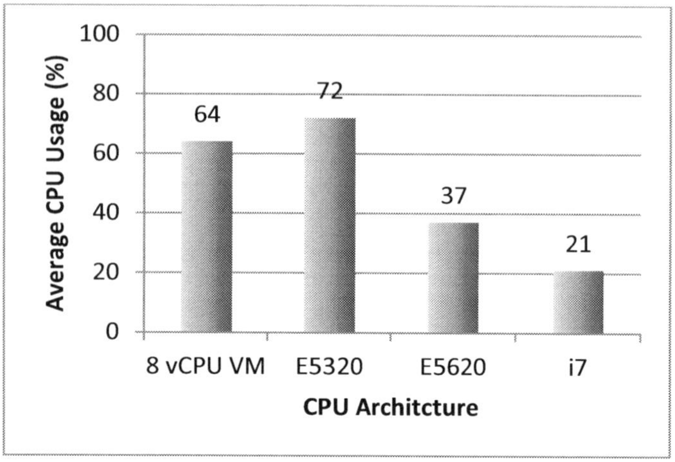

Figure 1.6 Average CPU usage (%) associated with the test results listed in Table 1.2

1.3.3 Hyper-Threaded or Non-Hyper-Threaded

Computer systems based on Intel-architecture typically come with the hyper-threading (HT) technology built-in, which may help improve application performance by as much as over 30%, as I observed and documented in my other book [Liu, 2009]. However, a challenging issue is how you would know HT has been enabled on your system. For example, with my i7-system, both the Task Manager and Computer Management views show that there are 8 CPUs or processors. See Figure 1.7. The question is how many physical cores or CPUs it actually has. It could have a single quad-core with HT enabled or two quad-cores with no hyper-threading. These two possible configurations could result in very different performance and scalability of an application, as an 8 physical core configuration would perform and scale better than a 4 physical core, HT-enabled system.

It used to be difficult to determine whether HT was enabled on an Intel-architecture based system prior to Windows 2008, as the only way was to reboot the system into BIOS mode and check if HT was enabled. This could be hard to do when your system is a server located in the data center of your company and you do not have physical access to it. Now with Windows 2008 and newer Windows, it is as simple as opening up an MS-DOS command prompt and executing the following command:

```
cmd>wmic cpu get numberOfCores
```

where 'wmic' in the above command stands for Windows Management Instrumentation Command-line. Then, if your system is a single quad-core, the output displays a '4' under the first line of 'NumberOfCores' or two '4's if you have a two-quad-core system or two '6's if you have a two six-core system, and so forth. With my i7 system, the above command outputs one '4' so it confirms that the system has a single quad-core with HT enabled. Therefore, the Task Manager and Computer Management views show eight hyper-threaded logical CPUs actually with one physical CPU split into two logical ones. Note that the above command does not apply to VMs, in which case, the only valid concept is virtual CPUs or vCPUs.

On a Linux system, issue the following command to get CPU info:

```
cat /proc/cpuinfo | grep "core id"
```

The # of `core id`'s output would be equivalent to the number of physical CPU cores on the system.

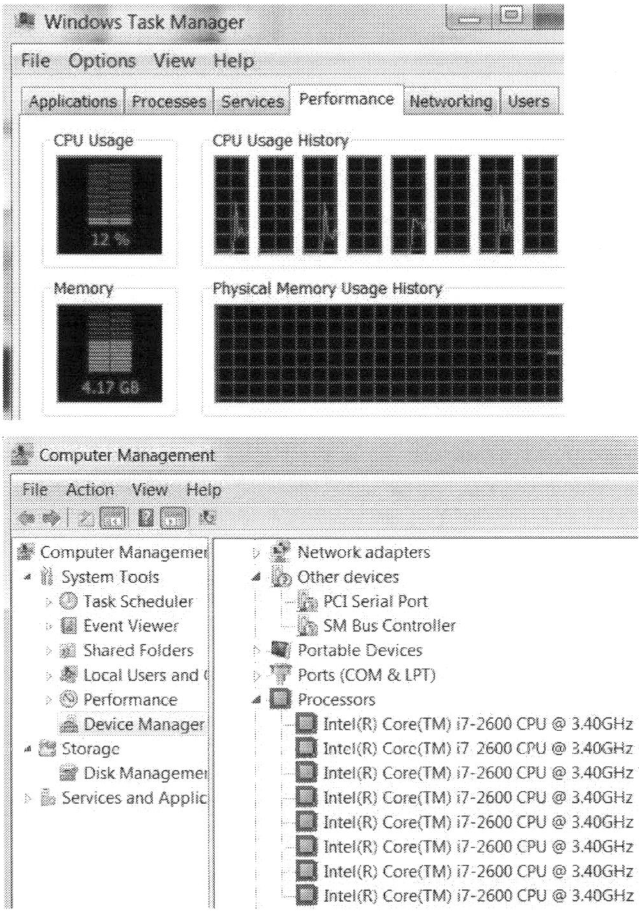

Figure 1.7 Task Manager (upper) and Computer Management (lower) views showing 8 CPUs on a Core™ i7-based system

1.4 PERFORMANCE VERSUS SCALABILITY

Enterprise applications must be high performing, scalable and reliable. While the reliability of an enterprise application is hard to define accurately, the performance and scalability requirements can be measured more quantitatively both in pre-production and in production environments. The *performance* aspect of an enterprise application can be quantified using the following two metrics, as we discussed in the section of *A Primer on Queuing Theory*:

- **Response Time**. This metric is used to quantify the amount of time a user experiences while performing certain actions, for example, logging into the application, opening a page, creating an item, saving a form, bringing up a report, etc. Although most of the actions initiated by a user should not exceed the two-second stringent requirement, certain less frequently initiated, aggregation-type of actions like running a report should be allowed to take longer, for example, up to a minute or even longer. In such cases, typically a progress pop-up is displayed to inform the user that "*this may take a while …*" so the user would not expect a fast return.
- **Throughput**. This metric is used to quantify how fast a background batch job could complete for a given amount of work to complete within a specified time window. In this case, no users get involved, and the batch jobs are scheduled to occur automatically at a specified time with a fixed schedule, for example, daily, weekly, or monthly.

The *scalability* aspect of an enterprise application is more concerned with how the system would perform with increasing load, for example, with more concurrent users or more work to complete in the background within a given period.

An enterprise application is said to be *scalable* if a wide range of customer load requirements can be met by using proper hardware. This is measured mostly by the CPU power of the hardware required to run the application. Accordingly, there are concepts of horizontal scaling and vertical scaling. As we discussed earlier, horizontal scaling requires implementing clustering and load balancing with more than one identical hardware systems, for example, web servers, application servers, or database servers, whereas vertical scaling simply implies adding more CPUs of the same power or upgrading the slower CPUs with faster CPUs for a given server system. Which type of scaling works better depends on many factors. For example, some practical limitations include whether the application can run on load-balanced servers without being modified for horizontal scaling, and whether vertical scaling alone can meet customer's requirements, etc.

No matter which type of scaling is chosen, the required scalability is the same, that is, one needs to test with increasing load in terms of the number of concurrent users or amount of background batch processing work to complete. Let's use the previous case study to help explain this next.

Specific user actions vary from application to application. However, a similar methodology can be used to measure the scalability of an application, that is, you can script and test a number of user actions with increasing number of concurrent users, and then use the response time averaged over all actions and all users to see how fast the average response time degrades with increasing number of users. Figure 1.8 shows such an example from the previous case study with the given hardware configuration of the Xeon E5620 for the JEE application server. It is seen that the average response time doubled when the number of concurrent users was doubled from 150 to 300. Different applications may exhibit different performance and scalability characteristics on different hardware systems, though.

Since the response time averaged over all users and all actions as shown in Figure 1.9 tends to smooth away those actions with large response times, it might be more helpful to show response times of actions averaged on all users on a per-action basis. In this case, it can be clearly seen how well each action performs so that further optimization and tunings might help bring the response times of those poorly performed actions down to acceptable levels. Using the same case study presented previously, Figure 1.9 shows the response times of the actions measured on the same JEE application server based on the E5620 CPU architecture with 150, 200, 250, and 300 concurrent users, respectively. As expected, the response time of each action became larger as more and more users were stressing the system, although not necessarily uniformly or proportionally across all actions.

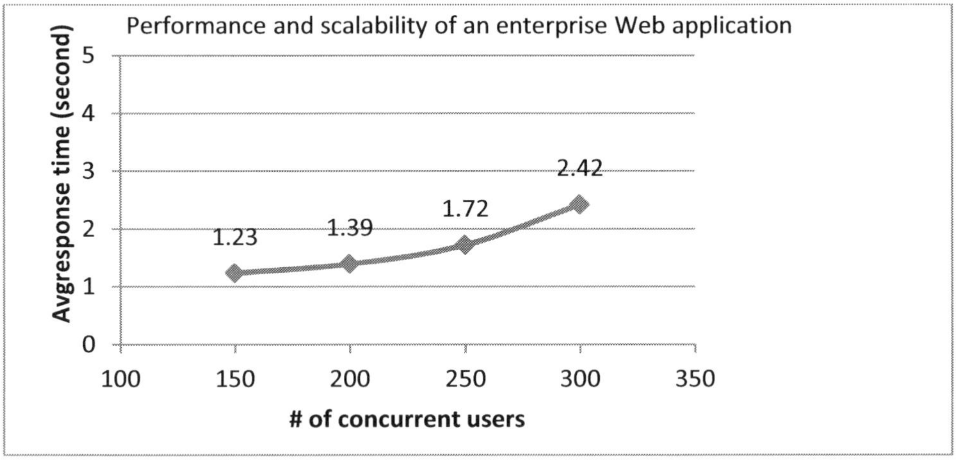

Figure 1.8 Measured average response times versus the number of concurrent users

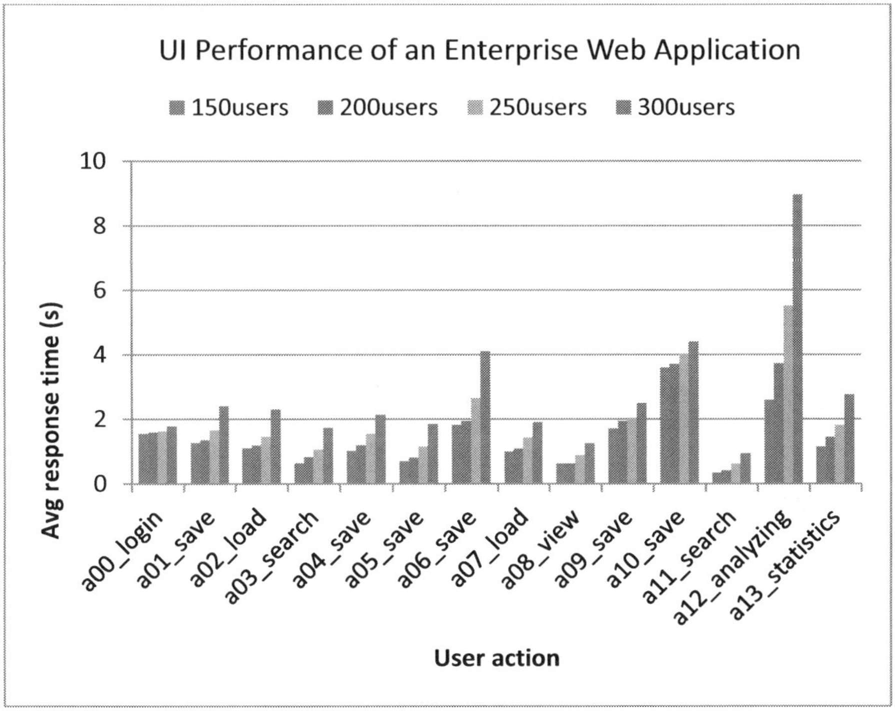

Figure 1.9 Average response times for a subset of actions versus the number of concurrent users

This kind of scalability testing gives valuable information on how many concurrent users an enterprise application can support with a given hardware configuration so that customers can plan for properly sized hardware in advance. Such performance and scalability testing activities typically should be integrated into the development process of an enterprise application for which meeting customer's performance and scalability requirements matters.

1.5 LINEAR SCALABILITY?

The concept of linear scalability is characterized by the linear relationship between the # of concurrent users and a critical system resource such as the CPU processing power of a server. The question is if linear scalability actually exists in reality. The answer is "yes, but not infinitely."

As an example of the statement that linear scalability does not extend infinitely, Figure 1.10 shows the scalability characteristics of the same real world case study presented previously, but with the 8 physical core JEE application server replaced with a hyper-threaded 12-core Windows 2008 R2 server. The straight line shows the ideally linear scalability, while the curve beneath it shows the measured scalability. It is seen that with the hardware configuration tested, it appears that the application could scale up to approximately 600 concurrent users. Note that with the test run of 700 concurrent users, the JEE application server average CPU usage actually dropped relative to the 600 concurrent user run. This was actually caused by massively failed transactions due to increased load and hence contentions, which led to less CPU consumptions in the JEE application server. Therefore, the load test results with 700 concurrent users was essentially invalid.

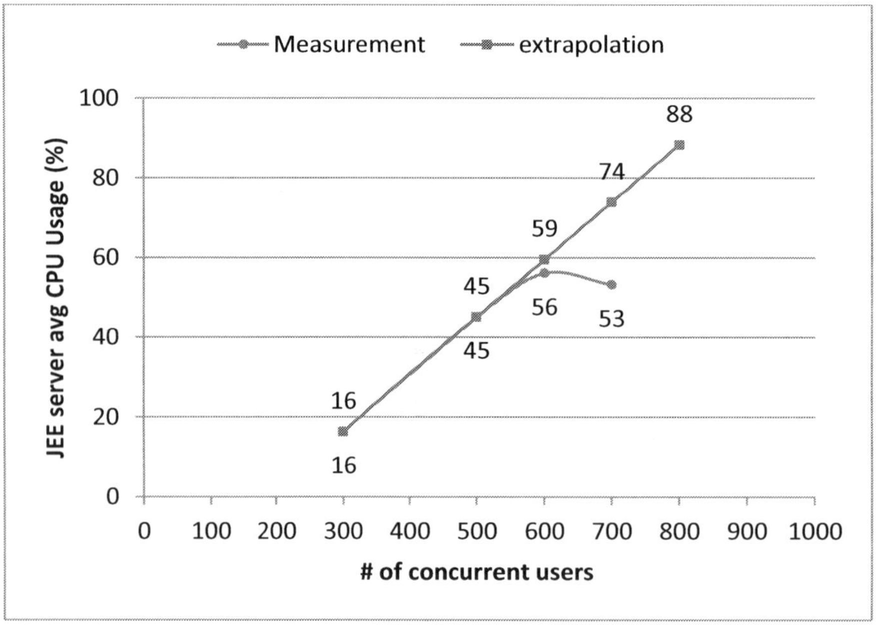

Figure 1.10 Scalability: linear versus measured

Although the test run with 700 concurrent users resulted in erroneous, invalid results, it helped provide valuable information for extrapolating the number of users that a system could support with more or less powerful hardware for the JEE application server with this product. For example, by upgrading the JEE application server from 12 CPU cores to 16 CPU cores with the same processor specs, the application may support up to 800 concurrent users. If the system only needs to support 400 concurrent users, the JEE application server could be scaled down to 8 CPU cores with the same processor specs. This kind of extrapolation exercise is useful when there are limitations to the availability of a wide range of hardware configurations for doing actual testing or when exhausting all hardware configuration permutations is virtually impossible.

1.6 SYSTEM PERFORMANCE COUNTERS

This section describes system performance counters on Windows and Linux for monitoring system resource utilizations, which provide most valuable information for trouble-shooting performance and scalability issues. In this section, we describe how to set up those counters to collect system resource usage data. Refer to my other text *Software Performance and Scalability: An Quantitative Approach* (Wiley, 2009) or similar texts for more in-depth description on how to interpret those counters to analyze a performance and scalability issue.

1.6.1 Windows

Table 1.3 lists a minimum set of performance counters that should be logged on a Windows system, useful for post-analyzing a performance and scalability test run. These counters are called *perfmon* counters. Note that the disk I/O counters are needed only on a database server in general. Also, since Windows does not provide a counter for `% busy time` for disk, you need to get the `% busy time` metric by using the conversion formula of 1 - `% idle time`. Besides, there are two %Processor Time counters: one for the Processor object and the other for the Process object. The former is normalized to 100% maximum, while the latter is aggregated across all CPUs including logical CPUs with the maximum value equal to the `# of CPUs x 100%`. Therefore, when you look at the %Processor Time for the Process object, you may see CPU utilizations exceeding 100%, which needs to be divided by the number of CPUs to compare with the %Processor Time for the Processor object.

Table 1.3 A minimum set of performance counters to be logged on Windows

Performance Object	Performance Counters
Processor	%Processor Time
System	Processor Queue Length
Process	%Processor Time Private Bytes Thread Count Virtual Bytes Working Set
Memory	Available MBytes

Disk (physical or logic)	%Idle Time Avg. Disk Read Queue Length Avg. Disk Write Queue Length Avg. Disk Bytes/Read Avg. Disk Bytes/Write Avg. Disk sec/Read Avg. Disk sec/Write Disk Read Bytes/sec Disk Write Bytes/sec Disk Reads/sec Disk Writes/sec
Network interface	Bytes Received/sec Bytes Sent/sec Bytes Total/sec

Performance counters can be set up and started on the Performance Monitor snap-in on a Windows system. It can also be configured to run by calling the *typeperf* command line utility program on Windows 2008 and newer systems. For example, to monitor the CPU utilizations on a computer, you can simply open up an MS-DOS command prompt, type and run the following command:

```
cmd>typeperf "\\<host>\Processor (_Total)\% Processor Time"
```

where <host> is the system name or IP to be monitored. For local systems, you can omit the part of "\\<host>".

I actually favor this tool over the Performance Monitor snap-in for two reasons:

1 You can put all counters in a text file and then execute it on an MS-DOS command prompt. This can help avoid accessing the Performance Monitor snap-in all the time.
2 You can collect performance counters on a remote system without having to log into that system, start up the Performance Monitor there, start up the job, and so on, which is too tedious when you have multiple systems to repeat the same procedure each time you start a run. This would allow you to collect performance logs on each individual machine from one system, and store them in one place without having to pull them over every time a test run is completed.

Listing 1.1 shows an example counter input file named *Mirabeau-perfLog.txt*. On that machine named Mirabeau or on a remote machine, you can execute it using the following *typeperf* command:

```
typeperf –f CSV –o MachineA-perfLog-001.csv -si 10 –cf  mirabeau-perfLog.txt -sc 70
```

The option *–f* specifies the output file format, *-o* output file, *-si* output interval in seconds, *–cf* input counter spec file, and *–sc* number of intervals.

Listing 1.1 Mirabeau-perfLog.txt

```
"\\mirabeau\Processor(_Total)\% Processor Time"
"\\mirabeau\System\Processor Queue Length"
```

In addition to writing *perfmon* counters into a log file for off-line analysis, Task Manager gives a real-time view of system resource utilizations, which should be used in conjunction with logged performance counters as listed in Table 1.3.

Figures 1.11 and 1.12 show the examples of CPU utilizations on the JEE application server obtained with the `Processor %Processor Time` as described above. They correspond to Test C and Test D listed in Table 1.2, respectively. Keep in mind that when you measure the average CPU usage, the head and tail parts should be excluded by moving the slider bars at both ends of the *time range* scale available under the Source tab of the *Performance Monitor Properties* Window.

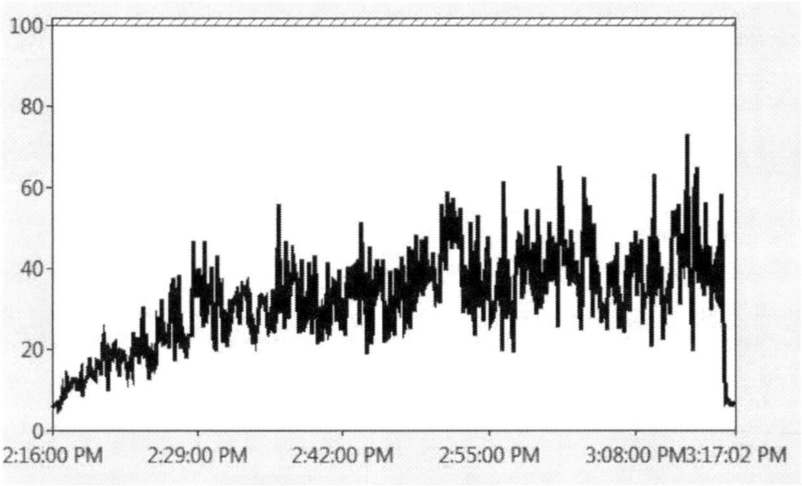

Figure 1.11 CPU utilizations on the E5620-based JEE application server corresponding to Test C listed in Table 1.2

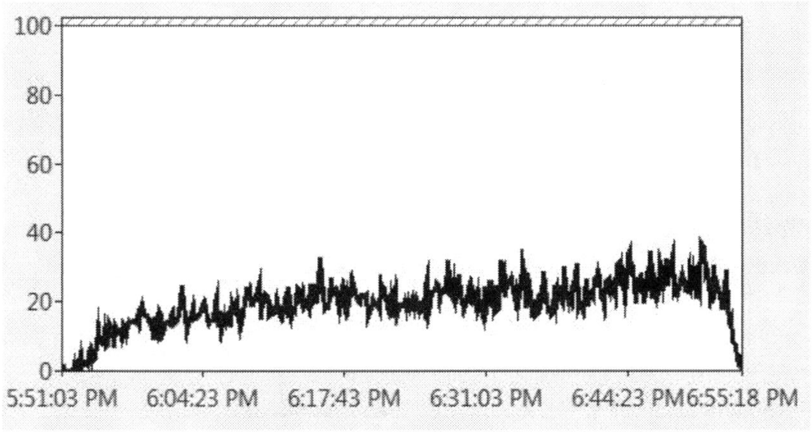

Figure 1.12 CPU utilizations on the i7-based JEE application server corresponding to Test D listed in Table 1.2

1.6.2 Linux

On Linux, I use the following `vmstat` command to log system resource utilizations:

vmstat –t –n 10 420 –SM > myLogFile.txt

which specifies logging with an interval of every 10 seconds for 420 intervals, amounting to about 70 minutes for covering a one-hour test duration. You can adjust the # of intervals based on the test duration you set with your test run. The other command switch options are explained as follows:

- The *–t* command switch enables logging timestamp. Note that some Linux variants, such as OpenSuSE, may not support this option. You can add pipe " `| awk '{now=strftime("%Y -%m -%d %T "); print now $0}'` " to precede each output line with a timestamp to be used with a graphing tool to circumvent the unsupported "*-t*" option..
- The *–n* command switch causes the header to be displayed only once rather than periodically.
- The *–SM* option specifies that memory counters report in the units of MB.

Table 1.4 explains all the counters logged with this `vmstat` command-line tool. Although other tools such as `ps`, `sar`, `iostat`, and so on, are also available, I found that this `vmstat` tool is most comprehensive and sufficient in diagnosing whether an application is CPU bound, memory-bound, or IO-bound. You can use this `vmstat` tool with the switch options as shown above to direct the output to a text file, and then use a program like Microsoft Excel to do statistical analysis and plot charts. Figures 1.13 and 1.14 show the Oracle database server CPU utilizations logged from this tool during the periods of Test C and Test D listed in Table 1.2, respectively.

Table 1.4 Linux `vmstat` Counters

Performance Object	Performance Counters
procs	**r** – The number of processes waiting for run time. This is equivalent to the Processor Queue Length counter on Windows. **b** – The number of processes blocked in uninterruptible sleep, waiting for resources such as I/O.
memory	**swpd** – The amount of virtual memory used. **free** – The amount of unused memory. **buff** – The amount of memory used as buffers. **cache** – The amount of memory used as cache.
swap	**si** – The amount of memory swapped in from disk. **so** – The amount of memory swapped out to disk. High so values over a long period may indicate that an application is leaking memory and the leaked memory is being swapped out.
io	**bi** – Input rate to a block device (blocks/s). **bo** – Output rate from a block device (blocks/s).
system	**in** – The number of interrupts per second, including the clock. **cs** – The number of context switches per second.

cpu	**us** – %user time. **sy** – % kernel time. **id** – % idle time. **wa** – % IO waiting time. **st** - %Time stolen from a virtual machine (not sure what this is about).
timestamp	Logging timestamp

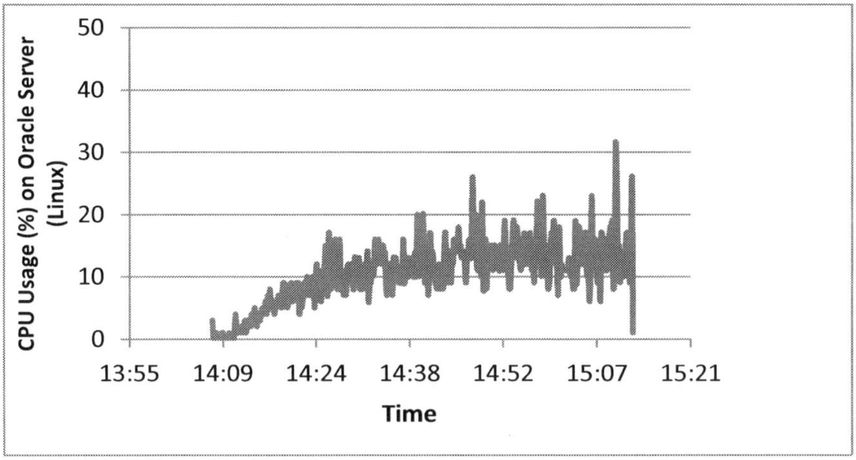

Figure 1.13 CPU usage of an Oracle database server collected with the `vmstat` tool on RedHat Linux corresponding to Test C listed in Table 1.2

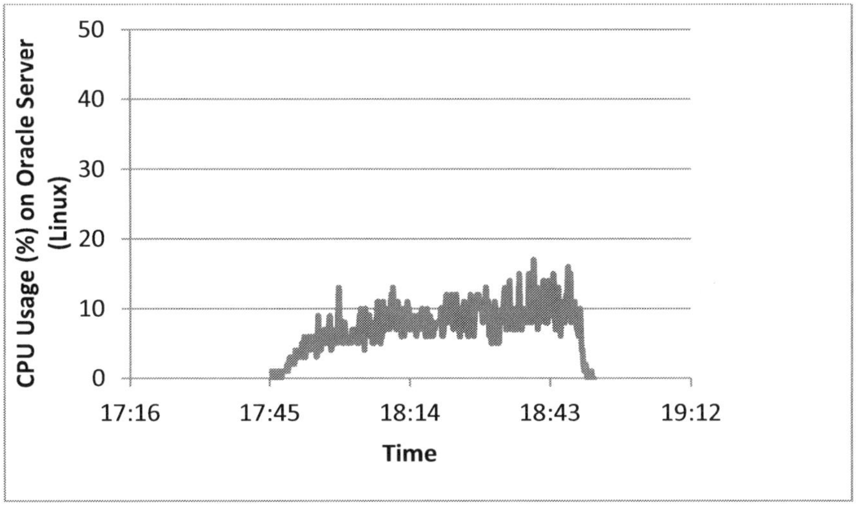

Figure 1.14 CPU usage of an Oracle database server collected with the `vmstat` tool on RedHat Linux corresponding to Test D listed in Table 1.2

Note the `cache` counter in the memory category listed in Table 1.4. This counter is related to Linux file system caching, which could be very detrimental if the Linux file system is used for storing database files. It may cause very large disk read and write times for database centric enterprise applications. My other book *Software Performance and Scalability: A Quantitative Approach* [Liu, 2009] covers this so-called "double-buffering" issue in detail. However, if you cannot place your database files on a third-party, non-Linux-native file system, you may need to reboot your server from time to time just to cleanse cached data when it becomes too large. For example, with the case study presented previously, that Linux file system cache could grow up to 10 GB, which was too large, given the fact that the server has 16 GB RAM total only. Whenever that happened, the only way to clean up that cache was to reboot the server. Some suggested using the following command to clean up the cache, but it doesn't work in my case.

```
prompt>sync; echo 3>/proc/sys/vm/drop_caches
```

In addition to the `vmstat` tool, you can use the `top` utility to monitor system resource utilizations interactively. This tool is similar to Task Manager on Windows. However, it's less appropriate for a long-running test for which it's more helpful to have an end-to-end view of the system resource utilizations covering the entire test period.

If you are interested in monitoring system resources on a per-process basis, you might want to try a script that I have been using for my own tests. This script logs three counters: `vsz`, `rss`, and `pcpu`, which represent the virtual memory size, resident memory size, and CPU usage associated with that process, respectively. Please refer to §8.4.8 for more information about this script.

1.7 SUMMARY

In this chapter, we started with a primer on queuing theory to set the theoretical foundation for optimizing and tuning Java application performance and scalability. We used an analogy between electrical circuits and computer systems to make it easier to understand all theoretical concepts and laws of computer system performance and scalability. Despite the differences in context, the two fields bear remarkable similarities in many aspects, from the similarity between the concept of electrical resistance in electrical circuits to that of resource contention in computer systems, to the similarities in the mathematical form of laws expressing relationships among the metrics in each context. Although brief, the primer provides us with a sufficient coverage on the response time laws, throughput laws, and Jackson's theorem, especially the concepts of service time and service demand, which are applied throughout the text to analyzing Java application performance and scalability issues.

We then used a real world case study to help explain the concepts of performance and scalability of enterprise software applications. With quantitative data, we also illustrated that computer server CPU typically is a critical factor in determining the performance and scalability of an application. This is very important to keep in mind when evaluating the performance and scalability of an enterprise application.

Some important skills learnt in this chapter include:

- How to determine if an Intel-architecture based system is hyper-threading enabled.
- How to use the linear part of a scalability curve to extrapolate the number of users an application may support with less or more powerful hardware.

- How to set up performance counters on Windows and Linux, which is always a necessary part of a performance and scalability testing project with an enterprise application.

The next chapter helps you get deeper with computer hardware architecture to help further enhance the notion that computer CPU architecture plays a critical role in determining the performance and scalability of an enterprise application. A basic understanding of hardware architecture, especially the state-of-the-art multicore CPU architectures, is valuable for enterprise application stakeholders to work more effectively to help meet the performance and scalability requirements for their customers.

EXERCISES

1.1 What makes electrical circuits and computer systems analogous to each other?

1.2 Explain the implications with the response time and throughput laws.

1.3 What's the essence of Jackson's theorem from the software performance and scalability tuning perspective?

1.4 How do you determine if a computer system is hyper-threading (HT) enabled on Windows? Why is it important to make sure whether a system is HT enabled or not?

1.5 What factor prevents software from scaling linearly infinitely?

1.6 Does *typeperf* apply to remote systems?

1.7 What command utility can help collect most common performance metrics on Linux and how do you use it?

REFERENCES

H. H. Liu, *Software Performance and Scalability: A Quantitative Approach*, Wiley, 2009.

J. R. Jackson, Jobshop-like Queuing Systems, *Management Science*, Vol. 10, No. 1, 131-142, 1963.

2 Computer Hardware Architecture

Using both queuing theory based performance laws and a real product based case study, we demonstrated in Chapter 1 the importance of underlying hardware in determining the performance and scalability of a Java application. We introduced a formula to describe the relationship between service time and response time of a computer system in Eq. (1.3) in the form of

$$\boldsymbol{R}esponse\ Time = \boldsymbol{S}ervice\ Time\ /\ (1 - \boldsymbol{U}tilization)\ \text{or}\ \boldsymbol{R} = \boldsymbol{S}\ /\ (1 - \boldsymbol{U})$$

This simple formula implies that in order to get smallest possible response time or best performance, two things must happen:

1. A *computer system* must be capable of running fast to produce smallest possible service time (***S***) as the numerator of the right-hand-side of the above equation.
2. An *application* must be designed, implemented and tuned properly so that it would require the least amount of resource (***U***) to run as designated by the denominator of the right-hand-side of the above equation.

A Java software stakeholder should be able to understand the above two factors sufficiently well to know how to strike a balance between the two. For example, when a performance and scalability barrier can be lifted with more properly configured, faster hardware, you may not want to pour in a huge amount of development time to dig on your application, which would not only cost more but also delay your product and potentially lose customers and eventually competition. On the other hand, if you know your application even doesn't perform and scale on state-of-the-art hardware, then you would not have much choice other than spending time on your application. This kind of decisions cannot be made just by tossing a coin – it requires a thorough understanding on both modern hardware and software performance and scalability engineering. It's not too exaggerating to say it imposes a high risk if a Java software stakeholder does not possess a minimum understanding on latest hardware technologies.

That's the purpose of this chapter, namely, helping you understand state-of-the-art computer hardware architecture so that you would be equipped with necessary hardware knowledge required to build performance and scalability into your Java application. All remaining chapters help you understand how to take an all-out approach to minimizing system resource utilizations to make your Java application perform and scale. To summarize, this chapter helps you understand the numerator of the above equation, whereas the rest of the book helps you work on the denominator in the above equation.

Because of its ubiquitous usage for both personal and enterprise computing, we use Intel processor architecture as the gateway to understanding computer hardware architecture. This should be a good choice, as whether you work on Windows or Linux or even Unix, most likely you're on an Intel box.

In this chapter, we first give a brief overview on the history of Intel processors. Intel architecture has evolved exponentially in terms of performance since the release of its first single-chip microprocessor 4004 four decades ago in 1971. However, its basic system structure still applies today. Therefore, we would start with the internal structure of an Intel i386 processor, which is simple, yet inclusive with all basic functions that even a modern computer processor has to offer. You might wonder why we even bother with such a very primitive Intel processor model developed decades ago. Our purpose is to pick something that's simple and easy to understand, rather than becoming a hardware engineer after reviewing this chapter. In addition, this brief coverage would help you understand the system performance counters introduced in Chapter 1 better. All in all, if you have a solid understanding of the modern computer processor architectures, you will be more effective and efficient in dealing with Java application performance and scalability issues with your product.

We wrap up this chapter by demonstrating how you can use some official CPU benchmarking results or one of my own benchmarking programs to help you trouble-shoot your application Java performance and scalability issues or asses your performance and scalability test results. Once again, real products are used to provide the context in which the benchmarking programs are demonstrated.

My minimum expectation is that after going through this chapter, you would be able to identify the hardware architecture (if an Intel-architecture based system) and assess its power with a give system you work on. Let us begin with the history of Intel processors next.

2.1 HISTORY OF INTEL PROCESSORS

Intel has been in the computer chip business for over four decades now, and has apparently come out of the fierce competition as the winner in chip business. It appears that Intel processor development has undergone three consecutive stages:

- Stage 1: From 4-bit to 32-bit computing
- Stage 2: From tens of MHz to multiple GHz CPU clock rates
- And stage 3: From single core to multicore CPUs

Following the above division, let us take a look at the initial stage of processor development at Intel next.

2.1.1 4-bit to 32-bit computing

Table 2.1 illustrates Intel's processor development activities in 1970's and 1980's. The first model 4004 had a CPU clock speed of 740 kHz and an address space of 640 bytes only. This tiny address space was limited by the 4-bit width of the registers used (a register in a computer processor is a storage structure that may contain an instruction, an address, a data item, the status value of some entities, or any other type of data that is required for various types of computing tasks at the processor CPU level). The milestones since then were measured by the number of register bits and hence the total capacity of the physical address space. You can see that it had taken one year to move from 4-bit up to 8-bit, six years from 8-bit to 16-bit, and three years from 16-bit to 32-bit, respectively. Unarguably, the advent of Intel's 32-bit processors once helped accelerate the arrival of the PC and Internet eras in early 90's.

Table 2.1 Intel Processor History up to 80846

Year	Model	CPU Clock Speed	Register width	Address Bus	Data bus	Address Space
1971	4004	740 kHz	4 bits	8 bits	8 bits	640 bytes
1972	8008	500 kHz	8 bits	8 bits	8 bits	16 KB
1974	8080	2 MHz	8 bits	16 bits	8 bits	64 KB
1978	8086	5 – 10 MHz	16 bits	20 bits	16 bits	1 MB
1979	8088	5 – 8 MHz	16 bits	20 bits	8 bits	1 MB
1982	80186	6 MHz	16 bits	20 bits	16 bits	1 MB
1982	80286	6 – 16 MHz	16 bits	24 bits	16 bits	16 MB
1985	80386DX	16 – 33 MHz	32 bits	32 bits	32 bits	4 GB
1988	80386SX	16 – 33 MHz	32 bits	24 bits	16 bits	16 MB
1989	80486DX	25-50 MHz	32 bits	32 bits	32 bits	4 GB

This first stage of Intel processor development was marked by the releases of 80386 and 80486 processors or i386 for 80386 and i486 for 80486 synonymously. This series of processors and some of the later releases are also termed *80x86* processors with "x" implied as a substitute for either '3' or '4' between 80 and 86. You may also often hear the term x86, which actually refers to a family of instruction set architectures (ISAs) based on the Intel 80x86 32-bit processors.

Let's clarify further on processor hardware architecture versus instruction set architecture. A specific CPU hardware architecture or vendor-specific microarchitecture classifies a PC configured with a specific type of processor, whereas the instruction set architecture denotes its applicable programming model defined by its native data types, instructions, registers, addressing modes, memory structure, interrupt and exception handling, external I/O interface, etc. The concept of an instruction set architecture helps hide the specifics of the underlying hardware so that applications developed based on the same instruction set architecture will run on the systems with different microarchitectures. In literature, you may also see the terms like "x86-32" and "x86-64," which refer to the more latest 32-bit and 64-bit Intel and AMD based PC architectures, respectively.

2.1.2 CPU GHz racing

Table 2.2 illustrates Intel's processor development activities from 1993 to 2006. This second stage is characterized by faster and faster CPU clock rates, ranging from 60 MHz Pentium, to faster Pentium Pro, Pentium II, Pentium III, Pentium 4, and all the way to Pentium D at 3.8 GHz. In fact, Pentium-based PCs are divided into three different categories: laptops, desktops, and servers (Xeon-based), with each category having its own optimization goals.

Table 2.2 Intel Pentium/Xeon processor history since P5/Pentium

Year	Microarchitecture /Model	CPU Clock Speed	Instruction cache	Data cache	L2 cache
1993	P5/Pentium	60 or 66 MHz	8 kB	8 kB	-
1995	P6/Pentium Pro	166 – 200 MHz	16 kB	16 kB	256 kB
1997	P6/Pentium II	300 – 450 MHz	32 kB	32 kB	512 kB
1999	P6/(Pentium III, Xeon)	0.6 – 2 GHz	32 - 64 kB	32 - 64 kB	512kB – 2 MB
2000 - 2006	Netburst/(Pentium 4, Pentium D)	1.3 – 3.8 GHz	32 kB	32 kB	256 kB - 4 MB

However, the performance of an application is not necessarily solely determined by the CPU clock rate of the PC on which the application runs. Another important factor is the proximity of data needed by the CPU. An application would perform poorly if the CPU constantly waits for data it needs to carry out the computing tasks in question. A large L1 cache (instruction cache + data cache) and a large L2 cache can help boost performance significantly by improving the proximity of data needed by the CPU.

In addition to faster and faster clock rates for the Pentium based PCs shown in Table 2.2, another notable advancement is in the microarchitectures behind each release of the Pentium processors. As is seen, the Intel microarchitecture had evolved from P5 to P6 and to Netburst during this period. A detailed discussion on each of those microarchitectures is beyond the scope of this text, but a high-level overview could be very beneficial both in general and in context of Java application performance and scalability.

Here are the highlights with each of those Intel's latest generations of microarchitectures:

- **P5**. This was Intel's fifth generation x86 microarchitecture. It is often called Intel's i586 architecture. It was an immediate extension to the 80486 architecture. In addition to the improvements such as dual integer pipelines, separate code and data caches, a faster FPU (floating point unit), a wider data bus (64-bit), MultiMedia eXtension (MMX: a single instruction, multiple data or SIMD instruction set), P5 introduced the superscalar concept, which had been a norm with super computers like Cray's CDC 6600 and RISC-based processors. The superscalar architecture works by enabling parallelism at the instruction level within a single processor. It is characterized by:

- Instructions are issued sequentially.
- The processor hardware dynamically checks for data dependencies at run time rather than checked by software at compile time.
- The processor can take multiple instructions per CPU clock cycle. This turned out to be a significant performance-boosting technique.

■ **P6**. This is the sixth generation Intel x86 microarchitecture or i686 architecture. The performance optimization techniques employed in the P6 include:

- Speculative execution (prefetching and branch prediction) and out-of-order execution (rather than wait for data for the current instruction, the next instruction is executed if its data becomes available first).
- Super-pipelining with P5's 5-stage pipeline extended to more than 10 stages.
- Physical address extension (PAE), which allows more than 4 GB RAM installed on a 32-bit x86 system, for example, 64 GB, but each process's linear address space still is capped to 4 GB. This feature is supported by almost all OS platforms including both Windows and Linux.
- Register renaming to avoid unnecessary serialization of program execution

■ **Netburst**. This microarchitecture was the successor to the P6 microarchitecture. Its main feature is the Hyper Pipelined Technology, which further bumped the number of pipeline stages from 10+ to 30+. However, this technique could introduce a series of complications, for example, penalty for mis-predicted branches. To compensate for any possible performance loss due to the Hyper Pipelined Technology, the concept of a Rapid Execution Engine was implemented, which double-pumps two ALUs in a CPU core so that they will be effectively operating at twice the core clock frequency. Consult Intel documentations for a more in-depth discussion on these advanced technologies.

2.1.3 Multicore processors

Prior to 2006, Intel had already made huge progresses in boosting computer system performance by improving CPU performance. Intel focused on several notable key performance areas such as expanding total physical address space from 4 bits to 32 bits, making CPUs crank faster and faster from sub-kHz to GHz, and adding larger and larger L1 and L2 caches for better data proximity, etc. Then, what's left after all these areas have been extensively explored? It turned out that the next big advance from Intel was the *Core* microarchitecture in place of the Netburst microarchitecture for better power efficiency. The Core microarchitecture was soon replaced by the *Nehalem* microarchitecture, which was in turn replaced by the *Sandy Bridge* microarchitecture, which is the latest as of this writing. Here is a summary of Intel's latest microarchitecture evolution (*Netburst → Core →Nehalem→Sandy Bridge*):

■ **Core microarchitecture**. This microarchitecture is characterized by lower CPU clock rates and better usage of both available clock cycles and power compared with the preceding NetBurst microarchitecture. It was used in Core 2 and Xeon microprocessors, produced with a 65 nm manufacturing process. These were the first Intel processors that supported Intel's x86-64 architecture. The term x86-64 is an extension to the 32-bit x86 architecture for 64-bit computing.

- **Nehalem microarchitecture**. This microarchitecture was built on the 45 nm process and supported producing the 1st generation of *Core i3*, *Core i5*, and *Core i7* microprocessors (note that these Core processors are not based on the Core microarchitecture despite their names with the prefix of Core). The performance considerations of the Nehalem microarchitecture include:
  - A 64 KB L1 cache (32 KB data + 32 KB instruction) per core, a 256 KB L2 cache per core, and a 4 – 12 MB L3 cache shared by all cores.
  - Hyper-threading reintroduced.
  - The legacy front side bus was replaced in high-end models with Intel *Quickpath Interconnect,* which is a point-to-point processor interconnect technology developed by Intel.
  - The traditional north-bridge was replaced in mid-range models with PCI Express or PCIe, which is a computer expansion card standard in place of older PCI, PCI-X and AGP bus standards.
- **Sandy Bridge microarchitecture**. This microarchitecture was built on a 32 nm process and supported producing the 2nd generation of Core i3, Core i5, and Core i7 microprocessors (note again that these Core processors are not based on the Core microarchitecture despite their names with the prefix of Core). The features of the Sandy Bridge microarchitecture include:
  - Roughly the same L1, L2 and L3 caches as with the Nehalem.
  - Two load/store operations per CPU cycle for each memory channel.
  - Advanced Vector Extensions (AVX), which is an extension to the x86 instruction set architecture. With AVX, the width of the SIMD register file is increased from 128 bits to 256 bits, resulting in wider vectors. It also has a new VEX coding scheme with a new set of code prefixes that extends the opcode space to allow instructions to have more than two operands.
  - Up to eight physical cores/sixteen logical processors with two hyper-threads per core

See Table 2.3 for Intel's multicore processor development activities across those three consecutive microarchitectures of *Netburst* → *Core* → *Nehalem* → *Sandy Bridge* since 2006. As of this writing, the most advanced Core i7 processors are from model 2600 with a CPU clock rate of 3.4 GHz, which was one of the systems I tested and mentioned in the real world case study presented in Chapter 1. Section 2.3 gives a high level overview on the performance features of the Core i7 processors.

Next, we take a closer look at the internals of Intel's processors, starting with the most influential 32-bit i386 microprocessors.

2.2 INTERNALS OF THE INTEL 80386 MICROPROCESSORS

Figure 2.1 shows a schematic diagram of the Intel 80386 microprocessor with all support subsystems. The clock generator provides the microprocessor and other components with necessary timing signals. It generates both full-cycle signals (CLK2) at 20 MHz for the 80386 processor and the half-frequency signals (CLK) for the 80286-compatible devices encompassed in the system, including RESET signals.

The 80386 microprocessor runs at 20 MHz, with 32-bit wide internal and external data paths and eight general-purpose 32-bit registers. It outputs 32-bit physical addresses directly, allowing for a maximum total physical memory capacity of 4 GBs. It also has a coprocessor running at 16 MHz for carrying out floating-point calculations.

To speed up data transfer, the 80386 microprocessor works with other crucial components such as a 32 kB cache, a cache controller, and a direct memory access (DMA) controller, which performs data transfers between main memory and external I/O devices such as hard disks, floppy disks, and communication channels without going through the processors.

Figure 2.2 illustrates the internal functional units of an 80386 microprocessor. It has a high-speed bus interface, address translation caches, pipelined instruction execution, memory management and multitasking support, all built on one chip. The pipelined architecture greatly enhances performance by allowing instruction fetching, decoding, execution, and memory management to occur in parallel.

Table 2.3 Intel Multicore Microarchitecture Processor History

Year	Model	Clock Speed	# of cores	L2 cache	L3 cache
2006	Core Solo/Duo	1 - 2.33 GHz	1-2	2 MB	-
2006 – 2008	Core 2 Solo/ Duo/ Quad/ Extreme	1.2 – 3.06 GHz	1-4	1 – 12 MB	-
2010-2011	Core i3	1.2 - 3.4 GHz	2	2x256 KB	3 – 4 MB
2010 - 2011	Core i5	1.2 – 3.6 GHz	2 - 4	2x256 – 4x256 KB	3 – 8 MB
2009 - 2011	Core i7 /Core i7 Extreme	1.2 – 3.5 GHz	2 - 6	2x256 – 6x256 KB	4 - 12 MB

Each of the six internal units of an 80386 microprocessor shown in Figure 2.2 functions as follows:

- **Bus Interface Unit**. The Bus Interface Unit processes signals for fetching code instructions and moving program data either among various internal units or between the processor and the external memory and I/O.
- **Code Prefetch Unit**. The Code Prefetch Unit fetches additional instructions from the instruction byte stream when the Bus Interface Unit is not transferring data or idle. This can potentially eliminate wait times for the next instruction.
- **Instruction Decoder Unit**. The Instruction Decoder Unit decodes the instructions fed from the prefetch queue into microcode, making them ready to execute for the Execution Unit.
- **Execution Unit**. The Execution Unit executes the instructions fed from the instruction queue as part of the Instruction Decoder Unit, assisted by the following three subunits:
    - The Control Unit that orchestrates microcode executions with special hardware that speeds multiply, divide, and effective address calculation.
    - The Data Unit that performs data load and store operations requested by the Control Unit. This is accomplished with an ALU, a file of eight 32-bit general-purpose registers, and a 64-bit barrel shifter, which is capable of performing multi-bit shifts in one clock,

- The Protection Test Unit that checks for segmentation violations under the control of the microcode.

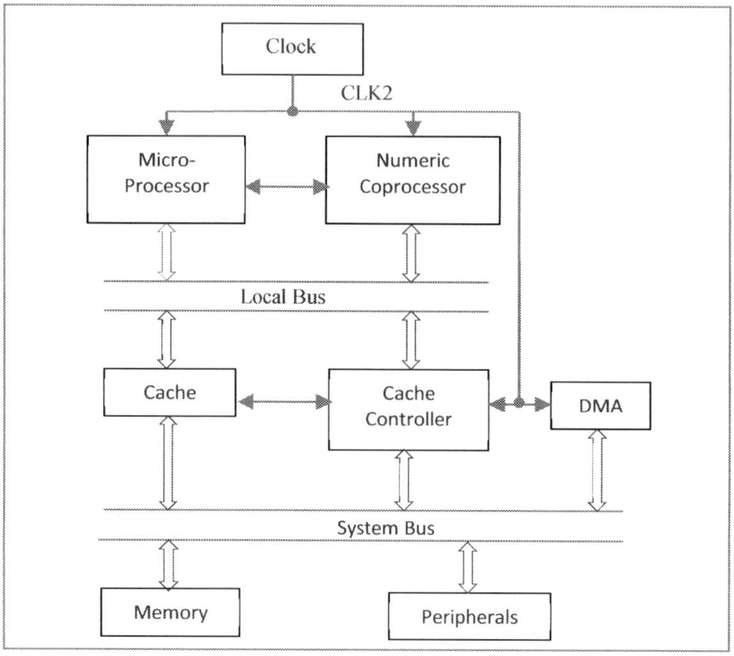

Figure 2.1 Intel 80386 microprocessor architecture

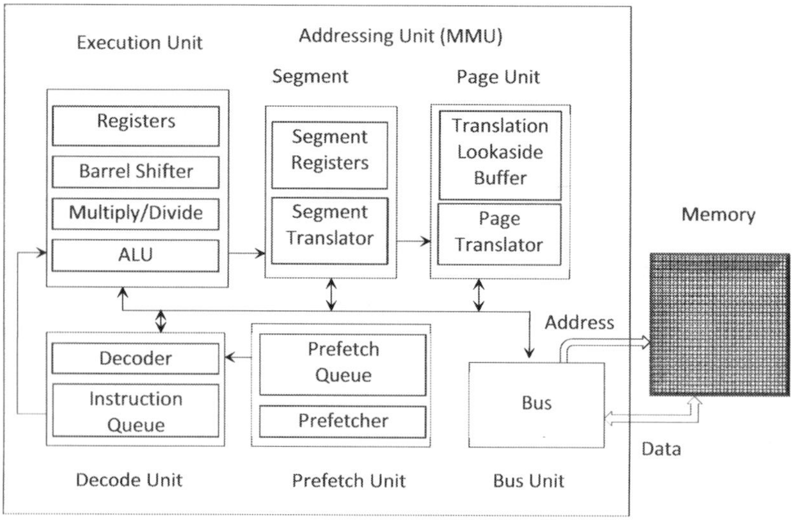

Figure 2.2 Internal functional units of an 80386 microprocessor

- **Segmentation Unit**. The Segmentation Unit translates logical addresses into linear addresses as requested by the Execution Unit. To speed up translation, an on-chip Segment Descriptor Cache is used to store the recently used segment descriptors.
- **Paging Unit**. The Paging Unit has two operating modes. When the paging mechanism is enabled, it translates linear addresses fed from the Segmentation Unit into physical addresses; otherwise, the linear addresses fed from the Segmentation Unit is used without translation as physical addresses. To speed paging, a Translation Lookaside Buffer is used to store recently used Page Directory and Page Table entries. The physical addresses out of the Paging Unit are fed to the Bus Interface Unit to perform memory and I/O operations.

Obviously, many new performance and scalability features have been introduced with the newer generations of Intel processors. The next section gives a high level overview of the performance features with the new Intel Core i7 processors, which are the most powerful processors for both single thread and multi-thread computing tasks at the time of this writing.

2.3 PERFORMANCE FEATURES OF THE INTEL CORE I7 PROCESSORS

Were you impressed with the outstanding performance of the i7-based system shown in Table 1.2? In this section, we examine several performance features of the Intel Core i7 processor based systems to understand why that i7-based system beat all other systems so handsomely with the real product based case study presented in the previous chapter.

2.3.1 Intel's New Microarchitecture

Figure 2.3 shows the differences between the previous generation of Intel microarchitectures and the new Core i7/Nehalem microarchitecture for a single-CPU system. It is seen that the previous Northbridge as a graphics and memory controller hub has been moved onto the CPU die, which reduces memory access latency and helps improve Core i7 family processor performance tremendously, as the latency to the memory DIMMs attached to a remote socket is considerably longer than to the local DIMMs. This integrated memory separates the cache coherency traffic and the memory access traffic, which results in a non-uniform memory access (NUMA). This enables an enormous increase in memory access bandwidth. A second advantage is that the memory control logic can run at processor frequency and thereby reduce the latency.

You might have noticed a few acronyms in Figure 2.3. They are explained as follows:

- FSB. This acronym stands for Front-Side-Bus. A CPU uses an FSB to transfer code and data, to and from other components, primarily the memory and I/O controllers. It has been called FSB, because the original L2 caches were added to the CPUs without being integrated in the silicon, so they had their own bus called the Back Side Bus.
- PCIe. This acronym stands for Peripheral Component Interconnect Express. It is the highest bandwidth I/O interface in an Intel-architecture based system. It's designed to replace the older PCI, PCI-X, and AGP bus standards.

- DMI. This acronym stands for Direct Media Interface. It has several serial links for transferring data between an I/O controller hub (ICH) and a CPU.

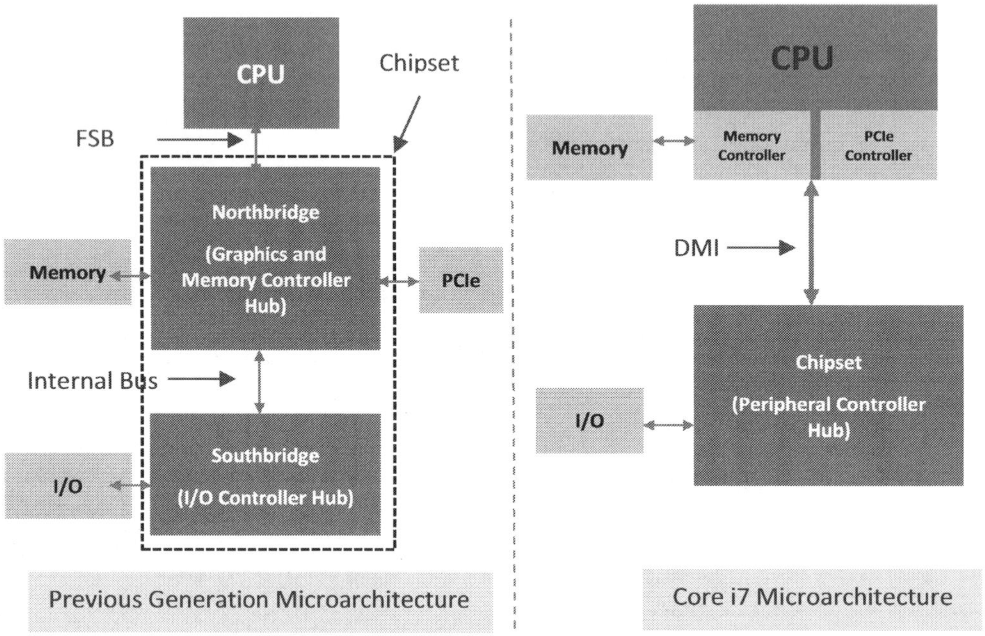

Figure 2.3 Microarchitecture comparison between previous generation and new Nehalem for Intel single-CPU based systems

2.3.2 Intel's QuickPath Interconnect Technology

In addition to moving the graphics and memory controller to the CPU die, Intel also introduced a distributed shared memory architecture using its QuickPath Interconnect (QPI) technology. As shown in Figure 2.4, this new point-to-point interconnect allows all CPU cores to access each other's local memory with up to 25.6 GB/s of total bidirectional throughput per link. It has made a much more significant impact on multicore systems than on single core systems.

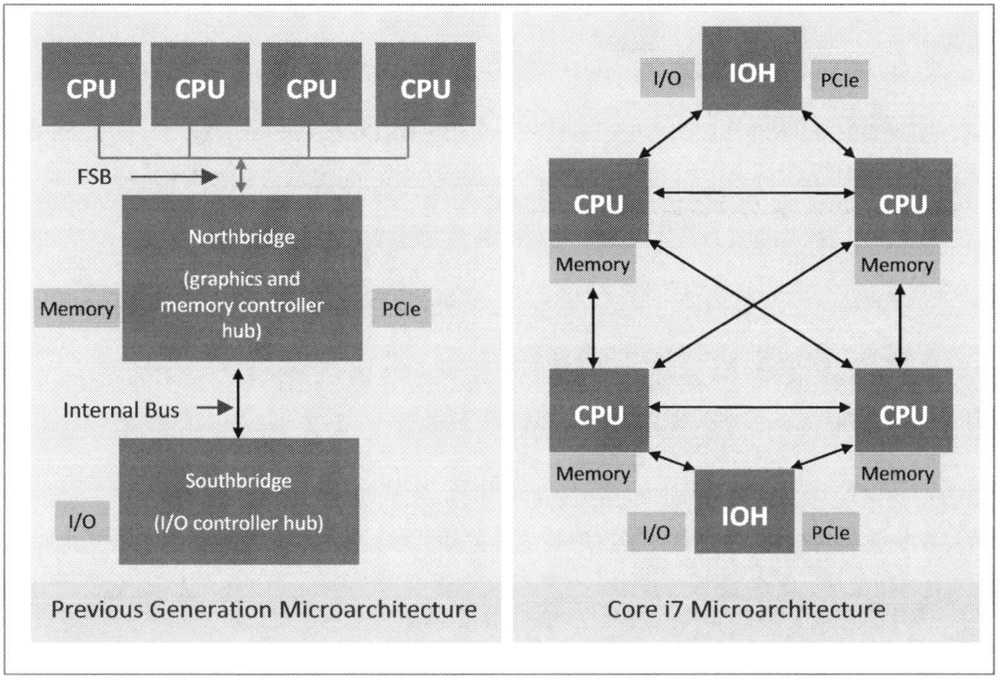

Figure 2.4 Microarchitecture comparison between previous generation and new Nehalem for Intel multi-core based systems

Notice that the original Northbridge has been integrated into the silicon, and the original Southbridge is now called IOH, which stands for Input/Output Hub. IOH is used for controlling I/O devices.

2.3.3 Intel's Turbo Boost Technology

Intel's Turbo Boost technology allows processor cores to dynamically switch clock rates between base operating frequency and higher, turbo boosted frequency when certain conditions are met. Using an i7 quad core system as an example, the following scenarios are possible:

- If there is no load to process, all four cores operate at their base clock rate, which helps reducing power consumption.
- If an application initiates four discrete execution threads, then all four cores start running at their turbo clock rate.
- If an application initiates two discrete execution threads, then two cores are put into low-power state by diverting their power share to the two active cores to allow them to run at turbo clock rate.
- Similarly, if an application initiates only one execution thread, then three cores are put into low-power state by diverting their power share to the active core to allow it to run at turbo clock rate.

This dynamic turbo boost technology helps guarantee that i7-based systems are ideal for both single threaded and multi-threaded applications. However, it must be configured properly. See Appendix A for a case study with Intel's Turbo Boost Technology on Linux.

2.3.4 Smart L3 Cache

Caching is one of the most effective performance optimization techniques at all levels. Figure 2.5 shows that the four cores of a quad core i7 based system have their local caches of L1 and L2 while sharing an inclusive L3 cache that can be up to 12 MB in size. A core can actually snoop other core's local caches (L1 & L2) to see if a data item it needs is available there. If not, it then checks in the larger L3 cache. If it is not available in the L3 cache, then it fetches data from the RAM. However, with the smart L3 cache, it is made inclusive and shared among all cores so that if a data item is not in the L3 cache, it is guaranteed that it's not in any other core's local caches, and thus caching snooping can be avoided. This helps eliminate core-to-core communications and thus helps improve performance.

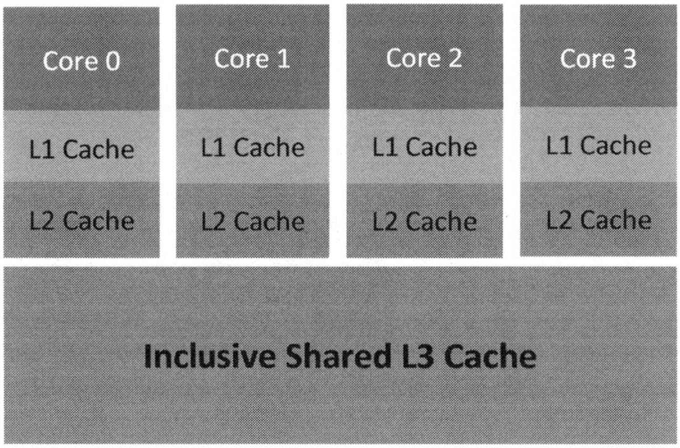

Figure 2.5 Quad core i7 local caches and inclusive shared L3 cache

2.3.5 Hyper-Threading Re-Introduced

As shown in Figure 2.6, HT technology makes two logical cores out of a physical core by sharing the resources of the physical core. Intel once stopped using HT when it introduced multicore processors, because the operating systems were not able to clearly differentiate between physical and logical processing cores. Since Windows 7 and newer operating systems have been made fully aware of the differences between physical and logical cores, Intel re-introduced HT into Core i7 based systems. Multi-threaded applications benefit more from the HT feature on Core i7 based systems, because of larger caches and increased memory bandwidth with Core i7-based systems.

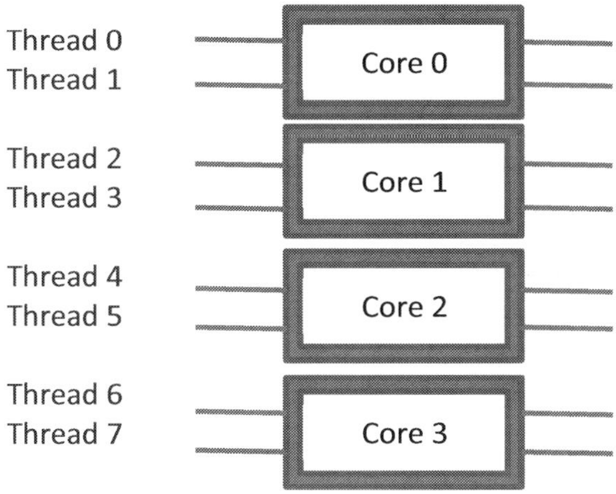

Figure 2.6 Hyper-threading re-introduced with Core i7-based systems

As you see, Core i7-based systems have taken care of both single-threaded and multi-threaded applications with the new performance features introduced above.

Because of the complexity of modern computer processors, whether Intel or other manufacturers, it is impossible to predict exactly how much performance improvement could be achieved for a given software product with a given processor performance feature or even a whole new faster processor based system. However, both the processor manufactures and customers are interested in knowing how those processors would perform relative to each other with a same given set of benchmarking programs and configurations. The next section provides some examples that you can try out with your own systems to help you evaluate potential performance and scalability benefits for your products. These examples may also help provide a reference point for you to decide what hardware you want to recommend to your customers to meet their performance and scalability requirements with your product.

2.4 CPU BENCHMARKING

Very pertinent to the case study presented in Chapter 1, Figure 2.7 shows the marks of both the Intel Xeon E5620 processor @ 2.40 GHz and Core i7-2600 processor @3.40 GHz, which were 4,600 and 8,898, respectively. These benchmarking marks were obtained by averaging over 1,300 standard benchmark programs with *PassMark* software, available at http://www.cpubenchmark.net/cpu.php?cpu=Intel+Xeon+E5620+%40+2.40GHz. It is seen that the ratio of i7's mark to E5620's mark is 8898/4600 = 1.9. Now refer back to Table 1.2 and notice that the average response time ratio between the i7 (test case D) and E5620 (test case C) based JEE application servers was about 3. This ratio of 3 is not exactly equal to the PassMark ratio of 1.9 mentioned above, but sufficiently indicative about a less known fact that Intel-architecture-based desktop systems are faster than their Xeon-based server systems for executing Java-based applications. Our test results presented in

Chapter 1 confirmed PassMark's ranking of i7-2600 at the #2 spot and E5620 at the #11 spot shown in Figure 2.7.

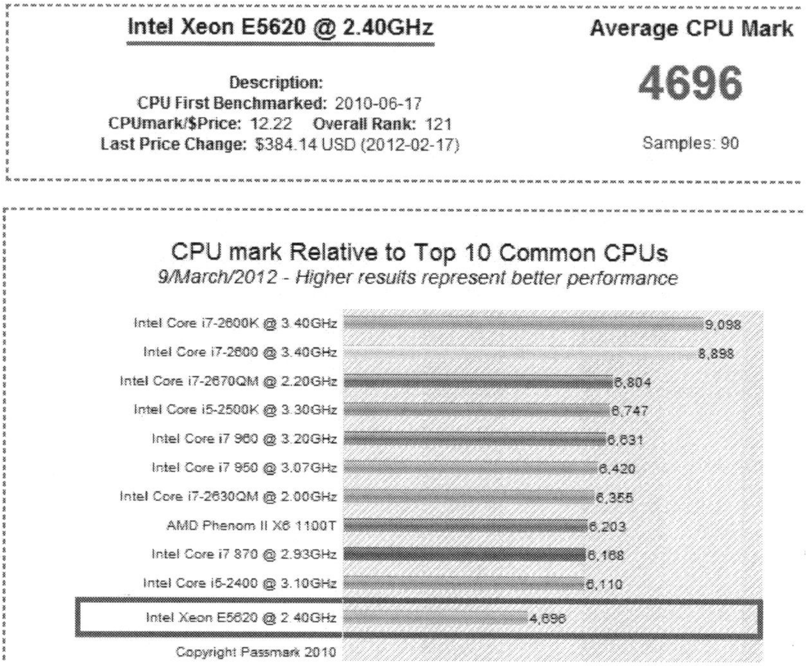

Figure 2.7 Xeon E5620 versus Core i7-2600

In addition to consulting PassMark's results, I developed a CPU benchmarking program named CPUCheck myself and I have used it frequently for a quick assessment of the relative power of the CPUs on one server versus those on others. For Xeon 5620 and i7-2600, my benchmarking program gave an execution time of 44.4 seconds and 21.9 seconds, respectively. The ratio of 44.4/21.9 = 2.0 is remarkably close to the ratio of 1.9 derived above from the PassMark's results. My program is much simpler than PassMark software, and therefore, much less comprehensive, but at least in this case, the two are close to each other (if you are interested in trying out my benchmarking program, see Appendix B for more information on where to download and how to run it).

Another experience I had was with the same JEE application presented in Chapter 1. With one particular action of viewing a model, it took 55 seconds to complete that specific action on a Xeon E5320 based server. I did the same test on an Intel Core 2 Duo E8500 based desktop system, which took 30 seconds. Since all test conditions were the same except the differences in the CPU configurations (Xeon E5320 versus Core 2 Duo E8500), it motivated me to compare both with my own benchmarking program as mentioned above. After running my CPUCheck program on both the E5320-based and the Core 2 Duo E8500-based desktop system, I got 83 seconds on the E5320 based server and 33 seconds on the E8500-based desktop system, respectively, resulting in a ratio of 83/33 = 2.5, which is quite close to 55 / 30 = 1.8 as tested with that application. This simple benchmarking helped us conclude that the performance disparity observed with the JEE application on those two different systems of Xeon E5320 versus Core 2

Duo E8500) was due to the differences in CPU models, not any JEE application server or application related configuration settings.

In general, Intel desktop CPUs are much faster than Intel server CPUs (Xeon's) released within about the same timeframe. This is a very unfortunate fact, as it implies that single-thread computing tasks on Xeon-based servers would run slower than on comparable Intel-architecture based desktop systems. This huge difference in server versus desktop performance compared on a single-thread basis needs to be factored in when testing and evaluating the performance and scalability of a Java application on Xeon-based servers. We need to keep in mind that without good single-thread performance, it's hard to achieve good multi-thread performance. I hope someday we could see that server systems would not only deliver better scalability but also comparable or better performance compared with the desktop systems of about the same release timeframe.

2.5 SUMMARY

This chapter focused on understanding computer hardware architecture, and specifically Intel architecture, which reinforces our notion introduced in Chapter 1 that hardware is one of the most critical factors in determining the performance and scalability of a software product, whether Java based or not. This brief coverage should be sufficient to help get a developer equipped with adequate knowledge to be able to diagnose or assess Java application performance and scalability issues from the hardware perspective. We also introduced the CPU benchmarking test results based on PassMark software, which provides very pertinent information on the relative performance strengths of Intel processors. Alternatively, you can use my CPU benchmarking program CPUCheck detailed in Appendix B to get a quick assessment on the relative performance strengths of the systems you have.

The next chapter discusses how Java virtual machines (JVMs) work, which is the runtime environment for a Java software product and certainly another critical factor in determining the performance and scalability of a Java application.

EXERCISES

2.1 What are the most critical specs of computer CPUs from the performance perspective?

2.2 Explain the concept of hyper-threading with Intel processors.

2.3 What's the difference between the concept of processor microarchitecture and instruction set architecture?

2.4 Why is single-thread performance also critical on server type of computer systems?

2.5 What consideration has made server CPUs lag desktop CPUs released in the same timeframe in performance significantly? How do you factor this in when you work on performance and scalability issues with your product?

REFERENCES

Intel, i386_1986.pdf for *Intel 80386 Programmer's Reference Manual*, 1986.

Intel, 1987_80386_Hardware_Reference_Manual.pdf for 80386 Hardware Reference Manual, 1987.

T. Langley and R. Kowalczyk, *Introduction to Intel Architecture The Basics*, available at http://download.intel.com/design/intarch/papers/321087.pdf, 2009.

Intel, Pentium Processor Family Developer's Manual, Vol. 3: Architecture and Programming Manual (1995_pentium_dev_manual_v3.pdf).

H. Messmer, The Indispensable PC Hardware Book, Addison Wesley, 2nd Edition, 1995.

3 Java Virtual Machine Fundamentals

As a high level programming language, Java is patterned heavily on C and C++ but has abandoned certain low level programming language constructs such as pointers. Pointers allow a programmer to manually allocate and de-allocate memory locations to objects directly, but at the same time, they leave a program more prone to memory leaks, which may eventually lead to unpredictable application behaviours and even crashes. Thanks to its garbage collectors, Java has unloaded memory management tasks from programmers.

Java is now also a high performing language. Java once was blamed for its poor performance during its early stage, but that drawback had been overcome soon after the concept of Just-In-Time (JIT) compilers was introduced and implemented in Java virtual machines (JVMs). A JIT compiler compiles sections of bytecode dynamically into native machine language and then caches them to help make an application run faster.

Today, numerous applications run on Java, from embedded devices to portable devices such as smart phones and tablets, and from desktops to enterprise servers, and so on. Accordingly, a variety of Java editions have been produced to meet the needs in each category. For example:

- Java ME (Micro Edition) for powering compact devices that require a small footprint because of very limited physical memory typically available on such devices.
- Java SE (Standard Edition) for powering desktop applications and enterprise applications, which are much less constrained by the amount of physical memory available.
- Java EE (Enterprise Edition) for large scale enterprise applications built with infrastructural features provided by products such as IBM WebSphere, Oracle Glass Fish and WebLogic Server, RedHat Jboss, and so on.

For a given category, developing software in Java starts with downloading a Java Development Kit (JDK), as running a Java application requires a Java Runtime Environment (JRE), which is also a part of a JDK. A JDK includes a compiler for compiling Java programs into bytecode, along with some monitoring tools such as *JConsole* and *VisualVM* for monitoring the execution of a Java program. A JRE consists of the following main parts:

- A Java Virtual Machine (JVM) as the main Java program execution engine with a JIT compiler and a garbage collector for memory management
- A runtime consisting of services and Java APIs as a set of standard class libraries

Figure 3.1 shows the complete stack of a Java application. It is seen that a Java application is OS platform neutral, whereas a JRE is not.

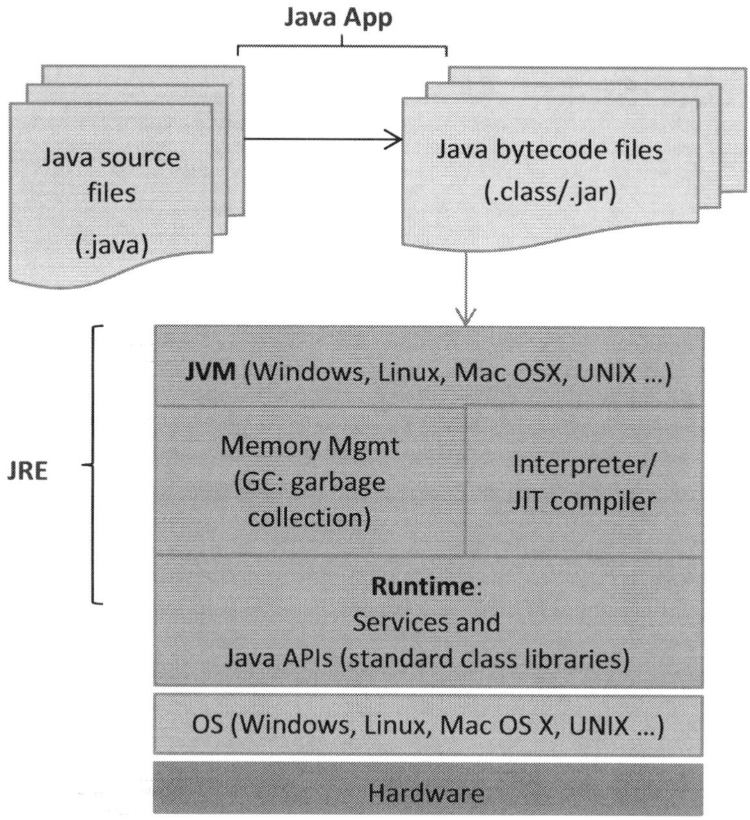

Figure 3.1 The complete stack of a Java application

Depending on which Java platform is in use, optimizations and tunings can be applied with different objectives. For example, with the Java ME platform, minimizing footprint while guaranteeing that a task is completed as fast as possible to meet real-time requirements should take the highest priority. For Java SE and Java EE based enterprise applications, optimizing and tuning for best possible performance and scalability take higher priority, although minimizing the footprint of an application is critical as well.

It is seen that Java application performance and scalability can be optimized and tuned at different levels, including hardware, OS, JVM and application itself. We emphasized the importance of understanding hardware architecture in order to be able to deal with Java application performance and scalability issues effectively and efficiently in the previous two chapters. In this chapter, we focus on understanding JVMs so that one would be able to tune Java applications for best possible performance and scalability.

3.1 JAVA VIRTUAL MACHINES (JVMS)

In order to optimize Java application performance and scalability, it's necessary to have an adequate understanding of how a JVM works, which is covered in this section.

3.1.1 Overview

A JVM is basically an execution engine for executing Java bytecode. However, programs written in other high-level programming languages such as Ada, C, Common Lisp, Pascal, JavaScript, etc., can also be compiled into Java bytecode and executed in a JVM. A JVM is not concerned with the source from which the bytecode is translated. It is concerned only with the format of the instruction set of which the Java bytecode is composed.

It's important to understand the differences between a JVM specification and a JVM implementation. A JVM specification is essentially a conceptual blueprint that provides an abstract description of all artifacts such as data types, instruction set, bytecode format, etc., on which a Java virtual machine should operate, whereas a JVM implementation is a real piece of software that executes Java bytecode according to the rules set in a JVM specification. Therefore, the relationship between a JVM specification and a JVM implementation is of one-to-many that many JVM implementations exist with a given JVM specification.

Since a JVM implementation is typically included in a JDK, most popular JVMs come with the JDKs offered by their vendors, such as:

- **Oracle JDKs/JVMs**. These are perhaps the most widely used JDKs/JVMs both on Windows and on Linux/UNIX platforms. In general, this is what you need for your project.
- **Oracle JRockit JDKs/JVMs**. JRockit is an alternative to Oracle JVMs, if you want to try something different. However, I once tried it with one of the real products I worked on, and saw little difference in performance compared with an equivalent version of Oracle JVM.
- **IBM JDKs/JVMs**. Sometimes when you are in a desperate situation of needing to squeeze as much performance and scalability as possible out of your Java application, you might want to try everything possible, including alternative JVMs with given hardware. IBM JDKs are certainly one of the few available alternatives, and they used to beat Oracle JVMs on Windows by an impressive performance boost of 2 – 3 times decades ago. However, it seems that IBM has bundled their JDKs/JVMs with their commercial Java software, which has made it impossible to download their JDKs standalone for a quick trial. It's not clear if the performance gap between IBM and Oracle JVMs on Windows has been closed, though.
- **OpenJDK**. This is a community, open source project, sponsored by Oracle. It's stated that it combines implementations from all three JDKs mentioned above. This certainly is a good option for those who are primarily interested in conducting research on JVMs.

A Java application is so portable that it can run on many hardware and OS platforms. Even on the same hardware with the same OS that supports both 32-bit and 64-bit memory addressing modes, you have a choice of running your Java application either in 32-bit mode or 64-bit mode without having to re-compile your application, in which case, all you need to do is select the proper JRE (32-bit or 64-bit). We will get more into this later.

Before taking an inside view of how a JVM works behind the scene, let's have a brief introduction to how a Java program is executed next. If you want to explore more, you can visit http://docs.oracle.com/javase/specs/jls/se7/html/index.html for a full coverage of the Java language specification for Java SE 7.

3.1.2 Java Program Execution

A JVM specification defines the format that Java bytecode must conform to as well as the operations that a JVM implementation must follow to execute Java bytecode, whereas a Java language specification defines basic Java language constructs such as types, variables, names, packages, interfaces, classes, fields, methods, constructors, arrays, exceptions, etc. Assuming that you are already familiar with the Java language, this section describes how a Java program is executed inside a JVM. To clarify, this subject is not covered in a JVM specification. Instead, it is covered in a Java language specification.

A Java program is executed as follows:

- **JVM start-up**. A JVM starts execution by invoking the method *main* of a class specified in the format of a *.class* file or a *.jar* file. It is initiated with a command like *java some_class* or *java –jar some_jar,* where "*java*" is the binary image of the JVM and "*some_class*" or "*some_jar*" is the Java program or some *jar* file to be executed.
- **Loading**. In order to execute the main method of a class, the *classloader* of a JVM attempts to find the binary image of the class to be executed. If the class is found, it is loaded into a memory area called a heap in the JVM.
- **Linking**. This is the process of preparing a binary form of a class or interface type into the runtime state of the JVM. This linking process consists of three steps: (1) Verifying that the binary representation of a class or interface is structurally correct, (2) Creating and initializing the static fields of a class or interface, and (3) Resolving each symbolic reference in a class or interface all at once (*static resolution*) or only when it is used (*lazy* or *late resolution*).
- **Initializing**. At this point, a class or interface is ready to be initialized. Note that before a class is initialized, its superclasses must be initialized if they have not been. However, the initialization of an interface does not require an initialization of itself or any of its superinterfaces – only its fields need to be initialized.
- **Creating new class instances**. Java is an object-oriented programming language. Thus, a JVM may need to create objects frequently from time to time. Whenever an object is created, memory space must be allocated to accommodate all the instance variables of the class type itself and of its superclasses. If there is insufficient memory space available to allocate memory for an object, the creation of the object fails and the program terminates abruptly with an *OutOfMmeoryError* (OOME). Otherwise, the object is created by calling the constructor of the class, and the reference to

the created object is returned as the result. Conceptually, such a reference is similar to a wrapped pointer in C/C++.

- **JVM exit**. When the method *exit* of class *Runtime* or class *System* is invoked, or when a program runs to completion, the JVM terminates the execution. However, a JVM has to complete a couple of important tasks before termination: (1) Finalizing the created objects that have not been garbage collected, and (2) Finalizing and unloading the classes and interfaces created. Here, the term *finalizing* means freeing the resources used by an entity, which could be an object, a class, or an interface.

As is seen, the execution of a Java program requires a carefully designed layout of the memory space allocated to a JVM. This subject is very pertinent to the performance and scalability of a Java application, which is described in more detail in the next section.

3.1.3 JVM Runtime Data Areas

Before delving into the subject of JVM runtime data areas, let us review the data types that determine how variables are stored in memory and handled. We assume that you are familiar with the basic Java language constructs such as types, variables, names, packages, interfaces, classes, fields, methods, constructors, arrays, exceptions, etc., mentioned in this section.

A JVM operates on two kinds of types: *primitive types* and *reference types*. There are, accordingly, two kinds of values that can be stored in variables, *primitive values* and *reference values*. With their corresponding *variables*, *primitive values* are passed as arguments, whereas *reference values* are returned by methods. A variable is an abstraction of a region of an addressable memory space. In addition to type and value, a variable has other attributes such as name, address size, scope and lifetime. However, of the two argument passing mechanisms, passing by value and passing by reference, Java language allows passing by value only.

The primitive data types supported by a JVM are: (1) the *numerical types* (*byte*, *short*, *int*, *long*, *char*, *float*, and *double*), and (2) the *returnAddress type* whose values are pointers to the *opcodes* of JVM instructions. The *returnAddress type* is not a Java language type, but is required in JVMs to maintain the order in which bytecode instructions are executed.

There are three kinds of reference types: *class types*, *interface types*, and *array types*. The values of these reference types are references to the dynamically created objects, arrays, or objects or arrays that implement interfaces.

Primitive types are also termed *value types* since their purpose is for holding values of primitive types. The major difference between value and reference types lies in how their values are allocated in memory. A value type holds actual value in memory allocated on the stack (or allocated as a part of a larger reference type object). The address of a reference variable sits on the stack, but the actual object is stored in the heap. In other words, the values of value types (e.g., integers) are stored on the stack, whereas the values of reference types (e.g., objects) are stored in the heap. When an object is allocated in the heap, its address is returned to a reference type variable.

The JVM specification defines an abstract notion of a *word* that has a platform-specific size. A word is usually the size of a pointer on the host platform, which is 32 bits on a 32-bit platform, and 64 bits on a

64-bit platform. We discuss the implications of the pointer size from 32-bit to 64-bit programming model later.

Since memory management is an important part of how a JVM operates, it's helpful to understand the runtime data areas set up in a JVM. A JVM has the following runtime data areas in memory:

- **Program Counter (pc) Register**. A pc register contains the address of a JVM instruction currently being executed. Since Java supports concurrency via a multi-threading model, a pc register is allocated for each thread of the multiple JVM execution threads.
- **JVM Stack**. A Java stack holds local variables and partial results in the form of *frames* on a per-thread basis. It plays an important role in method invocation and return. Two commonly seen errors, *StackOverflowError* and *OutOfMemoryError,* are associated with Java stacks. They occur when the execution of a thread requires a larger Java stack (*StackOverflowError*), or when the initial Java stack for a new thread cannot be created because of insufficient memory (*OutOfMemoryError).*
- **Heap**. A heap is a memory area shared among all threads. This is the runtime data area for allocating memory for all objects and arrays. A heap is managed automatically by an automatic memory management system such as an implementation specific garbage collector. The concept of a Java heap plays a predominant role in determining the performance and scalability of a Java application, and it is discussed in detail later.
- **Method Area**. A method area is shared among all threads. The method area is similar to the "text" segment in a UNIX process, or to the storage area for compiled code of a conventional language. It stores per-class structures such as the constant pool similar to a symbol table for a conventional programming language, field and method data, and the code for methods and constructors, including the special methods used in class, object and interface initializations.
- **Frames**. Frames are created to coordinate method invocations on the stack of a thread when a method is invoked. A frame may contain the local variables of a method, or an operand stack, or partial results, or a reference to the constant pool for the current method to support dynamic linking of the method code, etc.

We discuss more on these runtime data areas later when we discuss JVM memory management and garbage collections. Next, we briefly explain the JVM instruction set to help understand how Java bytecode is executed inside a JVM. This is one of the major areas that JVM vendors can help improve Java application performance and scalability significantly.

3.1.4 JVM Instruction Set

The JVM instruction set is characterized by two concepts: *opcode* and *operands*. An *opcode* specifies the operation type to be performed, whereas *operands* specify the objects to be performed upon. A JVM instruction consists of a one-byte opcode, followed by zero or more operands.

The following Java statement shows an example of operands:

```
k = i + j;
```

In the above example, `i`, `j` and `k` are operands, whereas '+' and '=' are operators, representing addition and assignment operations, respectively. Each type of operation has a corresponding opcode.

Note that in the above example, the operator '+' is placed between the two operands, `i` and `j`. This is called *infix notation*. It can also be expressed as `+ i j` or `i j +`, which are called *prefix* and *postfix notations*, respectively. The prefix and postfix notations are particularly suitable for constructing instructions for a machine to carry out the operation, as we will see below.

Some typical *opcodes* include *iload, istore, iadd, isub, imul, idiv*, etc., which operate on *integer* types. Similar *opcodes* exist for other data types. Each data type has its own fixed size in the JVM. Table 3.1 lists the length of each Java storage type and the corresponding computational type maintained internally in a JVM. Of these data types in Java, integers are 32-bits, and longs are 64-bits. Pointers maintained internally in a JVM are 32-bits in a 32-bit JVM and 64-bits in a 64-bit JVM. We will revisit this subtle difference later.

Table 3.1 Size in Bits for JVM Computational Types.

Java Type	Size in Bits	Computational Type
byte	8	int
char	16	int
short	16	int
int	32	int
float	32	float
long	64	long
double	64	double

The inner workings of a JVM could just be as simple as repeatedly executing the logic as shown below:

```
do {
    fetch an opcode;
    fetch operands if any;
    execute an instruction;
} while (there are more instructions to fetch);
```

As stated in the previous section, each thread in a JVM executes bytecode based on a data structure called a *stack*, namely, a JVM adopts a *stack-oriented* instruction set architecture. The counterpart of the stack-oriented architecture is the *register-oriented* architecture. The difference between a stack-oriented architecture and a register-oriented architecture lies in how operands are accessed. In a stack-oriented architecture, operands are maintained on a stack rather than in physical memory or physical registers, and hence the name *virtual* for *virtual machines*. In a register-oriented architecture, operands can be manipulated all at the register level or partially at the register level and partially in memory, resulting in register-register architecture and *register-memory* architecture. The register-register architecture also is called *load-store* instruction set architecture.

Now let's use an example to illustrate the differences between a stack-oriented architecture and a register-oriented architecture. The example we use is as simple as the following Java program, which performs the simple calculation of k = i + j as shown in the above example:

```
public class AddTwoIntergers {
    public static void main (String args[]) {
        int i = 135;
        int j = 246;
        int k;
        k = i + j;
    }
}
```

After this program is compiled into a *.class* file, its bytecode for the main method looks like the following:

```
1  0   sipush 135
2  3   istore_1
3  4   sipush 246
4  7   istore_2
5  8   iload 1
6  9   iload_2
7  10  iadd
8  11  istore_3
9  12  return
```

Let's interpret the above bytecode line by line as follows:

- Line 1: `sipush` is an opcode representing the operation of pushing a two-byte signed integer onto the operand stack. Note that the first column in the above bytecode listing represents the line number, and the second column represents the byte index.
- Line 2: `istore_n` is an opcode representing the operation of storing a value to location `n` in the variable table.
- Lines 3 and 4 are similar to lines 1 and 2.
- Line 5: `iload_n` is an opcode representing the operation of loading a value from location `n` in the variable table.
- Line 6 is similar to line 5.
- Line 7: `iadd` is an opcode representing the operation of adding two integers. Specifically, it pops two integers from the operand stack, adds them, and pushes the resultant integer back on to the stack.
- Line 8 is similar to line 2.
- Line 9: `return` is an opcode representing the operation of returning from a method.

An instruction set based on a register-oriented architecture may execute the statement of k = i + j as follows

```
load r1, i;  // load the value of variable i to register r1
load r2, j; // load the value of variable j to register r2
add r3, r1, r2;  // add r1 and r2 and store the result to register r3
store k, r3; // store the value of r3 to variable k.
```

The stack-based instruction set architecture can be viewed from a different perspective. Based on the number of operands required to follow an opcode, an instruction set can be said to be an `n`-operand instruction set, where n is an integer and can take a value of 0, 1, 2 or 3. In this sense, the instruction set for a stack machine is said to be a 0-operand instruction set because most opcodes implicitly operate on values on the top of the stack and store those values back on to the stack. The iadd opcode described above is such an example. A 1-operand instruction set corresponds to the accumulator architecture as the accumulator itself is an operand. A 2-operand instruction set corresponds to a register-memory architecture as one operand is a register and the other operand is a memory location. And a 3-operand instruction set corresponds to a register-register architecture as in one instruction it can have 3 registers as operands. See Table 3.2 for the subtle differences among these four types of instruction sets.

Table 3.2 Execution of k = i + j with four different types of instruction sets.

0-operand	1-operand	2-operand	3-operand
iload_1	load i	load eax i	load eax i
iload_2	add j	add eax, j	load edx, j
iadd	store k	store k, eax	add ecx, eax, edx
istore_3		store k, ecx	store k, ecx

Note: eax, ecx, and edx are integer registers for x86 family of processors.

A JVM specification only defines the bytecode format and what operations to perform in order to execute the bytecode. The actual memory layout of runtime data areas, the garbage collection algorithms, internal optimization of the JVM instructions, etc., are up to the discretion of a JVM implementer. Since a same JVM specification can be implemented by multiple vendors, which vendor's JVM to use may make a difference in terms of performance, scalability and reliably for your application. Unless you are locked in with a specific vendor, Oracle HotSpot JVM probably is the best choice in general. Throughout this text, we stick to this JVM, which is introduced next.

3.1.5 The HotSpot JVM

The HotSpot JVM was initially released in 1997 by Longview Technologies, LLC, a start-up formed in 1994. It was purchased by Sun Microsystems in 1997 and became the default Sun JVM in Java 1.3. Its name was derived from its feature of being capable of identifying and optimizing a Java program's "hot spots," which are repeatedly executed.

The HotSpot JVM technology actually refers to two JVMs, one optimized for client systems and the other for server systems. One of the major differences between the two is how memory is managed automatically. This will become clear after we review the memory management and various garbage collection algorithms in the next section.

3.2 JAVA MEMORY MANAGEMENT

With the execution of a computer program, objects are created and then destroyed when they are no longer referenced or become inaccessible. The objects that are still in use are called *live* objects, while the objects that are not in use or inaccessible are called *dead* objects or *garbage* objects. The memory occupied by garbage objects must be reclaimed, which is the major task of a garbage collector (GC). The key to understanding Java memory management is to understand how garbage objects are collected by a JVM.

Some high level programming languages such as C/C++ adopt explicit or manual memory management, which puts the burden of allocating and de-allocating memory on to programmers with the concept of *pointers* when objects are created and destroyed. In contrast, Java shifts such a burden from programmers to the JVMs that are equipped with garbage collectors, thus achieving automatic memory management. Because of the critical role of garbage collection in determining the performance and scalability of a Java application, it's worthwhile to get a deep understanding on how GC works, what GC options are available, how to size and tune a JVM heap, and which GC options should be used based on the concrete performance and scalability concerns. Let's start with understanding various garbage collection algorithms in the next section.

3.3 A SCALAR GARBAGE COLLECTION ALGORITHM

Since the criterion to determine whether an object is garbage is to check whether it still is referenced, a natural idea is to count the number of references that an object is referenced. If the reference count for an object is larger than zero, the object is live; otherwise the object is garbage. This idea led to the most intuitive garbage collection algorithm, as is discussed below. Also, as reference counting is more of a scalar type of operation without regard to the dependencies or the hierarchical relations among the objects, it's in nature a scalar garbage collection algorithm.

3.3.1 Reference Counting

With the reference counting garbage collection algorithm, the JVM keeps track of the number of references to an object. When a reference is assigned to or removed from an object, the reference count for that object is increased or decreased by one accordingly. When the reference count for an object reaches zero, that object is subject to garbage collection.

Let's use an example to help further illustrate how the reference counting garbage collection algorithm works. Let's arbitrarily pick a rental car management system as an example.

Suppose the rental car class, *RentalCar*, has such attributes as *ID*, *manufacturer*, *model*, etc. Suppose we have another class *Renter* with attributes of *name*, *carRented*, etc. Note that for convenience, we assigned only a few attributes to the classes we are concerned with.

Now consider the following two statements, which state that John rented a Toyota Camry and Sally rented a Honda Accord:

```
RentalCar rentalCar1  = new RentalCar (1, "Toyota", "Camry");
RentalCar rentalCar2  = new RentalCar (2, "Honda", "Accord",
```

```
Renter renter1 = new Renter ("John", rentalCar1);
Renter renter2 = new Renter ("Sally", rentalCar2);
```

At this point, the reference count for each object should look like Figure 3.2 (a). Suppose that Sally and John decide to share one rental car, the Toyota Camry, so Sally returns the Honda Accord she rented. Programmatically, this is equivalent to the statements of:

```
rentalCar2 = null;
Renter renter2 = new Renter ("Sally", rentalCar1);
```

Now reference counting for each object should look like Figure 3.2 (b). The object *rentalCar2* has become a garbage object and can be collected. The object *rentalCar1* has two references now.

The reference counting garbage collection algorithm has the advantage that it allows the memory occupied by an object to be reclaimed immediately as soon as its reference count becomes zero, without having to wait until sometime later when the total amount of free memory in the heap becomes insufficient. In contrast to a *stop-the-world* (STW) garbage collection algorithm that has to halt the application execution in order to collect garbage objects, this "*no waiting*" characteristic of the reference counting garbage collection algorithm is particularly suitable for those real-time applications that can't afford to pause and dedicate the entire CPU resource to collecting garbage objects.

However, because of its scalar nature in deciding when an object becomes garbage, a simple reference counting garbage collection algorithm like the one described above doesn't handle cyclic or self-referential reference structures well, as is discussed in the next section.

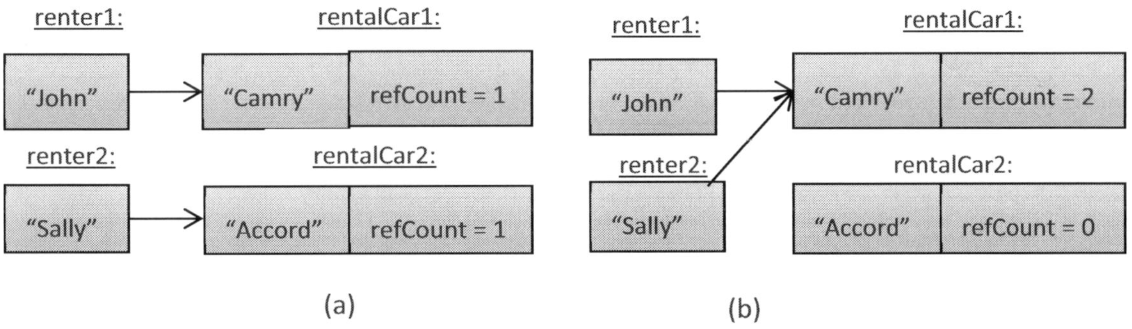

Figure 3.2 Changes of reference count with object allocation (a) and de-allocation (b)

3.3.2 Cyclic Reference Structures

Since a reference counting algorithm treats each object as an isolated island, it may not always fully collect all de-referenced objects. An obvious situation is when dealing with a cyclic reference structure as shown in Figure 3.3, which represents a singly-linked list. Figure 3.3 (a) shows that initially the first list node has a reference count of two, one from the head and the other from the tail of the list. When the head is de-referenced, the reference count of the first node becomes one, leaving a dangling circle that cannot be collected, as shown in Figure 3.3 (b).

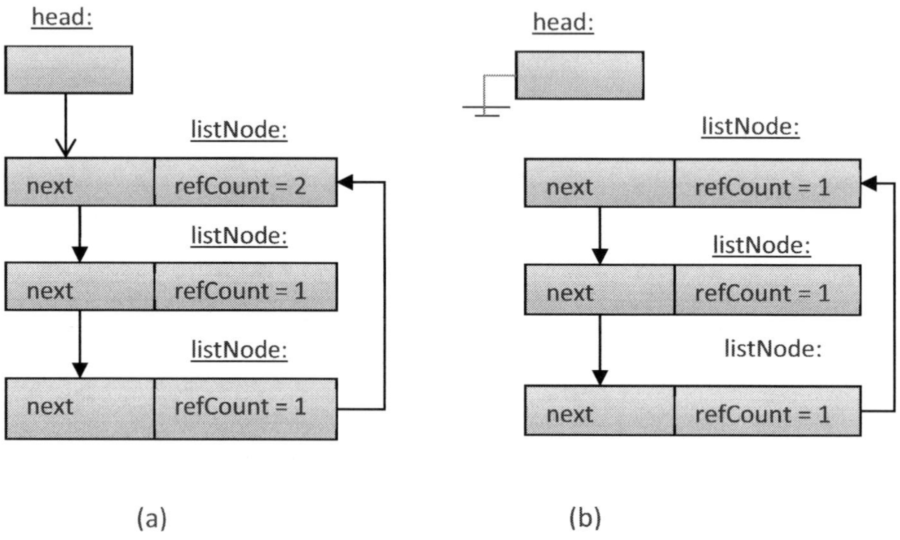

Figure 3.3 A cyclic reference structure in (a) becomes unreachable after the head node is de-referenced (b)

Despite the deficiency in coping with cyclic reference structure, the reference counting garbage collection method has been in use in Java RMI framework for collecting remote objects in an RMI server. Remote objects differ from local objects that they are referenced by objects in a separate JVM. Remote objects are not collected unless there are neither local nor remote references existing. A remote object that needs to be notified when it is de-referenced must implement the `java.rmi.server.Unreferenced` interface. In this sense, the memory of remote Java objects is not necessarily automatically managed.

This cyclic reference problem can be easily remedied with vectorial or tracing garbage collection algorithms, which trace the entire structure of a reference chain from node to node. The next section introduces some commonly used vectorial garbage collection algorithms to help establish a solid ground for understanding various garbage collection options built into a JVM.

3.4 VECTORIAL GARBAGE COLLECTION ALGORITHMS

All vectorial garbage collection algorithms start with determining whether an object is reachable. An object is reachable under one of the following two conditions:

- An object is reachable if it's a *root* object. In general, the objects referenced by global variables, local variables, function parameters, and so on, are root objects.

- An object is *transitively* reachable if it can be reached from a higher-level reachable object.

Let's start with the simplest vectorial garbage collection algorithm, the simple mark-and-sweep algorithm, in the next section.

3.4.1 Simple Mark-and-Sweep

The simple mark-and-sweep algorithm works by assigning a flag to each object in memory so that a JVM can mark or unmark an object. The marking and sweeping phases are illustrated with the following pseudo code:

```
// simple mark-and-sweep algorithm
mark all root objects;
for (each root object) { // marking phase
    mark all its descendent objects;
}
for (each object in memory) { // sweeping phase
    if (reachable) {
        unmark the object; // prepare for the next marking cycle
} else {
    reclaim the memory of the object;
    }
}
```

With the mark-and-sweep algorithm, cyclic reference structures are treated properly and no garbage objects are left behind. Figures 3.4 (a) through (c) illustrate the initial state, after marking and after sweeping with a linked list object structure. You can walk through the pseudo code described above with these illustrations. (Hint: In Figure 3.4 (b), two left-most leaf nodes are not marked, as they are not the descendants of the object directly above them.)

Although the mark-and-sweep algorithm resolves the potential problem with cyclic reference structures effectively, it results in additional problems:

- It has to suspend the application execution when garbage collection is in progress. This kind of STW nature makes it hard for real-time and time-critical applications to meet their stringent performance requirements.
- It examines the entire heap memory twice, once for marking and once for sweeping, resulting in redundancy and low efficiency.

Is it possible to have an algorithm that can deal with cyclic reference structures without requiring suspending the application execution and examining the entire object set twice? The answer is the tri-color algorithm as is discussed in the next section.

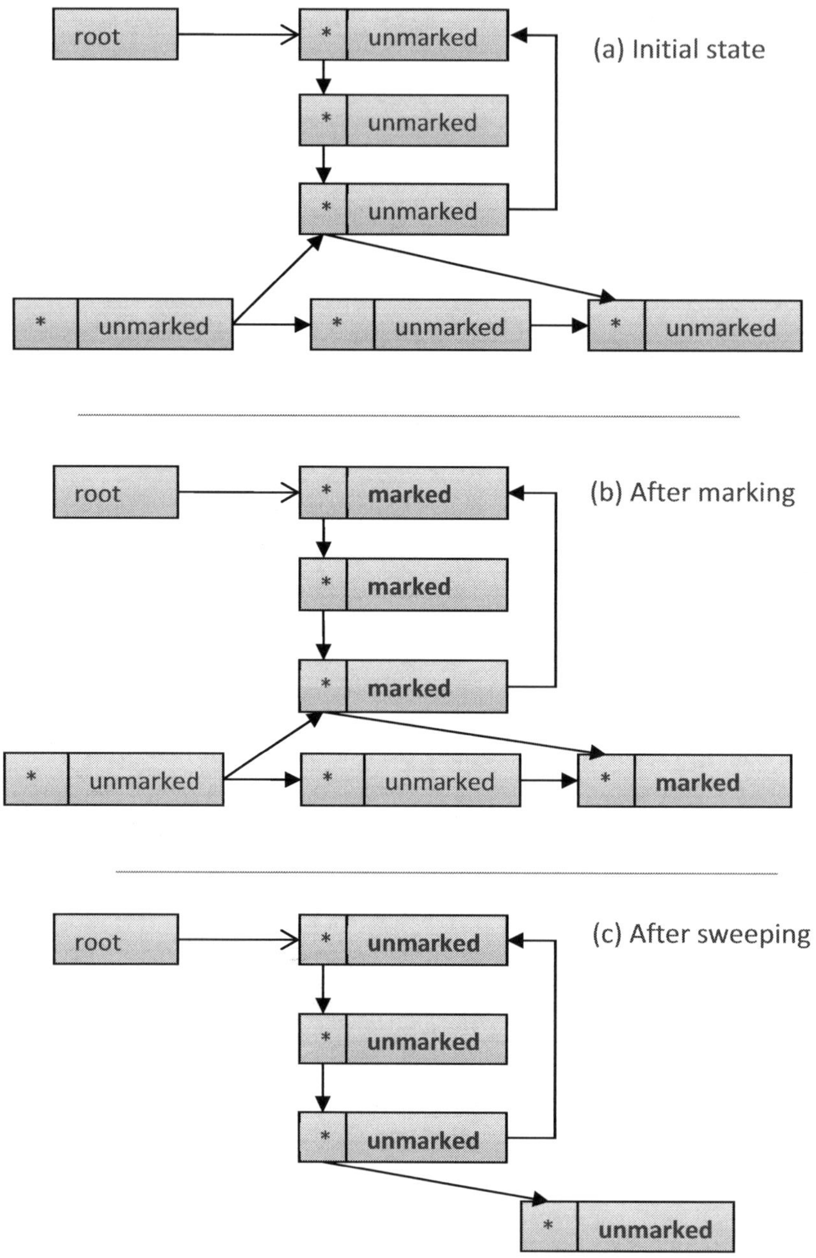

Figure 3.4 Mark-and-sweep GC: (a) initial state, (b) after marking, and (c) after sweeping

3.4.2 Tri-Colour Marking

The tri-colour GC algorithm is based on the concepts of a *root*, a *root set*, and a *mutator*. A *root* is a top-level object that holds references to objects that are *a priori* reachable. The *root set* contains a set of roots as a privileged collection, providing the starting points for determining all reachable objects. A *mutator* is the part of a garbage collection system that executes the user code, allocates and modifies (or mutates) objects. One can say that a garbage collection system consists of a mutator and a collector, each of which does its own job.

The tri-colour marking algorithm uses three sets (*white*, *grey*, and *black*) to designate the state of an object. Before we demonstrate this algorithm in pseudo code, let's state the purpose of each coloured set as follows:

- **White Set.** This set contains candidate garbage objects. It starts off with all non-root objects with the assumption that every object is subject to collection until its reachability is determined definitively.
- **Grey Set**. This set is a working set, which contains root objects only initially. It will also hold lower level reachable objects later.
- **Black Set**. This set contains live objects known to be reachable. It starts off empty with the same assumption that every object is subject to collection until its reachability is determined definitively.

The following pseudo code shows how the tri-colour algorithm works. The three steps are:

1. Sort out all objects based on its level (root or non-root) into the grey and white sets, respectively, with non-root objects in white set and root objects in grey set.
2. Process each object in the grey set by moving its direct descendent objects over from the white set and moving itself to the black set afterwards. Repeat this step until the grey set becomes empty.
3. At the end, collect all garbage objects in the white set, left over from step 2.

```
// tri-colour algorithm
tri_colour_gc (root_set) {
// 1. preparation
// set up three sets: white, grey and black;
mark all root objects grey;
mark all non-root objects white;
empty the black set;
// 2. determine the reachability of an object in the grey set
do {
        get the next grey object;
        grey all its direct descendent objects in the white set;
        mark the current object black;
    } while (grey set is non-empty)
// 3. collect garbage objects in the white set
for (each object in the white set) {
        reclaim the memory;
  }
}
```

Since objects can be mutated from white to grey and from grey to black but never from black to white, it's black-and-white clear which objects are garbage objects and can be collected once the grey set becomes empty. This is an important invariant preserved with the tri-colour algorithm. Figure 3.5 helps explain this notion further. Note that both the root set and memory regions containing all objects are shown as well to help illustrate the initial bootstrapping process of marking all root objects grey and marking all non-root objects white.

The tri-colour algorithm allows garbage objects to be collected on-the-fly without having to halt the system to perform garbage collection. The newly allocated or mutated objects stay in memory until being marked in the following cycle. Also, the need to visit the entire objects twice as was the case with the simple mark-and-sweep algorithm has been eliminated.

The above description conceptually explains how the tri-colour algorithm works. There are multiple strategies on how it can be actually implemented. This is the subject for the next section.

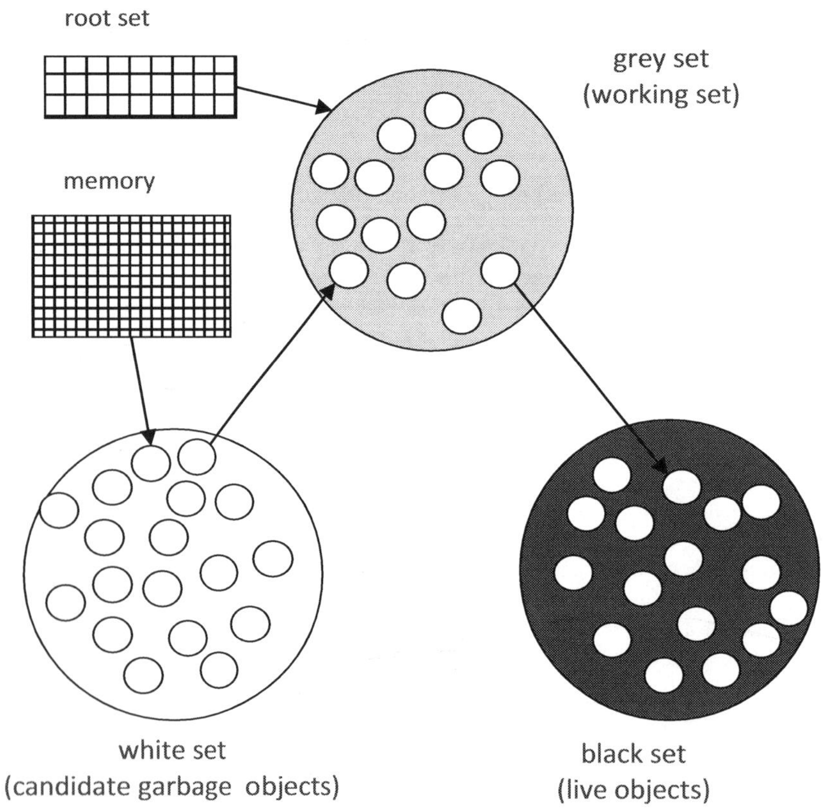

Figure 3.5 Tri-color mark-and-sweep GC algorithm

3.5 IMPLEMENTATION STRATEGIES

An algorithm only describes what needs to be done at each step but does not specify how it should be done. How each step described in an algorithm should be done is up to the implementer to decide based on the trade-offs with all major concerns taken into account. This section explores a few strategies about how the tri-colour algorithm described above can be implemented.

3.5.1 Serial versus Parallel

In the simplest case, garbage collection can be performed using a single thread serially even if more CPUs or threads are available. To speed up garbage collection, one can divide up the total garbage collection work and use multiple threads to collect all garbage in parallel. However, parallel collection may result in fragmentation. See Figure 3.6.

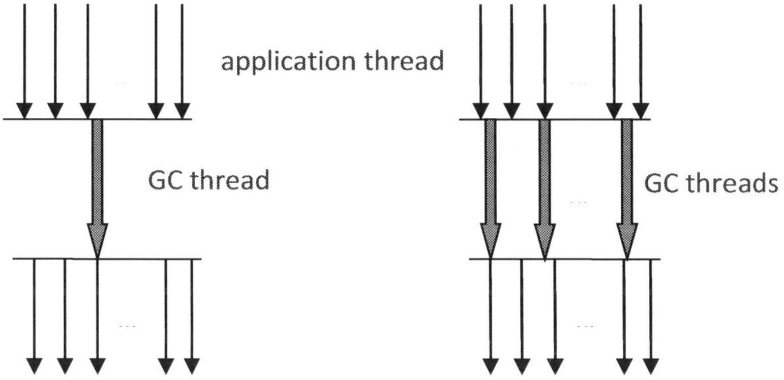

Figure 3.6 Serial (left) versus parallel (right) GC strategy

3.5.2 Non-Compacting versus Compacting versus Copying

First, refer back to step 3 in the previous pseudo-algorithm explaining the tri-colour mark-and-sweep GC algorithm. At step 3, the grey set becomes empty, and the white set and black set contain unreachable and reachable objects, respectively. At this point, a garbage collector adopts one of the following three strategies to reclaim the memory occupied by garbage objects:

- **Non-compacting Strategy**. This strategy operates on the unreachable objects that have been identified in the white set. It simply releases the unreachable objects on the spot with reachable objects left untouched. The benefit is faster completion of garbage collection, but with the drawback of fragmentation. Subsequent memory allocation for newly-created objects will have to depend on a free-list that keeps track of available memory locations.
- **Compacting**. This strategy relocates all the reachable objects together and reclaims the remainder of the entire memory area, which is now free as a large contiguous area. A new object can be allocated at the first free location. Allocating memory for subsequent newly created objects is just a matter of

moving the pointer to the next free location. This is also called *bump-the-pointer* technique [Hunt, 2012].

- **Copying Strategy**. This strategy operates on the reachable objects in the black set. It copies or evacuates all reachable objects that have been identified in the black set to a new memory area, updates all references to those reachable objects, and reclaims the entire memory occupied originally by both the unreachable and reachable objects. The benefit is that it eliminates fragmentation, but with the drawback that extra space is required for holding the reachable objects.

On first thought, it appears that the compacting strategy might result in worse performance, since presumably it would have more work to do. However, it turns out that the compacting strategy has the following advantages:

- The non-compacting strategy generally leaves many sporadic, non-contiguous "*holes*" or "*fragments*" on the spot after reclaiming the memory occupied by the unreachable objects. This would deteriorate the contiguity of the entire memory area. In contrast, the compacting strategy basically relocates all reachable objects to a contiguous memory area, not only increasing the chances of better locality for more correlated data to be pre-fetched together but also resolving the "fragmentation" problem left behind with the non- compacting strategy.
- With the compacting strategy, unreachable objects don't need to be visited individually, although it's true that reachable objects need to be visited individually when their references are being updated.

See Figure 3.7 for an illustration of non-compacting versus compacting versus copying GC strategies. In the first upper left frame, it shows the garbage and live objects. The upper right frame shows the compacting GC strategy, which leaves no fragmented memory regions. The lower left frame shows the non-compacting GC strategy, which leaves fragmented memory regions. The lower middle and right frames show the copying GC strategy, which copies the entire collection of live objects and leaves the original regions to be reclaimed entirely.

Because of the importance of keeping memory as contiguous as possible to avoid the fragmentation issue, which may eventually result in application crashing or require restarting the system periodically to clean up the fragmented memory, the compacting strategy should be favored over the non-compacting strategy if possible.

Before proceeding to the next section, it's necessary to point out that in some texts, the *copying* GC strategy is termed *moving* GC strategy. These two terms are interchangeable.

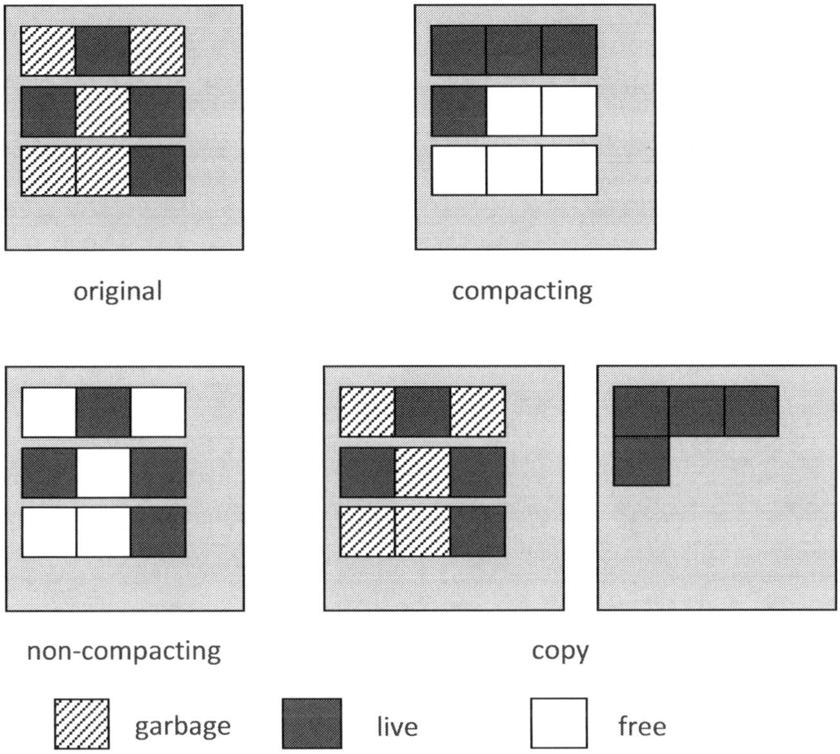

Figure 3.7 Non-compacting versus compacting versus copying GC strategy

3.5.3 Stop-and-Copy (or Two Space Collection) versus Concurrent

The stop-and-copy GC strategy requires the use of two separate spaces, a "*from-space*" and a "*to-space*." Initially, objects are placed in one of the two semi-spaces only until it becomes full and a garbage collection is triggered. At this point, the system stops executing the user code to copy the reachable objects (the black set) into the other semi-space, leaving the original semi-space entirely free. Then the system resumes executing the user code, letting object allocation continue in the new semi-space, and the same stop-and-copy process is repeated from one semi-space to the other until it becomes full.

See Figure 3.8 for an illustration of the stop-the-world versus concurrent GC strategies. It looks similar to Figure 3.6 showing the serial versus parallel GC strategies but different that it does not use all threads to conduct garbage collection.

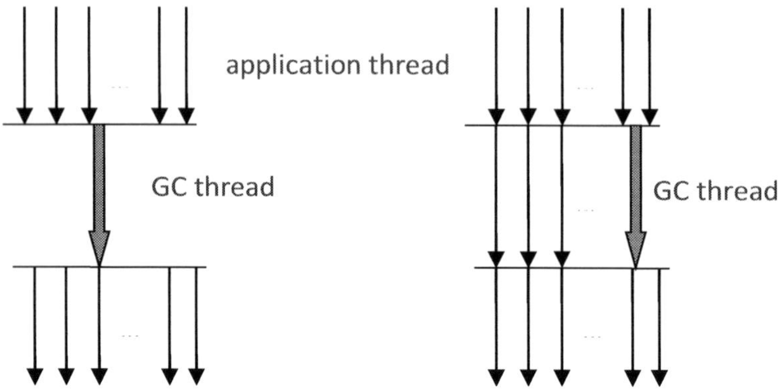

Figure 3.8 Stop-the-world versus concurrent GC strategy

Note also that this stop-and-copy strategy differs from the copying strategy described in the previous section as well, in which case, user code execution is not suspended, or in other words, user code execution and garbage collection can occur concurrently.

With a copying GC strategy, having two separate semi-spaces used alternately implies that the actual effective memory usage is below 50%. This situation can be improved with the generational collection strategy as discussed in the next section.

3.5.4 Generational Strategy

The generational garbage collection strategy is based on the observation that some objects may live longer than others, known as the *generational hypothesis*. The young generation contains relatively newly-created objects, which are marked white. The reachable objects in a black set out of the young generations are copied to an old generation region, which will not participate in the *minor* garbage collections performed more frequently on the young generations. The old generation region is examined only when it becomes full and then a *major* collection is performed on the old generation objects. This is apparently more efficient with the only risk that some unreachable objects in the white set may not be collected at once.

3.5.5 Incremental strategy

Much like the concurrent strategy, the incremental garbage collection strategy is devised to battle the obvious drawback of the stop-the-world strategy. The incremental strategy allows an entire collection cycle to proceed in several phases so that some user work can be done between two adjacent collection pauses. See Figure 3.9 for an illustration of one time versus incremental garbage collection.

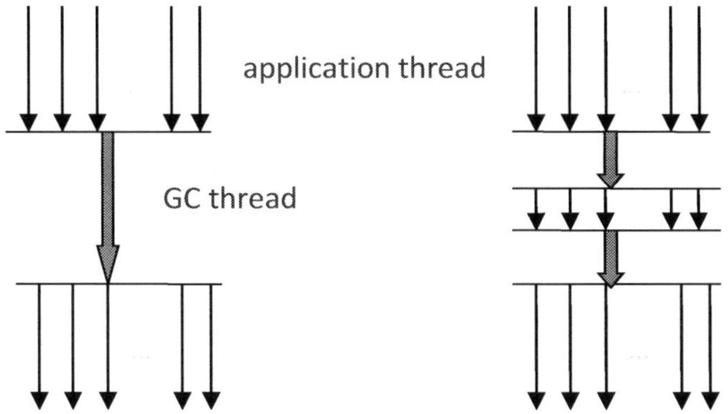

Figure 3.9 One time versus incremental GC strategy

In order to tune a JVM for best possible Java application performance and scalability, it is essential to understand various garbage collection algorithms and implementations conceptually we have introduced so far. For a more complete and deeper coverage of all GC algorithms and their variants, consult the latest text [Jones, 2011].

3.6 SUMMARY

In this chapter, we focused on understanding the Java platform from application performance and scalability perspectives. After a brief introduction to JVM internals, we reviewed Java memory management, especially from the garbage collection perspective. Various garbage collection algorithms and implementation strategies were discussed conceptually. With this preparation, it would be a lot easier to understand various daunting garbage collection options implemented in HotSpot JVMs, as covered in the next chapter.

EXERCISES

3.1 Explain the concept of an execution stack for Java. Is a stack for an entire JVM or each thread has its own stack?

3.2 What's the advantage of a stack-oriented instruction set architecture?

3.3 What's the difference between a mutator and a collector in context of a JVM? Which one of them would be suspended in a stop-the-world GC cycle?

3.4 Explain why objects in black set will never be moved to white set in a tri-color GC algorithm.

3.5 What's the difference between a parallel GC and a concurrent GC process? Which one is of stop-the-world collection in nature?

3.6 What is the main objective of the generational GC strategy? How does a generational GC strategy differ from an incremental GC strategy?

REFERENCES

JSE 7 JVM Specification: http://docs.oracle.com/javase/specs/jvms/se7/html/index.html.

C. Hunt, and B. John, *Java Performance,* Addison Wesley, 2012.

R. Jones, A. Hosking, and E. Moss, *The Garbage Collection Handbook: The Art of Automatic Memory Management*, Chapman and Hall/CRC, 2011.

4 HotSpot JVMs

The previous chapter focused more on the theoretical aspects of JVMs, especially on various garbage collection algorithms. In this chapter, we get real with real JVMs, or specifically with Oracle HotSpot JVMs. We begin with how Oracle JDKs have evolved since 1996 when Java débuted, with a particular focus on their performance and scalability features, including how garbage collections have been improved from release to release. We then delve into the details of various garbage collection schemes implemented with the latest releases of HotSpot JVMs. We wrap up the chapter by introducing JConsole and VisualVM, which are useful tools for monitoring and profiling Java applications to help resolve performance and scalability issues when they occur.

4.1 Oracle JDK Performance Features

In this section, let's first take a look at the Oracle JDK version history since the first release of JDK 1.0 in 1996 up to Java SE 7.0 as the latest. For each release, we cover only the release date and the major performance and scalability oriented features without enumerating all functionality enhancements.

4.1.1 Oracle JDK Version History

The release names of the Oracle JDKs have gone through the changes from JDK to J2SE, and to Java SE lately, as illustrated below:

- **JDK 1.0 (1/23/1996)**. Initial release that could execute bytecode.
- **JDK 1.1 (2/19/1997)**. Retooling of the AWT event model.
- **J2SE 1.2 (12/8/1998)**. JIT compiler introduced for the first time.
- **J2SE 1.3 (5/8/2000)**. HotSpot JVM with JIT compilation and adaptive optimization.
- **J2SE 1.4 (2/6/2002)**. Non-blocking NIO (New Input/Output).
- **J2SE 5.0 (9/30/2004)**. Concurrency utilities introduced.
- **Java SE 6 (12/11/2006)**. Dramatic performance improvements for the core platform, Swing and JVM in the areas of garbage collection algorithms and start-up performance.

- **Java SE 6 Update 10 or Java SE 6u10 (4/2008).** Default installation directory of jdk1.6.0_10, Java Quick Starter to improve cold start-up time, and improved Java2D graphics performance.
- **Java SE 6u12 (2/2/2009).** Performance improvements of Java and JavaFX applications as well as 64-bit browser support for Java Plugin and Java Web Start.
- **Java SE 6u14 (5/28/2009).** Extensive performance updates to the HotSpot JIT compiler, compressed pointers for 64-bit machines, as well as support for the experimental G1 (Garbage First) low pause garbage collector.
- **Java SE 6u31 (2/14/2012).** The latest stable release with many performance-oriented features enabled by default.
- **Java SE 7.0 update 4 (4/26/2012 – newest as of this writing).** New HotSpot JVM version 23 with some features merged from JRockit, formal support of G1 GC in place of the existing concurrent low-pause garbage collector (also known as CMS or Concurrent Mark-Sweep GC), and a new library for supporting parallel computing on multicore processors.

In the next few sections, we'll elaborate on some of the performance and scalability features mentioned above such as JIT compilation, adaptive optimization, NIO, concurrent utilities, cold start versus warm start, Java Quick Starter, and G1 GC.

4.1.2 JIT Compilation

A JIT compiler turns the bytecode of a Java program into OS platform specific native code at a proper time when the Java program is being executed, which brings the performance of a Java program up to par with a more traditional language such as C/C++. A JIT compiler can kick in for any arbitrary bytecode segment of a Java program when it is about to be executed and hence the name "just-in-time." This may cause a delay when it is invoked the first time but the compiled native code will run faster afterwards, and it typically is not a problem for applications that run for a long period of time with the compiled code executed repeatedly.

4.1.3 Adaptive Optimization

The HotSpot JVM contains an adaptive optimization technique, which performs runtime optimization and recompilation of portions of a program based on the current execution profile. It is capable of analyzing local data conditions and execution logic and then eliminating branches or using inline expansion to decrease context switching to speed up the execution of the application overall. This is an advanced optimization strategy based on the user code execution patterns that cannot be determined *a priori*.

4.1.4 New Input/Output (NIO)

The intrinsic I/O performance and scalability of a runtime such as the Java Runtime could have significant impacts on the performance and scalability of the applications it supports, since I/O activities have always been an important part of common computational tasks. Typical I/O scenarios include:

- Reading from and writing to internal memory arrays, external disk files and network sockets from the source/destination perspective

- Reading /writing binary or character data streams from the data format perspective

Java I/Os work on top of the underlying hardware level I/Os supported by the corresponding OS. At the Java platform level, the NIO APIs introduced in J2SE JDK 1.4 as a new package (`java.nio`) can save developers a lot of efforts in writing high-performance, scalable software that is I/O intensive. A few examples of the NIO APIs include:

- The API for scalable I/O operations on both files and sockets, making it easy to write server software that can scale to thousands of concurrent connections. It's also well suited for parallel processing by taking advantage of multi-threaded, multicore, and multiple processors.
- The fast buffered binary I/O API that has the ability to map files into memory. This is particularly suited for writing high-performance, I/O-intensive software that crunches streams or files of binary data.
- The fast buffered character I/O API for efficient handling of streams or files of character based data such as XML files and other types of text files.

Next, let's review the concurrent utilities offered since J2SE JDK 1.5.

4.1.5 Concurrent Utilities

To save developers efforts in coding software that requires use of significant concurrency, a new package of `java.util.concurrent` was included in JDK 1.5. It provides developers with ready-to-use concurrent utilities as basic building blocks for dealing with issues with thread pooling, asynchronous execution of tasks, concurrent access, and synchronization utilities such as counting semaphores, atomic variables, locks, and condition variables, and so on. It also has a very useful feature of nanosecond-granularity level timing through the `System.nanoTime` method. The conventional timing has a limited resolution of about 10 milliseconds.

In general, it's challenging to develop concurrent, thread-safe software. Obviously, those concurrent utilities can help developers write software with increased performance, scalability, reliability, and maintainability.

4.1.6 Java Quick Starter

Java Quick Starter (JQS) was introduced in JSE 6u10 to help improve the startup time of Java-based applications. When enabled, it pre-fetches some of the most heavily used files into memory to minimize the delay that would have incurred if not pre-fetched. Whether JQS is enabled depends on the OS on your system. Check it out if you feel you need this extra help in minimizing the startup time of your application.

4.1.7 Cold Start versus Warm Start

Conceptually, *cold start* means that a program is launched the first time since the system was rebooted, while *warm start* means that the program has been run more than once since the system was rebooted. You might have already had the experience that the warm start could be significantly faster than cold start with some applications on your system. What's behind the scene in terms of cold start versus warm start? It's simple: with cold start, all data necessary for a program to run must be all loaded into memory, while with warm start, some data might have already been cached in memory so less data needs to be loaded into memory during a startup. This is exactly how the Java Quick Starter works as described in the preceding section.

Cold versus warm start is an easy subject to understand. However, garbage collection is not. Although we have covered some basic garbage collection algorithms in the previous chapter from a theoretical point of view, we have not discussed about how garbage collection actually is implemented in the latest JDKs to be used in production environment. This is the subject of the next section.

4.2 Garbage Collectors in HotSpot JVMs

With the theoretical foundations laid down in the previous chapter about garbage collections in general, it should be a lot easier now to understand how garbage objects are collected in real world applications using the production quality JVMs such as the HotSpot JVMs included in Oracle JDKs. Let's review the concept of generations next.

4.2.1 Generations

Although GC algorithms and implementations may change from time to time, so far all GC implementations in Oracle JVMs seem to have stabilized on the notion of generational GC. Figure 4.1 shows the heap structure divided as generations used by the currently most popular Oracle 1.6.0_x JVM garbage collectors named Concurrent Mark and Sweep (CMS, to be discussed later). Let's establish a base first for understanding how Oracle JVM GCs collect garbage objects.

As shown in Figure 4.1, there are three regions in the heap: *Young*, *Tenured* (which is interchangeable with the term *Old*), and *Perm*. The Young generation region is further divided into three regions: *Eden* and two equally sized *Survivor* spaces. The purpose of each region is as follows:

- **The young generation**. Newly created objects are initially allocated in Eden. The other two survivor spaces play the role of stop-and-copy or two space collection strategy as discussed in the preceding chapter. Note that this is the GC model for Windows platforms. For Solaris, two equally sized spaces rather than one Eden + two smaller Survivors are used for copying.
- **The tenured generation**. Young live objects might be copied back and forth between the two survivor spaces, but eventually will be copied to the Tenured region after surviving several cycles of collection.
- **The permanent generation**. The Perm region holds metadata needed by the VM to describe objects such as class data structures, and so on.

Note that each region has a virtual space, which represents the virtual memory that has been virtually reserved but not allocated to physical memory until it is needed. Also, the heap structure shown in Figure 4.1 applies to all collectors except the throughput collector to be introduced later, for which the Young and Tenured regions are swapped, i.e., the Tenured region is placed in front of the Young region.

Next, let's explain a few GC performance metrics used to measure the performance of a GC process.

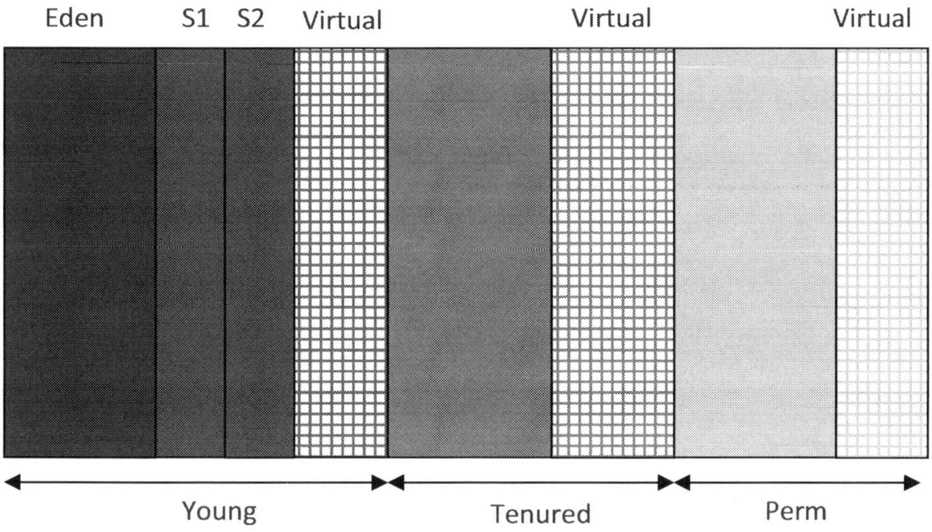

Figure 4.1 Heap structure for generational GC strategy with the HotSpot JVMs

4.2.2 GC Performance Metrics

The performance of a GC process can be measured with the following metrics:

- **Throughput**. This metric measures the percentage of total time not spent in garbage collection. Perhaps it's convenient to introduce a new metric *of GC duty factor,* which is equal to 1 – throughput. The metric of GC duty factor is an indication of how busy a GC has been collecting garbage objects. A GC duty factor of 2% means that the GC is collecting garbage 2% of the total time measured on average.
- **Footprint**. This metric measures the working set of a process, or the total memory required for a process. Note that this is not the same as the total heap size, as the latter is only a part of the former.
- **Promptness**. This metric measures the time from when an object is de-referenced to when its memory is reclaimed.
- **Pause**. This metric measures the duration when an application appears unresponsive because GC is occurring.
- **Frequency**. This metric measures how frequently garbage collection occurs.

Note that throughput is a relative metric whereas all other four are absolute metrics.

4.2.3 Garbage Collectors with the HotSpot JVMs

The most fundamental GC algorithm adopted by the HotSpot JVMs has been the serial mark-and-sweep with copying strategy. The collector implemented in this strategy is called a serial collector. Table 4.1 summarizes all four generational GCs available in the Oracle JDKs since 1.5. Here, the term "*parallel*" means multiple threads doing garbage collection versus only one thread, whereas the term "*concurrent*" means that user code execution and garbage collection occur concurrently without having any of the two tasks stopped to let the other proceed alone.

Table 4.1 Types of GC Collectors in Oracle/Sun JDKs

Collector	**Command Line Option**
Serial	-XX:+UseSerialGC
Throughput/Parallel	-XX:+UseParallelGC
Throughput/ParallelOld	-XX:+UseParallelOldGC
Concurrent Mark and Sweep (CMS)	-XX:+UseConcMarkSweepGC

Which collector is used is determined by the JVM based on the hardware capability such as the # of processors and the amount of physical memory. This is called Java *ergonomics*. However, by using a command option, you can specify which GC option to use, as is shown in Table 4.1.

The serial GC is mainly for client machines with limited number of CPUs. The guidelines for choosing which collector for enterprise Java applications are outlined as follows:

- Choose the *throughput* GC if:
    - Your system has more CPUs (as a rule of thumb, use ParallelGC if # of CPUs is < 8, or use ParallelOldGC otherwise).
    - Your application is multi-threaded that has many threads allocating objects, needing a large young generation.
    - Your application is more of batch-job type.
- Choose the *concurrent* GC if:
    - Your system has more CPUs.
    - You expect a large tenured generation.
    - You want to cut the major GC into multiple phases so that application execution and GC can occur alternately.
    - Your application is more of OLTP type and the user response time takes a higher priority.

Out of all the collectors, the CMS collector is the most complicated one. The next section describes how the CMS collector has been implemented in Oracle JVMs.

4.2.4 Concurrent Mark and Sweep (CMS)

It is interesting to see how low pauses during a major GC are achieved with the concurrent GC. Figure 4.2 shows the sequence of pauses with a CMS GC:

- **Phase I: Initial Marking**. At the beginning of a collection, the CMS collector stops all threads executing the user code for a brief pause and uses one thread for marking. During this initial marking phase, an initial set of live objects that are directly reachable from the root objects are identified. This phase is of *stop-the-world* (STW) and *serial*.

- **Phase II: Concurrent Marking**. The second phase is a concurrent marking phase, which marks the live objects that are transitively reachable from the set identified in the first phase. This phase is *concurrent* and *serial*.
- **Phase III: Remarking**. During this third phase, the application stops and the objects *touched* during the second phase are remarked in parallel. This phase is of *stop-the-world* (STW) and *parallel*.
- **Phase IV: Concurrent Sweeping**. The fourth phase, the final concurrent sweep phase, reclaims all garbage objects. This phase is *concurrent and serial*.

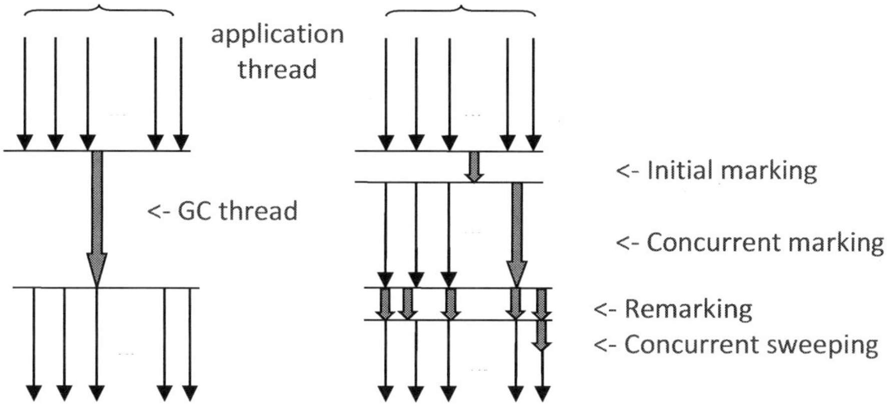

Figure 4.2 one-time, stop-the-world versus CMS GC

The CMS collector has a severe drawback that it's non-compacting, and it's the only collector in the HotSpot JVMs that doesn't compact. This is illustrated in Figure 4.3 where cross-hatch squares represent garbage objects, solid black squares live objects, and white squares free spaces. Essentially, the CMS collector trades low latency with memory fragmentation.

However, the CMS collector is the only proactive collector that it doesn't wait until the tenured generation becomes full. It also gives the user an option to set a threshold for the percentage of the occupied tenured region to trigger a GC so that it can be controlled externally. You can use the –`XX:+CMSInitiatingOccupancyFraction=n` command line option to specify your threshold, where `n` is an integer that represents the fraction in percentages (the default value for `n` is 68). The CMS collector can also be configured to run in incremental mode via the command line option –`XX:+CMSIncrementalMode`.

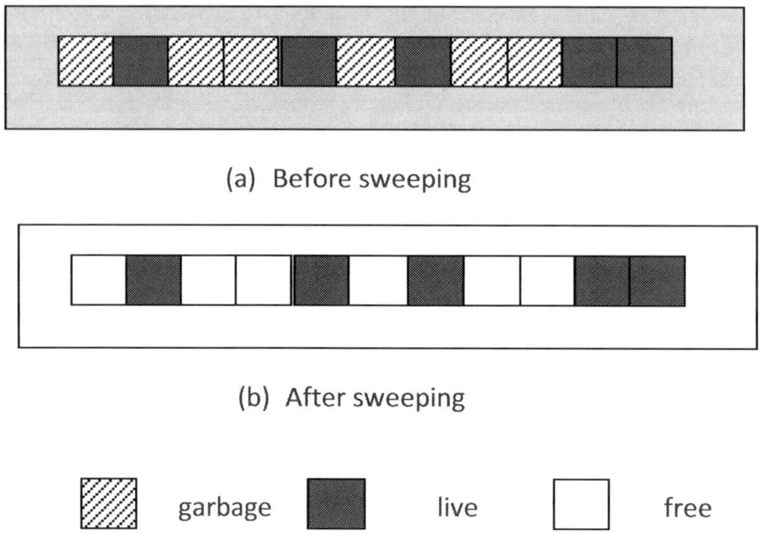

Figure 4.3 The CMS collector sweeps but does not compact the tenured generation, resulting in fragmented tenured region

See Tables 4.2 and 4.3 for the cross-collector comparisons about what strategies are implemented with a specific collector and a specific generation. These comparisons also put the CMS collector into perspective relative to other types of collectors.

Table 4.2 Features with Each Collector for Young Generation GC

Feature	Serial	Parallel	ParallelOld	CMS
Serial	✓	x	x	x
Parallel	x	✓	✓	✓
Copying	✓	✓	✓	✓
Compacting	x	x	x	x
Concurrent	x	x	x	x
Incremental	x	x	x	x

Table 4.3 Features with Each Collector for Tenured Generation GC

Feature	Serial	Parallel	ParallelOld	CMS
Serial	✓	✓	x	x
Parallel	x	x	✓	✓
Copying	✓	x	x	x
Compacting	✓	✓	✓	x
Concurrent	x	x	x	✓
Incremental	x	x	x	✓

In summary, the throughput collector favors batch job type of computing tasks, while the CMS collector favors OLTP type of applications such as Web applications. In reality, it's very likely that an application runs a mixed workload with some batch job type of tasks while serving online users at the same time. In such a hybrid scenario, the CMS collector should be considered first. Otherwise, it's necessary to verify that choosing the throughput collector doesn't hurt the UI performance of the application if the throughput collector is chosen.

4.2.5 Garbage First (G1) GC

G1 GC was included in JSE 6u14 for experimentation and formalized in Java SE 7u4 (http://www.oracle.com/technetwork/java/javase/7u4-relnotes-1575007.html). It has been marketed as the long-term replacement for the HotSpot low pause Concurrent Mark-Sweep GC (CMS) for quite some time. G1 GC has the following main features:

- **Still Generational**. G1 still works on the concept of young and tenured generations, but there is no more physical separation between *young* and *tenured* spaces on the heap. Instead, a single contiguous heap is split into many same-sized *regions,* both for young and tenured generations. Both young and tenured regions can be non-contiguous, providing the much needed flexibility in collecting garbage objects.
- **Compaction**. Unlike CMS, G1 takes the heap memory fragmentation issue seriously by performing heap compaction over time, which is very beneficial for long-lasting applications to run smoothly.
- **Parallelism and Concurrency**. G1 doesn't eliminate stop-the-world pauses as in CMS. It counts on more advanced hardware with more cores and threads to decrease the durations of stop-the-world pauses.
- **Predictability**. G1 has a built-in prediction model that helps meet a pause time target. This is made possible with its elimination of memory fragmentations.

An article at http://docs.oracle.com/javase/7/docs/technotes/guides/vm/G1.html gives more information about G1 GC. Also, I will use a real product based case study later in Chapter 6 to demonstrate how well G1 GC works in reality against the CMS GC.

Next, a brief section is added to help enhance a developer's garbage awareness, which should benefit all GCs, whether CMS or G1.

4.3 HELPING GARBAGE COLLECTORS

Java memory is managed automatically. However, this doesn't mean that programmers can take a hands-free approach to it. A garbage collector collects only unreferenced objects, and there are simple ways of letting a garbage collector know that an object is unreferenced. The simplest way to do this takes only one line of code, which is to assign the value `null` to a variable that refers to an object that is no longer needed. This way a garbage collector would know immediately that that object has become garbage and can be collected.

Assuming that a programmer has done all he could to help a GC work more efficiently, in the next section, let's see what knobs exist for tuning the performance and scalability of a HotSpot JVM.

4.4 GARBAGE COLLECTION TUNING

Garbage collection tuning is an indispensable part of every Java based enterprise application. All latest HotSpot JVMs have a feature called *ergonomics*, which helps select a collector and size a heap based on the number of CPUs and the amount of physical memory available on a machine. However, it's very rare that such an initial guessing will work best without requiring any tunings for a large scale enterprise Java application. For example, it is considered a server class machine if it has 2 or more CPUs and 2 GB or more physical memory. As we know, many laptop and desktop systems can exceed these requirements easily, but they are not necessarily to be meant to be server class machines.

Garbage collection tuning starts with sizing a heap properly. Before exploring the available sizing parameters with the HotSpot JVMs, let us first introduce the HotSpot JVM command line options in the next section.

4.4.1 HotSpot JVM Command Line Options

The HotSpot JVMs allow many configuration parameters to be passed in through specified command line options, which are categorized into *standard* options, *nonstandard* options, and *developer* options. These options differ as follows according to the number of X's:

- **Standard Options.** Standard options conform to the common JVM specification and are expected to be implemented by all JVM vendors.
- **Nonstandard Options.** As is implied, nonstandard options are JVM vendor specific. For HotSpot JVMs, nonstandard options are designated with a `-X` prefix.
- **Developer Options.** This class of options is designated with a `-XX` prefix. It has a few variations as follows:
    - *Boolean flags.* If a + or – sign is placed before the name of a variable, such as `-XX:+AggresiveOpts` or `-XX:-AggressiveOpts`, it enables or disables that option by setting that boolean variable to `true` or `false`.
    - Non-boolean flags. Non-boolean flags are expressed in the form of `-XX:OptionName=<N>` where `<N>` is some numerical value, which may be followed with a suffix of `k`, `m` or `g`, to indicate `kilo`, `mega` or `giga`- multipliers for the value indicated.

You will see many such options in the next few sections about tuning JVMs for best possible performance and scalability of your Java applications. For a complete list of all HotSpot VM options, visit http://www.oracle.com/technetwork/java/javase/tech/vmoptions-jsp-140102.html.

4.4.2 Sizing a Heap

The HotSpot JVMs have the following parameters available for tuning:

- **`-Xmsn`** and –**`Xmxn`**. These two options specify the minimum and maximum heap sizes, respectively. For example, adding the options of –Xms1024m –Xmx2048m would set the minimum and maximum heap sizes to 1024 MB and 2048 MB, respectively.
- **`-XX:MaxPermSize=n`**. This option specifies the maximum size of the perm region.

- `-XX:MinHeapFreeRatio=min` and `–XX:MaxHeapFreeRatio=max`. The collector will expand or shrink the heap to maintain the heap free ratios to the specified percentages. The default settings are 40 for min and 70 for max, respectively.

The heap sizing parameters apply to all collectors. Next, let's see how each collector can be tuned.

4.4.3 Tuning a Throughput Garbage Collector

A throughput garbage collector can be tuned with the following parameters:

- `-XX:ParallelGCThreads=n`. This option specifies the number of threads for garbage collection. The default setting is the number of CPUs. You may want to limit the number of threads for GC if you have many CPUs on your machine.
- `-XX:MaxGCPauseMills=n`. This option specifies that the max pause time should not exceed `n` milliseconds (but not guaranteed). There is no default for this setting.
- `-XX:GCTimeRatio=n`. This option specifies that for every (`n` + 1) units of time, 1 unit is spent on garbage collection. The default setting is `n` = 99.

Note that between pause time and throughput, the former takes a higher priority. Note also that the throughput garbage collector enables *adaptive heap sizing* by default, which can be disabled with the `–XX:-UseAdaptiveSizePolicy` Java startup command line option. The other garbage collectors do not have this feature associated with. The next section discusses more about adaptive heap sizing.

4.4.4 Adaptive Heap Sizing

Adaptive heap sizing constantly evaluates the allocation rates and lifetimes of application objects, and dynamically adjusts young and old generation spaces for optimal sizes. The objectives of adaptive heap sizing include:

- Having short-lived objects collected so that they would not be promoted to the old generation.
- Having long-lived objects promoted timely to the old generation so that they would not be copied between survivor spaces.

The initial settings for adaptive heap sizing can be specified with the following options:

- **–Xmn<n>[g|m|k]** – Sets the initial, min and max sizes for the young generation space. For example, -Xmn256m would set the initial, min and max sizes of the young generation space *all* to 256 MB.
- **-XX:NewSize=<n>[g|m|k]** – Sets the initial and minimum sizes for the young generation space. For example, -XX:NewSize=128m would set *both* the initial and minimum sizes for the young generation space to 128 MB.
- **-XX:MaxNewSize=<n>[g|m|k]** – Sets the maximum size for the young generation space. For example, -XX:MaxNewSize=1024m would set the maximum size for the young generation space to 1024 MB.
- **`-XX:NewRatio=`<n>** – Sets the ratio between the young generation size and tenured generation size. The default setting is 2 for a client JVM and 8 for a server JVM, respectively. Accordingly, for a server class machine, the size of the tenured region is eight times that of the young generation

region by default. Since n is an integer, the tenured region will be at least as large as the young region.

- **-XX:InitialSurvivorRatio=<n>** – Sets the initial ratio between each survivor space and Eden. The larger the value of n, the smaller the initial survivor space.

4.4.5 Tuning a CMS Garbage Collector

A CMS garbage collector has the following options to tune:

- **-XX:ParallelGCThreads=n.** This option specifies the number of threads for garbage collection. The default setting is the number of CPUs.
- **-XX:CMSIncrementalMode**. This option enables the concurrent phase to be done incrementally. It is disabled by default.
- **-XX:CMSIncrementalPacing**. This option allows the CMS garbage collector to control pacing adaptively based on the application behavior. It is disabled by default.
- **-XX:SurvivorRatio=<n>**–Sets the ratio between each survivor space and Eden. The default is 32, which means that the total young region can be measured as 34 equally sized blocks with 32 blocks for Eden and the rest 2 blocks for the two survivor spaces. Note that this option should not be used with a throughput garbage collector, in which case, use -XX:InitialSurvivorRatio as discussed in the previous section instead.

To experiment with various garbage collector tunings, it's very necessary to follow a strict procedure and adhere to the principle of "one single variable, comparable workload," which means that the workload for the comparison runs must be comparable if it's not possible to be exactly the same, and that there should be only one variable a time - the tuning variable under test. This principle is followed throughout all case studies presented in this text.

4.4.6 Dealing With OutOfMemoryErrors

A common problem with Java applications is the occurrence of massive OutOfMemoryErrors. Sometimes this is caused by memory leaks and sometimes it's just because the heap is not sized properly. Memory leaking shows a trend of increasing heap consumption over a period, while insufficient memory for normal use doesn't exhibit this trend. Whenever OutOfMemoryErrors messages appear, it's necessary to try to correlate them with the underlying causes based on several common factors, such as:

- **Undersized Java heap space**. This is an indication that new objects cannot be allocated on the heap because of insufficient memory. It can be mitigated by increasing the max heap size, or, you need to look for solutions at the code level, for example, if there are any bad code statements that prevent garbage objects from being collected. Use the tools to be introduced in the next section to help diagnose the problems at the source code level.
- **Undersized PermGen space**. This indicates that the permanent region is used out. This happens when an application loads a lot of classes dynamically, such as the dynamically created JSP pages. Using the option introduced in the previous section about sizing a heap to increase the perm size may help.

- **Requested array size exceeds VM limit**. This indicates that your application is requesting a large array, which cannot be satisfied on the current heap. This typically requires looking at your algorithm and making proper changes, for example, checking the data structures used and trying to limit the number of items to be processed at a time.

To analyze errors and to assess whether a chosen collector is working well with a Java application, one needs to use specialized tools to examine the JVM GC behaviors associated with the execution of the application. This is the subject of the next section.

4.5 GARBAGE COLLECTION MONITORING

JVM GC performance tuning starts with monitoring. For basic garbage collection information, you can simply add the following JRE command line options to your Java application startup script :

- `-XX:+PrintGC` for basic information at every collection.
- `-XX:+PrintGCDetails` for more detailed information at every collection.
- `-XX:PrintGCTimeStamps` for showing the time stamps of each collection. This option should be used together with one of the previous two options.
- `-Xloggc:<filename>` with one of the first two options described above to log GC data into a file for offline analysis. Many real applications actually use this option.

Two UI-based, built-in tools, JConsole and VisualVM, are available from Oracle JDK distributions since JSE 6. This section introduces how to use these two tools to monitor and tune your GC for the best possible performance and scalability for your Java-based application. Before kicking off your GC monitoring with these two tools, check out the JVM default options for your system on which your application is deployed to run, as is described next.

4.5.1 Java Ergonomic Defaults

Don't be intimidated by the term of *Ergonomic Defaults*. It merely means what default JVM options will be used on your system if you do not overwrite them. You can execute the command *java –XX:+PrintCommandLineFlags –version* to verify the ergonomic defaults on your system. For example, I executed this command on two of my systems, and obtained the following output messages with different versions of JDKs:

- **An 8 core, hyper-threaded Xeon E5620 @ 2.4 GHz system with 32 GB RAM running on Windows 2008 R2 64-bit**:
  - *C:**jdk1.6.0_24_64bit**\bin>java -XX:+PrintCommandLineFlags -version*

```
-XX:InitialHeapSize=536659328 -XX:MaxHeapSize=8586549248
-XX:ParallelGCThreads=13 -XX:+PrintCommandLineFlags
-XX:+UseCompressedOops -XX:-UseLargePagesIndividualAllocation
-XX:+UseParallelGC
java version "1.6.0_24"
Java(TM) SE Runtime Environment (build 1.6.0_24-b07)
Java HotSpot(TM) 64-Bit Server VM (build 19.1-b02, mixed mode)
```

- *C:\>C:**jdk1.7.0_04_64bit**\bin\java -XX:+PrintCommandLineFlags -version*

  -XX:InitialHeapSize=536659328 -XX:MaxHeapSize=4291581952
  -XX:+PrintCommandLineFlags -XX:+**UseCompressedOops**
  -XX:-UseLargePagesIndividualAllocation -XX:+**UseParallelGC**
  java version "1.7.0_04"
  Java(TM) SE Runtime Environment (build 1.7.0_04-b22)
  Java HotSpot(TM) 64-Bit Server VM (build 23.0-b21, mixed mode)

- **A quad-core, hyper-threaded Intel Core i7-2600 @ 3.4 GHz system with 8 GB RAM running on Windows 7 Professional 64-bit**:

  - *C:\ >c:**jdk1.6.0_24_64bit**\bin\java -XX:+PrintCommandLineFlags -version*

    -XX:InitialHeapSize=133514048 -XX:MaxHeapSize=2136224768
    -XX:ParallelGCThreads=8 -XX:+PrintCommandLineFlags
    -XX:+**UseCompressedOops** -XX:-UseLargePagesIndividualAllocation
    -XX:+**UseParallelGC**
    java version "1.6.0_24"
    Java(TM) SE Runtime Environment (build 1.6.0_24-b07)
    Java HotSpot(TM) 64-Bit Server VM (build 19.1-b02, mixed mode)

  - *C:\ >c:**jdk1.7.0_04_64bit**\bin\java -XX:+PrintCommandLineFlags -version*

    -XX:InitialHeapSize=133514048 -XX:MaxHeapSize=2136224768
    -XX:+PrintCommandLineFlags -XX:+**UseCompressedOops**
    -XX:-UseLargePagesIndividualAllocation -XX:+**UseParallelGC**
    java version "1.7.0_04"
    Java(TM) SE Runtime Environment (build 1.7.0_04-b22)
    Java HotSpot(TM) 64-Bit Server VM (build 23.0-b21, mixed mode)

It is seen that in all cases, `UseCompressedOops` and `UseParallelGC` options are enabled by default since JDK 1.6.0 update 24. The throughput garbage collector `UseParallelGC` option has been enabled by default since JDK 1.5, whereas the `UseCompressedOops` option was not enabled by default until JSE 1.6 update 23. Also, note that the throughput garbage collector `UseParallelGC` remains the default garbage collector even up to the latest JDK release of 1.7.0 update 4. Keep in mind that ParallelGC uses parallel and copying for young generation and serial and compacting for tenured region.

4.5.2 JConsole

JConsole is a simple tool for viewing very basic VM data and information. To use JConsole, start up your application and wait until it is fully up and running. Then, simply click on the `jconsole.exe` file in your JDK's `bin` directory on Windows. Using the CPUCheck sample included in this book, Figure 4.4 shows what you would see after you start up your JConsole. This sample contains two Java processes: The `AdminServer` and the client `ServiceDirectory`. See Appendix B for a detailed description about how to run this sample with both the server and the client.

At this point, you will be asked to select *Local* or *Remote Process*. For our demo purposes, select the `AdminServer` process and click *Connect*. Now you should see the JConsole window with six tabs of

Overview/Memory/Threads/Classes/VM Summary/MBeans. While having the JConsole connected to the Admin Server process, run the client a few times just to get some data to display.

Figure 4.4 JConsole startup page after the CPUCheck sample is started up

Cycle through all JConsole Tabs and get familiar with what information it provides. Given the extensive coverage on JVM garbage collection provided in the previous sections, it should be easy to correlate the information presented on this JConsole with the concepts we covered earlier. For example, a few interesting things you can observe under the Memory tab as shown in Figure 4.5:

- The top chart displays *Heap Memory Usage* with additional options available from that dropdown list. At the right upper corner is a *Perform GC* button for performing a forced garbage collection.
- The lower *Details* frame displays a summary of the GC activities, with a real-time display of the Heap and Non-Heap memory usages on the right side. The three bars above the *Heap* button represent the *Eden*, *Survivor* and *Old Gen* heap regions left to right, respectively, whereas the two bars above the *Non-Heap* button represent the *Code Cache* and *Perm Gen* regions from left to right, respectively. The first GC was a forced one (I clicked on the *Perform GC* button), whereas the next two were automatic ones. It reported that 1.591 seconds were spent on 24 PS (Parallel Scavenging) *MarkSweep* collections on the *Old Generation* and 0.319 seconds on 211 *PS Scavenge* collections on the *Young Generation*. Note that different collectors are used on different generations. Also, based on this reporting, it can be inferred that the throughput *ParallelGC* was used.

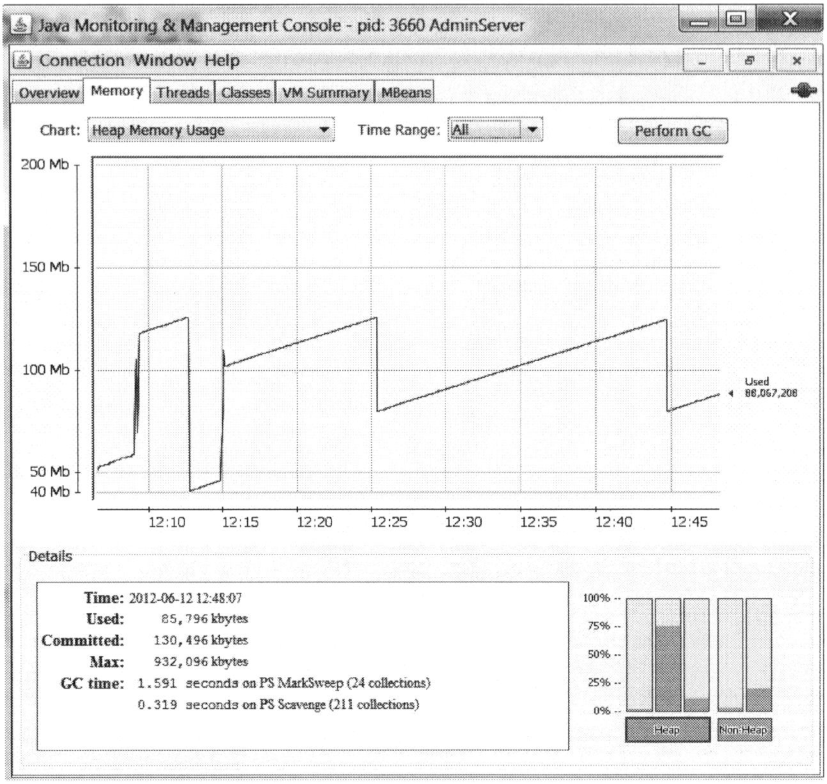

Figure 4.5 JConsole Memory Tab showing total GC times and algorithms

To explore further, I stopped both the sample and JConsole, and restarted the *AdminServer* with the –*XX:+UseConcMarkSweepGC* option to switch the garbage collector from the throughput GC to the low-latency CMS GC for the Admin Server. This option auto-enables *–XX:+UseParNewGC*, a multi-threaded GC for the young generation, along with the CMS for concurrent GC for the old generation. Refer to Figure 4.6 and compare it with Figure 4.5 to see how these two GC options differ in what GCs they use for young and old generations: The low-latency GC option of *–XX:+UseConcMarkSweepGC* sets the *ParNew* GC for the young generation and *CMS* for the old generation, respectively.

Figure 4.7 also shows the JConsole *Overview* page, which displays aggregated information on Memory, Threads, Classes and CPU Usage all in one place. It provides less information on each category, but is convenient for examining all in one place. However, most of the time, I recommend using the VisualVM tool, which covers both VM GC activity monitoring and application profiling. This is the subject of the next section.

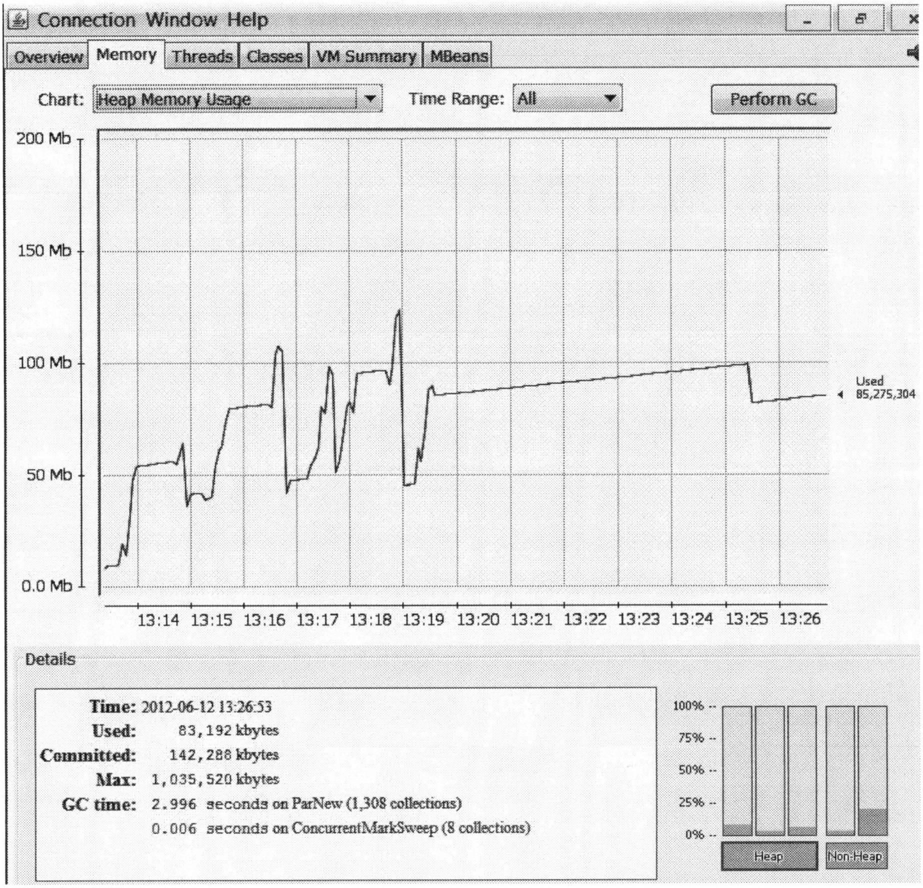

Figure 4.6 JConsole display with the *ParNew* and *CMS* collectors for the young and old generations, respectively

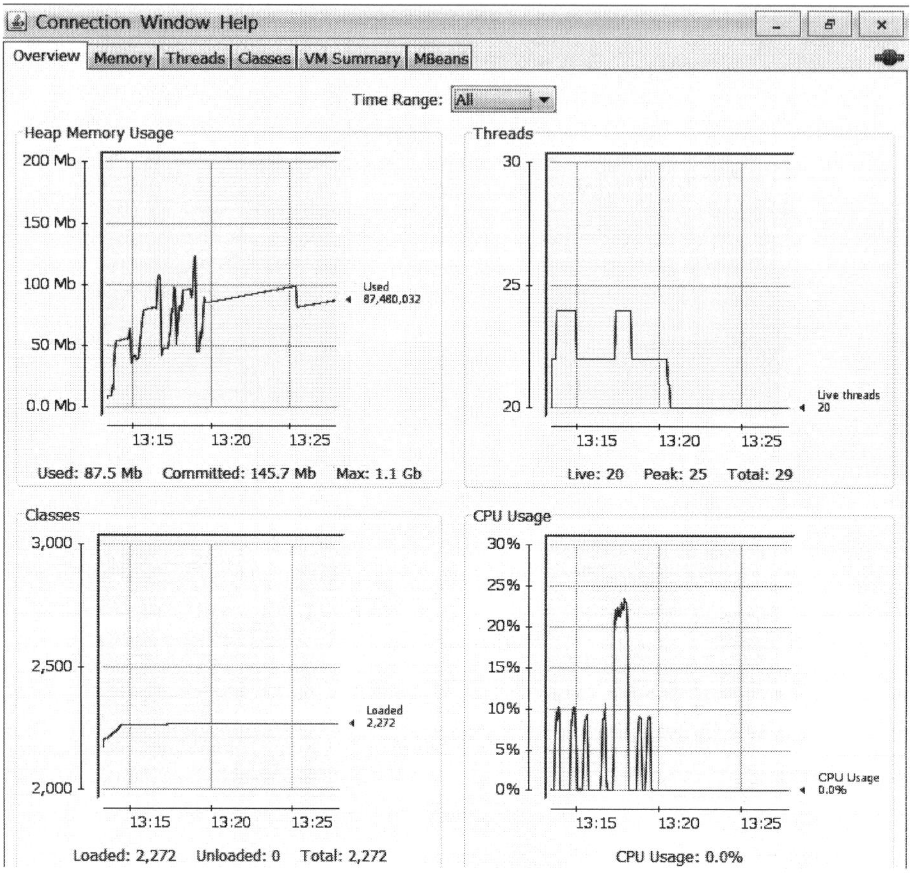

Figure 4.7 JConsole Overview page

4.5.3 VisualVM

VisualVM is an open-source tool with a series of standalone tools such as JConsole, jstat, jinfo, jstack, and jmap integrated together. To start it up, double-click on the image file *jvisualvm.exe* in the proper JDK *bin* folder.

Figure 4.8 shows the VisualVM startup page from my jdk1.6.0 update 31 install. You can see that it identified the two programs of the sample CPUCheck: *AdminServer* and *ServiceDirectory* client under *Local*. Visual VM can also monitor Java applications deployed on remote systems, although not all features available to local Java applications would be available to remote Java applications. In addition, you can take a snapshot of the state of a Java application at a given instant, and analyze it by selecting it afterwards under the node of Snapshots on VisualVM. Java applications are added or removed automatically as they are started up or shut down. Since configuring VisualVM to monitor a remote application is tedious with much fewer features available, we focus on monitoring *local* Java applications with VisualVM in this book. However, if your Java application is started up through a wrapper, you need to add the following lines in your `wrapper.conf` file (otherwise, you won't be able to see your Java process on your VisualVM console):

```
wrapper.java.additional.N=-Dcom.sun.management.jmxremote.port=xxxx
wrapper.java.additional.N=-Dcom.sun.management.jmxremote.ssl=false
wrapper.java.additional.N=-Dcom.sun.management.jmxremote.authenticate=false
```

You need to choose sequential integer numbers for "*N*" and an unused port number for "*xxxx*". Then, right-click on "*Local*" and "*Add JMX Connection…*" to connect to your Java process. If your Java application is started up with another program, you need to pass in these three JMX parameters as shown above to the JVM for your Java process similarly.

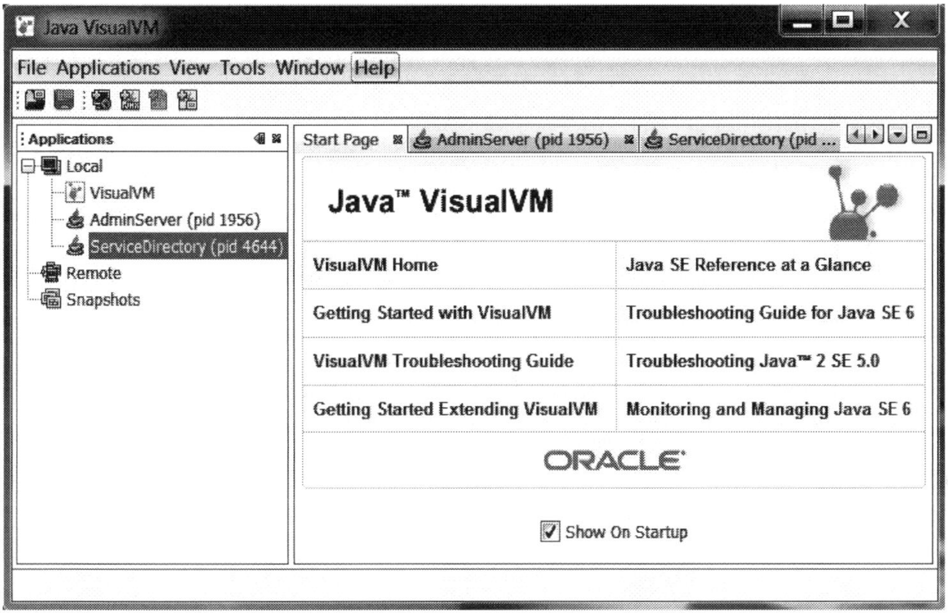

Figure 4.8 VisualVM start-up page

Now, let us use the CPUCheck program to demonstrate the features of VisualVM. Double-click on *AdminServer* to connect to the server admin process. You can also click the *ServiceDirectory* client application and switch between the server and client views. See Figure 4.8. Note the available tabs of Overview | Monitor | Threads | Sampler | Profiler. We describe how to use these features next.

- **Overview.** From this tab, you can see Main Class, Arguments, JVM, Java version, Java Home, JVM Flags, as well as Saved data, JVM arguments, and System properties, as shown in Figure 4.9.
- **Monitor**. From this tab, information displayed includes CPU (overall and GC activity), Heap/PermGen, Classes and Threads, as shown in Figure 4.10. You can also force a GC by clicking on the *Perform GC* button or take a heap dump by clicking on the *Heap Dump* button.

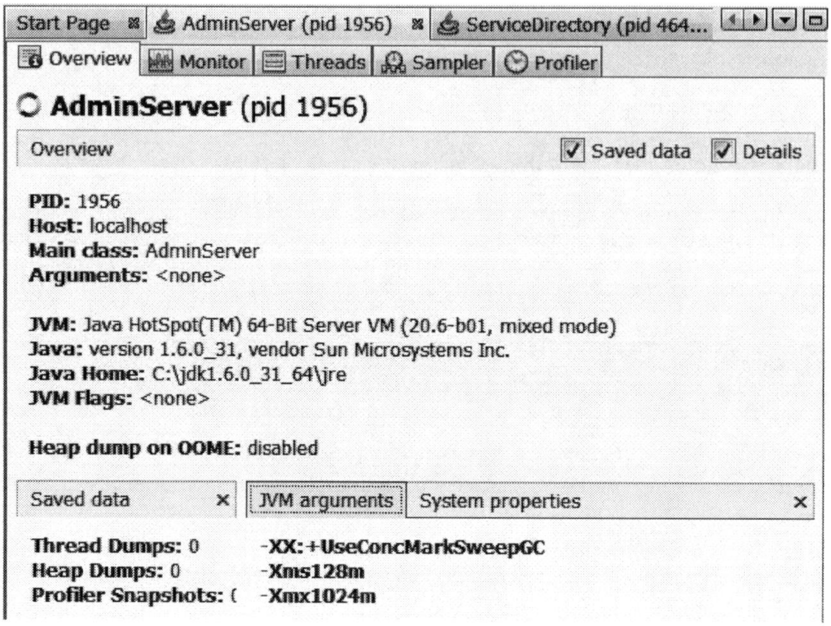

Figure 4.9 VisualVM *Overview* tab.

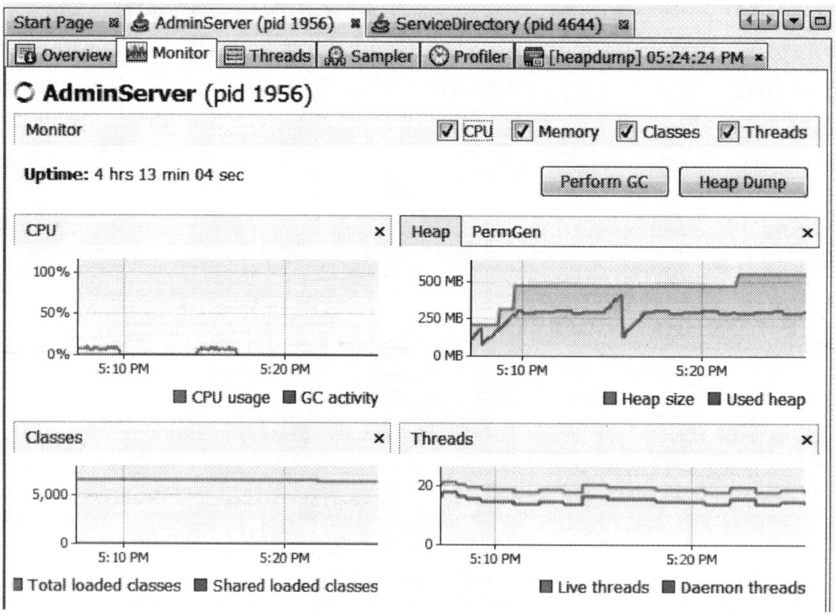

Figure 4.10 VisualVM *Monitor* tab

- **Threads**. From this tab, you can dig into every detail about the threads associated with the Java application being monitored. You can find out which threads are most active, and which threads are causing lock contention if any. You can choose one of the three perspectives (Timeline, Table, Details), as shown in Figure 4.11. Note that you can hide the charts that you don't want to see selectively.

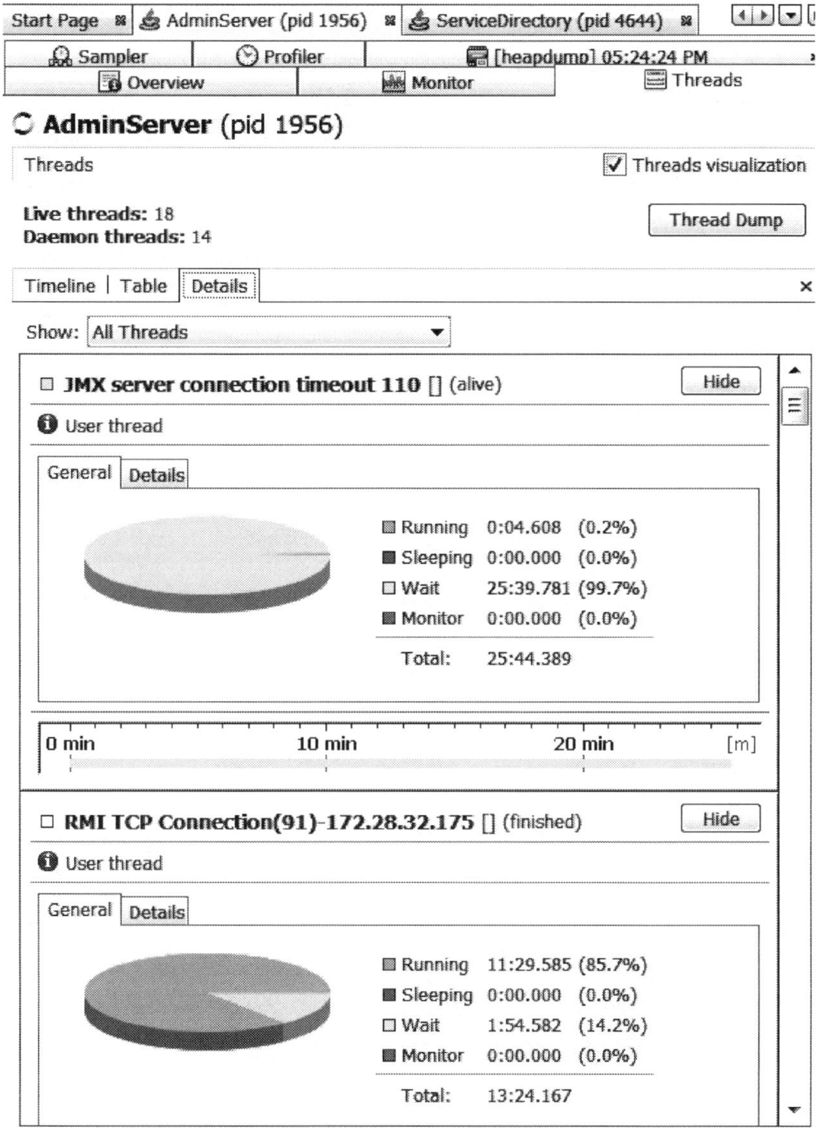

Figure 4.11 VisualVM Threads tab

- **Sampler**. This is where you can sample CPU and memory utilizations associated with your Java application to help diagnose performance issues. To sample CPU or memory, click on the *CPU* or

Memory button, and then click the *Stop* button to stop it when you need to. For each category of CPU or memory, you can pause/update/take a snapshot by clicking on the corresponding icon in the CPU or memory sampling frame. For CPU sampling as shown in Figure 4.12, the metric *Self Time* represents the time spent in that method only, namely, it does not include the times spent in other methods called from the method reported. Note the icons below CPU Samples. If you put your cursor over them, you would see *Pause live results* with the first icon and *Update live results now* with the second icon. You can flip their states by clicking on them.

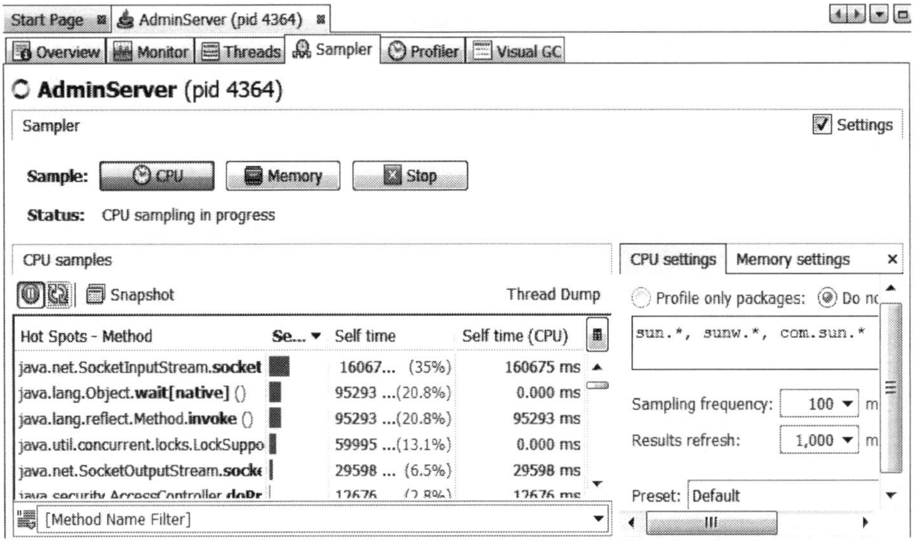

Figure 4.12 VisualVM Sampler tab / CPU sampling

- Figure 4.13 shows memory sampling, which displays the # of classes, object instances, and total bytes in the summary line as well as the # of instances and total bytes per Java type under *Class Name*. Note that you can check the *Settings* option at the upper right corner and configure how you want the Sampler to sample. For example, you can configure CPU sampling to include or exclude certain packages, and specify sampling frequency and results refresh interval. At the lower left corner, you can also filter classes to be sampled. For memory settings, you can specify Sampling and refresh rate.
- **Profiler**. The Profiler tab enables profiling CPU and memory utilizations at a finer granularity by instrumenting rather than sampling the methods on a per-invocation basis. Figures 4.14 and 4.15 show the CPU and memory profiling views, respectively. Note that the CPU profiling displays the # of invocations for each method in addition to *Self time,* whereas the Memory profiling displays generation information in addition to bytes. Compared with the Sampler settings, Profiler CPU settings remain the same, while memory settings differ.

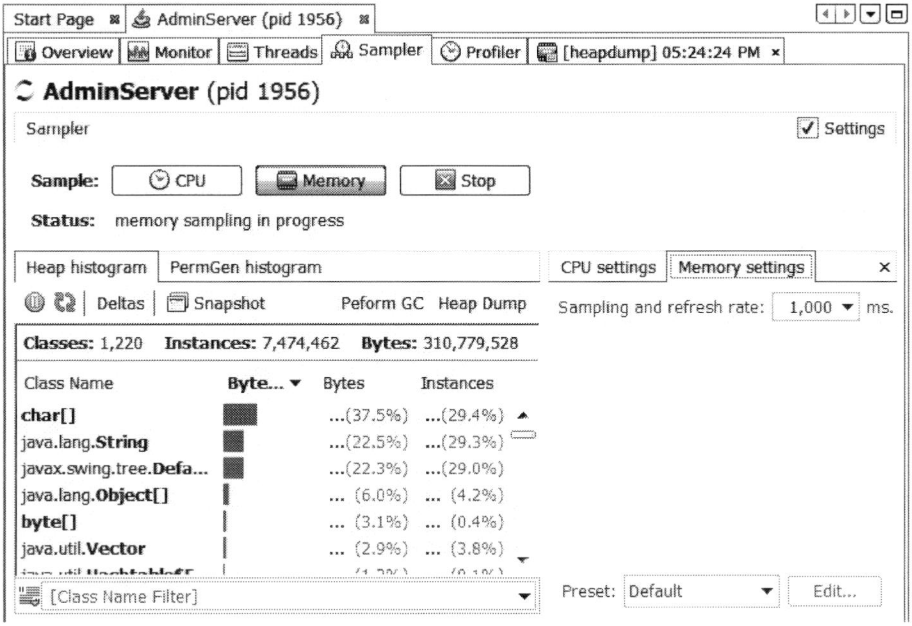

Figure 4.13 VisualVM Sampler tab / Memory sampling

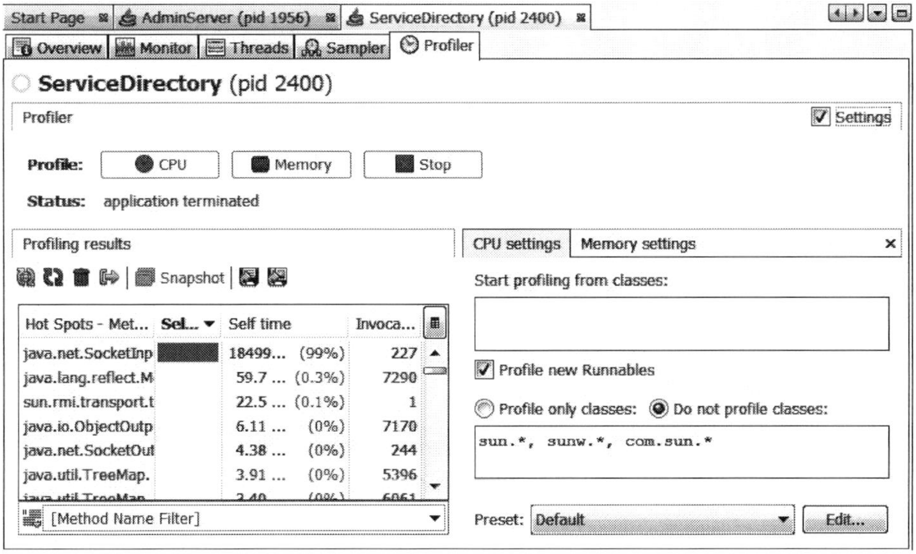

Figure 4.14 VisualVM CPU profiling

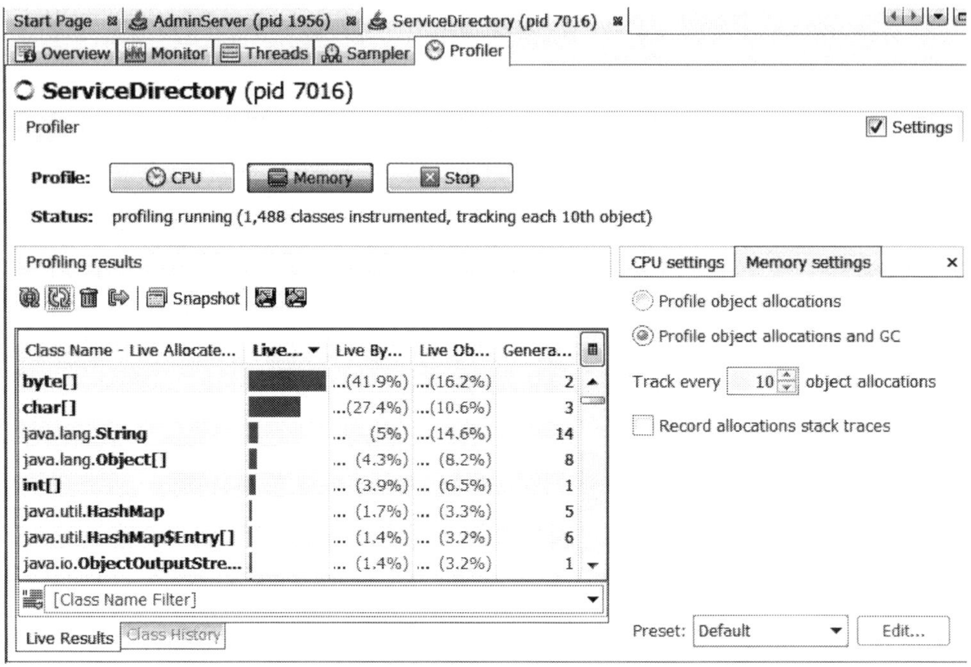

Figure 4.15 VisualVM memory profiling

Note the icons below *Profiling results* shown in Figures 4.14 and 4.15. If you put your cursor over them, you would see from left to right sequentially:

- Update Results Automatically
- Update Results Now
- Run Garbage Collection in Profiled Application and Update Results
- Reset Collected Results Buffer
- Take Snapshot of Collected Results
- Export to ...
- Save Current View to Image

In general, updating results automatically may not be needed and you can disable it and use the second icon to manually update results. This can help reduce overhead caused by profiling.

Also, as we pointed out earlier, when you use the Profiler feature of VisualVM to profile your application, you need to add the following option to the command that starts up your application:

```
-Xshare:off
```

Otherwise, your application may crash during profiling. This option essentially turns off class sharing. Class data sharing is a feature for enabling sharing classes across JVMs on the same system to help reduce their memory footprint. This feature may need to be turned off even if you use other commercial profiling tools.

You can also install plugins such as the VisualGC plugin for VisualVM. To add a plugin, click *Tools | Plugins*, and then, clicking on *Available Plugins* would bring up a window showing all installable plugins. Figure 4.16 shows the VisualGC plugin in action with the CPUCheck sample. Note that the VisualGC UI consists of three panels: Spaces, Graphs, and Histogram. The Histogram feature is available for the concurrent or serial GC only, namely, this feature is not available for the throughput GCs.

Next, we describe what information is contained on each panel of the VisualGC page as follows:

- **Spaces**. On this panel, you will see those bars moving up and down at fixed intervals in each space of *Perm*, *Old*, *Eden*, *S0* and *S1*. How much is occupied in each space indicates the usage of that space, whereas how quickly it is filled or emptied indicates the dynamic GC activities occurring in that space. The GC patterns to look for include:
  - *Minor GC frequency*. Minor garbage collections occur in the young generation. Each minor collection is indicated by a fill and drop in the Eden space. In addition, how often it happens indicates the minor GC frequency.
  - *Live object copying*. When a minor GC occurs, live objects are copied between the two survivor spaces of S0 and S1.
  - *Survivor spaces overflowing*. If you observe that after each minor GC cycle, the survivor spaces get full or nearly full, and in the meanwhile, the old space utilization increases, this indicates survivor spaces overflowing with short-lived objects copied into the old generation, which may cause performance problem. This is called *premature promotion*, which should be avoided with larger survivor spaces [Hunt, 2012].
  - *Major GC frequency*. When you observe a drop in Old space, it is a major GC. How quickly it happens indicates the major GC frequency. If your old space is not sufficiently large, then copying objects into it may fail during a minor GC, because there could be objects left when the old generation becomes full. This would trigger a full GC that collects the entire heap. This is called *promotion failure*, which may cause harm to the performance of an application if not prevented proactively.

- **Graphs**. This panel reports summary information on *Compile Time*, *Class Loader Time*, and *GC Time*. It then displays in the format of (*maxCapacity*, *currentCapacity*): *current utilization* for Eden space, S0, S1, Old Gen, and Perm Gen. Note that *maxCapacity* represents the max heap size (committed + uncommitted), while *currentCapacity* represents the current total heap size or committed memory for the heap. Use the formula *free* + *used* = *total* <= *maxHeapSize* to help you memorize these terms. You would see a white space region in a space if *maxCapacity* and *currentCapacity* are not equal for that space. In addition, a seesaw pattern for Eden Space implies minor garbage collections, an alternating pattern for the two survivor spaces implies copying live object activities, and a seesaw pattern in the Old Gen region, if any, implies major garbage collections.

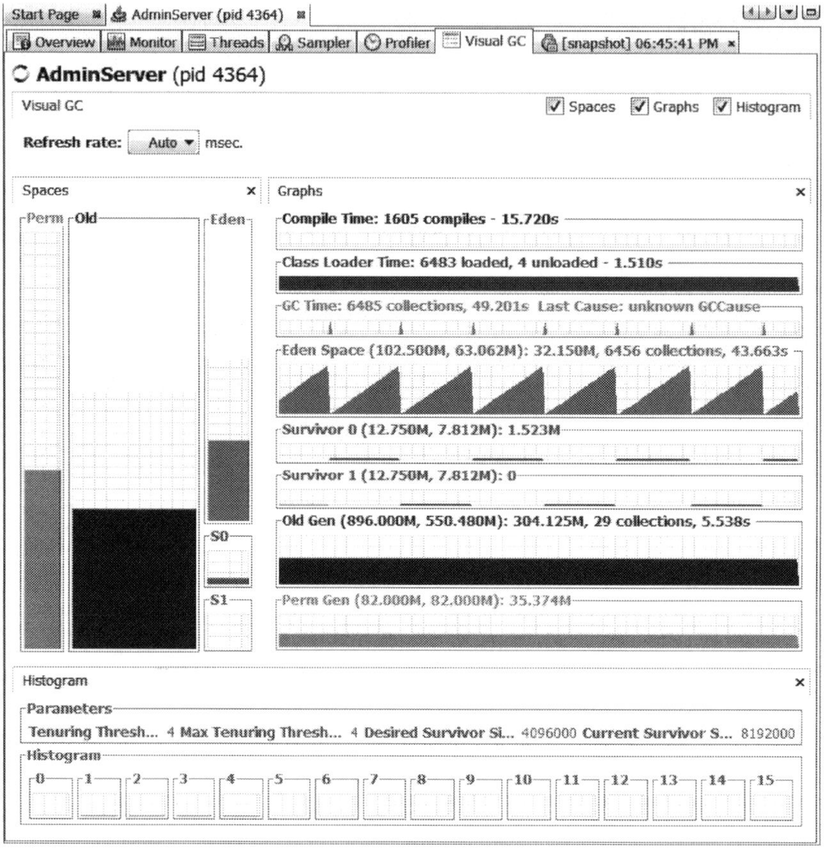

Figure 4.16 VisualVM/Visual GC plugin in action with the Service Admin sample

- **Histogram**. This panel has two subpanels: the Parameters subpanel and Histogram subpanel. The Parameters subpanel displays Tenuring Threshold, Max Tenuring Threshold, Desired Survivor Size and Current Survivor Size. Note that an object is moved from young to old generation based on the Tenuring Threshold, not the Max Tenuring Threshold. The Histogram subpanel is divided into 16 equally sized regions, with each region representing 100% of the active survivor space. Each region is labeled with its *age*, which is the number of minor collections that objects survived. For example, the "0" region represents of the percentage of fresh objects that have never endured a minor collection, while the "1" region represents the percentage of live objects survived one minor collection, and so forth.

Note that before using VisualVM to monitor or profile your application for diagnosing performance issues, it is necessary to quantify the overhead of the tool and its impacts on the performance of your application. After the next section about enabling remote access for VisualVM, we provide an example of quantifying the overhead of VisualVM using the CPUCheck sample.

4.5.4 Enabling Remote Access for VisualVM

Some real applications use a *server.xml* file to bind a JMX port. In such cases, you need to modify the JMX configuration element to enable remote JMX connections for VisualVM. For example, if your product uses Springsource with Tomcat web server, you can enable remote JMX connections for VisualVM by following a procedure similar to the following:

1. Add a Listener in Tomcat's *server.xml* file (all in one line. Remember to change *ip* and *port* to suit your needs):

<Listener accessFile="${catalina.base}/conf/jmxremote.access" authenticate="true" bind="10.20.136.33" className="com.springsource.tcserver.serviceability.rmi.JmxSocketListener" passwordFile="${catalina.base}/conf/jmxremote.password" port="7979" useSSL="false"/>

2. Add proper entries to the JAVA_OPTS env variable (all in one line) in the env configuration file:

```
JVM_OPTS="$JVM_OPTS -Dcom.sun.management.jmxremote.port=7979
-Dcom.sun.management.jmxremote.ssl=false
-Dcom.sun.management.jmxremote.authenticate=false"
```

3. Create the jmxremote.aceess file with the following contents:

```
#admin readonly
admin readwrite
```

4. Create the jmxremote.password file with the following contents:

```
# The "admin" role has password "mypassword".
admin mypassword
```

You can add a remote host by right-clicking the *Remote* tab on the VisualVM console and then *Add Remote Host…*, as shown in the below screenshot, taken in my environment.

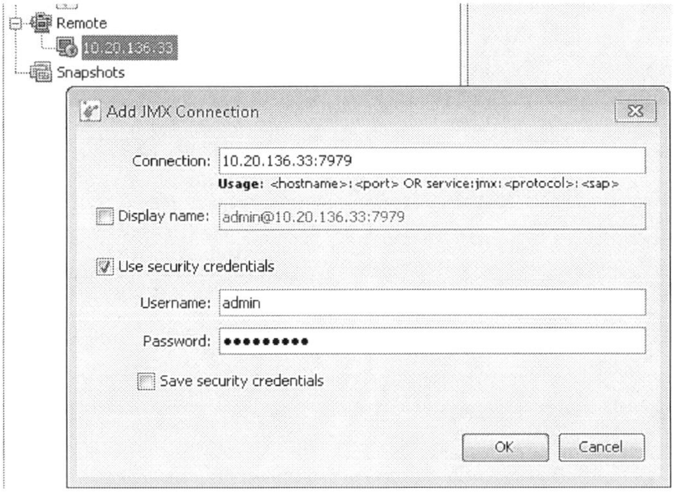

4.5.5 Overhead of VisualVM

To quantify the overhead of VisualVM, let's reconfigure the CPUCheck sample as follows:

- Edit the `services.properties` file and change *NUM_OF_LEVELS* from 6 to 7.
- Make sure *SUBSERVICES_PER_NODE* is set to 8.
- The admin server should be configured with `-XX:+UseConcMarkSweepGC -Xms128m -Xmx1024m -Xshare:off` in `runServer.bat`
- The client should be configured with `-Xms128m -Xmx2048m -Xshare:off` in `runClient.bat`

These settings would create 2,396,745 nodes or about 2.4 million elements in the service directory tree structure.

After making the above changes, open up an MS-DOS command prompt and cd to the folder that contains the sample. Execute `runServer.bat` with a proper JDK to start up the server, for example:

```
runServer C:\jdk1.6.0_31_64
```

Then open up another MS-DOS command prompt and cd to the same folder that contains the sample. Execute `runClient.bat` with a proper JDK to start up the client, for example:

```
runclient C:\jdk1.6.0_31_64
```

Table 4.4 lists the test results obtained on a single quad-core, hyper-threaded Intel i7-2600 @ 3.4 GHz, 8 GB RAM, Windows 7 Professional system. The baseline result of 139 seconds total execution time was obtained first without starting up VisualVM. It is interesting to see that:

- CPU profiling with Profiler resulted in a large overhead of 3.3 times the baseline.
- Memory profiling resulted in an overhead of 31%.
- The overheads with both CPU sampling and memory sampling were negligible.
- The overhead with VisualGC was negligible.
- The last row shows that the CPU profiling overhead was reduced to 7% after the java.*, javax.*, and sun.* Java packages were excluded. In general, these packages and any Java runtime packages should be excluded, because there is very little to tune there.

Table 4.4 Overhead of VisualVM measured with the CPUCheck sample

Test Condition	Total execution time (s)	Overhead
Baseline w/o VisualVM	142	baseline
Profiler | CPU (default settings)	614	3.3 times
Profiler | Memory	186	31%
Sampler | CPU	147	4%
Sampler | Memory	143	1%
VisualGC	142	0%

Profiler | CPU (excluded java.*, javax.*, sun.*)	149	7%

These numbers are specific to this sample and the system used for this testing. They may vary with different applications and systems.

4.5.6 Sampling Snapshots

A snapshot enables saving sampled or profiled data for offline analysis. This feature is available with both the Sampler and Profiler. To use it, you can start CPU sampling or profiling at some point of a long-lasting run, then take a snapshot, and stop sampling or profiling. Since the overhead with the Sampler is small, you can leave sampling running and take a few snapshots over the period of an entire run. The Profiler instrumentation could be very intrusive, so you might want to try the Sampler first.

After a snapshot is taken, you can save it by selecting it in the left frame, right-clicking on it and selecting *Save As* to save it to a folder of your choice in a file with the extension of `.nps`. Then you can re-open it through File | Load on VisualVM. Figure 4.17 provides an example snapshot saved while profiling the service directory client Java program with the Sampler, with the CPU settings of excluding java.* and javax.* applied in addition to the packages excluded by default.

You can view a saved snapshot either by *Call Tree* or *Hot Spots* or *Combined* as shown in Figure 4.18. Note that in a *Call Tree*, *Time* is inclusive that it includes times spent on other methods called in the method reported. This is opposite to *Self Time* that excludes times spent on other methods in the method reported.

For comparison purposes, during the same run as for the snapshot shown in Figure 4.17, another snapshot was taken with the default CPU settings that does not include java.* and javax.*. The resultant snapshot is shown in Figure 4.18, which includes more than just the main class of the service directory client shown in Figure 4.17. In general, these additional JRE classes are less interesting, because there is very little we can do about them. What we are most interested in is to find out the inefficiencies in the application or the JEE application server so that we can correct them to improve the performance and scalability of the application.

In principle, you can use the same procedure as stated above to take snapshots with the Profiler. However, when used with the service directory client, it did not capture the main method of the *ServiceDirectory* class, and the resultant snapshot contained totally different packages from those taken with the Sampler. It appears that the Profiler included in the VisualVM is much less useful than the Sampler, and therefore, use it at your discretion and with caution.

4.5.7 Application Snapshots

Application snapshot is one of the most useful features with VisualVM. You can right-click an application node and select Application Snapshot. Then a snapshot of the application will be displayed on your VisualVM with the tabs of *Overview*, *Monitor*, *Threads*, and *[threaddump] <timestamp>*. You can take a snapshot of an application any time the application is up and running. Chapter 6 uses this feature heavily to demonstrate how to tune the performance and scalability of a real Java application.

To learn more about VisualVM, visit http://visualvm.java.net/docindex.html .

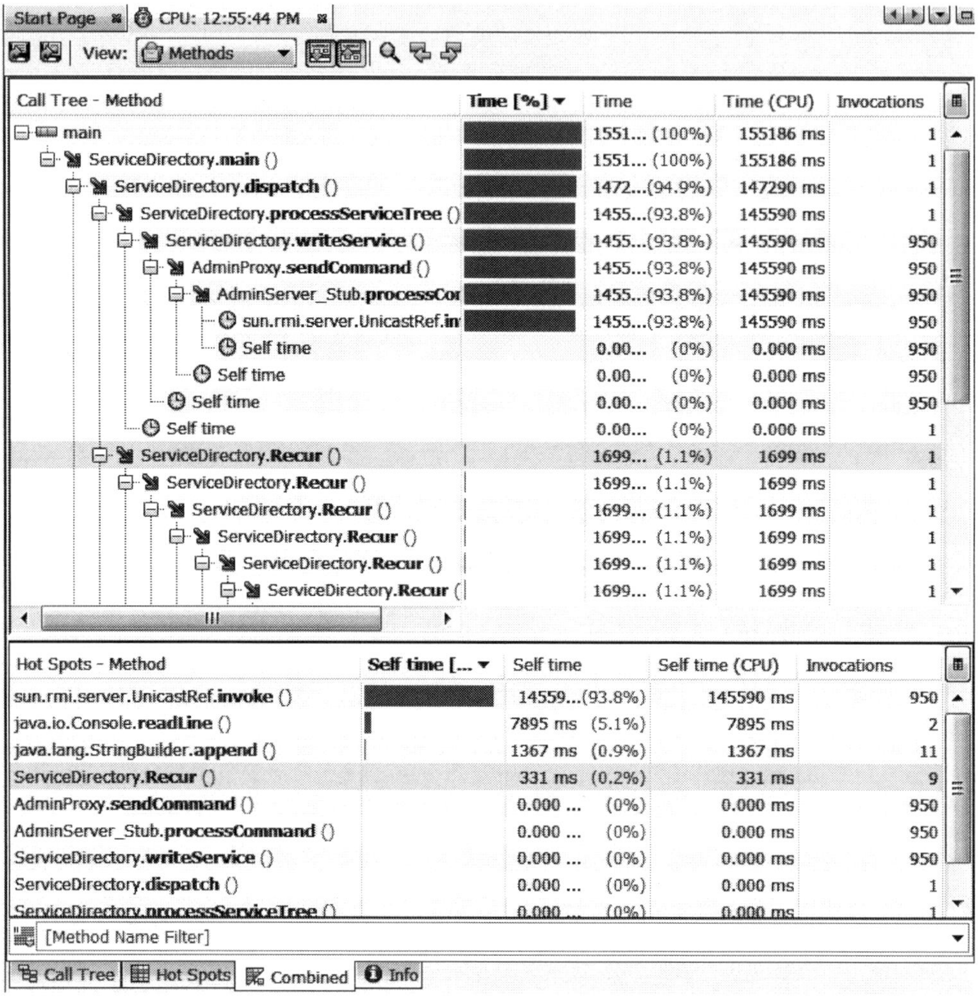

Figure 4.17 CPU profiling snapshot showing a Call Tree and Hot Spots

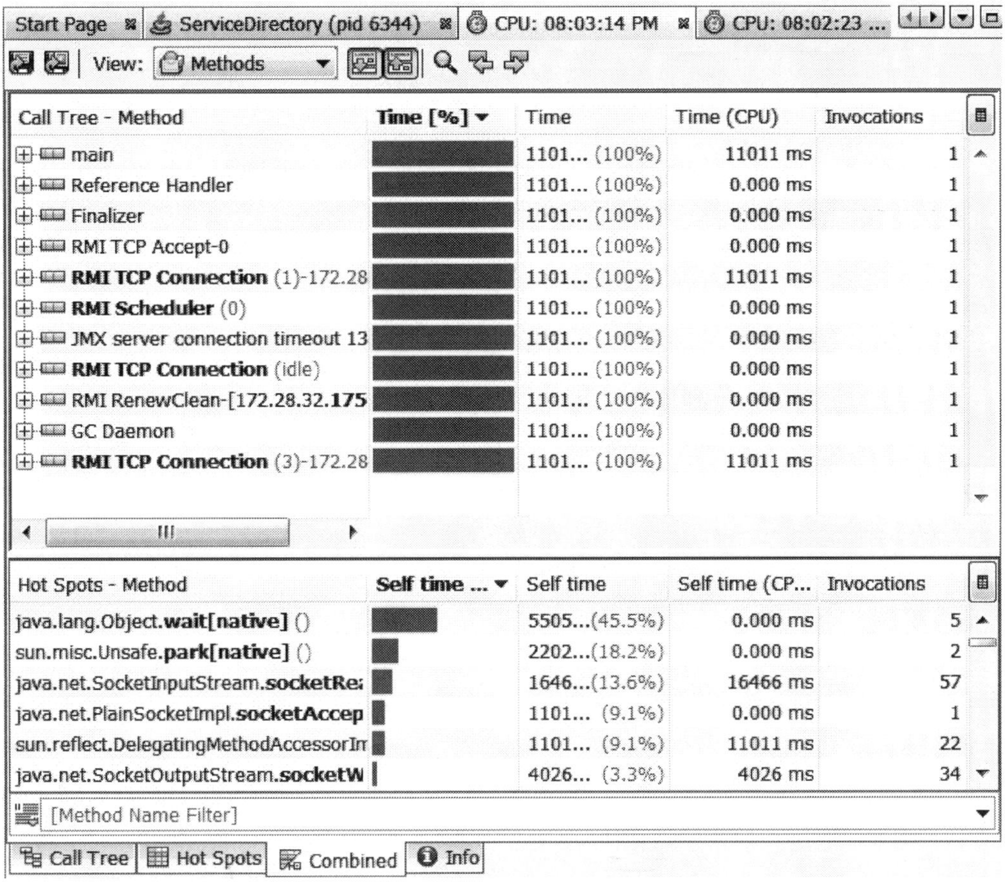

Figure 4.18 Sampler | CPU | Snapshot taken with the default CPU settings

4.5.8 Reading GC Logs

Before concluding this chapter, I'd like to summarize how to read GC logs from various GC log options. These options include:

- **–Xloggc:<file-name>**. Listing 4.1 shows an example of this GC log option. It was collected on a CentOS 7 Linux machine using my CPUCheck benchmark program. For each GC log output line, it begins with a timestamp relative to the program start, followed by a minor GC or Full GC line. For example, the first line is a minor GC, while the second line is a full GC. Whether a minor or full GC, the first two numbers flanking the "->" sign on a line like 2027K -> 608K(126464K) represent the combined size of live objects before and after the GC, respectively, while the number in the parentheses represents the total heap size at the time when that GC occurred. Therefore, the heap usage dropped from 2027/126464 = 1.% to 608/126464 = 0.48% after that GC. The last number is the GC time in seconds.

- **-Xloggc:sd-1.log -XX:+PrintGCDetails.** Listing 4.2 shows the combined GC options with PrintGCDetails added. Now you can see PSYoungGen, ParOldGen, and PSPermGen added to give more detailed GC activities in each region. GC times in terms of *user* time, *sys* time and *real* time are given as well for finer granularity. User and sys times are CPU times, while real time is wall-clock time. User time could be larger than real time if multiple threads were used for GC. A summary of the heap is also given at the end of the run. In fact, comparing Listing 4.2 with Listing 4.1 makes it immediately clear that the major difference between the two is that the PrintGCDetails option adds region-specific GC data. You can actually find from Listing 4.2 the numbers shown in Listing 4.1.
- **-Xloggc:sd-2.log -XX:+PrintGCDetails -XX:+PrintGCDateStamps -XX:+PrintGCTimeStamps.** As shown in Listing 4.3, the last two options add date and time for each GC logged. (For better clarity, address range parts in Heap summary have been removed.) Such information will be valuable for some GC viewer tools to display how GCs evolved over the period of collection.
- **-Xloggc:sd-3.log -XX:+PrintGCDetails -XX:+UseConcMarkSweepGC -XX:MaxGCPauseMillis=200.** Listing 4.4 shows the GC logs with the same test case. As you see, initially it started with a full GC for OldGen and PermGen, followed by many ParNew GCs. Then during the period of 8.786 – 9.486 = 700 ms, a full CMS GC occurred. I encourage you to read through the steps underlined for the entire CMS cycle and compare them with Figure 4.2, which explains how CMS works in general with four steps of initial marking, concurrent marking, remarking, and concurrent sweeping.

You can monitor a live Java program using the *jstat* utility as follows:

```
$ jstat -gcutil -t 6746 500ms 100
```

The above command was applied to the java process with a pid of 6746 and an interval of 500ms for 100 intervals while CMS was running behind the scene. Listing 4.5 shows the output. It should be read as follows:

- The first column is timestamp.
- The next several columns of S0, S1, E, O, and P represent %full (utilization) for each of these regions.
- YGC and FGC report the # of minor and full GCs, respectively.
- YGCT and FGCT represent total time spent for each of the young and old generations.
- The last column GCT represents total time for both minor and full GCs.

So, the following last line shows that at the end of the run, S0, S1, E, O, and P regions were 0%, 2.16%, 18.08%, 52.28%, 24.98% full, respectively, after 89 minor GCs and 3 full GCs occurred. The total GC times for minor and full GCs are 228ms and 31ms, respectively, resulting in a total GC time of 259ms, which was insignificant compared with the 34831ms total run time.

128.9 0.00 2.16 18.08 52.28 24.98 89 0.228 3 0.031 0.259

This concludes our introduction to HotSpot JVMs.

Listing 4.1 GC logs from -Xloggc:sd-0.log

```
[henry@localhost CPUCheck-1.0]$ java -Xshare:off -Xloggc:sd-0.log -Xms128m -Xmx2048m -DparameterFile=services.properties ServiceDirectory
continue? press Enter to go ...
start: Heap utilization statistics [MB]
Used/Free/Total/Max Memory:0/122/123/1820
admin proxy created with address and port:127.0.0.1:9999
started at Tue Nov 11 09:46:22 PST 2014
create a service directory tree of (l, m) = (6, 8) with 299593 service nodes
recursive ALGORITHM: 636 ms
Recursive call service tree size = 299592
100000 items processed over 17893 ms 5588.777734309507 items / s
200000 items processed over 29868 ms 6696.129637069774 items / s
processing service tree: 299592 nodes/40633 ms = 7373 nodes/second
recursive (ALGORITHM + processServiceTree): 41269 ms
end: Heap utilization statistics [MB]
Used/Free/Total/Max Memory:374/369/743/1820
total elapsed time = 41743 ms
press Enter to exit:
[henry@localhost CPUCheck-1.0]$ ls sd*
sd-0.log  sd.bat
[henry@localhost CPUCheck-1.0]$ cat sd-0.log | more
2.239: [GC 2027K->608K(126464K), 0.0337890 secs]
2.273: [Full GC 608K->534K(126464K), 0.1679140 secs]
2.838: [GC 34326K->9104K(126464K), 0.0800010 secs]
2.953: [GC 42896K->28302K(126464K), 0.1621250 secs]
3.963: [GC 62094K->43010K(160256K), 0.2062250 secs]
7.100: [GC 110594K->43034K(160256K), 0.0355180 secs]
8.507: [GC 110618K->43042K(204288K), 0.0681290 secs]
11.136: [GC 154658K->43074K(227840K), 0.0578900 secs]
13.325: [GC 154690K->43119K(336896K), 0.0933310 secs]
16.878: [GC 266351K->43175K(337408K), 0.0475710 secs]
19.038: [GC 266407K->43207K(445440K), 0.0415900 secs]
23.686: [GC 400583K->43263K(535040K), 0.0273280 secs]
28.436: [GC 465151K->43319K(685056K), 0.0310470 secs]
35.148: [GC 615735K->43447K(684544K), 0.0389310 secs]
40.511: [GC 615863K->43503K(761344K), 0.0017870 secs]
[henry@localhost CPUCheck-1.0]$
```

Listing 4.2 GC logs from -Xloggc:sd-1.log -XX:+PrintGCDetails

```
[henry@localhost CPUCheck-1.0]$ java -Xshare:off -Xloggc:sd-1.log -XX:+PrintGCDetails -Xms128m -Xmx2048m -DparameterFile=services.properties ServiceDirectory
continue? press Enter to go ...
start: Heap utilization statistics [MB]
Used/Free/Total/Max Memory:0/122/123/1820
......
end: Heap utilization statistics [MB]
```

Used/Free/Total/Max Memory:367/376/743/1820

total elapsed time = 32370 ms

press Enter to exit:

[henry@localhost CPUCheck-1.0]$ ls *.log

adminServer-0.log sd-0.log sd-1.log

[henry@localhost CPUCheck-1.0]$ cat sd-1.log

1.003: **[GC [PSYoungGen**: 2027K->608K(38912K)] 2027K->608K(126464K), 0.0032310 secs] [Times: user=0.00 sys=0.00, real=0.00 secs]

1.006: **[Full GC [PSYoungGen**: 608K->0K(38912K)] **[ParOldGen**: 0K->550K(87552K)] 608K->550K(126464K) **[PSPermGen**: 5135K->5133K(21504K)], 0.0176600 secs] [Times: user=0.02 sys=0.01, real=0.02 secs]

1.212: **[GC [PSYoungGen**: 33792K->5089K(38912K)] 34342K->9104K(126464K), 0.0131020 secs] [Times: user=0.02 sys=0.00, real=0.01 secs]

......

30.155: [GC **[PSYoungGen**: 572544K->128K(673792K)] 615147K->42819K(761344K), 0.0727210 secs] [Times: user=0.01 sys=0.13, real=0.07 secs]

Heap

PSYoungGen total 673792K, used 359524K

eden space 650752K, 55% used

from space 23040K, 0% used

to space 22528K, 0% used

ParOldGen total 87552K, used 42691K

object space 87552K, 48% used

PSPermGen total 21504K, used 5838K

object space 21504K, 27% used

[henry@localhost CPUCheck-1.0]$ java -XX:+PrintCommandLineFlags -version

-XX:InitialHeapSize=61904704 -XX:MaxHeapSize=990475264 -XX:+PrintCommandLineFlags -XX:+UseCompressedOops -XX:+UseParallelGC

java version "1.7.0_51"

OpenJDK Runtime Environment (rhel-2.4.5.5.el7-x86_64 u51-b31)

OpenJDK 64-Bit Server VM (build 24.51-b03, mixed mode)

[henry@localhost CPUCheck-1.0]$

Listing 4.3 GC logs from -Xloggc:sd-2.log -XX:+PrintGCDetails -XX:+PrintGCDateStamps -XX:+PrintGCTimeStamps

[henry@localhost CPUCheck-1.0]$ java -Xshare:off -Xloggc:sd-2.log -XX:+PrintGCDetails -XX:+PrintGCDateStamps -XX:+PrintGCTimeStamps -Xms128m -Xmx2048m -DparameterFile=services.properties ServiceDirectory

continue? press Enter to go ...

start: Heap utilization statistics [MB]

Used/Free/Total/Max Memory:0/122/123/1820

...

end: Heap utilization statistics [MB]

Used/Free/Total/Max Memory:354/389/744/1820

total elapsed time = 31165 ms

press Enter to exit:

[henry@localhost CPUCheck-1.0]$ cat sd-2.log

2014-11-11T10:55:53.359-0800: 1.104: [GC [PSYoungGen: 2027K->608K(38912K)] 2027K->608K(126464K), 0.0025850 secs] [Times: user=0.00 sys=0.00, real=0.00 secs]

2014-11-11T10:55:53.362-0800: 1.107: [Full GC [PSYoungGen: 608K->0K(38912K)] [ParOldGen: 0K->532K(87552K)] 608K->532K(126464K) [PSPermGen: 5126K->5124K(21504K)], 0.0164640 secs] [Times: user=0.02 sys=0.00, real=0.02 secs]

……

Listing 4.4 GC logs from -Xloggc:sd-3.log -XX:+PrintGCDetails --XX:+UseConcMarkSweepGC -XX:MaxGCPauseMillis=200

3.254: [Full GC3.254: [CMS: 0K->509K(87424K), 0.0176070 secs] 2803K->509K(126720K), [CMS Perm : 4657K->4655K(21248K)], 0.0177620 secs] [Times: user=0.01 sys=0.01, real=0.02 secs]

3.435: [GC3.435: [ParNew: 35072K->4352K(39424K), 0.0374210 secs] 35581K->9375K(126848K), 0.0375330 secs] [Times: user=0.07 sys=0.01, real=0.04 secs]

3.491: [GC3.491: [ParNew: 38838K->4352K(39424K), 0.0539960 secs] 43862K->32256K(126848K), 0.0541120 secs] [Times: user=0.09 sys=0.00, real=0.05 secs]

……]

8.786: [GC [1 CMS-initial-mark: 43715K(87424K)] 44463K(126848K), 0.0002180 secs] [Times: user=0.00 sys=0.00, real=0.00 secs]

8.787: [CMS-concurrent-mark-start]

8.834: [CMS-concurrent-mark: 0.047/0.047 secs] [Times: user=0.06 sys=0.01, real=0.05 secs]

8.834: [CMS-concurrent-preclean-start]

8.834: [CMS-concurrent-preclean: 0.000/0.000 secs] [Times: user=0.00 sys=0.00, real=0.00 secs]

8.834: [CMS-concurrent-abortable-preclean-start]

9.148: [GC9.149: [ParNew: 35115K->50K(39424K), 0.0006550 secs] 78831K->43772K(126848K), 0.0007340 secs] [Times: user=0.00 sys=0.00, real=0.00 secs]

9.452: [CMS-concurrent-abortable-preclean: 0.005/0.618 secs] [Times: user=0.16 sys=0.11, real=0.62 secs]

9.452: [GC[YG occupancy: 31706 K (39424 K)]9.452: [Rescan (parallel) , 0.0112900 secs]9.463: [weak refs processing, 0.0000300 secs]9.463: [scrub string table, 0.0002210 secs] [1 CMS-remark: 43721K(87424K)] 75427K(126848K), 0.0117060 secs] [Times: user=0.03 sys=0.01, real=0.01 secs]

9.464: [CMS-concurrent-sweep-start]

9.482: [CMS-concurrent-sweep: 0.018/0.018 secs] [Times: user=0.02 sys=0.00, real=0.02 secs]

9.482: [CMS-concurrent-reset-start]

9.486: [CMS-concurrent-reset: 0.003/0.003 secs] [Times: user=0.01 sys=0.00, real=0.00 secs]

9.505: [GC9.505: [ParNew: 35122K->54K(39424K), 0.0008470 secs] 75077K->40013K(126848K), 0.0009500 secs] [Times: user=0.00 sys=0.00, real=0.00 secs]

……

Listing 4.5 GC output from the jstat utility

[henry@centos7-1 ~]$ **jstat -gcutil -t 6746 500ms 100**

Timestamp	S0	S1	E	O	P	YGC	YGCT	FGC	FGCT	GCT
94.3	0.00	0.00	4.00	0.00	12.43	0	0.000	0	0.000	0.000

……

```
    97.8  0.00  1.65 92.40 51.72 24.95     7  0.161   3  0.031   0.192
    ......
    100.3  0.00  1.16 88.38 51.76 24.96    13  0.167   3  0.031   0.197
    ......
    101.8  1.67  0.00  2.01 51.79 24.96    18  0.170   3  0.031   0.201
    ......
    123.9  0.00  1.06 64.26 52.19 24.98    75  0.217   3  0.031   0.248
    ......
    128.4  0.00  1.05 76.31 52.27 24.98    87  0.226   3  0.031   0.257
    128.9  0.00  2.16 18.08 52.28 24.98    89  0.228   3  0.031   0.259
[henry@centos7-1 ~]$
```

4.6 SUMMARY

In this chapter, we focused on understanding various performance and scalability oriented features built into various releases of Oracle JDKs. We then covered all garbage collectors available in HotSpot JVMs, along with a command for checking default JVM options based on the hardware capabilities of a system. Keep in mind that for the young generation, either a serial or parallel GC with copying is used, while for the tenured generation, there are three options: (1) *Parallel* (default) with serial + compacting, (2) *ParallelOld* with parallel + compacting, and (3) *CMS* with parallel + concurrent + incremental. This kind of knowledge is important, as is demonstrated in Chapter 6 *Tuning Java Applications for Best Possible Performance and Scalability* that the version of JVM and the options enabled can have a profound impact on the performance and scalability of a Java application.

We also introduced the JConsole and VisualVM tools for monitoring and profiling Java applications. We quantified the overhead of VisualVM using my CPUCheck sample. It turned out that the Sampler method for profiling CPU and memory has very minimum overhead compared with the Profiler method, although both methods are based on the Java Virtual Machine Profiler Interface (JVM PI). In contrast to the sampling method that only *samples* periodically the stacks of all executing threads to find the most active stack traces, the profiling method captures the "method entry" and "method exit" events of every instrumented method of the profiled application, thus resulting in very significant overhead and making it much less usable.

We demonstrated how to install and use VisualGC as a plugin to VisualVM for monitoring garbage collection activities while your Java application is running. This VisualGC together with the snapshot feature from the Sampler should meet most of your needs in monitoring and profiling your Java applications for best possible performance and scalability, which is demonstrated fully in Chapter 6 with a case study based on a real product.

This chapter wraps up this first part of *Java Performance and Scalability: Basics*. In the next part of *Java Performance and Scalability: Practice*, by applying what covered in this first part, we present quantitative case studies on Java application performance and scalability, either based on real products I worked on or samples I developed myself. This way, theory and practice can cross-check with each other. This is an interesting process, because as we stated earlier, software performance and scalability field is both art and science.

EXERCISES

4.1 List six major performance features that have been built into the Oracle JDKs during the past several decades.

4.2 What's the major difference between Windows and Solaris regarding Java heap space structure? Is the Java heap space structure the same on Windows and Linux?

4.3 What is Java ergonomics? How do you check it out on a given system?

4.4 Does CMS GC perform compacting?

4.5 Does CMS GC wait for performing a collection in the old generation space until it becomes full?

4.6 Why would it help GC if a programmer explicitly sets an object variable to `null` at the end of its lifecycle?

4.7 Explain the concept of adaptive heap sizing. Does it apply to both throughput and CMS collectors?

4.8 Classify a few common types of OutOfMemoryErrors and the corresponding prescriptions to fix them.

4.9 Explain the differences between two different methods of sampling and profiling. Which one is more practical?

4.10 Given a VisualGC display, how do you calculate quickly the uncommitted memory for the heap and available memory on the heap?

REFERENCES

R. Jones, A. Hosking, and E. Moss, *The Garbage Collection Handbook: The Art of Automatic Memory Management*, Chapman and Hall/CRC, 2011.

C. Hunt, and B. John, *Java Performance,* Addison Wesley, 2012.

Part II Java Performance and Scalability: Practice

In this second part, we focus on presenting quantitative case studies on Java application performance and scalability, either based on real products or samples I developed myself. Specifically, this part consists of the following chapters:

- Chapter 5 64-Bit Enterprise Java Computing
- Chapter 6 Tuning Java for Best Possible Performance and Scalability
- Chapter 7 Java Performance and Scalability By Design
- Chapter 8 Java Performance and Scalability on Linux
- Chapter 9 Java Performance and Scalability on VMware vSphere

Let us begin with 64-bit enterprise Java computing next.

5 64-Bit Enterprise Java Computing

Enterprise computing is different from personal computing that it requires not only more powerful CPUs but also more memory or more bits in larger addressable units. The number of bits for data and addresses on which the processors operate has been one of the most important driving factors for computers to be more and more widely used for enterprise computing.

Note that 64-bit enterprise Java computing has rapidly left the 32-bit enterprise Java computing in the dust. To put it into perspective, this chapter starts with a brief overview on how the number of bits associated with data and addresses that processors deal with directly has evolved from 8-bit to 16-bit, 32-bit, and eventually to 64-bit over the last few decades. It then addresses how 64-bit JVMs, in particular, the Oracle 64-bit HotSpot JVMs, use a feature called `UseCompressedOops` to deal with the memory bloat issue that occurs when a Java application is moved from a 32-bit to a 64-bit environment. The chapter ends with a real world case study to demonstrate the efficacy of `UseCompressedOops` to make more efficient use of JVM heap spaces.

5.1 THE BITS

Although Chapter 2 already covered hardware architecture in detail from multiple perspectives, it is helpful to have a brief overview here again on the history of Intel processor advancement from a different perspective on the number of bits with which data and addresses are sized in the proximity of CPUs. This is a necessary preparation for us to understand what particular performance and scalability issues might arise in transitioning from 32-bit to 64-bit enterprise Java computing.

In addition to their clock rates, a computer's CPUs are measured by the contents that their integer registers can store as the addresses of any datum in the computer's virtual memory. Although there are a few other different types of registers in addition to integer registers, such as floating point registers, control registers and so on, in most modern processors, only integer registers can be used to address data in memory. Therefore, the size of the integer registers in a processor has become the limit to the amount of memory directly addressable.

A processor register is sized by its number of bits. The first microprocessor was byte-oriented, which was the 8-bit Intel 8008 processor designed and manufactured by Intel in 1972. Those 8-bit processors came with an external 14-bit address bus capable of addressing 16 kB memory. Then six years later in 1978, Intel introduced a 16-bit processor chip named 8086, with all internal registers and internal/external data buses being 16-bits wide as well. However, the external address bus was 20-bit wide, giving a 1 MB physical address space. It had eight general purpose 16-bit registers: AX (primary accumulator), BX (base, accumulator), CX (counter, accumulator), DX (accumulator and other functions), SI (source index), DI (destination index), BP (base pointer), and SP (stack pointer).

Seven years later in 1985, Intel released its first 32-bit processor 80386, which was also known as i386. It was once internally code-named P3, meaning that it was the 3rd generation processor in its x86 line. It had its registers, address and data buses all in 32-bits, which helped create a new era of computing with a sufficiently larger, 4-GB addressable memory space, together with an enormous proliferation of 32-bit applications. The terms of x86, IA-32, and i386 are interchangeable.

In 1989, Intel released its 4th generation processor 80486 (or i486), which was the first tightly pipelined x86 design. The i486 was the 4th generation of binary compatible processors since the original 8086, and it was the 2nd generation of x86 32-bit processors after the i386. Referring back to Table 2.1 about the evolution of the Intel processor family prior to the multicore microarchitecture introduced in 2005, it's seen that Intel stopped naming its processors with the usual 80-prefix when the first Pentium processor was released in 1993. That was due to a court ruling that prohibited using numbers for trade marking. Now in various references, you may see i586, which is meant for all Pentium family (or the P5 microarchitecture) processors.

From the performance perspective, a unique feature of the P5 microarchitecture is that it introduced the superscalar computing capability, which allows multiple instructions to be dispatched and executed within a single processor, thus increasing CPU throughput significantly. Other performance-oriented features of the i586 family of processors relative to its predecessors include dual integer pipelines, separate code and data caches, a wider 64-bit data bus, a faster FPU, reduced address calculation latency as well as MMX instructions for speeding up multimedia applications.

By definition, a 32-bit application means that it's developed to run on a commensurate 32-bit hardware machine, for example, on PCs based on i386/i486/i586. Although a total 4 GB addressable memory space is considered very large compared with what one could have with the 8-bit and 16-bit processors several decades ago, large-scale enterprise application software demands even much larger addressable memory space. This has spurred some competition in rushing into the 64-bit computing arena. In this regard, two noticeable platforms, the AMD64 platform and Intel EM64T platform, emerged.

In general, a 64-bit processor has its integer and addressing registers, internal data and address buses all in 64-bits, although its external data and/or address buses could have larger sizes than their internal counterparts. 64-bit processors have existed in supercomputers for scientific computing since 1960s and in RISC-based machines since early 1990s. However, the competition started in 2003 when it was realized that the high-end servers were a much more lucrative market than the low-end PC market. While Intel was focusing on developing its first pure 64-bit processor named Itanium, AMD took a shortcut and developed its 64-bit line of processors by extending x86 architecture. One of the advantages that the AMD64 has is that it's fully backwards compatible with 32-bit code without any performance loss. This minimizes the application porting efforts from 32-bit to 64-bit tremendously, and thus was welcomed hilariously by the industry. The most prominent features with the AMD64 processors from the performance and scalability perspective are:

- **Larger and more integer registers**. AMD64 processors doubled the number of integer registers from eight in x86-32 to 16 in x86-64, in addition to doubling their sizes from 32-bits to 64-bits. Specifically, AMD64 processors upgraded from eight 32-bit integer registers of `eax`, `ebx`, `ecx`, `edx`, `ebp`, `esp`, `esi`, and `edi` to 16 64-bit integer registers of `rax`, `rbx`, `rcx`, `rdx`, `rbp`, `rsp`, `rsi`, `rdi`, `r8`, `r9`, `r10`, `r11`, `r12`, `r13`, `r14`, and `r15`. More registers mean that more local variables can be held on registers rather than on the stack, providing a performance advantage. However, pure 64-bit processors have even more registers. For example, many RISC architecture based machines have 32 64-bit registers, and the IA 64 (Intel / HP Itanium) has 128 64-bit registers.
- **64-bit addressing capability**. All memory-to-register, register-to-memory operations as well as pushes and pops on the stack are always in 8-byte strides, and pointers are 8 bytes wide.
- **Larger addressable spaces**. In principle, a 64-bit processor can address up to 16 EB (ExaBytes, 2^{64} or 18,446,744,073,709,551,616 bytes), or 4 billion times larger than the 4 GB limit of a 32-bit processor. Current processors implementing the AMD64 architecture can address up to 256 TB (TeraBytes, or 2^{48} or 281,474,976,710,656 bytes), or 64 thousand times larger than the 4 GB limit of a 32-bit processor.

Intel's counterpart to AMD64 is Intel EM64T (Extended Memory 64-bit Technology). Intel's first EM64T processor was its multi-socket processor Xeon released in 2004. Xeon is the brand name for Intel's server-oriented processors. Note that IA64 (Intel/HP Itanium) is not compatible with x86-64 (AMD64 and Intel EM64T), while x86-32 is compatible with x86-64. Here, the term *compatible* means that 32-bit applications can run on x86-64 systems without being modified.

It is comforting that 32-bit applications can run seamlessly in a 64-bit environment. However, that's not the purpose for 64-bit systems. 64-bit systems are developed for running 64-bit applications beyond the 4 GB addressability inherent with 32-bit systems. For those applications that need to scale beyond the 4 GB limit tied to 32-bit machines, moving to 64-bit is a natural choice.

However, for an application, moving from 32-bit to 64-bit will inevitably incur a memory bloat, which compromises the potential benefits from 64-bit systems. The next section explains what this memory bloat from 32-bit to 64-bit is about.

5.2 MEMORY BLOAT FROM 32-BIT TO 64-BIT

Perhaps it's more beneficial to start off from a computer science point of view. A computer program arranges data in different types. Based on the size of each data type, different programming models exist. Pertinent to our discussion here about moving from 32-bit to 64-bit computing, two programming models are relevant: ILP32 and LP64.

With the ILP32 programming model, integers, longs and pointers are all 32-bit wide, whereas with the LP64 programming model, both longs and pointers are 64-bit wide while keeping integers still at 32-bits. This means that the size of a *long* or a *pointer* is doubled immediately from 32-bit to 64-bit, resulting in a memory bloat on a per-object basis. Since Java has a *long* as a 64-bit even in 32-bit mode, strictly speaking, a 32-bit Java application does not fall into the ILP32 programming model.

As shown in Table 3.1, most Java types are implemented as integer types internal to a JVM. Therefore, it's safe to assume that a Java application is predominated by integer types and pointers. Without making it more complicated, let's compare how much space it takes to store an integer type and a reference type in a 32-bit environment. Keep in mind that although pointers are not exposed directly to programmers in Java, a JVM internally needs to use pointers so that it can manage memory automatically for objects on a heap. An integer and a pointer would take 32-bits for the address of the integer, and 32-bits for the pointer, for a total of 64 bits on the heap. In a 64-bit environment, it would take 32-bits and 64-bits, respectively, for a total of 96 bits on the heap. This means that potentially the heap footprint of a 32-bit Java application would be bloated to roughly 1.5 times larger in a 64-bit environment.

In reality, it is impossible for a machine to have as much as the total 64-bit addressable amount of physical memory – the 16 EB limit as we calculated in the preceding section. Therefore, a question is if we can save memory by compressing a pointer from 64-bits to, say, 32 + 4 bits. This would lift the 4-GB limit of a 32-bit system to 64 GB, which is much less than 16 EB, but still very desirable for many enterprise class applications.

Next, let's see how some of the 64-bit JVMs implemented the above option for circumventing the memory bloat problem that occurs when an application is moved from a 32-bit environment to a 64-bit environment.

5.3 64-BIT JVMS

With the prior introduction of an ILP32 programming model versus an LP64 programming model, it's clear that many of the Java data types are not doubled in size from 32 bits on a 32-bit system to 64 bits on a 64-bit system. In fact, the only change is the pointer size. Since a pointer is not a Java built-in type, a 100% pure Java program is not affected and it does not need to be migrated or even re-compiled. However, most JVMs are internally implemented with C/C++, which heavily depends on pointers. Therefore, 64-bit JDKs, 64-bit JREs, and 64-bit JVMs are expected.

Sun then now Oracle started releasing 64-bit JDKs for SPARC, IA64-Itanium, AMD64 and Intel EM64T as early as JDK1.4.2 update 11. For AMD64 and EM64T on Windows, the start versions of operating systems are Windows Server 2003 and Windows XP. Sun started supporting 64-bit for AMD64 and EM64T on Linux since JDK 1.5.0 update 2. Therefore, if you are interested in running your Java application on AMD64 or EM64T, a latest stable release of 64-bit JDK is available.

Note that Oracle's 64-bit JDKs do not have both client and server versions: The server version is the only version. Perhaps this is because a 4 GB addressable space is sufficient for personal computing. On the Windows platform, a 64-bit JDK is installed standalone, just like how a 32-bit JDK is installed. When you want to run a Java program in 64-bit, just use the java.exe binary from your 64-bit JDK or JRE installation. On Solaris, the procedure is the same except that you may need to install a 32-bit JDK first before you install a 64-bit JDK. Such subtleties can be verified from the website for the latest JDK release that you are interested in.

The next section discusses the memory bloat issue when an enterprise Java application is moved from a 32-bit system to a 64-bit system. Newer Oracle JVMs have a feature to help mitigate this issue. We will see how effective it would be with a real product based case study.

5.4 COMPRESSING ORDINARY OBJECT POINTERS WITH USECOMPRESSEDOOPS FLAG

Before we explain what ordinary object pointers (OOPs) are, perhaps it's handy to review what a point is at first.

A pointer is a variable that holds the memory address of another object. For example, if a variable called x holds the address of another variable called y, then x is said to point to y. To help understand how a pointer is used in a C/C++ program, the following program is provided.

```
#include <iostream.h>
main ()
{
    int *x, y;
    y = 13579;
    x = &y;
    cout << *x;
    return 0;
}
```

The above program uses the form of (type *pointer-name) to declare a pointer x that points to an integer object. Then it assigns an integer number as the address to an integer variable y. The ampersand operator (&) denotes the address value of an object. In this example, the address of the integer variable y is assigned to the integer pointer variable x. The next statement prints the content of the pointer variable x ,which would be 13579.

Seeing what a pointer can do, it should be clear why in the previous sections about garbage collection we emphasized why it's easy to use a pointer to locate the next available free slot for a new object if the memory is contiguous, in contrast to looking up the next free slot from a free-list that tracks non-contiguous free slots.

Now let's come back to the question of what an ordinary object pointer is. According to Oracle's definition, an ordinary object pointer is a managed pointer to an object. Then, what is a managed pointer? A managed pointer is a handle to an object in the managed heap. Another two types of pointers supported by a runtime are: unmanaged pointers and unmanaged function pointers. Thus, it's clear that a managed pointer refers to a pointer that holds the address of a Java reference type in a JVM.

Looking at it another way, since the HotSpot JVMs are written in C/C++, they definitely use C/C++ pointers to manage Java reference types. Therefore, we can say that managed pointers are used to manage object memory allocation and de-allocation for Java applications at the JVM layer.

An Oracle JVM compresses oops by extending a 32-bit address to 35 bits, thus extending the 4 GB limit to 32 GB accordingly. The compression involves two operations: the decoding operation, which converts a compressed oop address into a 64-bit native address in the managed heap, and the inverse operation is encoding. Oracle also details what and when oops are compressed, but they are beyond comprehension for most readers who are not familiar with how HotSpot JVMs are coded. Note that the Permanent Generation (PermGen) memory space is not compressed, though.

This feature of compressing oops is enabled in the Oracle JVMs since 1.6.0 update 14 via the command line option `-XX:+UseCompressedOops`. As we pointed out previously, it has been made a default option since JDK 1.6.0 update 23. In the next few sections, we will see how it actually worked out with a real product.

5.5 CASE STUDY: USECOMPRESSEDOOPS

In this case study, oops-specific test results are presented based on a real product built with Java. The application context is less important, so we would focus on how much enabling oops flag had helped. We start with the specs of the system tested first in the next section.

5.5.1 The 64-bit System Under Test: AMD64 Opteron

With that real product I tested, the system under test was an AMD64 system with eight Opteron dual-core 8218 processors. The OS was Microsoft Windows Server 2003 Enterprise x64 Edition with Service Pack 2. The total physical memory was 64 GB. The system had a L1 cache with 64 kB for data and 64 kB for instructions. The L2 cache size was 1 MB. The disk storage was a RAID 0 stripped across three local disks for a total capacity of 135 GB.

5.5.2 The Principle of "Comparable Workloads, One Single Variable"

The purpose of the test was to see how much memory could be saved for that large-scale enterprise application when the option of compressing ordinary pointers available in the JDK 1.6.0_14 was enabled. As is the case with any kind of comparison tests, two major factors will determine the comparison results given everything else the same (hardware, OS, application configurations, etc.): one is the workload, and the other is the variable under test. This pertains to the principle I call "*comparable workloads, one single variable*." Here we can only require the workloads to be comparable, as it's extremely difficult to require them to be exactly the same. The second requirement of "*one single variable*" states that the variable under test should be the only parameter varied. If a test were conducted with more than one variable introduced in a run, it would be hard to interpret the test results.

The application was a multi-tier, multi-component enterprise application with a backend database tier, a mid-tier consisting of several collaborating components, and a front-tier providing a user interface for users. A combined number of internal and external objects, which were processed by the system over a period, characterized the workload. To guarantee that the tests were conducted with extra care and precision, the object flow was monitored on an hourly basis over a period of five days for each round of tests, with and without that option of `-XX:+UseCompressedOops` enabled.

For this case study, Figure 5.1 shows the workloads of hourly object processing rates experienced with runs #1 – 3, with the first run represented by a solid line, the 2nd run by a dotted line, and the 3rd run by a dashed line. The first run had the option of `UseCompressedOops` enabled and was successful, while the second run had `UseCompressedOops` disabled and had failed, as is seen that the object processing rate dropped to about 2k objects/hour in about 20 hours. After the problem caused the second run to fail was identified and fixed, the 3rd run with `UseCompressedOops` disabled was launched, which ran to completion successfully. Although the object processing rates between enabling and disabling the option of UseCompressedOops were not exactly the same, they were comparable. In fact, the first run processed a total number of 1,501,681 objects, whereas the 3rd run processed 1,408,195 objects (about 7% less).

The next section presents the oops related measurements.

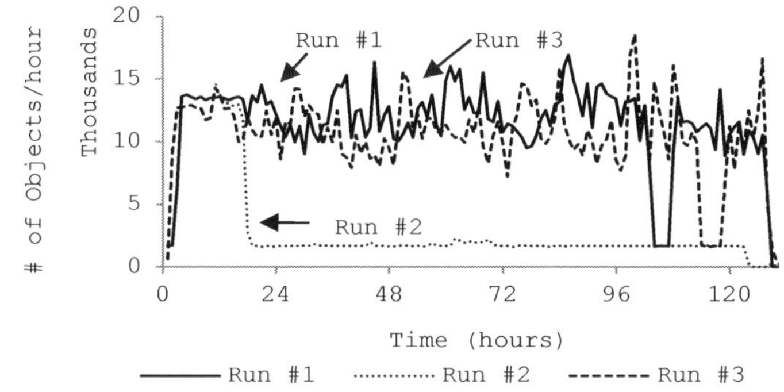

Figure 5.1 Three test runs for investigating the effects of compressing ordinary object pointers. The second run failed. The 1st and 3rd runs demonstrated comparable workloads

5.5.3 The Measurements and Comparisons

With this multi-component based enterprise application, we examined two memory intensive Java-based components for the effects of compressing ordinary object pointers on the memory usage of each component. For convenience, we call those two components *AppServer* and *AnalyticalEngine* throughout this section, respectively. The actual functions of each component are not important in this context.

Other relevant details common to all the test runs include:

- The min and max heap sizes were set to 512 MB and 12.288 GB for each component, respectively.
- The JVM used was Oracle's JDK 1.6.0 update 14. By the time when the tests were done, JDK 1.6.0 update 18 was the most up-to-date stable release but it was not QAed with the product yet.
- In order not to complicate the issue, no manual manipulation was applied to garbage collection in either case. According to Sun's JVM ergonomics, the throughput collector was used for each of the components involved.

Figure 5.2 shows the evolution of the heap used space, Eden space, and tenured space with time for the component of AppServer, with the option of UseCompressedOops off and on, respectively. It is seen that the heap space used had been reduced considerably, mostly due to savings with the tenured space when the ordinary object pointers were compressed. The Eden space remained the same with or without having ordinary object pointers compressed.

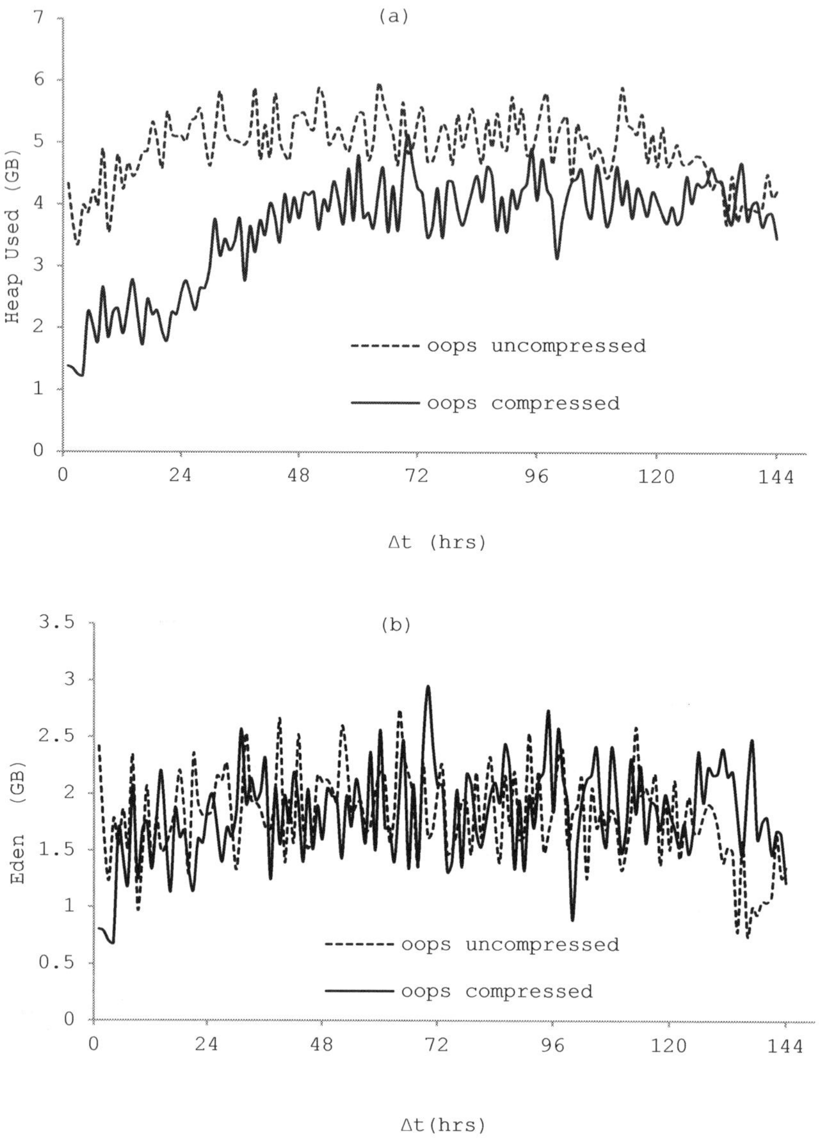
(a)
Heap Used (GB)
7
6
5
4
3
2
1
0
0
24
48
72
96
120
144
oops uncompressed
oops compressed
Δt (hrs)
(b)
Eden (GB)
3.5
3
2.5
2
1.5
1
0.5
0
0
24
48
72
96
120
144
oops uncompressed
oops compressed
Δt(hrs)

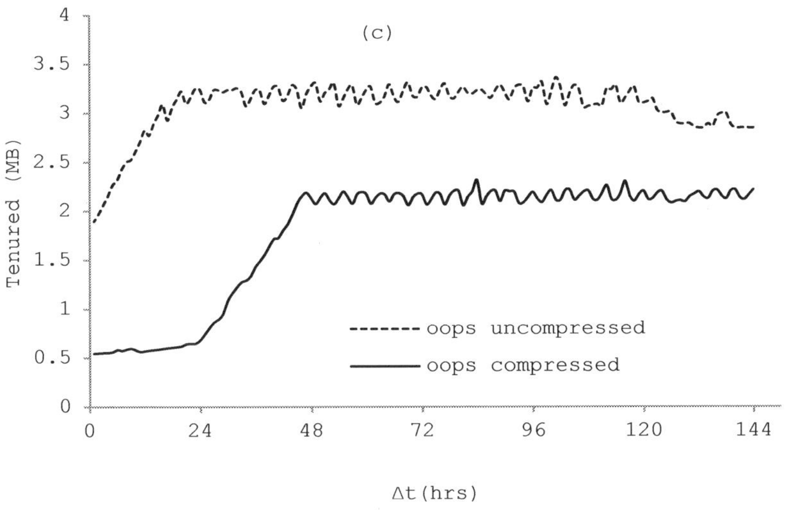

Figure 5.2 AppServer: The effects of oops compression on (a) heap usage, (b) Eden space, and (c) tenured space

Figure 5.3 shows the statistical average occupancies of the objects in different heap regions for the component of AppServer, including code cache and PermGen regions, with and without having ordinary object pointers compressed. It's seen that the code cache and PermGen regions were not affected by the `UseCompressedOops` JVM option, which was expected as we described previously. The survivor region was compressed by about 24%, indicating that only objects in the young generation region and the old generation region are subject to having their pointers compressed.

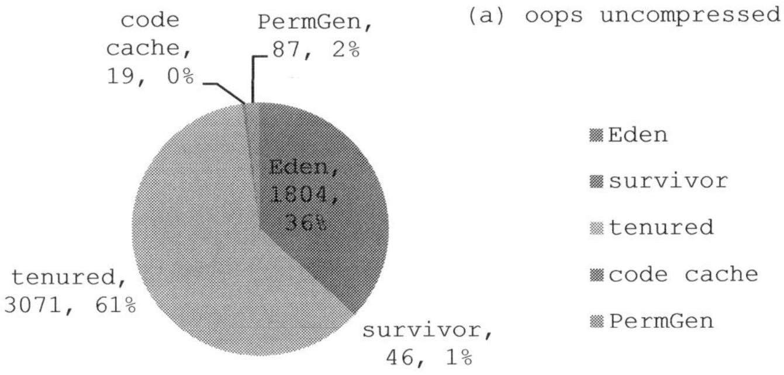

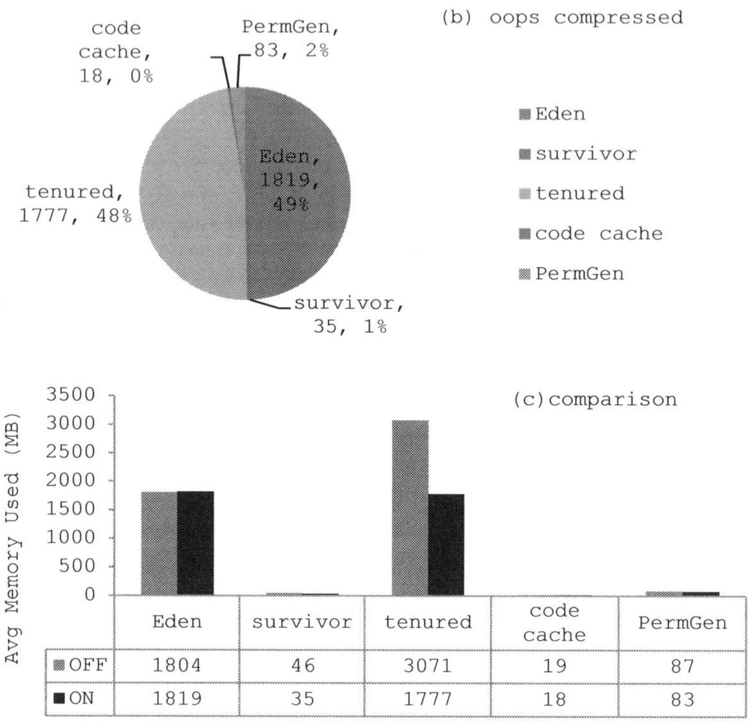

	Eden	survivor	tenured	code cache	PermGen
OFF	1804	46	3071	19	87
ON	1819	35	1777	18	83

Figure 5.3 AppServer: (a) average size of each heap region without oops compression, (b) with oops compression and (c) comparison between without and with oops compression

Figure 5.4 shows the evolution of the heap used space, Eden space, and tenured space with time for the component of AnalyticalEngine, with the option of `UseCompressedOops` off (upper curve) and on (lower curve), respectively. It is seen that the heap space used had been reduced considerably as well, but due to savings with both the Eden and tenured spaces when the ordinary object pointers were compressed. This differs from what was observed on AppServer, in which case Eden space stayed about the same. This might have something to do with the fact that AppServer is more of an OLTP application, while AnalyticalEngine is more of a batch-job type application.

(a)

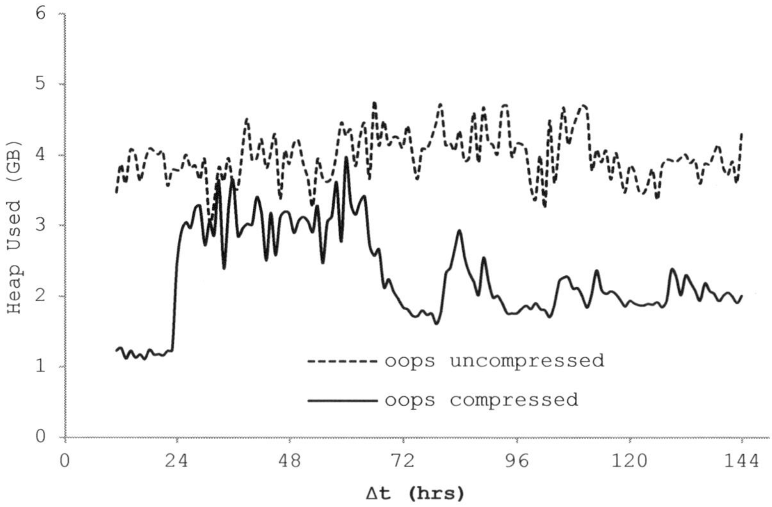
6
5
4
3
2
1
0
Heap Used (GB)
oops uncompressed
oops compressed
0
24
48
72
96
120
144
Δt (hrs)

(b)

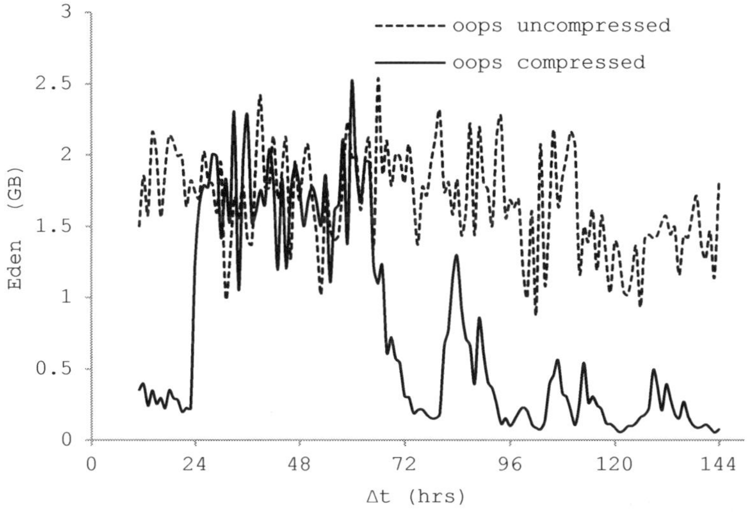
3
2.5
2
1.5
1
0.5
0
Eden (GB)
oops uncompressed
oops compressed
0
24
48
72
96
120
144
Δt (hrs)

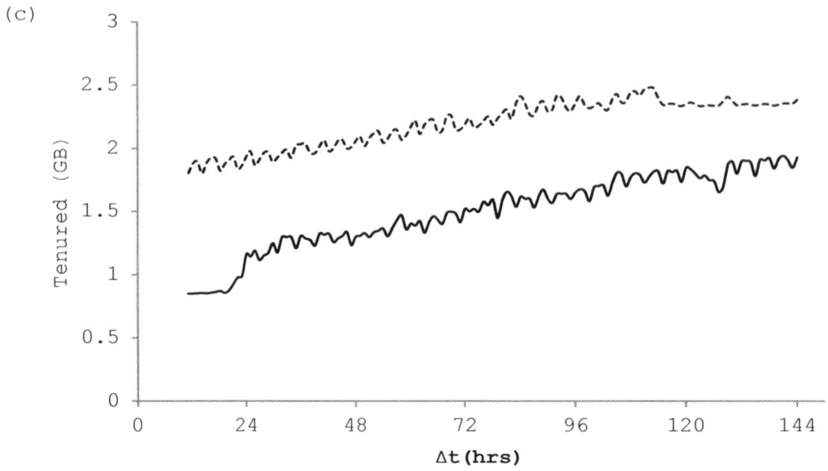

Figure 5.4 Analytical Engine: The effects of oops compression on (a) heap usage, (b) Eden region and (c) tenured region (upper – oops uncompressed; lower: oopscompressed)

Figure 5.5 shows the statistical average occupancies of the objects in different heap regions for the component of AnalyticalEngine, including code cache and PermGen regions, with and without having ordinary object pointers compressed. Once again, the code cache and PermGen regions were not affected as expected. Both the Eden region and the survivor region seem to have been compressed considerably, indicating again that only objects in the young generation region and the old generation region are subject to having their pointers compressed.

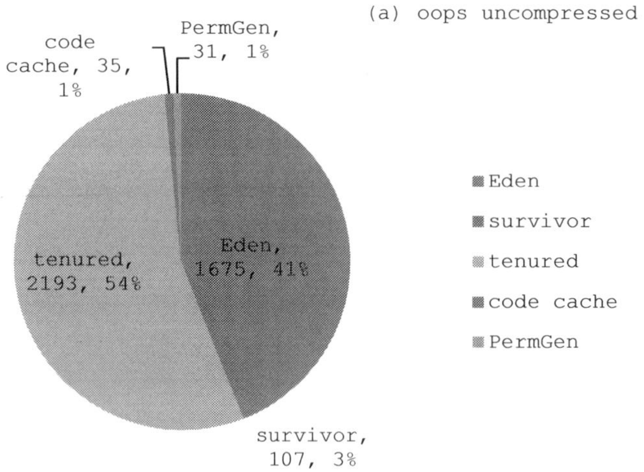

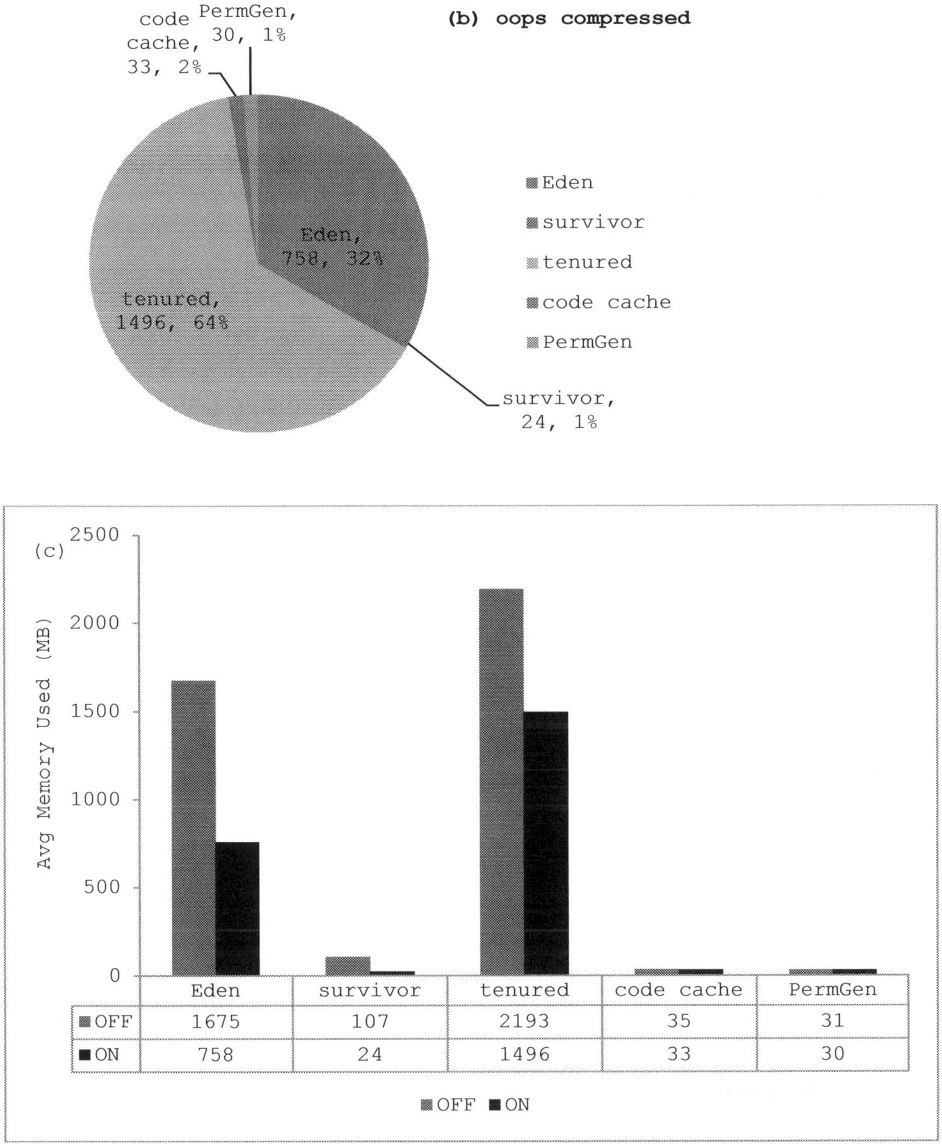

Figure 5.5 Analytical Engine: (a) average size of each heap region without oops compression, (b) with oops compression and (c) comparison between without and with oops compression

The measurements presented so far have clearly shown the significant benefits of compressing ordinary object pointers in reducing the heap occupancies in both young and old generation regions. Next, we discuss the impacts of oops on the working set of each component discussed above.

Sizing memory is somewhat different from sizing CPUs. CPUs can reach 100% busy and then come down without causing an application to mal-function or crash. However, when an application reaches certain limit to its memory utilization and `OutOfMemoryErrors` ensue, then the application typically immediately starts to mal-function or crash. This means that it's important to pay attention to the peak working set of an application under a certain load to make sure that it does not poke through a certain limit. Therefore, one should monitor the evolution of the working set of a process to make sure that the possibly reduced working set at the end of a test is not mistakenly used to size the memory of the process.

Figure 5.6 shows how the working set of each of the components evolved with time when the option of `UseCompressedOops` was turned off and on, respectively. It's seen that a 13% and a 15% reduction in peak working set of the two components have been achieved with the option of `UseCompressedOops` turned on, respectively. Those percentage savings correspond to over 1 GB saving in memory on average for each component, which is significant. We emphasize again that the working set of AnalyticalEngine fluctuated from time to time, and one should use its peak value instead of the value near the end of the run to plan for the amount of memory required by this component.

Figure 5.7 shows the CPU usage for the entire system on which all components were installed, with oops uncompressed and compressed, respectively. It is seen that the total CPU utilizations were not affected much by the technique of oops compression. Note that the average total CPU usage in each case was relative to the total max CPU usage of 100%.

Figure 5.8 shows the CPU usage for the component of AppServer, with oops uncompressed and compressed, respectively. Here the metric of average process CPU usage is used, which means that the numbers were accumulative across all CPUs, or relative to the max CPU usage of 1600% for the 16-CPU system used here. Statistically, the CPU usage for AppServer was reduced from 22% to 19% with oops compressed, which does indicate that compressing oops can help reduce CPU utilizations of a Java application as well, although not very significantly.

Figure 5.9 shows the CPU usage for the component of AnalyticalEngine, with oops uncompressed and compressed, respectively. Once again, here the metric of average process CPU usage was used, which means that the numbers were accumulative across all CPUs, or relative to the max CPU usage of 1600% for the 16-CPU system used here. Statistically, the CPU usage for AnalyticalEngine was reduced from 67% to 47% with oops compressed, which does indicate again that compressing oops can help reduce CPU utilizations of a Java application as well, although not very significantly.

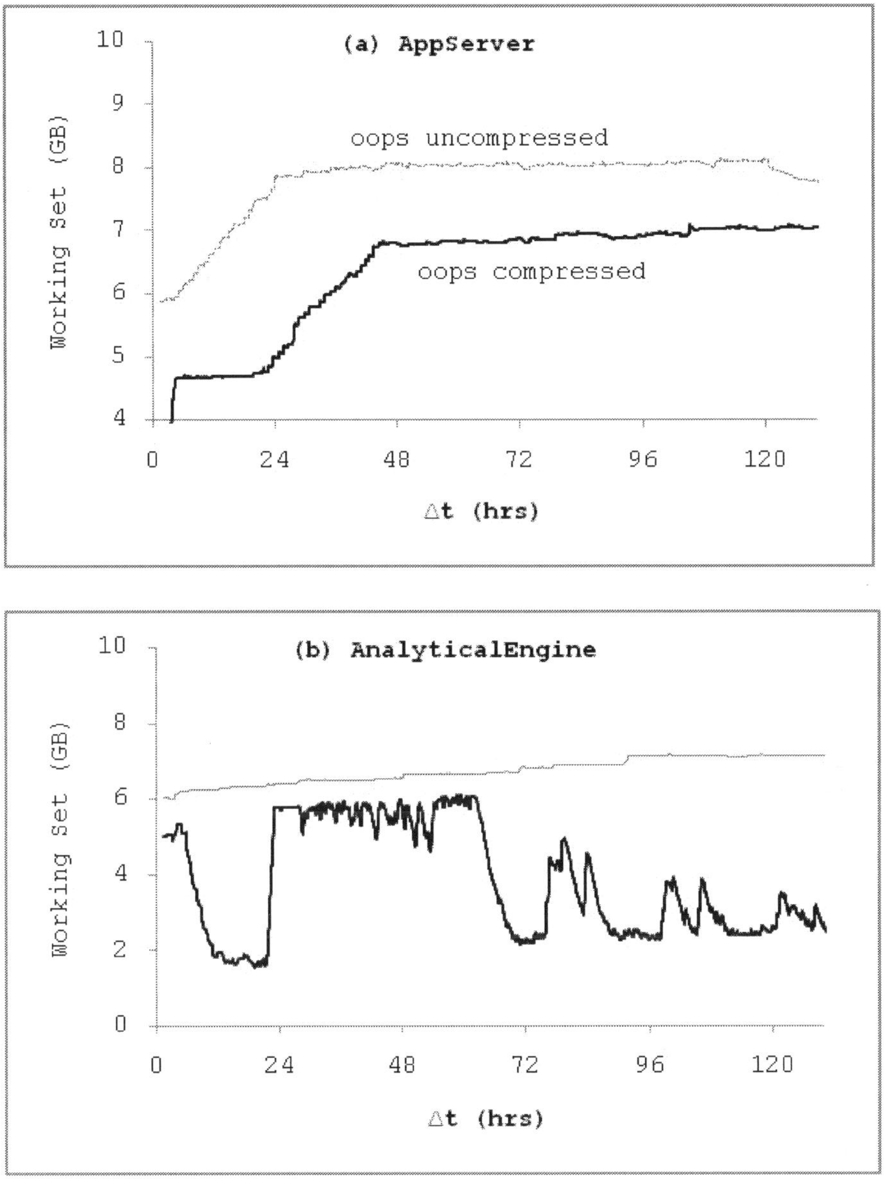

Figure 5.6 Working set comparison. In each chart, the upper curve corresponds to oops uncompressed, and the lower curve to oops compressed

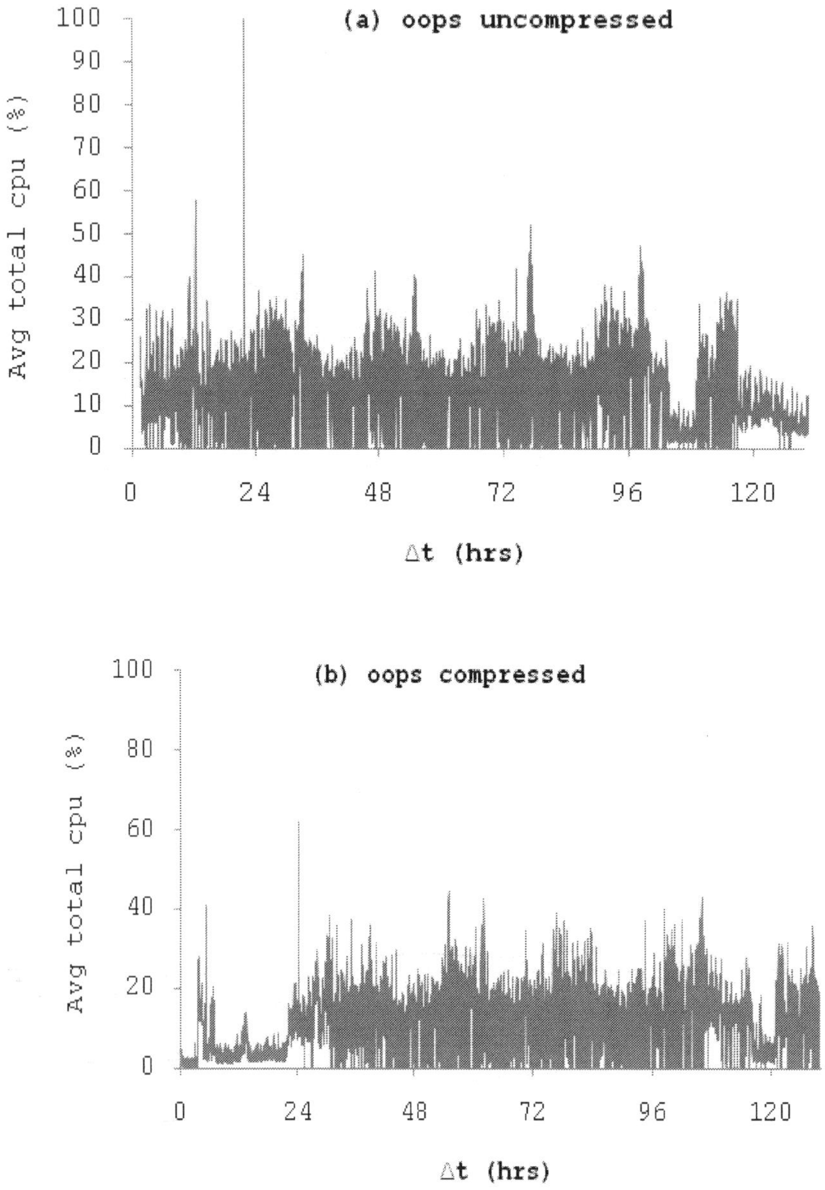

Figure 5.7 Comparison of the average total CPU usage for the entire system

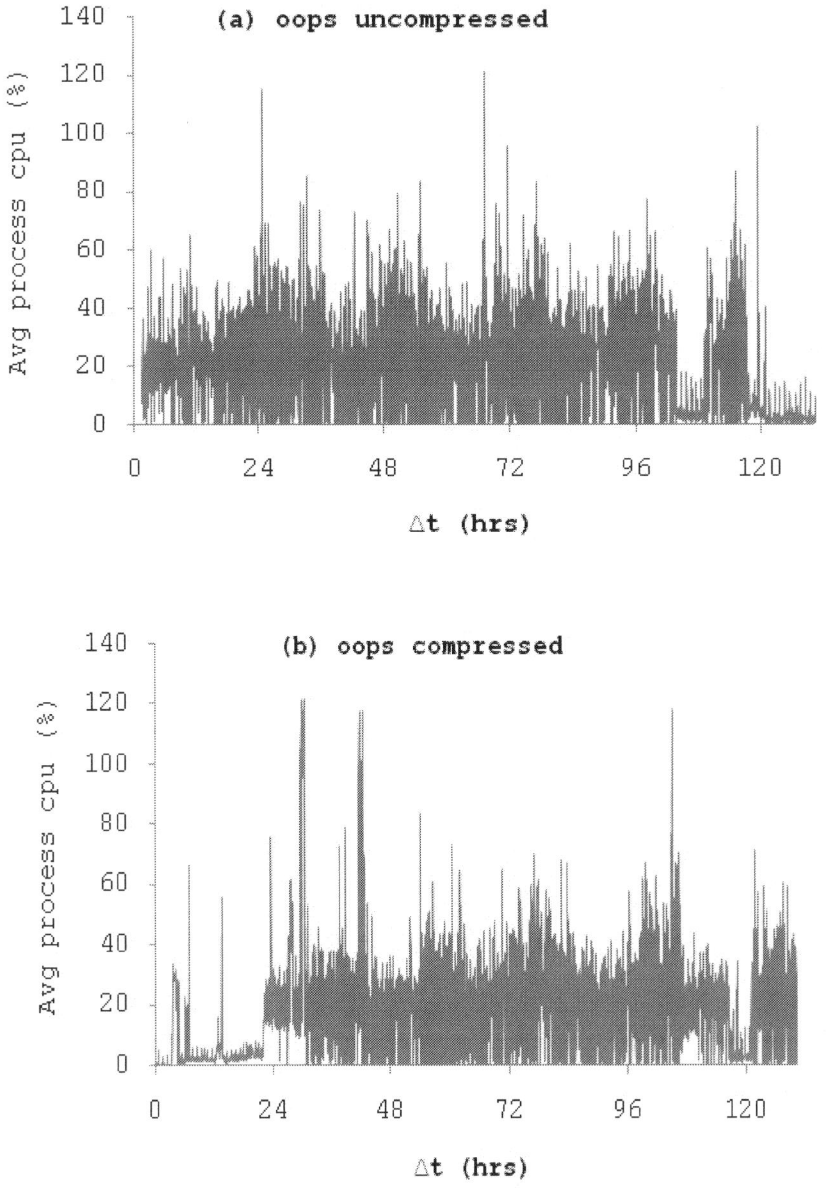

Figure 5.8 Comparison of the average process CPU usage for the AppServer

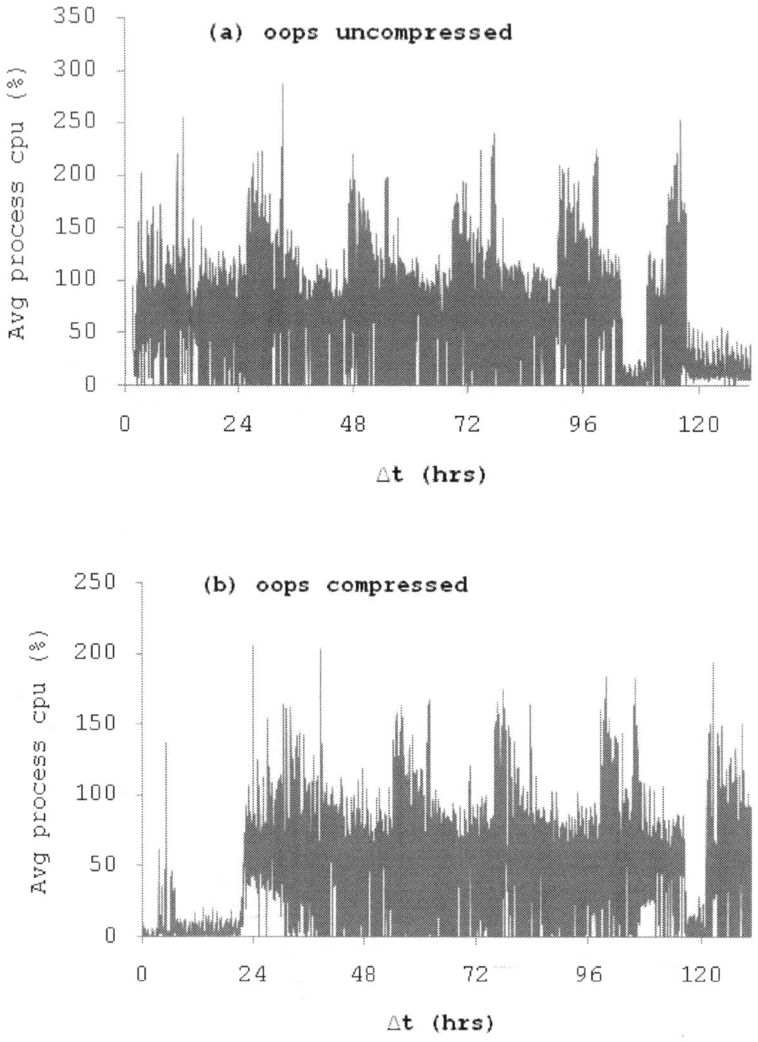

Figure 5.9 Comparison of the average process CPU usage for the AnalyticalEngine

Based on this case study, it seems that the effects of the oops compression technique is more on heap space reduction than on CPU utilization reduction. The good thing is that no side effects were observed and this feature turned out to be safe in addition to the benefits described above. Finally, note that if you are using an Oracle JDK newer than 1.6.0 update 23, this feature is enabled by default so that you don't have to enable it explicitly. Refer to section 4.5.1 on how to verify this on your system.

5.6 SUMMARY

This chapter started with a brief overview on the evolution of Intel processors from 8-bits to 16-bits and 32-bits to help illustrate how we got to where we are today with the massively ubiquitous 32-bit computing – both personal and enterprise computing. Yet, the 4 GB addressable space limit inherent with a 32-bit environment turned out to be a significant obstacle to enterprise computing. This obstacle was overcome with the advent of AMD64 and Intel EM64T technologies, which provide much needed support for 64-bit based enterprise computing.

However, wasted memory space because of the doubled pointer size from 32-bit to 64-bit has become a concern. Fortunately, the HotSpot JVMs since 6u14 provide a built-in mechanism to help combat the memory bloating issue for running 32-bit Java applications in 64-bit mode with the AMD and Intel 64-bit machines. This mechanism is exposed as a Java command line option of `-XX:+UseCompressedOops` so that it can be enabled easily. The quantitative case study presented in this chapter demonstrated that the oops compression technique is an effective approach to containing the memory bloat issue arising from running 32-bit Java applications in 64-bit environment. Since the application used for the case study was a real world, large-scale Java application, the benefits demonstrated should be compelling to encourage more users to consider the oops compression for their applications if they are in a similar situation.

The next chapter focuses on how to tune Java application performance and scalability from multiple perspectives.

EXERCISES

5.1 What are ordinary object pointers (oops)? Did you notice that a 32-bit Java application takes a much larger footprint in a 64-bit environment than in a 32-bit environment? In other words, for performing the same amount of work, a 32-bit Java application uses more memory in a 64-bit environment than in a 32-bit environment. What are the underlying causes for this memory bloating issue from a 32-bit environment to a 64-bit environment?

5.2 Does oops compression technique improve more on heap space or CPU utilizations? Did you try oops compression with your Java application? If yes, what were your observations and any discrepancies compared with the case study presented in this chapter?

5.3 From which version of Oracle JDK on is oops enabled by default?

REFERENCES

Oracle, *Java HotSpot Virtual Machine Performance Enhancements*, available at http://docs.oracle.com/javase/7/docs/technotes/guides/vm/performance-enhancements-7.html

Oracle, *CompressedOops*, available at https://wikis.oracle.com/display/HotSpotInternals/CompressedOops

C. Hunt, and B. John, *Java Performance*, Addison Wesley, 2012.

6 Tuning Java for Best Possible Performance and Scalability

To achieve best possible performance and scalability for your Java application, proper design and implementation with performance and scalability taken into account are the two most important proactive measures to take during the development process. Even so, it is very rare that a Java application would perform and scale without having to be tuned. In general, it's necessary to tune your Java application for best possible performance and scalability after coding is complete because of a few factors as follows:

- Performance and scalability testing requires much more powerful systems than the development boxes used for developing and QA-testing the application.
- Performance and scalability testing requires a much larger data volume than development and QA, both of which typically tend to use a much smaller data set to validate that the application works in an un-contended environment.
- Performance and scalability testing is a different process than designing, coding and QA, and requires a totally different set of skills in order to carry it out properly.

This chapter uses a real product to demonstrate how to tune a Java application to make it perform and scale after it has been designed, implemented and QA-ed. It is divided into the following three categories:

- Profiling the application and trying to understand the root causes responsible for preventing the application from performing and scaling better.
- Tuning the tunable JVM parameters for best possible performance and scalability for the application.
- Tuning system configurations for maximum performance and scalability potentially achievable with the application.

The next chapter discusses how to design and implement performance and scalability into a Java application.

6.1 QUANTIFYING PERFORMANCE AND SCALABILITY ISSUES

When tuning a Java application, the first step is to quantify the performance and scalability issues properly. This quantification process should include the following:

- The application architecture such as the major technologies used to build the application, components and/or layers that the application consists of and their inter-communications protocols, the backend database if applicable, etc.
- The performance and scalability test environment for the application. This should mimic customer production environment as much as possible so that any sizing guidelines and best performance and scalability practices derived from internal tests would be applicable to customer production environments.
- Hardware specs of the systems under test. Note that most of the time one may need to have an environment with mixed virtual and physical systems. Virtual systems are appropriate for development and QA, but they typically would be significantly undersized compared with the systems required both for internal performance and scalability testing and for customer production environment. CPU-intensive components such as database servers and Java application servers, and so on, should be installed on properly sized physical systems. Also, you should know your hardware rather than pounding on it blindly. If your hardware is new to you, you can check it out with my CPUCheck program, which is introduced in Appendix B, to know instantly how powerful it is relative to other hardware you used. If database is involved, you can also check out the I/O throughput of your I/O subsystem instantly with my other program named DiskCheck, which is introduced in Appendix C.
- Use cases, workload, and load test tools for testing the performance and scalability of your Java application.
- Informal brief interim reports based on the performance and scalability test results indicating performance and scalability issues with the application.

Next, we quantify the performance and scalability issues with the application in question by following the above guidelines.

6.1.1 Application Architecture

The application architecture of the Java application used as the case study in this chapter is characterized by its heavy dependency on a JEE application server. It's an OLTP type of enterprise application that has a GUI for online users as well as a backend database for storing user and enterprise data. Users access the application via a UI based on the HTTP protocol. Based on this information, we can infer immediately that the performance and scalability of this application would be measured by response times and the number of concurrent users it can support with a given deployment environment.

6.1.2 Test Environment

The test environment was the same as is shown in Figure 1.5, as it was the same application as we discussed in Chapter 1. Since it's an EJB-based application, you probably have already guessed that the EJB server would be the most CPU-intensive component, as it surely was.

6.1.3 Hardware Specs

Since as anticipated, the JEE application server was the most CPU-intensive component that limited the performance and scalability of the application, a physical server was used. Accordingly, we only list the specs for the JEE application server used as follows:

- CPU Model – Intel Xeon E5620 two quad cores with hyper-threading enabled @ 2.4 GHz for a total number of 16 processors (physical cores + hyper-threaded).
- Amount of RAM – 32 GB.
- OS – Windows 2008 R2 Enterprise Server Service Pack 2 (64-bit).

6.1.4 Load Testing

Load testing for this application was conducted with the load test tool *Silk Performer*. Five silk scripts were developed, which covered about 50 typical user actions in total. The queuing workload model was used and configured with a test period of one hour, along with different number of users out of a total of 300 concurrent users assigned to different scripts.

6.1.5 Performance and Scalability Issues

The performance and scalability issue with this application was related to upgrading the JEE application Server from version 4 to version 5. For convenience, throughout this chapter we would call it Java Enterprise Application Server (JEAS), and JEAS 4 and 5 accordingly.

Various internal tests indicated significant performance degradation from JEAS 4 to JEAS 5. Initial single user, manual tests shown that setting `enableAudit` to `false` with the `JNDIBasedSecurityManagement` bean on JEAS 5 could help avoid massive auditing activities on the EJBs. Otherwise, the default setting of `enableAudit = true` would totally derail the migration with intolerable performance and scalability degradation. By setting this parameter to `false`, extensive and also expensive, unnecessary audits on EJB invocations can be avoided, which helps save a lot of CPU cycles from JEAS 5. However, my Silk Performer load testing with hundreds of concurrent users demonstrated that this setting was insufficient to completely mitigate the degradation due to upgrading the application from JEAS 4 to JEAS 5, as discussed below.

The performance and scalability of the application were tested with JEAS 4 first with two runs: one with 200 concurrent users and one with 400 concurrent users. Then the tests were switched to JEAS 5 on the same JEE application server with everything else the same as with JEAS 4. Two JEAS 5 runs were conducted with 200 and 400 concurrent users as well, respectively, for an apple-to-apple comparison between the two versions of JEAS. The test results are presented next.

Figure 6.1 shows the response times averaged over all user actions, obtained with 200 and 400 concurrent users on JEAS 4 and 5, respectively. First, it is seen that with JEAS 4, the average response time increased from 1.86 seconds with 200 concurrent users to 2.14 seconds with 400 concurrent users, while with JEAS 5, the average response time increased from 2.27 seconds with 200 concurrent users to 3.63 seconds with 400 concurrent users. This means that, as is shown in Figure 6.2, upgrading the application from JEAS 4 to JEAS 5 caused 22% and 70% performance degradations for 200 and 400 concurrent users, respectively.

It's even more alarming from the JEAS CPU utilization perspective. Refer to Figures 6.3 and 6.4, and notice that for the same number of concurrent users, JEAS 5 consumed a lot more CPU cycles than JEAS 4. For example, with 400 concurrent users, the average total CPU utilization on JEAS 4 was merely 34%, while with JEAS 5, it increased to 68% on average or close to 100% for the majority part of the test duration after the run started. This means that JEAS 5 would have no further capacity for more concurrent users, imposing a threat to the scalability of the application.

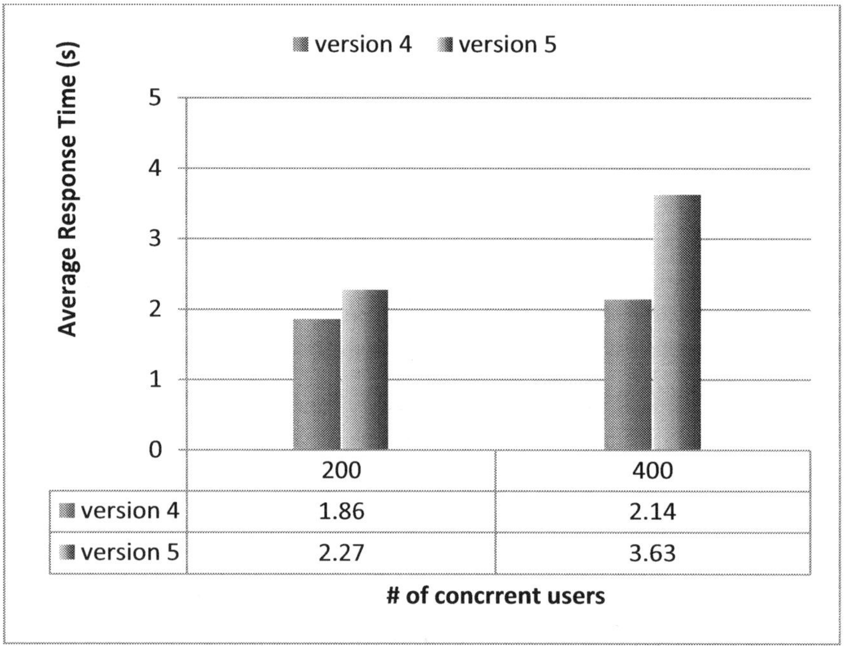

Figure 6.1 Application UI average response times measured with 200 and 400 concurrent users with two different versions of JEAS

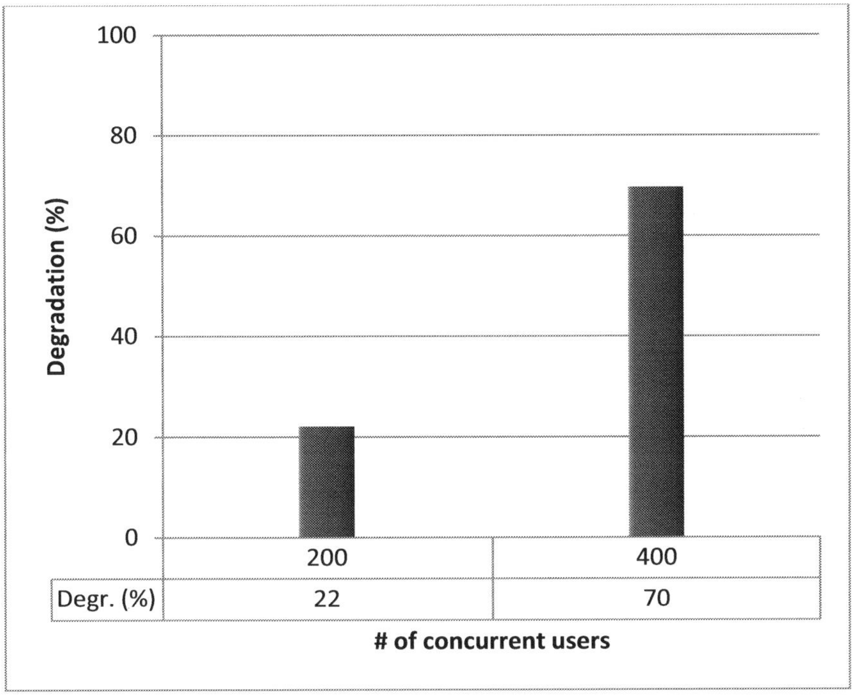

Figure 6.2 Application UI performance degradation caused by upgrading the application from JEAS 4 to JEAS 5

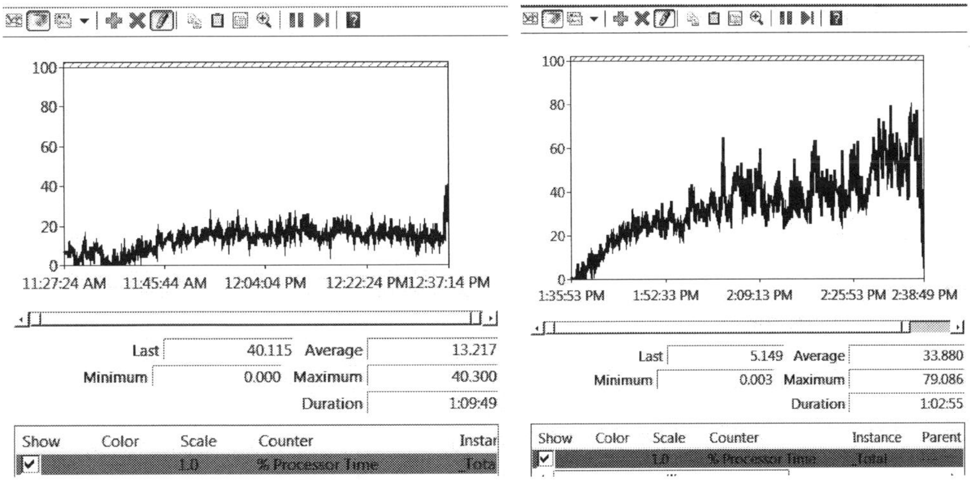

Figure 6.3 Average CPU utilizations with 200 (left) and 400 (right) concurrent user runs on JEAS 4

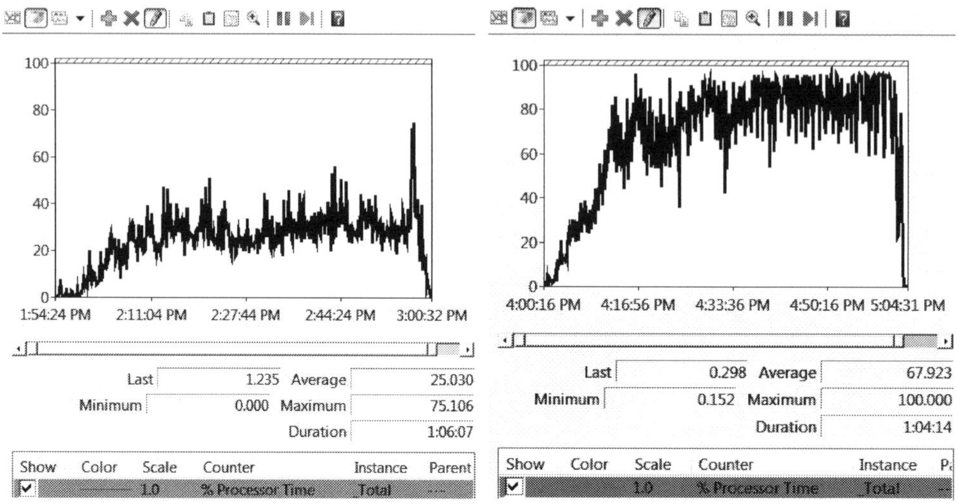

Figure 6.4 Average CPU utilizations with 200 (left) and 400 (right) concurrent user runs on JEAS 5

At this point, we felt that it's time to profile the application to find out exactly what was causing the large performance degradation when the application was upgraded from JEAS 4 to JEAS 5. The next section summarizes the profiling efforts for this purpose.

6.2 APPLICATION PROFILING

First, I have to say that profiling a real application might be quite a different experience than profiling a simple sample application like the *CPUCheck* program we used in Chapter 4 for demonstrating the profiling features of VisualVM. The challenge comes from the fact that the scope might be orders of magnitude larger with a real application than with a simple sample, and many unanticipated issues may arise accordingly. Since we were eager to find out why the JEE enterprise application server average CPU utilization doubled from version 4 to version 5 with the same 400 concurrent user workload as shown in Figures 6.3 and 6.4, I jumped to it directly with VisualVM in the hope that the puzzle could be solved immediately. However, it only turned out to be an interesting adventure, which I would share with you in the next section just in case you might run into a similar situation and wonder why profiling with VisualVM was not working.

6.2.1 Profiling the 400 Concurrent User Run with VisualVM

First off, after re-conditioning the test environment, I added the option of `-Xshare:off` to the start-up script and started up the application. Then after starting up VisualVM from the JDK1.6.0 update 31 install on the same server, a pop-up window appeared as shown in Figure 6.5, which performed initial JDK calibration.

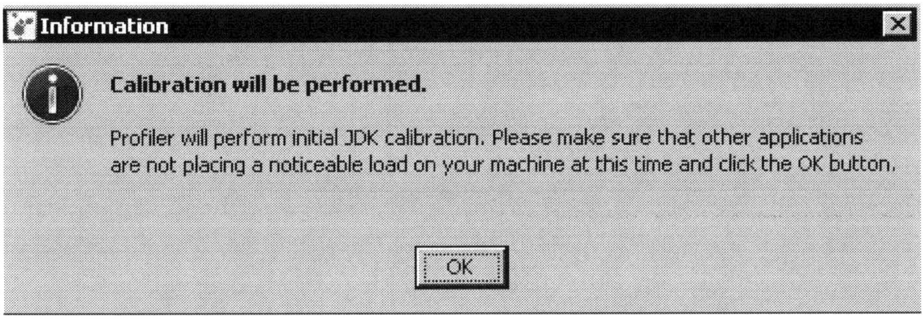

Figure 6.5 VisualVM calibration

Then, the application became visible on VisualVM. With a double-clicking on the application process, VisualVM was attached to the application. Then I launched the one-hour duration, 400 concurrent user run and switched back to the VisualVM console. The Monitor and VisualGC features worked well, but the Sampler feature failed to work at all that after I clicked the CPU icon, the Snapshot icon and Stop icon stopped responding. Rather than being stuck with the Sampler CPU profiling, I focused on the Monitor and VisualGC features. This experience is summarized next.

With this run, the minimum and maximum heap sizes were set to the same value of 3072 MB, and MaxPermSize was set to 512 MB. These were the same settings used throughout all runs presented in this chapter. In addition, this was a run with JEAS 4.

Figure 6.6 shows the Monitor page at the end of the one-hour duration run. Note the following statistics:

- **CPU chart**. This chart (top left) shows that the CPUs on the JEE application server were not stressed with 400 concurrent users. Note that GC activity was very light, from which we could eliminate GC as an issue.
- **Heap chart**. The GC pattern (top right) is characterized by an initial linear uptrend, followed by a sudden dip, indicating a major collection. Then three similar, faster uptrends ensued. The last part is essentially flat. The peaks and dips within each uptrend curve prior to a major collection indicate minor collections, with the delta between a peak and a subsequent dip representing the amount of heap space freed in the young generation.
- **Classes chart**. This chart (lower left) shows the number of classes loaded with the application. In this application, about 20k classes were loaded. This perhaps is one way to measure the size of the application.
- **Threads chart**. This chart (lower right) shows that at the end of the one-hour run, threads statistics had changed to *Live* (553), *Live peak* (555), *Daemon* (448), and *Total started* (1,211,472). It's amazing to see that a total of over 1.2 million threads were created over a one hour period, or at a rate of 337 threads/second. This had been a lot of work for the JEE application server.

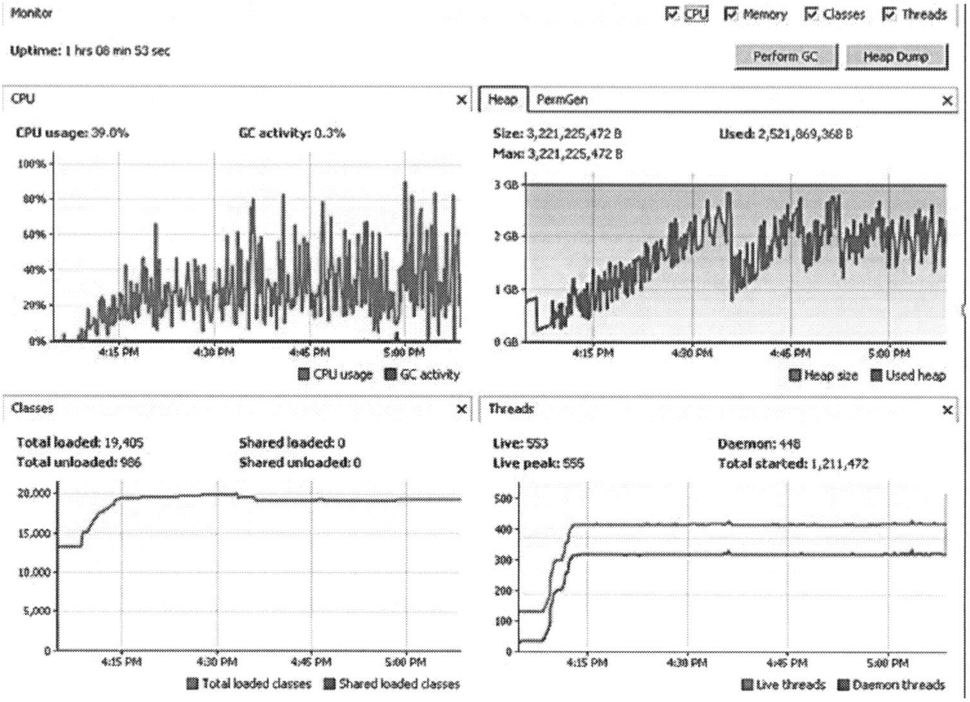

Figure 6.6 VisualVM Monitor page with the application at the end of the run

Figure 6.7 shows the VisualGC page at the end of the run. From this page, note the *Compile Time* of 1m54s for 5660 compiles or 20 ms/compile, *Class Loader Time* of 20s for 20392 loads or 1 ms/load, *GC Time* for *Eden* of 3m17s for 2004 minor collections or 98 ms/minor collection, and *GC time* for *Old Gen* of 51 seconds for 13 major collections or 1.538 seconds/per major collection. Apparently, those major collections took too long per collection. We will discuss this issue later when we discuss switching from the throughput collector to the CMS collector.

That 377 threads per second thread creation rate might explain why the Sampler CPU sampling never worked, even after I reduced the number of concurrent users from 400 to 200. Figure 6.8 shows what happened with the Sampler during the runs that both CPU and Stop buttons greyed out.

Since the VisualVM CPU Sampler did not work for full scale load tests with hundreds of users, I tried the commercial tool JProfiler with no success at all. After the Save Snapshot icon was clicked, JProfiler was stuck with the *Saving snapshot (Please wait)* progress window, which never finished. Eventually, I had to use the Task Manager to end the JProfiler process, which stopped JProfiler progress window, but it did not seem to end the JProfiler agent process as I could not attach it to the JEE application server again afterwards. I had to reboot the JEE application server to get it completely cleaned. At that point, I concluded that a full scale load test run was too large in scope for both VisualVM and JProfiler, so I devised an alternative approach to profiling in single threaded mode to keep going, which worked well as discussed in the next section.

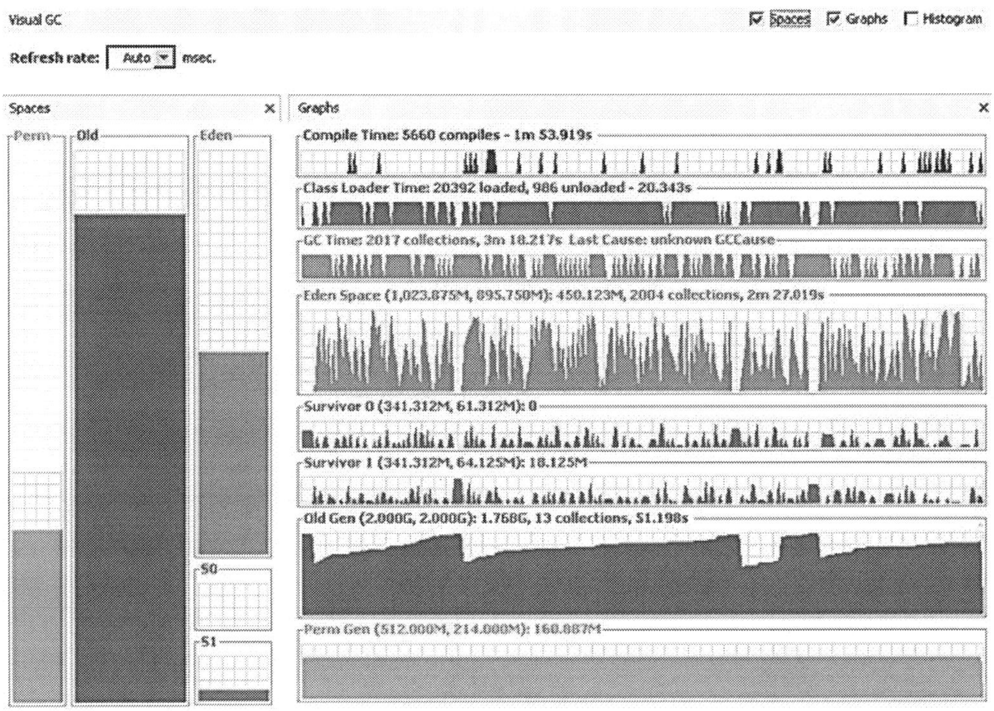

Figure 6.7 VisualGC page at the end of the run

Figure 6.8 VisualVM Sampler did not work with 200 – 400 concurrent user runs

6.2.2 Profiling in Single Threaded Mode

Because of the enormous difficulties with profiling the application running in full-scale load test mode with hundreds of concurrent users, I realized that I should use the *Try Script* feature of Silk Performer to profile, which allows running a Silk script in single threaded mode with think time ignored. This turned out to be a perfect alternative, as we were most interested in comparing JEAS 4 and JEAS 5 profiles, so a single-threaded run driven with a single script rather than all five scripts with hundreds of concurrent users was sufficient. The profiling results from this alternative approach with VisualVM Sampler for CPU sampling are presented next.

First, a single-threaded run using the Try Script feature of Silk Performer took 1m42s on JEAS 4, whereas the same run took 2m51s on JEAS 5. This means that the same test took 68% longer on JEAS 5 than on JEAS 4. See Table 6.1 to compare average response times between JEAS 4 and JEAS 5 on an action-to-action basis. It is seen that some actions were degraded more than others. The last row represents the overall response time averaged over all eight actions, indicating a 67% degradation from JEAS 4 to JEAS 5.

Table 6.1 Average Response Time Comparison between JEAS 4 and 5

Action	JEAS 4	JEAS 5	Degradation (%)
a01_login	1.625	2.094	29
a02_clickPlans	2.594	4.756	83
a03_clickNew	3.094	4.684	51
a04_save	1.256	2.286	82
a05_clickAll	2.642	4.281	62
a06_manageAssignmentTemplates	0.325	0.59	82
a07_loadDefaultAssignments	0.322	0.524	63
a08_logout	0.094	0.157	67
average	1.678	2.798	67

It turned out that the data generated with this alternative profiling approach was sufficient for diagnosing the application performance degradation from JEAS 4 to JEAS 5. Figures 6.9 and 6.10 show the HotSpots methods reported from the JEAS 4 and 5 profiles, respectively. Table 6.2 summarizes the top two hot classes that differed significantly in CPU time from JEAS 4 to JEAS 5, including the total elapsed times for both runs. A brief explanation about these two classes is given as follows:

- `javax.management.StandardMBean`. To understand this class, we starts with the concept of an MBean. An MBean is a managed bean, which is a Java object representing a resource to be managed. MBeans can be *standard* or *dynamic*. A standard MBean exposes the resource to be managed directly through its attributes and operations, whereas a dynamic MBean defines its management interface at runtime. Anyway, it's clear that this class is attributable to the JEAS kernel.
- `java.security.AccessController`. This apparently is associated with the JAVA security feature of both JEAS 4 and 5. We needed to drill down deeper with this class as described next.

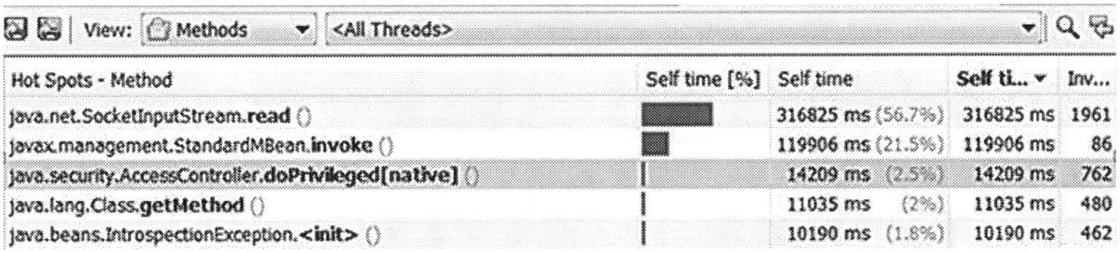

Figure 6.9 HotSpots methods sorted by Self Time (CPU) from the JEAS 4 profile

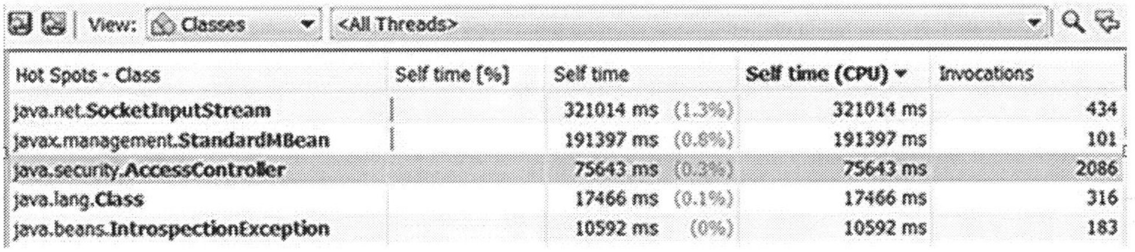

Figure 6.10 HotSpots methods sorted by Self Time (CPU) from the JEAS 5 profile

Table 6.2 Two Hot Methods Showing Significant Increase in CPU Time from JEAS 4 to JEAS 5 with the Same Workload Executed on the Same JEE Application Server (to Put it into Perspective, Total Elapsed Times for both Runs are Included as well)

Class	JEAS 4	JEAS 5
javax.management.StandardMBean	119.906 seconds	191.397 seconds
java.security.AccessController	14.209 seconds	75.643 seconds
Script execution wall-clock time	102 seconds	171 seconds

VisualVM has a very useful feature called *Back Traces* that can help display callers of a hot method. To use this feature, right-click on a hot method and then select *Show Back Traces*. By comparing the back traces of the `java.security.AccessController` class with both runs, it turned out that a lot of additional callers that did not appear in the JEAS 4 profile appeared in the JEAS 5 profile. See Figure 6.11 for the JEAS 4 profile and Figure 6.12 for the JEAS 5 profile, all in method view (back traces can also be shown in class and package views). Note that the first two top callers from the JEAS 4 profile appeared in the JEAS 5 profile as well with comparable CPU times. However, a lot of additional callers that did not appear in the JEAS 4 profile appeared in the JEAS 5 profile. This explained the performance degradation from JEAS 4 to JEAS 5 in question.

	Time [%]	Time	Time (CPU)	Invocations
doPrivileged[native] ()		14...(11.9%)	14209 ms	762
.ejb.SecurityActions.**setContextID** ()		11...(10.1%)	11986 ms	560
ne.commons.logging.LogFactory.**getCo**		21... (1.8%)	2100 ms	99
.resource.adapter.jms.JmsCred$GetCr		42.... (0%)	42.1 ms	3
.security.plugins.SubjectActions.**setCo**		21.... (0%)	21.1 ms	1
.security.SimplePrincipal.**equals** ()		20.... (0%)	20.1 ms	1
.security.plugins.SubjectActions.**getAc**		19.... (0%)	19.4 ms	1
.resource.connectionmanager.BaseCor		19.... (0%)	19.2 ms	1
urity.auth.login.LoginContext.**invokePr**		0.0... (0%)	0.000 ms	3
JRLClassLoader.**findClass** ()		0.0... (0%)	0.000 ms	2
ne.commons.logging.LogFactory.**getRe**		0.0... (0%)	0.000 ms	1

Figure 6.11 Back traces in *method view* for the hot method of `java.security.AccessController.doPrivileged` from the JEAS 4 profile

	Time [%]	Time	Time (CPU)	Invocations
.**doPrivileged[native]** ()		75643 ... (40%)	75643 ms	2086
s.ejb.SecurityActions.**setConte**		11390 ... (6%)	11390 ms	221
s.security.plugins.authorization.		7880 ms (4.2%)	7880 ms	148
s.ejb.plugins.SecurityActions.**ge**		6702 ms (3.5%)	6702 ms	131
s.ejb.plugins.security.SecurityA		5892 ms (3.1%)	5892 ms	112
s.security.plugins.authorization.		5585 ms (3%)	5585 ms	160
s.ejb.SecurityActions.**getSecur**		4994 ms (2.6%)	4994 ms	96
s.security.jacc.SubjectPolicyCon		4267 ms (2.3%)	4267 ms	76
s.ejb.plugins.SecurityActions.**po**		3699 ms (2%)	3699 ms	115
s.ejb.plugins.SecurityActions.**is**		3629 ms (1.9%)	3629 ms	103
s.ejb.plugins.PerTxEntityInstanc		3368 ms (1.8%)	3368 ms	71
s.security.authorization.module		2501 ms (1.3%)	2501 ms	46
s.ejb.plugins.SecurityActions.**au**		2223 ms (1.2%)	2223 ms	354
s.ejb.plugins.SecurityActions.**pu**		2076 ms (1.1%)	2076 ms	73
he.commons.logging.LogFactor		1954 ms (1%)	1954 ms	35
s.security.javaee.AbstractJavaEl		1650 ms (0.9%)	1650 ms	31
s.ejb.plugins.security.SecurityA		1339 ms (0.7%)	1339 ms	25
s.ejb.plugins.security.SecurityA		1303 ms (0.7%)	1303 ms	27
s.ejb.plugins.SecurityActions.**ge**		1259 ms (0.7%)	1259 ms	25
s.ejb.plugins.security.SecurityA		1101 ms (0.6%)	1101 ms	20
s.ejb.plugins.security.SecurityA		1099 ms (0.6%)	1099 ms	22
s.ejb.plugins.security.SecurityA		948 ms (0.5%)	948 ms	17
s.ejb.plugins.security.SecurityA		695 ms (0.4%)	695 ms	30
s.web.tomcat.security.SecurityA		77.0 ms (0%)	77.0 ms	2

Figure 6.12 Back traces in method view for the hot method of `java.security.AccessController.doPrivileged` from the JEAS 5 profile

6.3 RESOLUTION

According to the profiling analysis presented at the end of the preceding section, the different security execution paths between the two versions of the JEE application server caused the observed performance degradation issue after the application was upgraded from JEAS 4 to JEAS 5. It's unclear how that happened with that JEE application server, because the option `-Djava.security.manager` was not specified on the start-up command of that application. Therefore, this issue is different from the one mentioned in the section *Presence of Security Manager* in *Java Performance* [Hunt and John, 2012], which reported that this option resulted in 33% reduction in throughput.

Since the application was not in fault, other potential remedies as described as follows were attempted:

- Using newer JDKs with more performance and scalability features incorporated.
- Upgrading the hardware for the application JEE server to compensate for the extra security calls invoked by the new version of the JEE application server JEAS 5.

Improvements obtained with these remedies are presented next.

6.3.1 Newer JDKs

We explored the potential performance improvements using newer JDKs relative to the results presented in section 6.1 obtained with the 64-bit JDK 1.6.0 update 21. A 400 concurrent user run was conducted with JDK 1.6.0 update 24 on JEAS 5. With this change, the performance degradation with JEAS 5 was reduced from 70 % with JDK 1.6.0 update 21 64-bit down to 59% with an average response time of 3.41 seconds. Encouraged by this improvement, another 400 concurrent user run was conducted with the latest JDK 1.6.0 release of update 31 64-bit, and the degradation was further reduced from 70% with JDK 1.6.0 update 21 to 41% with an average response time of 3.03 seconds. To see whether JDK 1.6.0 update 31 would make a difference with JEAS 4, a 400 concurrent user run was conducted, which resulted in an average response time of 2.01 seconds. This 2.01 second average response time represents a 13% improvement over the run with JDK 1.6.0 update 21 on JEAS 4. This smaller improvement was expected, as the 400 concurrent user run on JEAS 4 consumed much less CPU cycles (compare Figure 6.3 and 6.4). See Table 6.3 for a summary of all these runs.

Table 6.3 Improvements with Newer JDKs on the Application Performance on JEAS 5 (the Same 400 Concurrent User Workload and the Same Xeon E5620 Based JEE Server was Used for all the Runs)

JEAS and JDK Version	Average Response Time (s)	Degradation (%)
JEAS 4: JDK 1.6.0 update 21	2.14	JEAS 4 baseline
JEAS 5: JDK 1.6.0 update 21	3.63	70%
JEAS 5: JDK 1.6.0 update 24	3.41	59%
JEAS 5: JDK 1.6.0 update 31	3.03	41%
JEAS 4:JDK 1.6.0 update 31	2.01	New JEAS 4 baseline

Figure 6.13 shows the JEAS CPU utilizations with 400 concurrent users on JEAS 4 (left) and JEAS 5 (right), respectively, after the JDK 1.6.0 update21 was replaced with JDK 1.6.0 update 31 for both cases. It is seen that even JDK 1.6.0 update 31, JEAS 5 still consumed a lot more CPU cycles on the JEE application server than JEAS 4.

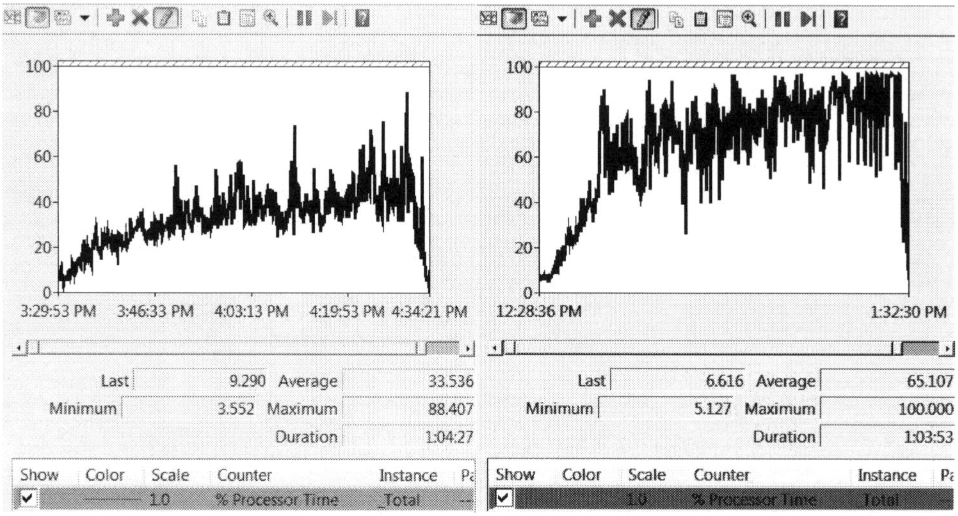

Figure 6.13 Average CPU utilizations with JEAS 4 (left) and JEAS 5 (right) runs for 400 concurrent users with JDK 1.6.0 update 31 in place of 1.6.0 update 21

6.3.2 Faster Hardware

The faster hardware found for the newer version of JEAS 5 was a system equipped with two Xeon X5550 quad cores @ 2.67 GHz, hyper-threaded, 24 GB RAM, running on Windows 2008 Enterprise Server SP2, while the system used previously was equipped with two Xeon E5620 quad cores @ 2.4 GHz, hyper-threaded, 32 GB RAM, running on Windows 2008 R2 Enterprise Server. Table 6.4 compares the specs between these two Intel CPU models. Refer back to Table 1.2 and note the outstanding performance obtained with an Intel Core i7 based system. In fact, Core i7 and Xeon 5500 shares the same microarchitecture of Nehalem. Therefore, it's anticipated that X5550 would be faster than E5620, although their specs don't seem to differ much.

To have a quick evaluation on the relative performance of these two Intel Xeon CPU models, I looked up the *Passmark* scores for each CPU model, which shows that X5550 is 10% faster than E5620. I also ran my own CPU benchmark named *CPUCheck* on both E5620 and X5550, and to my surprise, X5550 turned out to be 65% faster than E5620, as shown in Table 6.4. To really appreciate the high performance of Xeon X5550, you might want to refer back to Section 2.3 *Performance Features of the Intel Core i7 Processors* to know more about it, as X5550 and Core i7-2600 share the same microarchitecture of Nehalem.

Table 6.4 Intel Xeon X5550 versus Xeon E5620 (Both Hyper-Threaded)

Spec	X5550	E5620
# of cores @ GHz	2x4 @ 2.67 GHz	2x4 @ 2.4 GHz
Cache	8 MB	12 MB
QPI (QuickPath Interconnect)	6.4 GT/s	5.86 GT/s
# of QPI links	2	2
Launch date	Q1'09	Q1'10
PassMark	5170 (10% faster)	4696
Henry's benchmark	27 seconds (67% faster)	45 seconds

To make the comparison more apple-to-apple, all system configurations remained the same except two variables: JEAS version and JEE application server CPU model. All runs were conducted with the same number of 400 concurrent users, same JDK version of 1.6.0 update 31, and same JVM options. Figure 6.14 shows the test results.

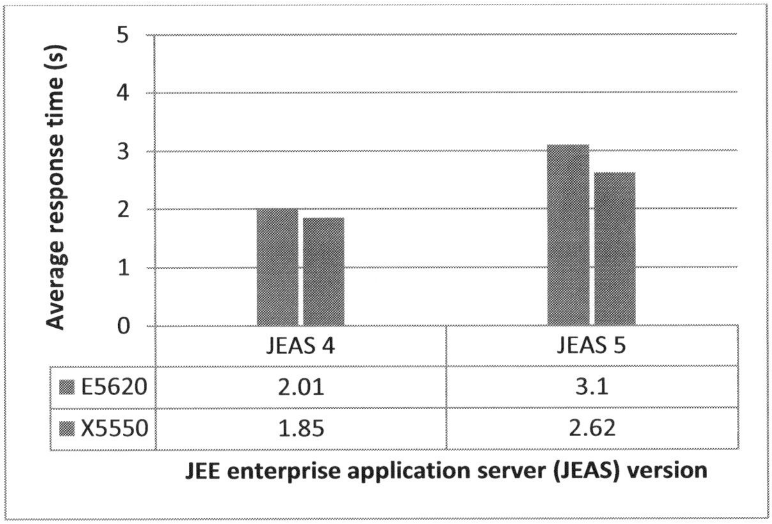

Figure 6.14 Average response time comparison between Xeon E5620 and X5550 based JEE servers (400 concurrent users and JDK 1.6.0 update 31 were used for both cases)

According to the test results shown in Figure 6.14, by moving the JEE application server from an E5620-based system to an X5550-based system, the average response time of the application with 400 concurrent users was reduced from 2.01 seconds to 1.85 seconds with JEAS 4, and from 3.1 seconds to 2.62 seconds with JEAS 5. The former corresponds to a 9% gain, whereas the latter corresponds to a 18% gain. A larger gain was achieved with JEAS 5 because the application consumed more CPU cycles with JEAS 5 than with JEAS 4 with the same number of 400 concurrent users. Note that the original average response time was 3.63 seconds with JDK 1.6.0 update 21 on a Xeon E5620 based JEE server.

By upgrading the JDK from 1.6.0 update 21 to 1.6.0 update 31 and upgrading the JEE server from a Xeon E5620-based system to a Xeon X5550-based server, that 3.63 second average response time had been reduced to 2.62 seconds, which corresponds to a total improvement of 39% overall. However, that 2.62 second average response time with JEAS 5 was still about 42% higher than the average response time of 1.85 seconds with JEAS 4 on the same Xeon X5550-based system.

Next, let's compare JEAS 4 and 5 profiles obtained on this new Xeon X5550-based JEE server, similar to what we did in the last section with the JEAS 4 and 5 profiles obtained on that Xeon E5620-based JEE server.

Table 6.5 shows the following relevant statistics:

- The CPU time for `StandardMBean`: 88 seconds with JEAS 4 and 128 seconds with JEAS 5.
- The CPU time for `AccessController`: 8 seconds with JEAS 4 and 49 seconds with JEAS 5.
- The total elapsed time for the script executed to drive the runs: 68 seconds with JEAS 4 and 107 seconds with JEAS 5. Refer back to Table 6.1 for the actions included in this script.

It is seen that JEAS 5 still lagged JEAS 4 significantly on every account listed in Table 6.5 even on this Xeon X5550-based system. However, a comparison between Table 6.5 and Table 6.2 indicates that the JEAS 5 script execution time of 107 seconds on this X5550-based server were much closer to the JEAS 4 script execution time of 102 seconds obtained on that E5620-based server, except the `AccessController`.

Table 6.5 Two Hot Methods Showing Significant Increase in CPU Time from JEAS 4 to JEAS 5 with the Same Workload Executed on the Same JEE Application Server Based on the Xeon X5550 CPUs (to Put it into Perspective, Total Elapsed Times for both Runs are Included as well)

Class	JEAS 4	JEAS 5
javax.management.StandardMBean	88 seconds	128 seconds
java.security.AccessController	8 seconds	49 seconds
Script execution	68 seconds	107 seconds

We can examine the above results from a different perspective, that is, we look at how much improvement was obtained with the different JEAS versions on the same hardware. Table 6.6 shows the comparison for JEAS 4, while Table 6.7 shows the comparison for JEAS 5. Note that the X5550-based server was 60% faster than the E5620-based server in single thread mode. This appears to be more consistent with my CPUCheck benchmarking number of X5550 67% faster than E5620 as shown in Table 6.4.

Table 6.6 Single-Thread Execution Performance Comparison between E5602-Based and X5550-Based JEE Servers with the Same Version of JEAS 4

Class	E5620	X5550	Speed-up (%)
StandardMBean	120 seconds	88 seconds	36%
AccessController	14 seconds	8 seconds	75%

Script execution	102 seconds	68 seconds	50%

Table 6.7 Single-Thread Execution Performance Comparison between E5602-Based and X5550-Based JEE Servers with the Same Version of JEAS 5

Class	E5620	X5550	Speed-up (%)
StandardMBean	191 seconds	128 seconds	49%
AccessController	76 seconds	49 seconds	55%
Script execution	171 seconds	107 seconds	60%

To help re-evaluate the performance degradation from JEAS 4 to JEAS 5 on this X5550-based JEE application server, Figures 6.15 and 6.16 show the hot spot methods with JEAS 4 and JEAS 5, respectively. Note the large difference in Self Time (CPU) for `AccessController` between these two VisualVM profiles (7.865 seconds with JEAS 4 versus 49.268 seconds with JEAS 5).

Hot Spots - Method	Self time [%]	Self time	Self time (CPU) ▼	Invocations
t.StandardMBean.invoke ()		88122 ms (59.2%)	88122 ms	25
ons.beanutils.PropertyUtils.isWriteable ()		16374 ms (11%)	16374 ms	384
essController.doPrivileged[native] ()		7856 ms (5.3%)	7856 ms	449
ossatx.BaseTransactionManagerDelegate.suspend ()		7816 ms (5.3%)	7816 ms	153
.OraclePreparedStatementWrapper.executeQuery ()		5471 ms (3.7%)	5471 ms	293
.OracleStatementWrapper.executeQuery ()		2509 ms (1.7%)	2509 ms	78
.OracleResultSetImpl.next ()		1965 ms (1.3%)	1965 ms	32
na.core.ApplicationFilterChain.doFilter ()		1872 ms (1.3%)	1872 ms	1094
notify[native] ()		1718 ms (1.2%)	1718 ms	95
.plugins.JaasSecurityManager.getPrincipal ()		1613 ms (1.1%)	1613 ms	91
nt.OracleXAResource.end ()		1574 ms (1.1%)	1574 ms	83
.plugins.JaasSecurityManager.getCacheInfo ()		875 ms (0.6%)	875 ms	47
ossatx.BaseTransactionManagerDelegate.resume ()		797 ms (0.5%)	797 ms	43
nt.OracleXAResource.start ()		786 ms (0.5%)	786 ms	43
nt.OracleXAResource.commit ()		660 ms (0.4%)	660 ms	36
etDeclaredMethods ()		579 ms (0.4%)	579 ms	30
.OraclePreparedStatementWrapper.executeUpdate..		562 ms (0.4%)	562 ms	28

Figure 6.15 HotSpots methods sorted by Self Time (CPU) from the JEAS 4 profile obtained on the Xeon X5550 based JEE application server

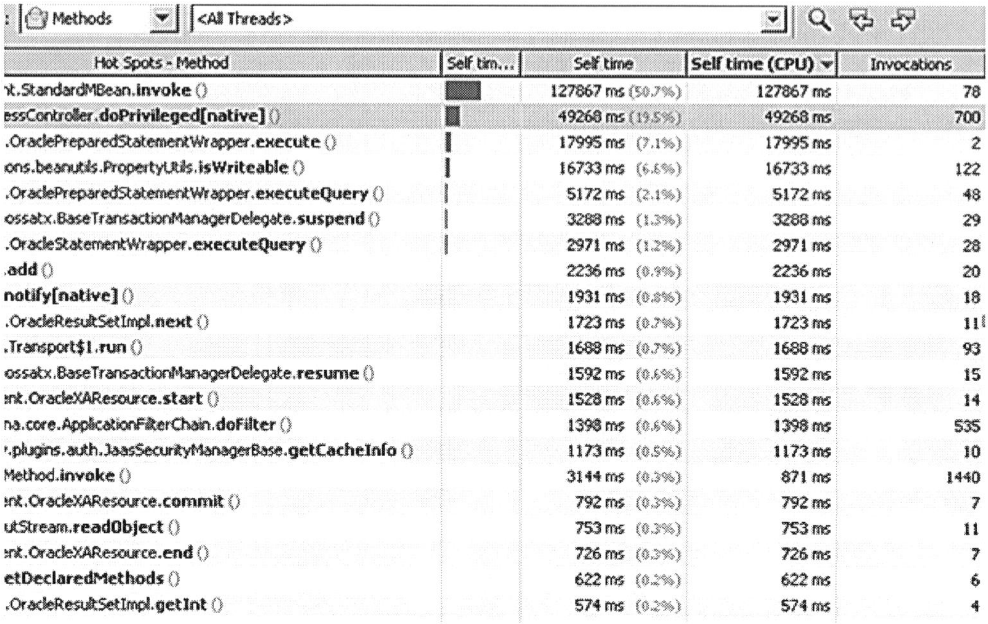

Methods | <All Threads>

Hot Spots - Method	Self tim...	Self time	Self time (CPU)	Invocations
ıt.StandardMBean.invoke ()		127867 ms (50.7%)	127867 ms	78
essController.doPrivileged[native] ()		49268 ms (19.5%)	49268 ms	700
.OraclePreparedStatementWrapper.execute ()		17995 ms (7.1%)	17995 ms	2
ons.beanutils.PropertyUtils.isWriteable ()		16733 ms (6.6%)	16733 ms	122
.OraclePreparedStatementWrapper.executeQuery ()		5172 ms (2.1%)	5172 ms	48
ossatx.BaseTransactionManagerDelegate.suspend ()		3288 ms (1.3%)	3288 ms	29
.OracleStatementWrapper.executeQuery ()		2971 ms (1.2%)	2971 ms	28
.add ()		2236 ms (0.9%)	2236 ms	20
notify[native] ()		1931 ms (0.8%)	1931 ms	18
.OracleResultSetImpl.next ()		1723 ms (0.7%)	1723 ms	11
.Transport$1.run ()		1688 ms (0.7%)	1688 ms	93
ossatx.BaseTransactionManagerDelegate.resume ()		1592 ms (0.6%)	1592 ms	15
ent.OracleXAResource.start ()		1528 ms (0.6%)	1528 ms	14
na.core.ApplicationFilterChain.doFilter ()		1398 ms (0.6%)	1398 ms	535
'.plugins.auth.JaasSecurityManagerBase.getCacheInfo ()		1173 ms (0.5%)	1173 ms	10
Method.invoke ()		3144 ms (0.3%)	871 ms	1440
ent.OracleXAResource.commit ()		792 ms (0.3%)	792 ms	7
utStream.readObject ()		753 ms (0.3%)	753 ms	11
ent.OracleXAResource.end ()		726 ms (0.3%)	726 ms	7
etDeclaredMethods ()		622 ms (0.2%)	622 ms	6
.OracleResultSetImpl.getInt ()		574 ms (0.2%)	574 ms	4

Figure 6.16 HotSpots methods sorted by Self Time (CPU) from the JEAS 5 profile obtained on the Xeon X5550 based JEE application server

Figures 6.17 and 6.18 show the back traces of the `java.security.AccessController` class with the JEAS 4 run and JEAS 5 run, respectively. Note again that the first two top callers from the JEAS 4 profile appeared in the JEAS 5 profile as well with comparable CPU times. However, similar to what was found out on the previous E5620-based JEE server, a lot of additional callers that did not appear in the JEAS 4 profile appeared in the JEAS 5 profile, except that they ran faster on the X5550-based JEE server than on the E5620-based JEE server.

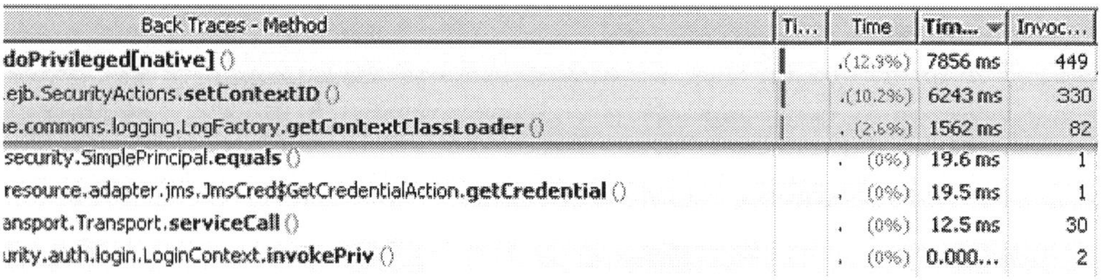

Back Traces - Method	Ti...	Time	Tim...	Invoc...
doPrivileged[native] ()		.(12.9%)	7856 ms	449
.ejb.SecurityActions.setContextID ()		.(10.2%)	6243 ms	330
ie.commons.logging.LogFactory.getContextClassLoader ()		.(2.6%)	1562 ms	82
security.SimplePrincipal.equals ()		.(0%)	19.6 ms	1
resource.adapter.jms.JmsCred$GetCredentialAction.getCredential ()		.(0%)	19.5 ms	1
ansport.Transport.serviceCall ()		.(0%)	12.5 ms	30
urity.auth.login.LoginContext.invokePriv ()		.(0%)	0.000...	2

Figure 6.17 Back traces for `java.security.AccessController` from the JEAS 4 profile obtained on the Xeon X5550 based JEE application server

	Time [%]	Time	Time (CPU) ▾	Invocations
doPrivileged[native] ()		4926...(39.5%)	49268 ms	700
:.ejb.SecurityActions.**setConte**		5973... (6.8%)	5973 ms	56
:.security.plugins.authorization.		5426... (6.2%)	5426 ms	49
:.security.plugins.authorization..		3771... (4.3%)	3771 ms	50
:.ejb.plugins.SecurityActions.**ge**		3527... (4%)	3527 ms	32
:.ejb.SecurityActions.**getSecur**		3430... (3.9%)	3430 ms	31
:.ejb.plugins.SecurityActions.**is**		3412... (3.9%)	3412 ms	40
:.ejb.plugins.security.SecurityA(		2724... (3.1%)	2724 ms	25
:.ejb.plugins.PerTxEntityInstanc		2621... (3%)	2621 ms	24
:.security.jacc.SubjectPolicyCon		2491... (2.9%)	2491 ms	21
he.commons.logging.LogFactor		2385... (2.7%)	2385 ms	22
:.ejb.plugins.SecurityActions.**po**		2343... (2.7%)	2343 ms	36
:.security.authorization.modules		1648... (1.9%)	1648 ms	15
:.ejb.plugins.security.SecurityA(		1313... (1.5%)	1313 ms	12
:.ejb.plugins.SecurityActions.**au**		1229... (1.4%)	1229 ms	112
:.security.javaee.AbstractJavaEl		1173... (1.3%)	1173 ms	11
:.ejb.plugins.SecurityActions.**pu**		1099... (1.3%)	1099 ms	20
:.ejb.plugins.security.SecurityA(		934 ... (1.1%)	934 ms	13
:.ejb.plugins.security.SecurityA(		882 ... (1%)	882 ms	9
:.ejb.plugins.security.SecurityA(		809 ... (0.9%)	809 ms	7
:.ejb.plugins.security.SecurityA(		795 ... (0.9%)	795 ms	8
:.ejb.plugins.security.SecurityA(		756 ... (0.9%)	756 ms	7
:.web.tomcat.security.SecurityA		218 ... (0.3%)	218 ms	2
:.ejb.plugins.SecurityActions.**ge**		206 ... (0.2%)	206 ms	2
naming.internal.VersionHelper:		90.0 ... (0.1%)	90.0 ms	1
:.remoting.transport.bisocket.Bi		0.00... (0%)	0.000 ms	1
:urity.auth.login.LoginContext.**in**		0.00... (0%)	0.000 ms	1
ransport.Transport.**serviceCal**		0.00... (0%)	0.000 ms	93

Figure 6.18 Back traces for `java.security.AccessController` from the JEAS 5 profile obtained on the Xeon X5550 based JEE application server

For an enterprise Java application, proper JVM tunings are necessary in addition to profiling in order to achieve the best possible performance and scalability for the application. The next section summarizes the JVM tunings applied to the application in question.

6.4 JVM TUNING

Since VisualVM has very low overhead with its Monitor feature and VisualGC plugin, the full-scale, one-hour duration, 300 concurrent user workload was used to drive all test runs throughout the entire JVM tuning cycle with this same application. If you did not skip the previous sections of this chapter, you should already be familiar with the context of this application. Let us start with the problem quantification directly in the next section.

6.4.1 Quantifying the Performance and Scalability Issues

To simplify, we would not list all performance and scalability test results for all 50 actions averaged over 300 concurrent users from Silk Performer runs with this application. Instead, we look at the response times for the actions contained in one of those five scripts, as shown in Table 6.8. In this table, both average response times and max response times are listed in seconds. Note that as a convention, each action is prefixed with a label like *a01_login* to indicate that it's action #1 of *login*, and so forth. It is seen that the average response times are below 2 seconds for all actions, but the max response times for actions #3 and #5 exceeded six seconds (6.062 and 6.718 seconds, respectively, to be exact). The question was what we could do to help reduce those large response times to help prevent potential customer performance escalations.

Table 6.8 Average/Max Response Times in Seconds for 8 Typical User Actions (300 Concurrent Users, Throughput GC)

Action	Average/Max Response Time (seconds)
a01_login	1.167/1.687
a02_clickPlans	1.191/3.656
a03_clickNew	1.745/**6.602**
a04_Save	0.613/1.078
a05_clickAll	1.574/**6.718**
a06_ManageAssignmentTemplates	0.183/1.734
a07_loadDefaulAssignments	0.177/0.329
a08_logout	0.036/0.063
Average/max	0.913/**6.718**

6.4.2 Baseline with the Throughput GC

To help answer the above question, I have to mention that the test results shown in Table 6.8 were obtained with the default throughput garbage collection algorithm from JDK 1.6.0 update 31 (64-bit) for the JEE application server. Since all throughput garbage collectors are of the *stop-the-world* (STW) collectors, user requests would accumulate when the application execution was suspended in order to let garbage collection tasks complete, resulting in large response times for certain user actions. To help confirm that this is the case, let's take a look at a few VisualVM screenshots taken prior to and at the end of the run.

First, Figure 6.19 shows the Monitor screenshot taken prior to the run. From this figure, note the following interesting statistics:

- **CPU**. From the top left chart, it's seen that CPU activity was close to zero, which means that that server was dedicated to the JEE application server and no other applications were running actively on that machine. This is a necessary condition to help make sure that whatever activities observed on that system were from the application in question alone.
- **Heap**. From the top right chart, it's seen that both min and max heap sizes were set to about 3.2 GB, out of which about 435 MB were used.
- **Classes**. From the lower left chart, it's seen that about 13k classes loaded and no shared classes loaded. This number of 13k classes was the initial number of classes loaded and more would be loaded later.
- **Threads**. From the lower right chart, it's seen that there were 144 *Live* threads with a peak of 148, 39 *Daemon* threads, and 1,164 total started threads. These numbers would increase a lot at the end of the run, as shown shortly.

Next, Figure 6.20 shows the VisualGC screenshot taken prior to the run. From this screenshot, note the *Compile Time* of 22.848s, *Class Loader Time* of 10.338s, *GC Time* of 294.588ms for 6 collections, *GC time* for *Eden* of 260.661ms, and *GC time* for *Old Gen* of 33.926ms. Also, note the size information displayed in the format of (*maxCapacity*, *currentCapacity*): *current in use* for each space. For example, for *Eden Space*, *maxCapacity* and *currentCapacity* were 1 GB and 768 MB, respectively, out of which 262 MB were in use at the instant when the screenshot was taken. You can find similar information for *S0, S1, Old Gen* and *Perm Gen* spaces.

Figure 6.21 shows the Monitor screenshot taken at the end of the run. Notable statistics include:

- **CPU**. From the top left chart, it's seen that average CPU usage was below 20%, despite occasional spikes at various points during the run.
- **Heap**. From the top right chart, note the garbage collection pattern with heap usage peaks close to 3 GB .
- **Classes**. From the lower left chart, it's seen that about 19k classes loaded and no shared classes loaded. Compared with the initial number of 13k classes shown in Figure 6.20, about 6k classes were loaded during the one-hour run. This number of 19k loaded classes can be used as an indicator about the scope or size of the application.
- **Threads**. From the lower right chart, note *total started threads* of 919,425 – almost one million threads started.

Figure 6.22 shows the VisualGC screenshot taken at the end of the run. From this screenshot, note the *Compile Time* of 1m19.620s or *14ms per compile*, *Class Loader Time* of 15.541s or *< 1ms per load*, *GC Time* of 1m30.160s or *65ms per collection* (including both *minor* and *major*), *GC time* for *Eden* of 1m18,855s or *57ms per minor collection*, and *GC time* for *Old Gen* of 11.305s or *2.8s per major collection*. Also, note the current capacity of *Eden*: 903 MB, *S0*: 31 MB, *S1*: 61 MB, *Old Gen*: 2 GB, and *Perm Gen*: 324 MB. The heap usage data available here provides valuable information for setting some parameters when switching from the current throughput collector to the CMS collector, as discussed in the next section. However, before jumping to the next section, let's review once again what we learnt in Chapter 4 about throughput GC versus CMS GC as follows (refer to Tables 4.2 and 4.3):

- Throughput GC
  - Young generation: parallel and copying
  - Old generation: serial or parallel and compacting
- CMS GC
  - Young generation: Parallel and copying (unchanged)
  - Old generation: parallel, concurrent, incremental, but non-compacting

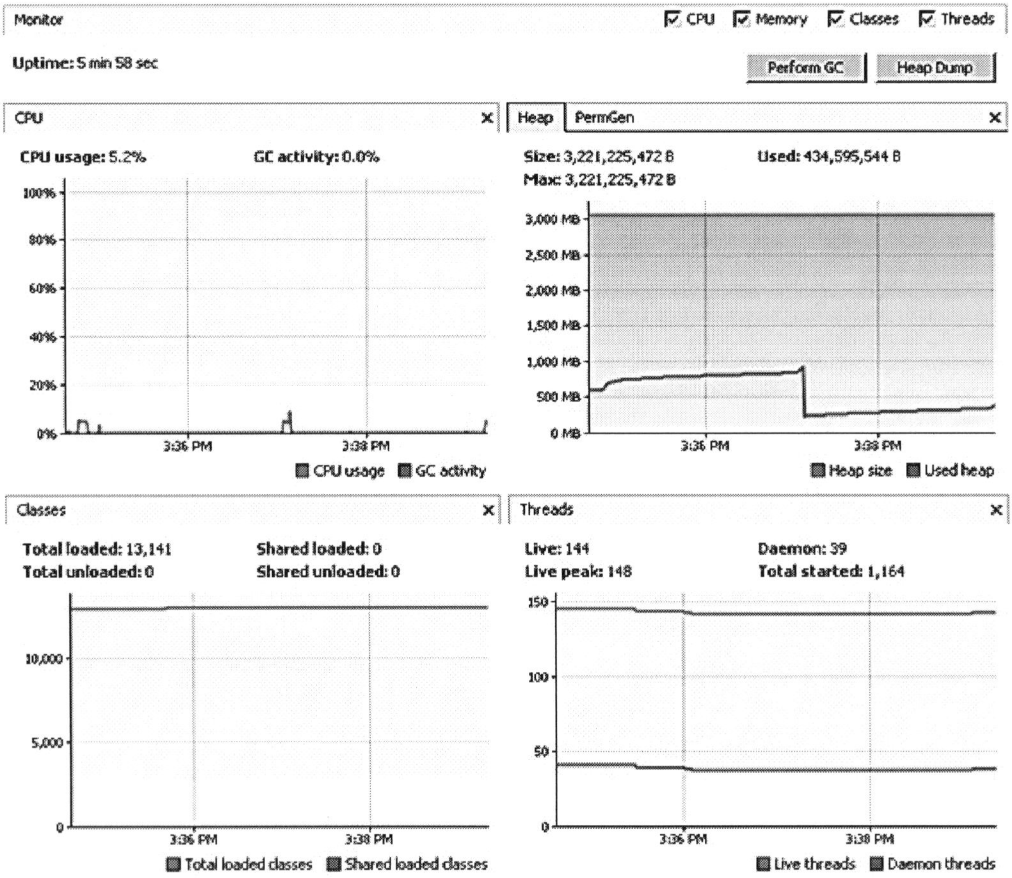

Figure 6.19 *CPU*, *Heap*, *Classes* and *Threads* statistics prior to the run

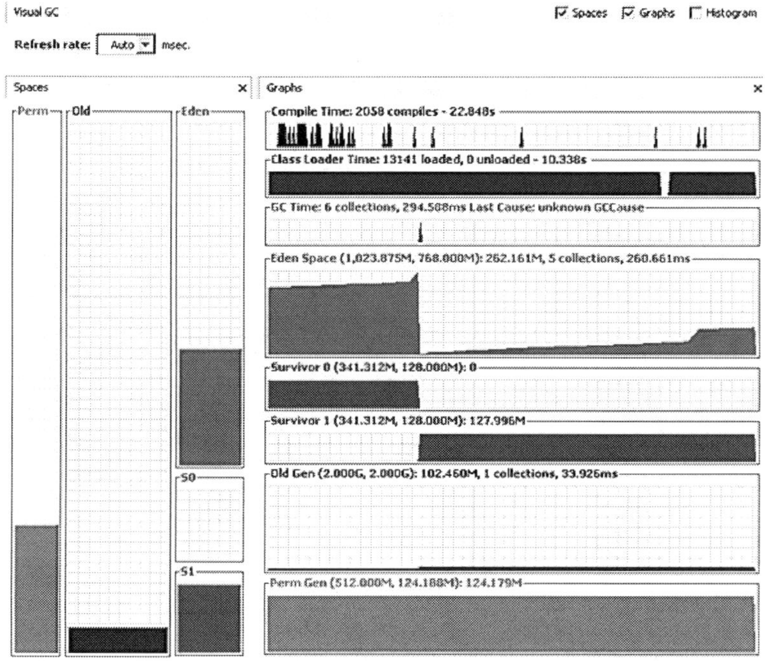

Figure 6.20 *Visual GC* statistics prior to the run

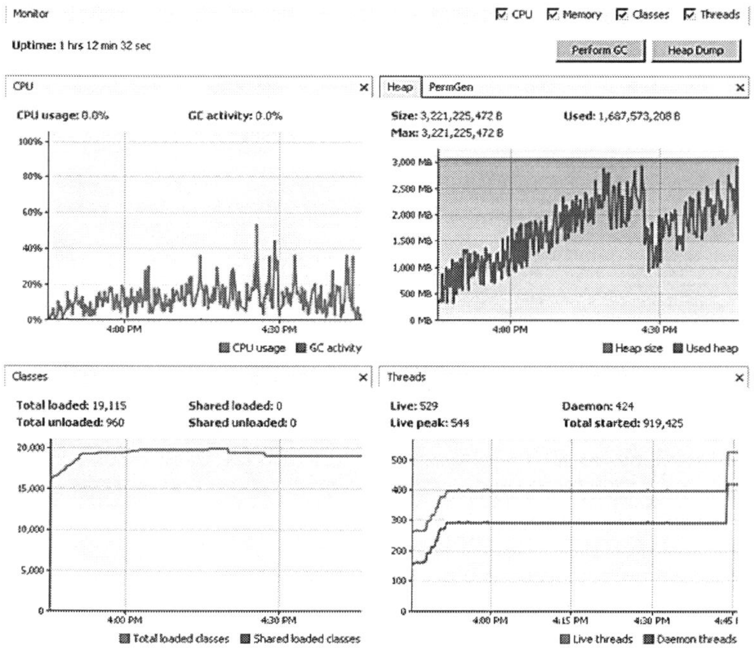

Figure 6.21 *CPU*, *Heap*, *Classes* and *Threads* statistics at the end of the run

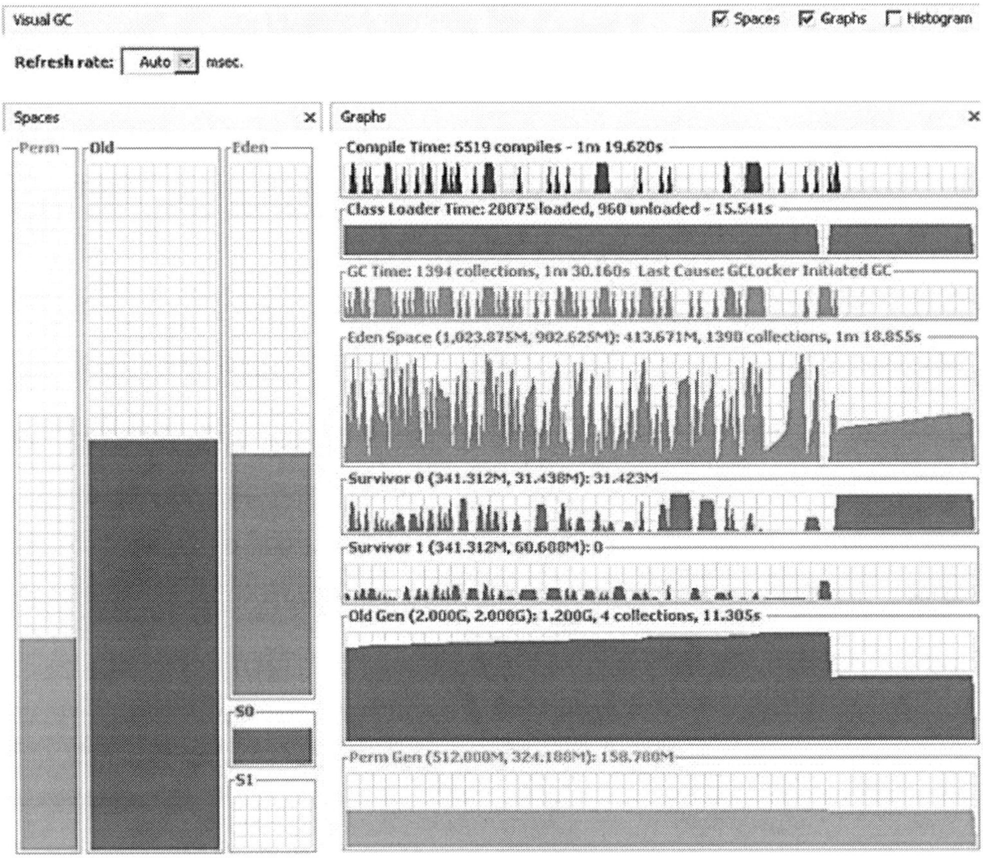

Figure 6.22 *Visual GC* statistics at the end of the run

6.4.3 Switching to the CMS GC

By looking at both the seesaw, fast-climbing GC pattern shown in Figure 6.21 and the large Old Gen average collection time of 2.8 seconds per collection shown in Figure 6.22, it's clear that some GC tunings should be attempted. Since this is an OLTP type of application with online users accessing it, a better choice would be to use the low-latency garbage collector or CMS GC, which could be enabled with the JVM command line option of `–XX:+UseConcMarkSweepGC`. As the JDK used was 1.6.0 update 31, the *oops compression* option was enabled automatically. Also, with `–XX:+UseConcMarkSweepGC` specified, the option `–XX:+UseParNewGC` was enabled automatically as well (this is a multithreaded, stop-the-world, parallel collector for the young generation). The JVM tuning parameters that should be used jointly include:

- –Xmn<n>, which was set to –Xmn1000m based on the *current capacity* information displayed in Figure 6.22 for Eden and Survivor spaces. It was arrived at with (903 + 31 + 61) = 995, which was rounded to 1000.

- –XX:SurvivorRatio=<n>, which was set to –XX:SurvivorRatio=20 based on the *current capacity* information displayed in Figure 6.22 for Eden and Survivor spaces. It was arrived at with 903 / [(31 + 61)/2] = 20.

With the above GC tunings applied, the test was re-conditioned and launched. Table 6.9 shows the average and max response times from this run, in comparison with the baseline run results shown in the second column. It is seen that the max response times of those two actions (a03 and a05) had been cut by 47% and 69%, respectively, or more than 3 seconds and 4.7 seconds were eliminated by replacing the throughput collector with the CMS collector, respectively. The throughput measured in # of transactions per second decreased from 0.59 to 0.58, which was 2% lower only and very insignificant. Also, note from the last row in Table 6.9 that the average response time increased from 0.913 seconds to 0.955 seconds, which was about 5% only and very insignificant. This is the essence of using the CMS GC with a Java-based web application: throughput and average response times are compromised slightly while having large, worst-case response times reduced significantly. This tuning can help prevent your customers from complaining to you that some users experience very bad performance with your application.

Table 6.9 Average/Max Response Times in Seconds for 8 Typical Actions (300 Concurrent Users, Column 2 – Throughput GC, and Column 3 – CMS with –Xmn1000m and –XX:SurvivorRatio=20)

Action	**Throughput GC**	**CMS**
a01_login	1.167/1.687	1.180/1.594
a02_clickPlans	1.191/3.656	1.294/3.672
a03_clickNew	1.745/**6.602**	1.784/**3.531**
a04_save	0.613/1.078	0.641/1.235
a05_clickAll	1.574/**6.718**	1.650/**2.094**
a06_manageAssignmentTemplates	0.183/1.734	0.183/0.718
a07_loadDefaulAssignments	0.177/0.329	0.189/0.391
a08_logout	0.036/0.063	0.040/0.079
Average/amx	0.913/**6.718**	0.955/**3.672**

Figures 6.23 and 6.24 show the Monitor and VisualGC screenshots corresponding to this run, respectively. The charts on the Monitor page remained similar, while the statistics on the VisualGC page had changed, due to switching to the CMS collector. See Table 6.10 for a comparison of average GC times between the throughput collector and the CMS collector. It is seen that average major GC time had decreased from 2800 ms to 595 ms, while the # of major collections increased from four to six.

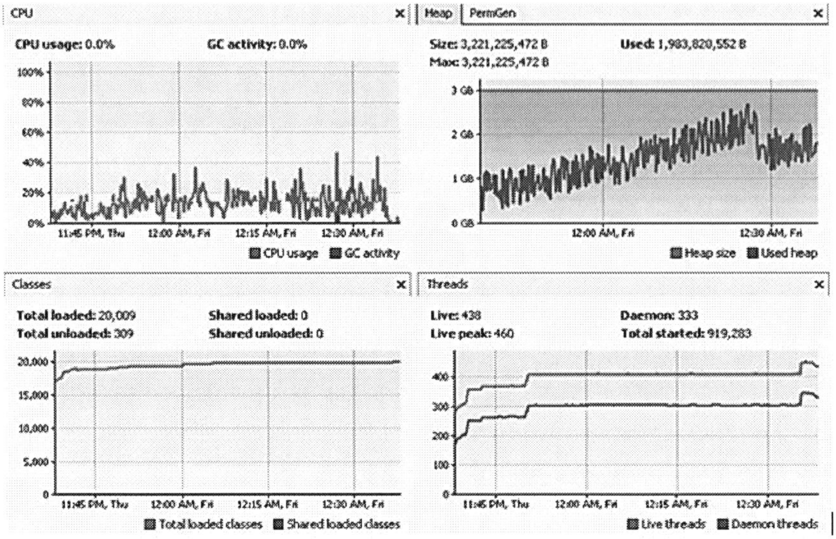

Figure 6.23 *CPU*, *Heap*, *Classes* and *Threads* statistics at the end of the run using the CMS garbage collector (`-XX:+UseConcMarkSweepGC -Xmn1000m -XX:SurvivorRatio=20`)

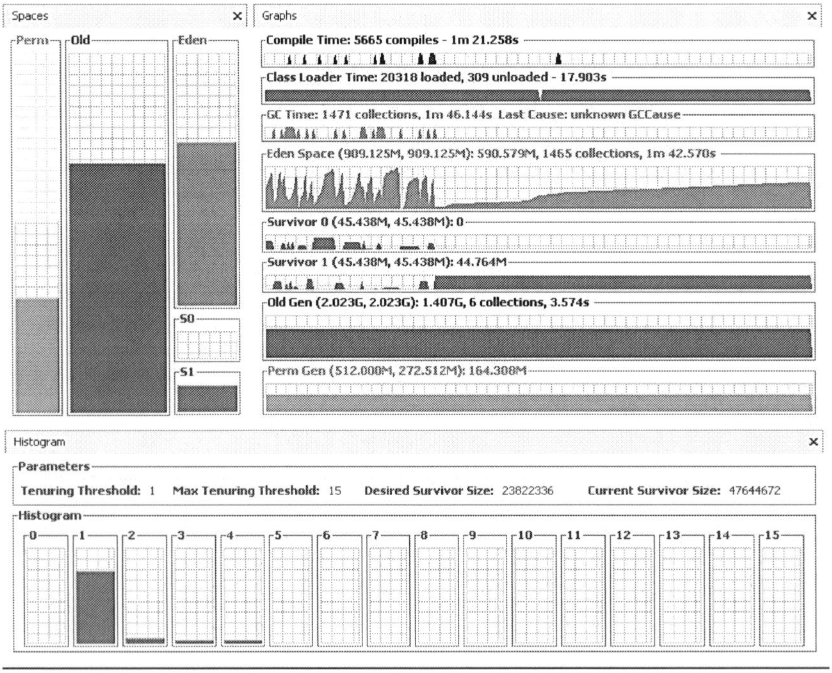

Figure 6.24 *VisualGC* statistics at the end of the run with `-XX:+UseConcMarkSweepGC -Xmn1000m -XX:SurvivorRatio=20`

Table 6.10 Average GC Time Comparison between the Throughput and CMS Garbage Collectors

Collection	Throughput GC	CMS GC
Total (minor + major)	65 ms	72ms
Eden (minor)	57 ms	70 ms
Old Gen (major)	2800 ms	595 ms

6.4.4 Verifying the Parameters Used In Conjunction with `-XX:+UseConcMarkSweepGC`

To see the effects of the two parameters of `-Xmn` and `-XX:SurvivorRatio`, one additional run was conducted with the CMS collector by changing the other two parameters from `-Xmn1000m and -XX:SurvivorRatio=20` to `-Xmn944m and -XX:SurvivorRatio=24`. The average/max response times with all these three runs are updated in Table 6.11.

Table 6.11 Average/Max Response Times in Seconds for 8 Typical Actions (300 Concurrent Users, Column 2 – Throughput GC, Column 3 – CMS with –Xmn1000m and –XX:SurvivorRatio=20, and Column 4 with –Xmn944m and –XX:SurvivorRatio=24)

Action	Throughput GC	CMS (#1)	CMS (#2)
a01_login	1.167/1.687	1.180/1.594	1.107/3.203
a02_clickPlans	1.191/3.656	1.294/3.672	1.237/3.453
a03_clickNew	1.745/**6.602**	1.784/**3.531**	1.784/**3.109**
a04_save	0.613/1.078	0.641/1.235	0.638/1.828
a05_clickAll	1.574/**6.718**	1.650/**2.094**	1.626/**3.297**
a06_manageAssignmentTemplates	0.183/1.734	0.183/0.718	0.179/0.360
a07_loadDefaulAssignments	0.177/0.329	0.189/0.391	0.188/1.000
a08_logout	0.036/0.063	0.040/0.079	0.047/0.078
Average/max	0.913/**6.718**	0.955/**3.672**	0.937/**3.453**

With CMS run #2, the throughput reported by Silk was 0.59 transactions/s, which was the same as run #1. Those large max response times resulting from the throughput GC had been reduced more than half similarly, although not significantly different from the CMS run #1, which means that the JVM tunings of `-XX:+UseConcMarkSweepGC -Xmn1000m -XX:Survivorratio=20` could be retained for this application.

For comparison purposes, Figures 6.25 and 6.26 show the Monitor and VisualGC screenshots from the second CMS run described above, respectively. The average GC times for all those three runs are updated in Table 6.12. It is seen that the average per collection time for the Old Gen space had increased from 595 ms with the first CMS run to 683 ms with the second CMS run. It appears that the method for calculating the values for `-Xmn` and `-XX:SurvivorRatio` parameters described previously is effective.

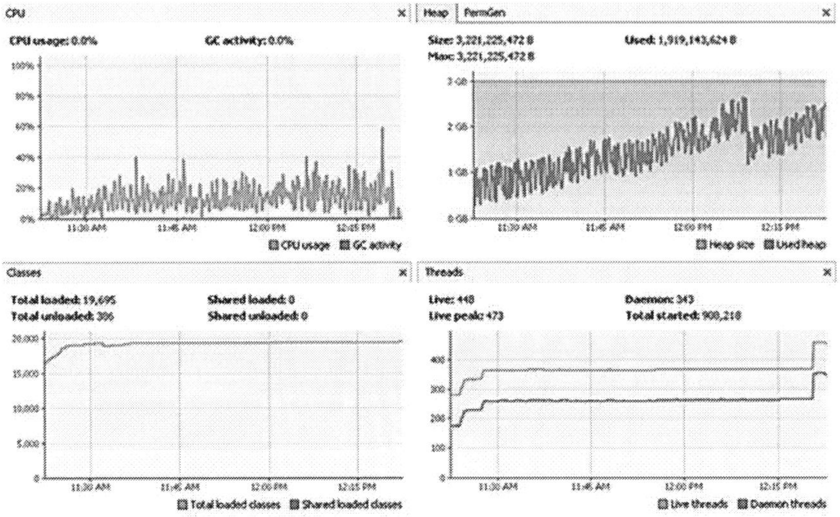

Figure 6.25 *CPU*, *Heap*, *Classes* and *Threads* statistics at the end of the run `-XX:+UseConcMarkSweepGC -Xmn944m -XX:SurvivorRatio=24`

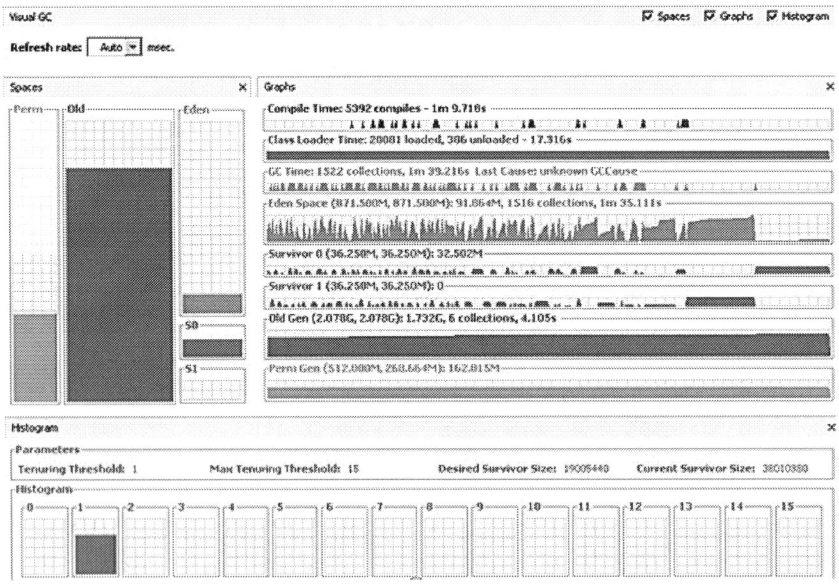

Figure 6.26 *VisualGC* statistics at the end of the run with `-XX:+UseConcMarkSweepGC -Xmn944m -XX:SurvivorRatio=24`

Table 6.12 Average GC Time Comparison between the Throughput and CMS Garbage Collectors

Collection	Throughput	CMS GC (#1)	CMS (#2)
Total (minor + major)	65 ms	72ms	65 ms
Eden (minor)	57 ms	70 ms	63 ms
Old Gen (major)	2800 ms	595 ms	683 ms

Since the JVM tunings were performed with a specific workload of 300 concurrent users, it's necessary to conduct scalability tests further to help understand better on:

- How this application would scale with more concurrent users.
- Eventually on what resources the application would be bottlenecked.
- What additional measures can be taken to make the application even more scalable.

The next section covers systematical tunings to help answer the above questions.

6.5 SYSTEMATICAL TUNINGS FOR BEST POSSIBLE PERFORMANCE AND SCALABILITY

For an enterprise Java application, the ultimate goal is to deliver best possible performance and scalability while meeting all functional requirements for customers. Best possible performance and scalability don't just come as a windfall. Instead, it requires substantial, systematic tunings at all levels and from all perspectives. This section serves as an example about how to carry out such a process for your reference. It covers the following topics:

- Establishing a solid baseline
- Quantifying your baseline
- JDBC tunings
- Sizing thread pools
- JVM statistics

Let us begin with establishing a solid baseline next.

6.5.1 Establishing a Solid Baseline

Establishing a baseline means more than just an initial, out of the box run with all default configuration settings. It should include the following items:

- *Use Cases and Load Test Scripts*. You need to have a well-defined list of use cases and quality load test scripts to actually drive your performance and scalability tests.
- *Data Volume, Representativeness and Validity*. You need to have data properly populated into your database, which is not only sufficiently large in volume but also representative of what most of your customers would have in their production environment. Your data must be valid so that it would not drive out torrents of exceptions and errors to make your test results erroneous and invalid.
- The systems under test should be properly sized. Depending on whether your application is CPU-bound, I/O-bound, memory-bound, or network-bound, you should have taken proper measures so

that you would not conduct your performance and scalability tests in a test environment that can only support a few concurrent users. Also, your environment should not have limitations that customer's environment doesn't. For example, try to avoid using a single local disk to store your entire data for your database. Customers typically use SANs in their production environment.

- You should already know all tunable knobs with your application, including both application specific configuration settings and various performance and scalability sensitive settings with various server systems, for example, settings specific to the performance and scalability of your Web server, database server, application server, and other edge systems with your test environment.

Assuming that you have taken care of all the items as summarized above, establish a baseline with a neither too light nor too heavy workload. Then quantify your baseline run really well, as illustrated next.

6.5.2 Quantifying the Baseline

We already know that batch jobs are measured in throughput, whereas OLTP applications are measured in user response times. Although the metric of throughput is also used for benchmarking OLTP applications, it's more appropriate to use the metric of response times to benchmark OLTP applications. Online users do not perceive whether an application is fast based on throughput or the number of requests the system can support. Instead, they perceive whether an application or a website is fast or slow based on the response times or how fast the system can respond to their requests with responses they expect.

In addition, even if you use response times to quantify the performance and scalability of your Java application, there are a few different methods to quantify. For example:

- One can use a single number of an overall average response time as a single metric, averaged over response times from all users. This method is acceptable sometimes, for example, in evaluating the performance regression or improvement of your application internally from one release to another.
- Sometimes, the method of using a single metric is insufficient. This is especially true when you need to generate a customer-oriented report to demonstrate how your application would perform and scale under different load levels typically measured in number of concurrent users. In this case, rather than giving one number like the average response time of the application is n seconds for m concurrent users, it's necessary to come up with a subset of actions that customers would be most interested in and report the response times on a per-action basis. This can be done easily with a commercial-quality load test tool like Silk Performer, which allows custom timers to be inserted into a script during the process of recording a script. Then, after a run is complete, it can report the timing statistics specific to those custom timers built into the load test scripts. This is my so-called *action-oriented load testing approach*, which emphasizes more on the response times of user actions rather than throughput like # of transactions per second or hits per second for OLTP-type of applications.

Using the same EJB-based enterprise web application as we have used in the previous sections of this chapter, we established a baseline within the following periphery:

- The workload consists of five scripts, each of which simulates a specific uses case. Each script has custom timers built in for measuring various user actions, with each action measured as a whole with a corresponding custom timer rather than a series of individual HTTP requests. A different number of concurrent users were assigned to each script, with a total summed up to 300 for this baseline run.

- The Silk Performer queuing workload model was used with the specified workload. This model simulates an equilibrium condition with an hourly, per-user steady transaction rate assigned to the main transaction of each script. A user logins first in a *TInit* transaction, performs the actions specified in the *TMain* transaction part of the script *n* times where *n* is an hourly, single-user transaction rate, and finally logs out in the *TEnd* transaction.
- The most critical system was the JEE application server as we mentioned previously. It was a Xeon X5550-based, two quad-cores @ 2.67 GHz, hyper-threaded, 64-bit Windows 2008 server. The 64-bit JDK 1.6.0 update 31 was used throughout the tests presented in this section.

Table 6.13 shows the baseline average response times for a subset of user actions, obtained with a 300 concurrent user run over a one-hour period. The last row represents the response time averaged over these 14 actions. The total CPU utilizations averaged over the last 50 minutes for the JEE application server, Oracle database server, and the authentication server were 16.5%, 0.4%, and 4.4%, respectively.

Table 6.13 Baseline Average Response Times for a Subset of User Actions

Action	Average Response Time (Seconds)
a00_login	1.034
a01_saveNewPlan	0.634
a02_loadDefaultAssignments	0.182
a03_searchPlan	0.789
a04_saveNewLineItem	0.383
a05_saveAttachment	0.237
a06_saveNewAssignment	1.328
a07_loadAssignment	0.966
a08_viewAssignment	0.287
a09_saveNewScope	2.37
a10_saveMyPage	0.545
a11_searchScope	0.155
a12_analyzingMerits	2.052
a13_viewPlanStatistics	2.079
average	**0.93**

Figure 6.27 shows the relevant Oracle Application Workload Repository (AWR) report segments collected during this baseline run. The purpose for including these screenshots is to show that the database is not a bottleneck at all so that we could focus on finding issues in other places.

Cache Sizes

	Begin	End		
Buffer Cache:	1,344M	1,344M	Std Block Size:	8K
Shared Pool Size:	2,496M	2,496M	Log Buffer:	34,104K

Top 5 Timed Foreground Events

Event	Waits	Time(s)	Avg wait (ms)	% DB time	Wait Class
DB CPU		1,566		99.63	
SQL*Net message to client	7,958,480	14	0	0.92	Network
latch: cache buffers chains	6,835	7	1	0.45	Concurrency
enq: TX - row lock contention	27	7	244	0.42	Application
log file sync	11,474	3	0	0.19	Commit

Memory Statistics

	Begin	End
Host Mem (MB):	15,951.8	15,951.8
SGA use (MB):	4,160.0	4,160.0
PGA use (MB):	160.8	283.6
% Host Mem used for SGA+PGA:	27.09	27.86

SQL ordered by Elapsed Time

- Resources reported for PL/SQL code includes the resources used by all SQL statements called by the code.
- % Total DB Time is the Elapsed Time of the SQL statement divided into the Total Database Time multiplied by 100
- %Total - Elapsed Time as a percentage of Total DB time
- %CPU - CPU Time as a percentage of Elapsed Time
- %IO - User I/O Time as a percentage of Elapsed Time
- Captured SQL account for 47.1% of Total DB Time (s): 1,572
- Captured PL/SQL account for 7.5% of Total DB Time (s): 1,572

Elapsed Time (s)	Executions	Elapsed Time per Exec (s)	%Total	%CPU	%IO	SQL Id	SQL Module
114.47	5	22.89	7.28	99.92	0.00	a8r4t201tuuvq	JDBC Thin Client
101.29	2,832	0.04	6.44	99.13	0.00	4by16qwsdy9tv	JDBC Thin Client
89.30	1,025	0.09	5.68	99.92	0.00	0yqtu8xpp15k3	JDBC Thin Client
40.50	3,052	0.01	2.58	96.97	0.00	dncm9h1r81s7z	JDBC Thin Client
39.35	410,307	0.00	2.50	95.84	0.00	48xvudqm4ywb8	JDBC Thin Client
36.81	374	0.10	2.34	95.87	0.00	4m0hczqyxnqhr	JDBC Thin Client
28.34	508,833	0.00	1.80	96.52	0.00	8fysjyj01qqjb	JDBC Thin Client

Figure 6.27 Oracle AWR report statistics collected during the baseline run

Figure 6.28 shows the Monitor view at the end of the baseline run. Note the CPU and GC patterns shown for this baseline run. Becoming familiar with the GC patterns with your application can help you become proficient with tuning your JVM for best possible performance and scalability for your application.

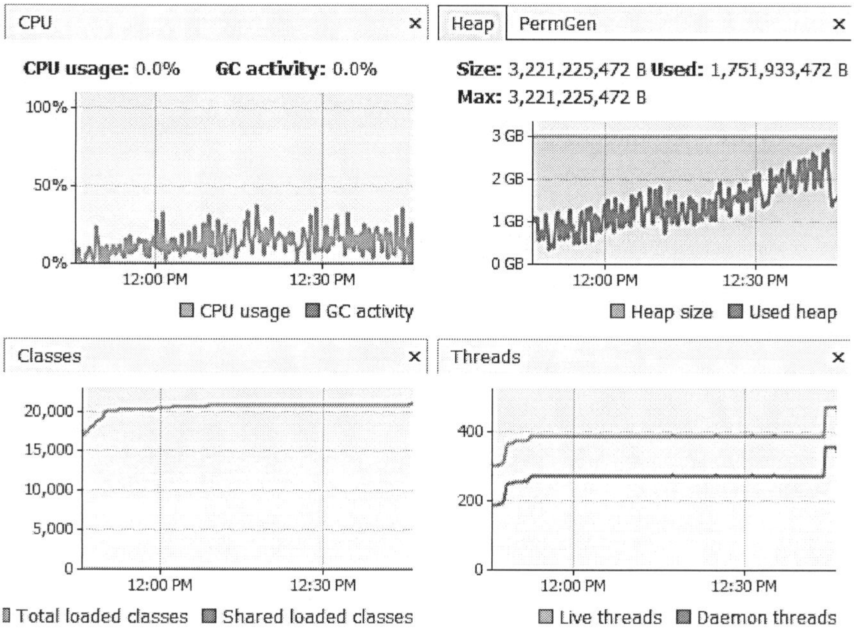

Figure 6.28 VisualVM Monitor view taken at the end of the baseline run

6.5.3 JDBC Tunings

JDBC (Java Database Connectivity) is a generic connection protocol used for communications between a Java application server and a database server. JDBC connection pools are tunable with various parameters externalized in an XML configuration file. Typically, two JDBC connection pools are available: A local transaction pool and a distributed or global transaction pool. A local transaction pool is used when only one database resource is involved, whereas a global transaction pool is used when multiple database resources are involved, in which case, the concept of two-phase commit gets into the picture. It's important to make sure that an XA pool is not used unless absolutely needed from a performance perspective.

With this application in question, at the time of testing, only the XA JDBC pool was used. Listing 6.1 shows the portion of the distributed or global tx data source. Listing 6.2 shows additional tunable JDBC connection pool parameters that apply to both local and global pools.

JDBC connection pool tunings may include the following attributes:

- **<min-pool-size>**. This attribute specifies a minimum number of connections to set up initially. Somehow, this JEE application server seems to create twice the min-pool-size connections at start-up. Check this out with your application server.

- **<max-pool-size>**. This attribute specifies an upper limit to the number of connections that can be maintained in the pool. To be safe, you can specify a large number without causing performance overhead, as the extraneous connections are not created if they are not needed. Somehow, this JEE application server seems to create more than max-pool-size connections if needed. Check this out with your application server.
- **<track-statements>**. If this parameter is set to true, the application server takes care of closing Statements and ResultSet if they are not coded to be closed explicitly in the application.
- **<blocking-timeout-millis>**. This attribute specifies a maximum amount of time in milliseconds to block while waiting for a connection before throwing an exception. The default value is 5000.
- **<idle-timeout-minutes>**. This attribute specifies a maximum amount of idle time in minutes before a connection is closed if it's not used.
- **<prepared-statement-cache-size>**. This attribute specifies the number of Statements to be cached and reused *per connection* in the application server.
- **<shared-prepared-statements>**. This attribute specifies that if two requests are executed in the same transaction the prepared statement cache should return the same statement. It should be used jointly with the preceding attribute.
- **defaultFetchSize.** This parameter specifies how many rows to fetch with a query in a single round trip. The default value is 10. So if you have 50 rows to fetch, 5 round trips would be needed. It is equivalent to the ARRAY SIZE concept in Oracle. Keep in mind that a too large fetch size may incur out of memory (OOM) errors.
- **tcp....** There are a few TCP related tuning parameters as specified in Listing 6.3. The default TCP packet size is 32 kB, and doubling it to 64 kB or larger may help sometimes.

These JDBC tunings were actually attempted with the application in question, and only a 5% performance improvement was observed, which is insignificant. This was expected because this application was not bottlenecked on the database. The tunable JDBC parameters are included here just in case your application uses JDBC and is database intensive so that you know what to tune on your JDBC connection pools.

Listing 6.1 Global Transaction Datasource Defined in oracle-xa-ds.xml

```
<datasources>
 <xa-datasource>
  ......
   <min-pool-size>20</min-pool-size>
   <max-pool-size>1520</max-pool-size>
   <blocking-timeout-millis>5000</blocking-timeout-millis>
   <idle-timeout-minutes>15</idle-timeout-minutes>
    ......
</datasources>
```

Listing 6.2 Additional Tunable JDBC Pool Parameters

```
<!-- additional JDBC tunings -->

   <prepared-statement-cache-size>30</prepared-statement-cache-size>
```

```
<shared-prepared-statements>true</shared-prepared-statements>
<connection-property name="defaultFetchSize">50</connection-property>
<connection-property name="tcpSndBuf">65534</connection-property>
<connection-property name="tcpRcvBuf">65534</connection-property>
<connection-property name="tcpNoDelayBuf">true</connection-property>
```

6.5.4 Sizing Thread Pools with PSI-Probe and VisualVM

Since this application is JEE-based and uses JDBC to connect to the backend Oracle database, it's important to quantify how many threads and JDBC connections are actually used during a test run. Table 6.14 lists the pools that are pertinent to this application.

Table 6.14 Thread Pools Associated with the Application

Pool	Purpose
HTTP thread pool	Handling HTTP requests
AJP thread pool	Clustered Web server (not used)
JDBC connection pool	Connecting to backend database

To help size these pools, it's necessary to monitor how many threads or connections are in use with each of these pools. Different JEE application servers may provide different tools for tuning application server specific thread pools. However, typically, JEE thread pools such as system pools, JMS pools, etc., require no tuning at all. The only thread pools that need to be tuned are the HTTP thread pools and JDBC connection pools as listed in Table 6.14. Next, I will demonstrate how to use third party tools such as the PSI-Probe and VisualVM to help size these pools.

PSI-Probe is intended to be an advanced manager and monitor for Apache Tomcat. You can also make it work easily with some of the JEE application servers. This is a very useful tool for monitoring HTTP and JDBC pools. Consult PSI-Probe's website about how to install PSI-Probe to work with your application server.

After your *Probe* is up and running, check out the following items:

- Under the *Applications* tab, locate your Web application and check out the number under the column of `SESS.`, which indicates how many sessions are open with your application.
- Under the *Data Sources* tab, locate your data sources and check out the numbers under the M, E, and B columns, which represent the **M**aximum number of connections in the pool, the number of **E**stablished connections that can be reused, and the number of **B**usy connections that are not available for re-use.
- Under the *Threads* tab, you can flip the icon right below the Applications tab to see `Running Threads` or `Thread Pools`. The `Thread Pools` page lists `CURRENT THREAD COUNT`, `CURRENT THREADS BUSY`, and `MAX THREADS` for your HTTP and AJP pools.

You can also find similar information with VisualVM using the procedure described below (except the JDBC pool), which works but is slightly inconvenient. First, take an application snapshot and a thread dump near the end of your test, copy/paste the thread dump content displayed on your VisualVM into a text file, and make the following queries on an MS-DOS command prompt:

- **HTTP Thread Pool**: `find /c "http-" <yourThreadDumpfile>`
- **Application Thread Pool**: `find /c "Thread-" <yourThreadDumpfile>`
- **JEE System Thread Pool**: `find /c "System Threads" <yourThreadDumpfile>`
- **JCA Thread Pool**: `find /c "JMS SessionPool Worker-" <yourThreadDumpfile>`
- **Total # of threads**: `find /c "nid=" <yourThreadDumpfile>`

Table 6.15 shows the thread pool usage associated with the baseline run presented in this section, with the max pool size configured given as well when applicable. Note that pools sizes in decreasing order are HTTP thread pool, application thread pool, JDBC pool, JCA pool, and system thread pool.

Table 6.15 Thread Pool Usage Associated with the Baseline Run

Pool	Used/Max	Monitored With
HTTP thread pool	303/2400	VisualVM
System thread pool	2/16	VisualVM
JCA thread pool	5/100	VisualVM
Application	101/NA	VisualVM
Total	493/NA	VisualVM
JDBC connection pool (XA)	M:200|E:40|B:6 /(20/200)	PSI-Probe

Figure 6.29 shows the thread pool snapshot taken at the beginning, mid-point, and end of the run with PSI-Probe. From top to bottom in each snapshot are a JDBC XA pool, System Thread Pool, JCA pool, and a JDBC local pool that was not used by the application). For the JDBC XA pool, the minimum pool size was 20 and the JEE application server created 40 established connections at start-up. This peculiarity needs to be taken into account when setting the min/max pool size for a JDBC pool.

Figure 6.29 Thread pools monitored with PSI-Probe at the beginning, mid-point, and the end of the run

Next, we take a look at the JVM statistics associated with the baseline run, before we discuss more about how to tune these pools as a part of scalability testing.

6.5.5 JVM Statistics

After each run, it's important to take a look at how the JVM performed. Such information is available from VisualVM's VisualGC view at the end of a run. Instead of showing the screenshot of a VisualGC view, Table 6.16 shows various timings characterizing various JVM activities for this baseline run. It is seen that the average times for Eden and Old Gen collections are 63 ms and 457 ms, respectively.

Table 6.16 JVM activities associated with the baseline run

Activity	Count	Total Time	Average Time (ms)
Compile	5669	1m15.24s	13
Class Loader	21504	17.16s	0.8
GC (all)	1467	1m36s	65
Eden	1461	1m33s	63
Old Gen	6	2.742s	457

6.6 SCALABILITY TESTING

After establishing a solid baseline with 300 concurrent users on a high-end Xeon X5550-based system for the JEE application server, it's time to push the envelope with more concurrent users to see ultimately how many concurrent users the product can support with this given environment. This would provide customers with a reference point for them to deploy the product in their production environment. In addition, we would continue to optimize and tune in order to achieve truly best performance and scalability for the product. I will share some detailed procedures along the way in case you want to use them for your own project as well.

One procedure followed consistently throughout all tests was to recondition the test environment prior to each run. The steps for reconditioning the test environment include:

- Restoring the same database dump so that all runs would be re-calibrated to the same start point. Since the database was Oracle, it means dropping users and importing an analyzed dump with same data restored.
- Restarting the authentication server. This is required as the authentication server authenticates users against the database.
- Restarting the JEE application server.
- Resetting the number of concurrent users in Silk Performer.
- Re-attaching VisualVM to the newly started JEE application server process.
- Restarting PSI-Probe to get ready for monitoring the application session, JDBC connection pool and the HTTP thread pool.
- Taking an Oracle snapshot for generating an AWR report for the run to be launched.

- Starting up *Perfmon* on the Windows systems for the authentication server and the JEE application server as well as executing the command of "`vmstat -t -n 10 420 -SM >run_xxxx.txt`" on the Linux system for Oracle to collect system resource utilization data for post-analysis of the run. All *Perfmon* jobs should be configured with a stop condition of roughly 10 minutes longer than the test duration.
- Launching the run on Silk Performer Workbench.
- Jotting down the # of errors and # of concurrent connections on Silk Performer Workbench roughly every 5 minutes.
- Jotting down the # of sessions, JDBC connection pool max/established/busy connections, and HTTP thread pool count/busy/max using PSI-Probe roughly every 5 minutes.
- At the end of the run, do the following:
    - Taking another Oracle AWR snapshot.
    - Take a thread dump and an application snapshot on VisualVM for offline analysis. Also, take a screenshot of the VisualGC view on VisualVM for offline JVM activity analysis as well.
    - Saving the Silk result into an HTML file so that it would be easier to examine offline.
    - Generating an AWR report in HTML format.
    - Gathering all data into one place on a system for book-keeping purposes.

To save some time, you can start to recondition your test environment while you examine your test results and decide what to do next. Because of the large volume of data, it took me about 30 minutes to recondition my test environment.

Next, we take a look at how the application performed and scaled with 500 and 700 concurrent users, relative to the baseline of 300 concurrent users. Note that with these additional three runs, the only variable was the number of concurrent users. Then we would settle down on 700 concurrent users and see how we could optimize and tune further to the point when no more performance bits could be squeezed out.

The scalability testing results are presented in the following sequence:

- Average response times
- System resource utilizations
- JVM activity analysis
- Thread pool analysis
- Database activity analysis
- Fine-tuning JDBC connection pool
- Further tuning with JVM options –XX:+AggressiveOpts and –XX:+DoEscapeAnalysis
- Scaling beyond
- Trials with G1 GC

6.6.1 Average Response Times

Our first concern was how the average response time would degrade with more concurrent users accessing the application. Table 6.17 shows the results for 300 (baseline), 500, and 700 concurrent users.

It is seen that without further optimization, the application could support up to 500 concurrent users with good response times.

Table 6.17 Average Response Times in Seconds for a Subset of User Actions out of Three Runs with 300 (baseline), 500 and 700 Concurrent Users

Action	**300**	**500**	**700**
a00_login	1.034	1.041	1.050
a01_saveNewPlan	0.634	0.738	1.063
a02_loadDefaultAssignments	0.182	0.218	0.325
a03_searchPlan	0.789	1.101	2.472
a04_saveNewLineItem	0.383	0.538	0.721
a05_saveAttachment	0.237	0.286	0.406
a06_saveNewAssignment	1.328	1.708	8.393
a07_loadAssignment	0.966	1.115	1.35
a08_viewAssignment	0.287	0.369	0.514
a09_saveNewScope	2.37	2.8	3.436
a10_saveMyPage	0.545	0.616	0.895
a11_searchScope	0.155	0.199	0.323
a12_analyzingMerits	2.052	2.295	6.471
a13_viewPlanStatistics	2.079	2.343	3.048
average	**0.93**	**1.10**	**2.18**

The 500 concurrent user data point is good as the JEE application server used was a mid-range 8 core system only. With a 16-core system based on the identical CPUs, the application could potentially support up to 1000 concurrent users. However, we would not just stop here – we would continue to optimize and tune so that the application might be capable of supporting up to 700 concurrent users with this same hardware for the JEE application server. If that happens, customers would not have to spend extra on a more powerful system for the JEE application server. This requires carefully analyzing the test results and look for opportunities to improve the performance and scalability of the application further. We start by looking at the system resource utilizations next.

6.6.2 System Resource Utilizations

Figure 6.30 shows CPU and heap GC patterns with 300, 500, and 700 concurrent users from top to bottom. It's seen that the average CPU utilizations went beyond 80% with 700 concurrent users, which explains why average response time was high with this test run. We will see how we can reduce it later in this section.

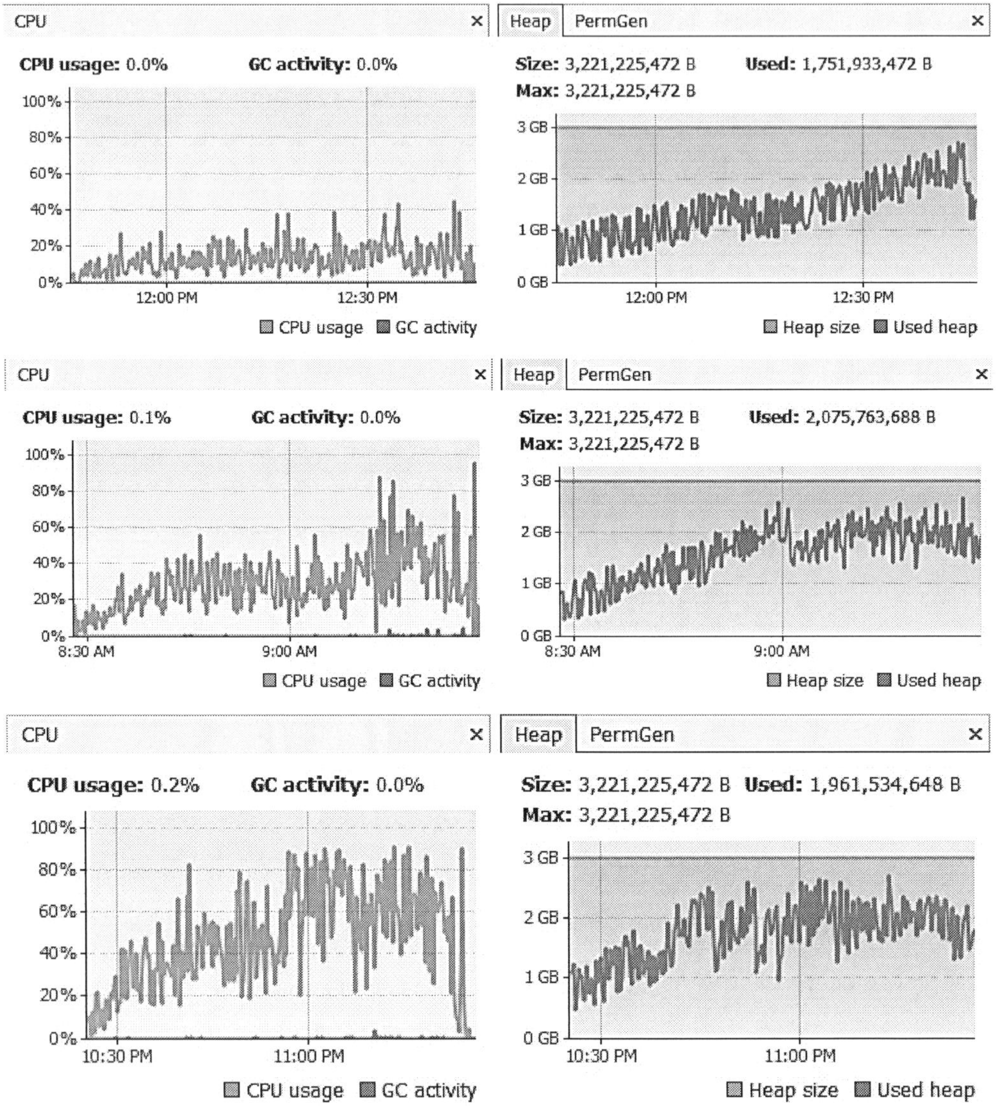

Figure 6.30 CPU and Heap GC patterns with 300, 500, and 700 concurrent users from top to bottom

6.6.3 JVM Activity Analysis

Tables 6.18 to 6.21 show average compile times, class loading times, Eden and Old Gen GC times with those three runs of 300, 500, and 700 concurrent users. It's seen that a minor collection in the young generation space took about 66 ms, while a major collection in the old generation space took about 540 ms on average. Note that the # of major collections in the old generation region increased significantly as the number of concurrent users increased from 300 through 500 to 700, as shown in Figure 6.21, which is due to rapidly increased contention levels associated with increasing number of threads.

Table 6.18 JVM Compile Activities with Increasing # of Concurrent Users

Metric	300	500	700
Count	5669	5965	6670
Total Time	1m15.24s	1m29.8s	1m42.73s
Average Time	13 ms	15 ms	15 ms

Table 6.19 JVM ClassLoader Activities with Increasing # of Concurrent Users

Metric	300	500	700
Count	21503	21563	21709
Total Time	17.16s	17.6	16s
Average Time	0.8 ms	0.8 ms	0.7ms

Table 6.20 JVM Eden GC Activities with Increasing # of Concurrent Users

Metric	300	500	700
Count	1467	2700	3685
Total Time	1m36s	3m38s	4m4.7s
Average Time	63 ms	81 ms	66 ms

Table 6.21 JVM Old Gen GC Activities with Increasing # of Concurrent Users

Metric	300	500	700
Count	6	57	137
Total Time	2.742s	37.9s	1m11s
Average Time	457 ms	665 ms	518s

The next section summarizes thread pool analysis based on the data collected during those three runs. The analysis helps size various pools properly as we will see.

6.6.4 Thread Pool Analysis

In this section, we present the thread pool statistics sampled manually with PSI-Probe roughly every five minutes during each run, along with the maximum number of concurrent connections reported at the same time by Silk Performer. It is important to understand that a load test tool emulates Web browsers with the concept of virtual users. Each virtual user may have multiple concurrent TCP/IP connections to the Web server, depending on which browser it emulates. For example, Microsoft Internet Explorer 6 and 7 could have at most 4 HTTP 1.0 connections and 2 HTTP 1.1 connections, whereas IE 8 and Fire Fox 3 could have at most 6 connections for both HTTP 1.0 and HTTP 1.1 protocols.

Table 6.22 shows the maximum number of concurrent connections reported by Silk Performer as well as the maximum number of application sessions, maximum global JDBC Established and Busy connections, and maximum HTTP thread pool count and busy, all reported by the tool of PSI-Probe, for the 500 and 700 concurrent user runs.

Table 6.22 Maximum Connections, Application Sessions, and Threads Observed During 500 and 700 Concurrent User Runs

Pool	500	700
Concurrent Connections	1229	1654
Sessions	538	896
JDBC XA Established/Busy Connections	88/9	132/52
HTTP Current Thread Count/Busy	510/407	730/533

Note that in Table 6.22, we cannot simply configure the maximum concurrent connections and application sessions in external files, as they are determined by the number of virtual users specified in a Silk Performer load test run. The JDBC connection and HTTP thread pools, however, can be configured externally. For these runs, the min/max pool size for JDBC XA pool were set to 20/200, and the max pool size for HTTP thread pool was set to 2400. For JDBC XA pool, the maximum number of established connections exceeded the min size of 20 with all three runs, which means that the min pool size should be elevated. The undersized JDBC XA connection pool would be corrected later based on the analysis here. We will refer back to this analysis when we get there in the section of *Fine-Tuning JDBC pool* later.

Also, we lifted the `maxThreads` setting for the HTTP thread pool from its default value of 250 to 2400, because we already knew that 250 would be insufficient.

Next, we present database activity analysis associated with these runs.

6.6.5 Database Activity Analysis

Although this application was not bottlenecked on the backend database, it doesn't mean that there is no need to perform a database activity analysis. Since this application had a backend database on Oracle 11g R2, the most useful performance trouble-shooting tool would be the Oracle AWR report. Figures 6.31 through 6.33 show the top five timed events from the AWR reports for 300, 500, and 700 concurrent user runs. As is seen, with 700 concurrent users, the *enq: TX – row lock contention* event had an average wait time of 10.907 seconds versus 244 milliseconds with 300 concurrent users and 567 ms with 500 concurrent users. The Oracle *enq* wait event indicates that lock contentions occurred with the application. As you can see, the level of contention intensified with increasing number of concurrent connections as can be measured by the % DB times of 0.42%, 2.16%, and 40.59% for 300, 500, and 700 concurrent user runs, respectively. Since the CPU utilizations on the JEE application server were high, the contention was possibly caused by long queues of requests on the JEE application server. In the next section, we will see if we could somehow tune this wait event down for 700 concurrent users to achieve better scalability for this application.

Top 5 Timed Foreground Events

Event	Waits	Time(s)	Avg wait (ms)	% DB time	Wait Class
DB CPU		1,566		99.63	
SQL*Net message to client	7,958,480	14	0	0.92	Network
latch: cache buffers chains	6,835	7	1	0.45	Concurrency
enq: TX - row lock contention	27	7	244	0.42	Application
log file sync	11,474	3	0	0.19	Commit

Figure 6.31 Top five events for 300 concurrent user run

Top 5 Timed Foreground Events

Event	Waits	Time(s)	Avg wait (ms)	% DB time	Wait Class
DB CPU		3,336		96.93	
enq: TX - row lock contention	131	74	567	2.16	Application
SQL*Net message to client	16,796,648	37	0	1.07	Network
latch: cache buffers chains	17,581	27	2	0.79	Concurrency
resmgr:cpu quantum	316	7	23	0.21	Scheduler

Figure 6.32 Top five events for 500 concurrent user run

Top 5 Timed Foreground Events

Event	Waits	Time(s)	Avg wait (ms)	% DB time	Wait Class
DB CPU		5,292		58.61	
enq: TX - row lock contention	336	3,665	10907	40.59	Application
SQL*Net message to client	24,556,822	65	0	0.71	Network
latch: cache buffers chains	25,560	37	1	0.40	Concurrency
latch free	96,597	31	0	0.34	Other

Figure 6.33 Top five events for 700 concurrent user run

6.6.6 Fine-Tuning JDBC Connection Pool

This section presents the test results from fine-tuning the JDBC XA connection pool for this application. Referring back to Table 6.22, we could infer that the minimum pool size of 20 specified was too small for the 500 and 700 concurrent user runs, since the maximum established pool sizes recorded during those two runs were 88 and 132, respectively. This indicated that the minimum size for the JDBC XA connection pool needed to be lifted so that the JEE application server would not have to create additional connections while processing torrents of user requests.

Table 6.23 shows the test results of a run with the JDBC XA connection pool's min/max sizes changed from 20/200 to 200/1520. The new minimum pool size of 200 was chosen based on the recorded actual established pool size of 132 as shown in Table 6.22. It is seen that the average response times for two actions had been reduced drastically: from 8.393 seconds to 2.394 seconds for the "a06" action and from 6.471 seconds to 3.779 seconds for the "a12" action.

Table 6.23 Comparison between Two 700 Concurrent User Runs with JDBC XA Pool min/max set to 20/200 for Run #1 and 200/1520 for Run #2

Action	**Run #1**	**Run #2**
Options Explicit?	No	No
JDBC XA (min/max)	20/200	200/1520
a00_login	1.05	1.221
a01_save	1.063	0.988
a02_load	0.325	0.308
a03_search	2.472	2.531
a04_save	0.721	0.701
a05_save	0.406	0.394
a06_save	**8.393**	**2.394**
a07_load	1.35	1.374
a08_view	0.514	0.484
a09_save	3.436	3.744
a10_save	0.895	0.854
a11_search	0.323	0.275
a12_analyzing	**6.471**	**3.779**
a13_statistics	3.048	2.865
average	**2.18**	**1.57**

Four your reference, Figure 6.34 shows the CPU and GC patterns, while Figure 6.35 shows the Oracle top five wait events corresponding to these two runs. It is seen that the enq wait event essentially subdued down to a negligible level after applying the above JDBC XA connection pool size tuning (%DB time associated with the enq wait event decreased from 40.59% to 2.92%). Actually, many Oracle performance experts most likely would point the issue to the application or suggest digging for the SQLs that caused this wait event (you could easily confirm this by typing in that enq wait event on Google and search). However, as you can see that it was resolved by simply adjusting the JDBC connection min pool size to allow more connections created upfront when the JEE application server was being started up.

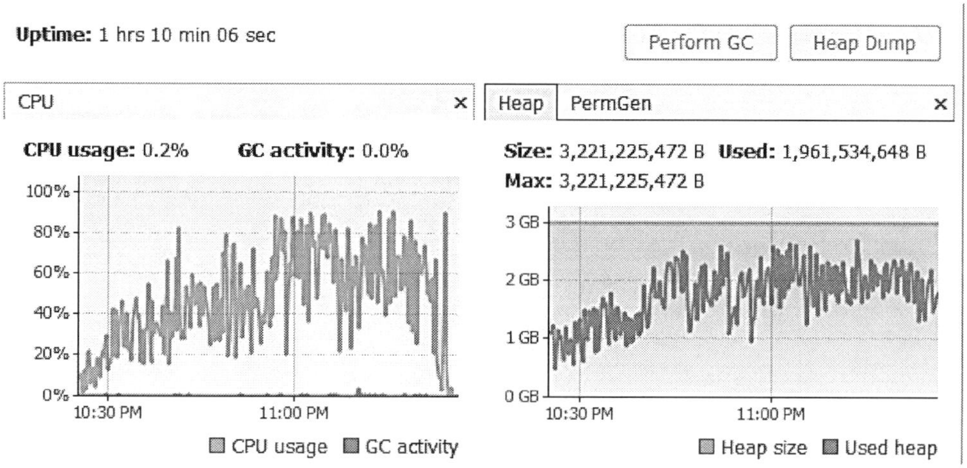

(a): JDBC XA pool min/max = 20/200

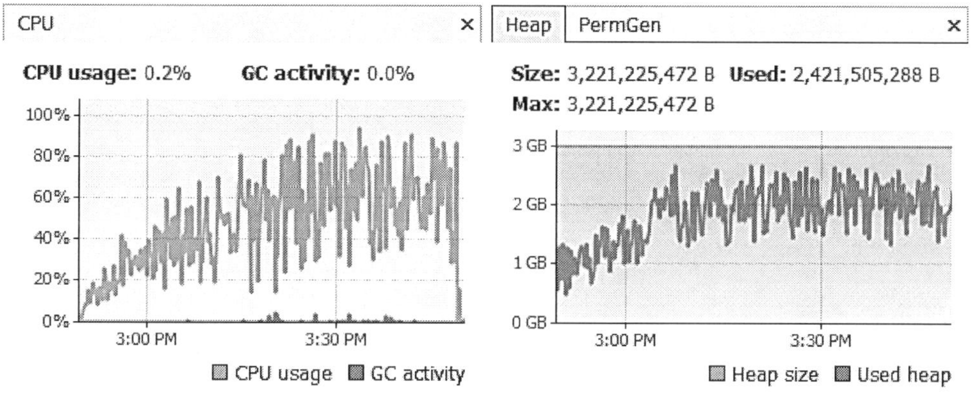

(b): JDBC XA pool min/max = 200/1520

Figure 6.34 CPU and GC patterns versus JDBC connection pool sizes, corresponding to those two runs shown in Table 6.23 (other conditions: 700 concurrent users with CMS GC)

Top 5 Timed Foreground Events

Event	Waits	Time(s)	Avg wait (ms)	% DB time	Wait Class
DB CPU		5,292		58.61	
enq: TX - row lock contention	336	3,665	10907	40.59	Application
SQL*Net message to client	24,556,822	65	0	0.71	Network
latch: cache buffers chains	25,560	37	1	0.40	Concurrency
latch free	96,597	31	0	0.34	Other

Top 5 Timed Foreground Events

Event	Waits	Time(s)	Avg wait (ms)	% DB time	Wait Class
DB CPU		5,167		96.16	
enq: TX - row lock contention	217	157	722	2.92	Application
latch: cache buffers chains	32,747	40	1	0.74	Concurrency
SQL*Net message to client	24,656,223	27	0	0.50	Network
latch free	89,638	26	0	0.48	Other

Figure 6.35 Top five wait events corresponding to those two runs shown in Table 6.23

6.6.7 Further Tuning with JVM options `-XX:+AggressiveOpts` and `-XX:+DoEscapeAnalysis`

Two HotSpot JVM options, `-XX:+AggressiveOpts` and `-XX:+DoEscapeAnalysis`, might be helpful in improving the performance of a Java application. The `-XX:+AggressiveOpts` option is simple that it enables all latest HotSpot JVM performance features, while the `-XX:+DoEscapeAnalysis` option needs a little bit more explanation. Escape analysis determines whether an object on the heap is referenced only locally in a method by the thread itself. If yes, the runtime can allocate the object on the stack or in registers instead of in the heap. Since no other threads can allocate the object, the runtime can remove acquiring and releasing locks on the object (lock elision). It is supposed to help improving performance and scalability by mitigating lock contentions among multiple threads.

Some literature mentioned that the JVM option `-XX:+AggressiveOpts` helped reduce response times by 8%, whereas the option `-XX:+ DoEscapeAnalysis` helped reduce response times by as much as 40%. Therefore, I decided to try these options out on the application in question as well.

To be cautious, I first conducted a few quick runs with my CPUCheck program just to see how the above two options might work out. I used the same Xeon X5550 based server and ran my CPU benchmarking program CPUCheck on it. Table 6.24 shows the results obtained with either none or both options applied to the server and client simultaneously. It turned out that the best case was with the last version of JDK 1.6.0 update 31 with or without these two options set explicitly, as is shown in the second and last rows (the results were almost exactly the same). Also, note the significant performance improvement from update 21 to update 31 with or without these two options set explicitly.

So how did these two options `-XX:+AggressiveOpts` and `-XX:+DoEscapeAnalysis` do with the application in question? Table 6.25 shows the test results with the same workload of 700 concurrent users, compared with the JDBC connection pool fine-tuned run as presented in the previous section. The run designated as Run #3 used exactly the same test conditions just to confirm the results of Run #2 with these two JVM options of `-XX:+AggressiveOpts` and `–XX:+DoEscapeAnalysis` enabled explicitly. It is seen that Run # 2 and Run #3 performed about the same with a small difference of 2% in average response time, which confirmed that the test result was reproducible. However, both runs even helped degrade the performance of the application, which was in line with what was found out with my CPUCheck program as shown in Table 6.24. Figures 6.36 and 6.37 the CPU and GC patterns as well as Oracle top 5 wait events associated with those runs.

Table 6.24 Execution Times in Seconds with and without –XX:+AggressiveOpts and –XX:+DoEscapeAnalysis Options

jdk1.6.0	AggressiveOpts	DoEscapeAnalysis	Runs (#1/#2#3)	Evaluation
update21	×	×	43s/42s/37s	poor
update31	×	×	27s/27s/26s	best
update21	√	×	27s/42s/41s	unstable
update 31	√	×	42s/26s/26s	fair
update 21	×	√	42s/42s/43s	poor
update 31	×	√	31s/25s/27s	good
update 21	√	√	42s/42s/41s	poor
update 31	√	√	27s/26s/27s	best

Table 6.25 Effects of -XX:+AggressiveOpts and –XX:+DoEscapeAnalysis in Comparison with the JDBC Connection Pool Fine-Tuned Run (Run #1) (all Three Runs were Conducted with JDBC Connection Pool min/max Set to 200/1520)

Action	Run #1	Run #2	Run #3
Options Explicitly Set?	No	Yes	Yes
JDBC XA (min/max)	200/152	200/1520	200/1520
a00_login	1.221	1.656	1.085
a01_save	0.988	1.054	1.038
a02_load	0.308	0.334	0.293
a03_search	2.531	3.001	2.511
a04_save	0.701	0.776	0.768
a05_save	0.394	0.438	0.411
a06_save	2.394	2.689	2.435
a07_load	1.374	1.507	1.405
a08_view	0.484	0.586	0.531

a09_save	3.744	3.548	3.679
a10_save	0.854	1.004	0.987
a11_search	0.275	0.304	0.313
a12_analyzing	3.779	5.473	6.313
a13_statistics	2.865	2.998	3.014
average	**1.57**	**1.81**	**1.77**

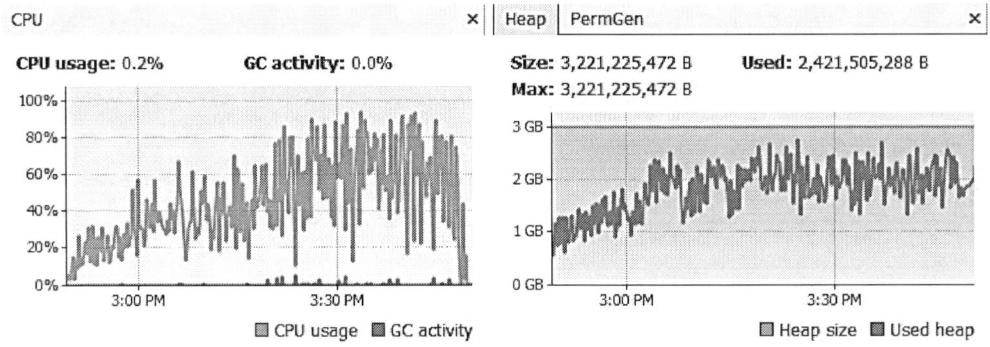

(a) JDBC fine-tuned run w/o -XX:+AggressiveOpts and –XX:+DoEscapeAnalysis

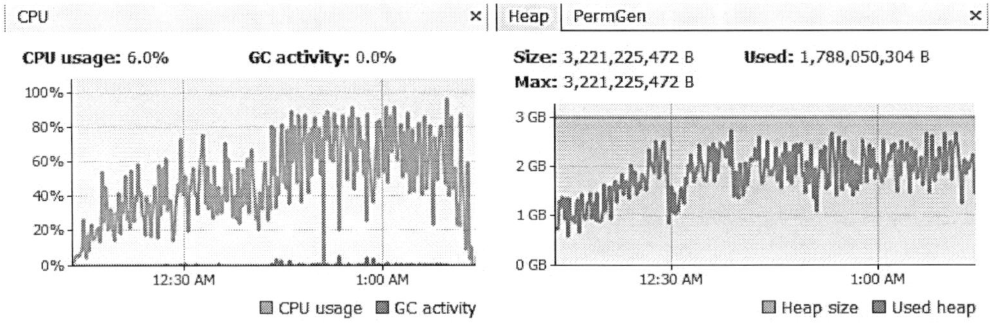

(b) 1st run with -XX:+AggressiveOpts and –XX:+DoEscapeAnalysis

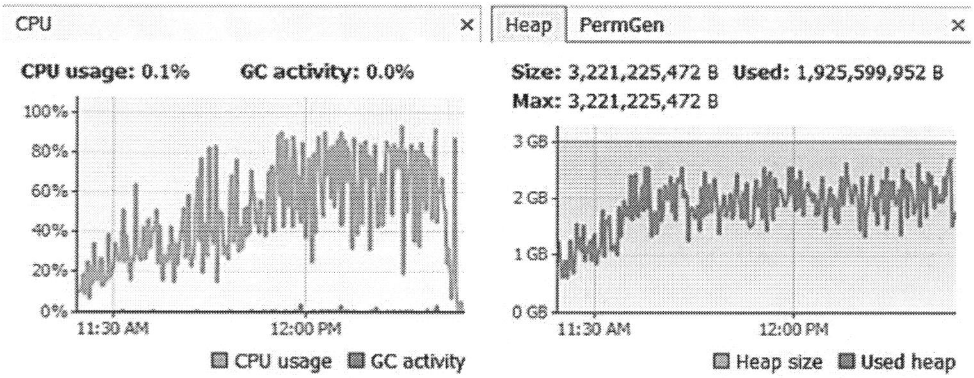

(c) 2nd run with -XX:+AggressiveOpts and –XX:+DoEscapeAnalysis

Figure 6.36 CPU and GC patterns corresponding to runs #1 – 3 shown in Table 6.25 from top to bottom.

Top 5 Timed Foreground Events

Event	Waits	Time(s)	Avg wait (ms)	% DB time	Wait Class
DB CPU		5,167		96.16	
enq: TX - row lock contention	217	157	722	2.92	Application
latch: cache buffers chains	32,747	40	1	0.74	Concurrency
SQL*Net message to client	24,656,223	27	0	0.50	Network
latch free	89,638	26	0	0.48	Other

(a) JDBC fine-tuned run

Top 5 Timed Foreground Events

Event	Waits	Time(s)	Avg wait (ms)	% DB time	Wait Class
DB CPU		5,175		97.07	
enq: TX - row lock contention	209	119	568	2.23	Application
latch free	96,383	29	0	0.55	Other
latch: cache buffers chains	28,500	29	1	0.54	Concurrency
SQL*Net message to client	24,468,785	27	0	0.50	Network

(b) 1st run with -XX:+AggressiveOpts and –XX:+DoEscapeAnalysis

Top 5 Timed Foreground Events

Event	Waits	Time(s)	Avg wait (ms)	% DB time	Wait Class
DB CPU		5,339		97.13	
enq: TX - row lock contention	176	120	681	2.18	Application
SQL*Net message to client	24,701,342	65	0	1.19	Network
latch free	90,664	27	0	0.48	Other
latch: cache buffers chains	19,836	20	1	0.37	Concurrency

(c) 2nd run with -XX:+AggressiveOpts and –XX:+DoEscapeAnalysis

Figure 6.37 Top five wait events corresponding to runs #1 – 3 shown in Table 6.28 from top to bottom.

6.6.8 Scaling Beyond

One might wonder what would happen if we just kept increasing the # of concurrent users, say, to 800. I indeed carried out a run with 800 concurrent users, following the JDBC fine-tuned 700 concurrent user run. It turned out that the average response time had increased to 2.68 seconds in contrast to the 1.57 second average response time for 700 concurrent users as shown in Table 6.25. The average response times for action #3 (a03) and #12 (a12) had increased to 7 and 11 seconds, respectively. This was not a surprise given the high level CPU utilizations with 700 concurrent users as shown in Figure 6.36. See Figure 6.38 for the CPU & GC patterns and Figure 6.39 for the top five events on the database associated with this 800 concurrent user run. For this application, scaling beyond 700 concurrent users requires an even more powerful system for the application server if only a few hundred concurrent users more needed to be supported, or scaling out should be considered if thousands of concurrent users need to be supported, which is beyond the scope of this text at this point.

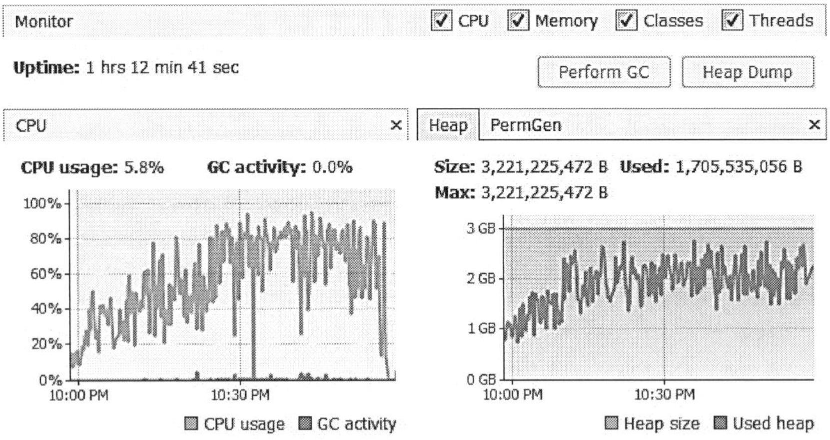

Figure 6.38 CPU & GC patterns with the 800 concurrent user run

Top 5 Timed Foreground Events

Event	Waits	Time(s)	Avg wait (ms)	% DB time	Wait Class
DB CPU		7,813		94.65	
enq: TX - row lock contention	307	355	1157	4.30	Application
SQL*Net message to client	26,971,878	76	0	0.92	Network
latch free	125,104	40	0	0.49	Other
log file sync	29,041	32	1	0.39	Commit

Figure 6.39 Top five wait events on the database with the 800 concurrent user run

6.6.9 Trials with G1 GC

As we introduced earlier, G1 GC is experimental for Java 1.6 and formally enabled for Java 1.7 to replace the CMS GC. To evaluate if the G1 GC could help improve the performance and scalability of the application in question, I replaced the CMS GC with the G1 GC using the flags of `-XX:+UnlockExperimentalVMOptions -XX:+UseG1GC` and conducted 3 runs with 300, 500, and 700 concurrent users using the otherwise same test conditions as used with the CMS collector. I didn't expect anything better, because I already checked it with my CPUCheck program that it was actually worse than the CMS collector.

As is shown in Figure 6.40, the performance and scalability of the same application actually degraded significantly after substituting the CMS GC with the G1 GC. With the CMS GC, the average response time was 0.9, 1.1, and 1.6 seconds for 300, 500, and 700 concurrent users, respectively. With the G1 GC, however, these numbers increased to 3.2, 8.3, and 24.2 seconds with 300, 500, and 700 concurrent users, respectively. Table 6.26 shows the actual data used for plotting Figure 6.40, just in case you want to see response time comparisons on an action-to-action basis.

So what has caused this huge disparity in terms of performance and scalability for this application after the garbage collector switched from CMS to G1 (the JDK used was the 64-bit 1.6.0 update 31)? Figure 6.41 shows the CPU patterns with those six runs as listed in Table 6.26. The left column top to bottom is for 300, 500, and 700 users with CMS, while the right column top to bottom is for 300, 500, and 700 users with G1. It is clear that the CPUs of the JEE application server were a lot busier with G1 than with CMS in collecting garbage objects.

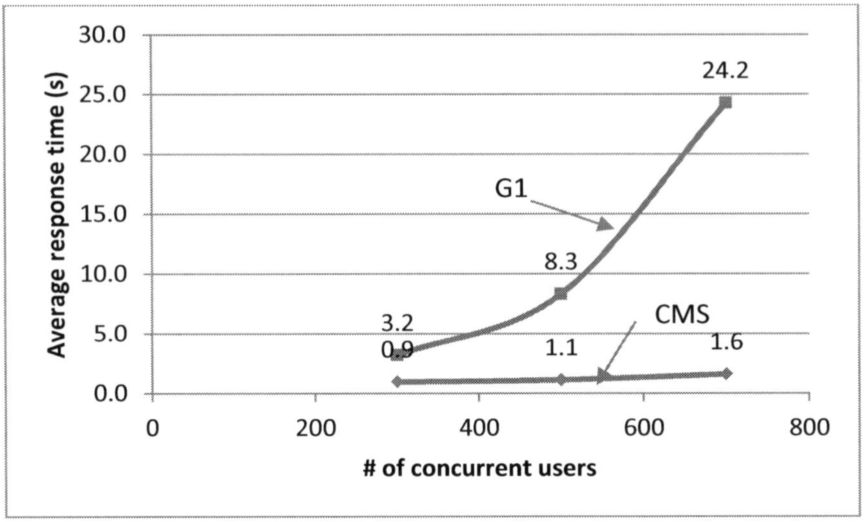

Figure 6.40 Performance and scalability comparison between the G1 (upper) and CMS (lower) garbage collectors with a real enterprise Java application

Table 6.26 Average Response Time Comparison between the G1 GC and CMS GC on an Action-to-Action Basis.

GC	CMS	G1	CMS	G1	CMS	G1
action/# of	**300**	**300**	**500**	**500**	**700**	**700**
a00_login	1.034	1.282	1.041	2.768	1.221	7.394
a01_save	0.634	2.582	0.738	5.634	0.988	11.505
a02_load	0.182	2.483	0.218	2.179	0.308	4.138
a03_search	0.789	1.101	1.101	13.571	2.531	62.443
a04_save	0.383	2.606	0.538	3.866	0.701	8.194
a05_save	0.237	1.719	0.286	3.459	0.394	6.564
a06_save	1.328	5.807	1.708	10.333	2.394	43.452
a07_load	0.966	4.386	1.115	6.701	1.374	9.691
a08_view	0.299	1.936	0.369	2.742	0.484	5.868
a09_save	2.37	4.709	2.8	12.203	3.744	23.318
a10_save	0.545	6.447	0.616	10.201	0.854	17.103
a11_search	0.155	0.564	0.199	2.618	0.275	7.065
a12_analyzing	2.052	2.656	2.295	30.182	3.779	115.282

a13_statistics	2.079	6.111	2.343	9.632	2.865	17.298
average	**0.9**	**3.2**	**1.1**	**8.3**	**1.6**	**24.2**

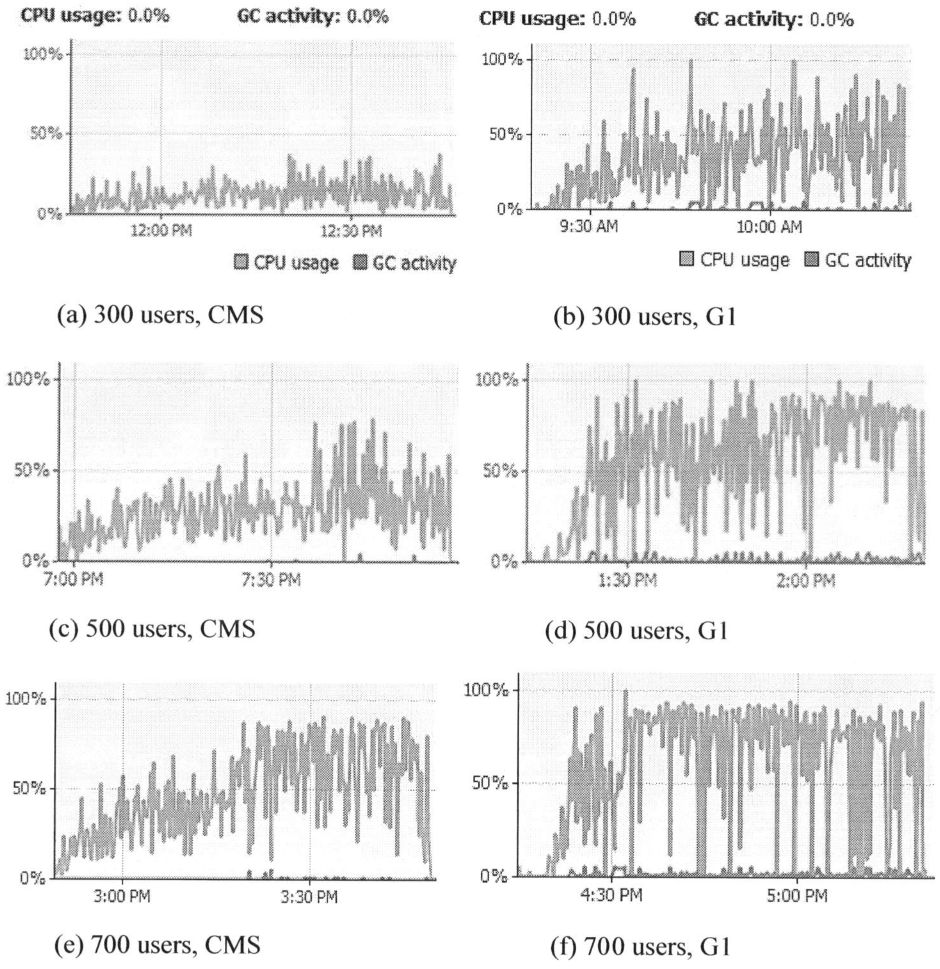

Figure 6.41 CPU pattern comparison between CMS and G1

Figure 6.42 shows the Oracle top 5 wait event comparison between the G1 GC run and CMS GC run, both of which were for 700 concurrent users corresponding to the last two charts shown in Figure 6.41. Note the "`enq: TX - row lock contention`" wait event with the G1 run, which was due to the CPUs on the JEE app server driven too busy with collecting garbage objects by the G1 collector, perhaps compacting, which is one of its major differences from the CMS collector.

Top 5 Timed Foreground Events

Event	Waits	Time(s)	Avg wait (ms)	% DB time	Wait Class
enq: TX - row lock contention	1,376	14,840	10785	81.25	Application
DB CPU		3,301		18.07	
SQL*Net break/reset to client	202	123	610	0.67	Application
SQL*Net message to client	13,005,956	38	0	0.21	Network
latch free	42,163	13	0	0.07	Other

Top 5 Timed Foreground Events

Event	Waits	Time(s)	Avg wait (ms)	% DB time	Wait Class
DB CPU		5,167		96.16	
enq: TX - row lock contention	217	157	722	2.92	Application
latch: cache buffers chains	32,747	40	1	0.74	Concurrency
SQL*Net message to client	24,656,223	27	0	0.50	Network
latch free	89,638	26	0	0.48	Other

Figure 6.42 Top 5 wait event comparison between the G1 run (upper) and CMS run (lower) with the 700 concurrent users

Based on these trials, it appears that G1 still is experimental, at least for Java 1.6. Whether G1 can substitute CMS in Java 1.7 for better performance is yet to be seen.

6.7 SUMMARY

In this chapter, we demonstrated how to profile a Java application with VisualVM to help diagnose and improve the performance and scalability of a Java application. We then demonstrated how to leverage the HotSpot JVM low-latency, CMS garbage collection algorithm to help reduce worst-case response times. An empirical approach to determining the values for the parameters to be used in conjunction with the CMS GC option was demonstrated. We also covered how to perform scalability testing and analysis to help achieve the best possible performance and scalability for an enterprise Java application. A few best enterprise Java performance and scalability tuning practices that might be helpful for your application as well are presented below:

- If your application still is running with an older version of JDK, it's worthwhile to try a newer version of JDK, for example, the latest 1.6.0 HotSpot JDK of update 31.
- You can use PSI-Probe to help fine-tune your JDBC connection pool if JDBC is part of your application. Your minimum pool size should be above the maximum number of established connections your application would need for normal operations. However, for this JEE application server, somehow twice min pool size JDBC connections are created at start-up. For example, if you specify 20, 40 JDBC connections would be created at server start-up. You need to verify if this is the

case with your application server, and this needs to be taken into account when you specify the min pool size for a JDBC connection pool. Your maximum pool size should cover the maximum number of established connections your application would need for peak hours.

- If your application is run on Oracle and the "`enq: TX - row lock contention`" wait event shows large wait times, try to lift up your JDBC pool thresholds (both min and max pool sizes) before digging for SQLs that might have caused contention or asking developers to investigate which part of the application might have caused the contention.

We also attempted the G1 GC with the same application and test conditions, and it turned out that G1 doesn't appear to be promising for the moment for replacing the CMS collector, at least for Java 1.6.

The next chapter covers how to build performance and scalability into an enterprise Java application by design to avoid a common pattern of "design, build, and then panic" when torrents of performance escalations flood in from customers.

EXERCISES

6.1 Describe how you would quantify a Java application performance and scalability issue. Why is this quantification process a very important step toward solving a Java application performance and scalability issue?

6.2 Is it practical to use VisualVM sampling feature with a full-scale Java application performance and scalability test run? How would you work around this issue?

6.3 How would you determine the initial settings to be used with the CMS GC?

6.4 How do you use PSI-Probe to monitor Java application session pool, JDBC connection pool, and HTTP thread pool? How do you size these pools based on the statistics you collect with PSI-Probe?

6.5 Why is it important to make sure you have a sufficiently large minimum JDBC connection pool size to start with for your scalability testing? If this parameter is not sufficiently large, explain what issue it may cause.

6.6 How do you use VisualGC plugin for VisualVM to collect GC related statistics at the end of a Java application performance and scalability run?

6.7 A load test tool emulates Web browsers that may use multiple concurrent connections. Let's say in your load test run you specify *n* virtual users and each virtual user may use up to 6 concurrent connections to your Web server. Does that mean that you may need up to 6 **n* threads with your Web container HTTP thread pool and up to 6**n* connections with your JDBC connection pool? Why or why not?

6.8 If your enterprise Java application uses Oracle as its backend database, and you observe a significant average wait time with the wait event "`enq - Tx row lock contention`" from an AWR report. How would you attempt to resolve such an issue before calling for digging SQLs immediately?

REFERENCES

J. Hunt and B. John, *Java Performance*, Addison Wesley, 2012.

PSI-Probe tool, http://code.google.com/p/psi-probe/.

H. Liu, *Software Performance and Scalability: A Quantitative Approach*, Wiley, 2009.

H. Liu, *Oracle Database Performance and Scalability: A Quantitative Approach*, Wiley, 2011.

7 Java Performance and Scalability by Design

Java has been in use for building all kinds of applications for more than two decades. It has been one of the few most popular platforms for building enterprise applications. However, a Java project may succeed or fail, depending on many factors. One of the most common factors is that developers just keep coding without worrying about the performance and scalability at all. Sometimes, a product might be rushed to customers without going through a bare minimum performance and scalability engineering cycle. Then performance and scalability concerns are given proper attention only when the team is flooded with customer escalations.

This chapter does not attempt to address all performance and scalability issues with a Java application, which is a too big scope for this text or any text. Instead, I'd like to emphasize that performance and scalability should be taken into account as early as during the product design and implementation stage. I understand that this is easy to say than to do, but still we should not give up our hope that performance and scalability can actually be taken into account during the early stage of designing and implementing a product. This chapter uses my CPUCheck sample, which emulates a service admin console, to demonstrate the importance of deciding on and implementing algorithms for a product that can result in either good or poor performance and scalability for the product later. However, algorithmic design is not necessarily all we need for performance and scalability with a Java product. You need to properly size and tune your deployment environment as we demonstrated in the preceding chapter.

7.1 The CPUCheck Program

I developed a CPUCheck program several years ago for two main purposes. One is that I could use this program to check how fast a PC or server is relative to all PCs I purchased over time and all servers I have been using for my work. The other is that I could use this program to help myself understand Java performance based on many factors such as algorithmic design, actual implementation, JDK evolution, hardware advancements, and so on. This is a simple, yet very convenient utility that within minutes it would help you know how fast your system is and also how you can speed up your application by, for example, implementing some well-known performance optimization and tuning best practices or by trying out newer JDKs, new JVM options, or new hardware. If you are a professional software performance engineer, you can check out the power of your system with my program before you actually start your testing on it.

The CPUCheck program is a Java RMI-based client/server program that emulates a service admin console application. Figure 7.1 shows the structure of the CPUCheck program, taken from my Eclipse IDE. In the next few sections, we go over how it is coded in Java.

Figure 7.1 CPUCheck program structure

7.1.1 The Admin Server

The `AdminServer` consists of three Java classes: The `AdminInterface.java` class, `AdminServer.java` class, and `AdminConsole.java` class. The `AdminInterface` defines only one method of `processCommand`, as shown in Listing 7.1. The `AdminServer` class extends the `AdminInterface` by adding entries to an `AdminConsole` object. Listing 7.2 shows the `AdminServer` class, while Listing 7.3 shows the `AdminConsole` class. Let us go through these two classes quickly next.

The `AdminServer` has the following methods:

- **main**: Simply creates an instance of an `AdminServer`.
- **`AdminServer` () constructor**: Creates a registry for the `AdminServer` at the TCP port 9999 on the local host, and then creates an `AdminConsole` object by calling the `createAdminConsole` method.

- **createAdminConsole**: Creates an instance of `AdminConsole` with the normal logistics like setting look and feel, etc.
- **processCommand**: Takes a command from a caller and then calls the corresponding method of the `AdminConsole` class to perform various operations on and display the service directory tree structure on the service admin console GUI, which pops up when the `AdminServer` is started.

The `AdminConsole` has many methods for operating on a service directory. In addition, it has a utility method of `checkMemory` that prints heap information such as `used`, `free`, `total`, and `max` memory.

Listing 7.1 AdminInterface.java

```
import java.rmi.*;
public interface AdminInterface extends Remote {
    void processCommand(String command) throws RemoteException;
    void processCommand(String[] commands) throws RemoteException;
}
```

Listing 7.2 AdminServer.java

```
import java.rmi.*;
import java.rmi.registry.*;
import java.io.Console;
import java.net.*;
import javax.swing.*;
import java.util.*;

public class AdminServer extends java.rmi.server.UnicastRemoteObject implements
        AdminInterface {
    int port;
    String uri;
    Registry registry;
    static AdminConsole adminConsole = null;
    public void processCommand(String[] commandBuffer) throws RemoteException {
        for (String command: commandBuffer) {
            if (command.contains(" ")) processCommand (command);
        }
    }
    public void processCommand(String command) throws RemoteException {
        StringTokenizer st = new StringTokenizer (command, " ");
        String commandName = st.nextToken();
        if (commandName.equals("addNode")) { // top siblings
            String nodeName = st.nextToken();
            adminConsole.addNode (nodeName);
        } else if (commandName.equals("addContainer")) {
            String containerName = st.nextToken();
            String containeeName = st.nextToken();
            adminConsole.addContainer (containerName, containeeName);
```

```
        } else if (commandName.equals("addContainee")) {
            String containerName = st.nextToken();
            String containeeName = st.nextToken();
            adminConsole.addContainee (containerName, containeeName);
        } else if  (commandName.equals("addEntry")) { // leaf
            String leafNodeName = st.nextToken();
            String entryName = st.nextToken();
            adminConsole.addEntryToLeafNode(leafNodeName, entryName);
        } else if  (commandName.equals("removeNode")) {
            String nodeName = st.nextToken();
            adminConsole.removeNode(nodeName);
        } else if  (commandName.equals("removeAll")) {
            adminConsole.removeAll ();
            adminConsole.reload(); // added 2/10/2009
        } else if  (commandName.equals("getLeafNodeEntryCount")) {
            String path = st.nextToken();
            System.out.println (adminConsole.getLeafNodeEntryCount (path));
        } else if  (commandName.equals("reload")) {
            adminConsole.checkMemory ("before reload:");
            adminConsole.reload();
            adminConsole.checkMemory ("after reload:");
        } else if (commandName.equals("checkMemory")) {
            adminConsole.checkMemory ("admin server:");
        } else {
            if (command.length() > 1) { // allow empty command
                System.out.println ("command " + command + " with command name " +
                    commandName + " is invalid");
            }
        }
        //adminConsole.reload(); // call reload for each cmd to get UI updated
        // 2/10/2009: this causes AWT exceptions for a large service tree
    }

    public AdminServer() throws RemoteException {
        try {
            uri = (InetAddress.getLocalHost()).toString();
        } catch (Exception e) {
            throw new RemoteException("can't get inet address.");
        }
        port = 9999;
        //uri = "127.0.0.1";
        System.out.println("uri =" + uri + " , port=" + port);
        try {
            registry = LocateRegistry.createRegistry(port);
            registry.rebind("AdminServer", this);
        } catch (RemoteException e) {
            throw e;
```

```
        }
        createAdminConsole ("Content");
    }
    static public void main(String args[]) {
        try {
            AdminServer s = new AdminServer();
        } catch (Exception e) {
            e.printStackTrace();
            System.exit(1);
        }
    }
    public static void createAdminConsole (String root) {
         setLookAndFeel ();
        adminConsole = new AdminConsole(root);
        adminConsole.setDefaultCloseOperation(JFrame.EXIT_ON_CLOSE);
        adminConsole.setVisible(true);
    }
    public static void setLookAndFeel () {
        try {
         // UIManager.setLookAndFeel(
          //       UIManager.getCrossPlatformLookAndFeelClassName());
            UIManager.setLookAndFeel
                ("com.sun.java.swing.plaf.windows.WindowsLookAndFeel");
       }
       catch (UnsupportedLookAndFeelException e) { }
       catch (ClassNotFoundException e) { }
       catch (InstantiationException e) { }
       catch (IllegalAccessException e) { }
    }
}
```

Listing 7.3 AdminConsole.java

```
import java.awt.*;
import javax.swing.tree.*;
import javax.swing.JFrame;
import javax.swing.JScrollPane;
import javax.swing.JTree;
import javax.swing.tree.DefaultMutableTreeNode;
import javax.swing.tree.TreeNode;
import java.util.*;

public class AdminConsole extends JFrame
{
      private DefaultMutableTreeNode root;
      private DefaultTreeModel model;
      private JTree tree;
```

```
    private Hashtable items = new Hashtable (10000);
    private static final int WIDTH = 600;
    private static final int HEIGHT = 800;
public AdminConsole(String rootName)
{
  setTitle("Service Admin Console");
  setSize(WIDTH, HEIGHT);
  // construct tree
  root = new DefaultMutableTreeNode(rootName);
  model = new DefaultTreeModel(root);
  tree = new JTree(model);
  tree.setEditable(true);

  JScrollPane scrollPane = new JScrollPane(tree);
  getContentPane().add(scrollPane, BorderLayout.CENTER);
}
// add a node to root
public void addNode (String nodeName) {
    //System.out.println ("calling addNode: " + nodeName);
    DefaultMutableTreeNode node = new DefaultMutableTreeNode (nodeName);
    addNode (node);
}
public void addNode (DefaultMutableTreeNode node) {
    //System.out.println ("\tcalling addNode with node " + node.toString());
    if (!isDuplicate (root, node)) {
        int index = root.getChildCount();
        model.insertNodeInto(node, root, index);
    } else {
          System.out.println ("ERROR: cannot add duplicate node  " + node.toString());
    }
}
public boolean isDuplicate (DefaultMutableTreeNode parent,
  DefaultMutableTreeNode child) {
    Enumeration children = parent.children();
    boolean found = false;
    while (children.hasMoreElements()) {
        DefaultMutableTreeNode c = (DefaultMutableTreeNode) children.nextElement();
        if (c.toString().equals (child.toString())) {
            found = true;
        }
    }
    return found;
}
// get a node as a child of the root node
public TreeNode getNode (String path) {
    int count = root.getChildCount();
    TreeNode child = null;
```

```
        String nodeName = path;
        if (path.contains("/")) {
            nodeName = path.substring(0, path.indexOf("/") - 1);
        }

        for (int i = 0; i < count; i++) {
            child = root.getChildAt (i);
            if (child.toString().equals(nodeName)) break;
        }
        return child;
    }
    public TreeNode getLeafNodeByName (String name) {
        Enumeration depth = root.depthFirstEnumeration();
        TreeNode node = null;
        while (depth.hasMoreElements()) {
            node = (TreeNode) depth.nextElement();
            if (!node.isLeaf()) continue;
            if (node.toString().equals(name)) break;
        }
        return node;
    }
    // add a new container to an existing containee node
    public void addContainer (String container, String containee) {
        //System.out.println ("calling addContainer");
        DefaultMutableTreeNode p = new DefaultMutableTreeNode (container);
        addNode(p);
        DefaultMutableTreeNode child = (DefaultMutableTreeNode) getNode (containee);
        if (!isDuplicate(p, child)) {
            p.insert(child, 0); // container is new
        } else {
            System.out.println ("containee duplicate " + containee );
        }
    }
    // add an existing containee node to an existing container node
    public void addContainee (String container, String containee) {
        //System.out.println ("calling addContainee");
        DefaultMutableTreeNode p = (DefaultMutableTreeNode) getNode (container);
        DefaultMutableTreeNode c = (DefaultMutableTreeNode) getNode (containee);
        int index = p.getChildCount();
        if (!isDuplicate(p, c)) {
            model.insertNodeInto(c, p, index);
        } else {
            System.out.println ("container / containee duplicate "
                    + container + "/" + containee );
        }
    }
    public void addEntryToLeafNode (String leaf, String entry) {
```

```
        //System.out.println ("calling addEntryToLeafNode: " + leaf + " " + entry);
        DefaultMutableTreeNode p = (DefaultMutableTreeNode) getLeafNodeByName (leaf);
        if (p != null) {
            int index = p.getChildCount();
            TreeNode[] path = p.getPath ();
            String pathName = path[0].toString();
            int count = path.length;
            for (int i = 1; i < count; i++) {
                pathName += "/" + path[i];
            }
            if (!items.containsKey (pathName)) {
                ArrayList al = new ArrayList (1000);
                al.add(entry);
                items.put (pathName, al);
            } else {
                ArrayList al = (ArrayList) items.get (pathName);
                al.add(entry);
                items.put (pathName, al);
            }
        } else {
            System.out.println ("leaf node " + leaf + " doesn't exist");
        }
    }
    public String getLeafNodeEntryCount (String path) {
        if (items.containsKey (path)) {
            ArrayList al = (ArrayList) items.get(path);
            return path + " contains " + al.size() + " entries";
        } else {
            return path + " entered does not exist";
        }
    }
    public int getCount () {
        return root.getChildCount();
    }
    public int printAllContainers () {
        Enumeration children = root.children();
        while (children.hasMoreElements()) {
            DefaultMutableTreeNode c = (DefaultMutableTreeNode) children.nextElement();
            System.out.print (c.toString() + "/");

        }
        System.out.println ("-------");
        return getCount ();
    }
    public void reload () {
        model.reload();
    }
```

```
    public void removeNode (String nodeName) {
        Enumeration breadth = root.breadthFirstEnumeration();
        TreeNode node = null;
        while (breadth.hasMoreElements()) {
            node = (TreeNode) breadth.nextElement();
            if (node.toString().equals(nodeName)) {
                model.removeNodeFromParent((DefaultMutableTreeNode)node);
                break;
            }
        }
    }
    public void removeAll () {
      root.removeAllChildren();
    }
      public static void checkMemory(String comment) {
        int mb = 1024*1024;
        Runtime runtime = Runtime.getRuntime();
        System.out.println(comment + " Heap utilization statistics [MB]");
        //Used memory
        System.out.println("Used Memory:"
                + (runtime.totalMemory() - runtime.freeMemory()) / mb);
        //Free memory
        System.out.println("Free Memory:"
                + runtime.freeMemory() / mb);
        //Total available memory
        System.out.println("Total Memory:" + runtime.totalMemory() / mb);
        //Maximum available memory
        System.out.println("Max Memory:" + runtime.maxMemory() / mb);
        }
}
```

7.1.2 The Client

The client side consists of three Java classes as well: `AdminProxy.java`, `AdminClient.java`, and `ServiceDirectory.java`. The function of each program is described as follows:

- The `AdminProxy` class has a constructor for setting up a connection to the Admin Server with a given server name or IP and a TCP port. It has only one method: `sendCommand (String command)`, which calls the `processCommand` method on the Admin Server. See Listing 7.4 for how the `AdminProxy` class is coded.
- The `AdminClient` class is also a very simple program. It looks up an `AdminServer` instance with a given IP and a port number, and then executes a command as one of the input parameters. See Listing 7.5 for how the `AdminClient` class is coded.
- The class `ServiceDirectory` is the main part of this CPUCheck program. Its responsibility is to construct a service directory expressed as a uniform tree structure of *m* levels and *n* child nodes for each non-leaf node. Each *node* in a service directory represents a *service* and each of its immediate

child node is a *subservice*. Using a properties file named `services.properties` that defines all parameters for a CPUCheck test run, it then sends this service directory structure to the Admin Server for displaying the service directory on the Admin Console GUI. Since this is the main driver for the CPUCheck program, we describe it in more detail in the next section.

Listing 7.4 AdminProxy.java

```
import java.rmi.*;
import java.rmi.registry.*;
import java.net.*;

public class AdminProxy
{
  private AdminInterface adminServer;
  private String serverAddress;
  private String serverPort;

  public AdminProxy (String sa, String sp)
  {
    serverAddress = sa;
    serverPort = sp;
    try{
      Registry registry=LocateRegistry.getRegistry(
        serverAddress,
        (new Integer(serverPort)).intValue()
      );
      adminServer=
        (AdminInterface)(registry.lookup("AdminServer"));
    }
    catch(RemoteException e){
      e.printStackTrace();
    }
    catch(NotBoundException e){
      e.printStackTrace();
    }
  }
  public void sendCommand (String command) {
   try{
       adminServer.processCommand(command);
    }
    catch(RemoteException e){
      e.printStackTrace();
     }
  }
  public void sendCommand (String[] commands) {
   try{
       adminServer.processCommand(commands);
```

```
        }
        catch(RemoteException e){
            e.printStackTrace();
        }
    }
}
```

Listing 7.5 AdminClient.java

```
import java.rmi.*;
import java.rmi.registry.*;
import java.net.*;

public class AdminClient
{
    static public void main(String args[])
    {
        AdminInterface adminServer;
        Registry registry;
        String serverAddress = args[0];
        String serverPort = args[1];
        String command = args[2];
        try{
            registry=LocateRegistry.getRegistry(
                serverAddress,
                (new Integer(serverPort)).intValue()
            );
            adminServer=
              (AdminInterface)(registry.lookup("AdminServer"));

            adminServer.processCommand(command);
        }
        catch(RemoteException e){
            e.printStackTrace();
        }
        catch(NotBoundException e){
            e.printStackTrace();
        }
    }
}
```

7.2 THE SERVICEDIRECTORY PROGRAM

First, if you are interested in looking at the source code of this program, refer to Listing B.7 `ServiceDirectory.java`. It is shown there as it is kind of too bulky to be put here. We go through it here to help explain how algorithmic design and implementation can help build performance and scalability into a product in the first place.

The main programmatic logic of this program works as follows:

- The `init()` method. This method reads and populates all parameters from an external properties file `services.properties`. It then creates an `adminProxy` object if USE_PROXY is set to `true` and clears the service tree on the Service Admin GUI if CLEAR_SERVICE_TREE is set to `true`. Finally, it creates a file that will contain all summary information for the run, including all parameters specified in the `services.properties` file.
- The next step is to dispatch to an algorithm for creating the service directory tree structure based on the parameter `ALGORITHM` specified in the `services.properties` file. This parameter can have one of the three values: *static*, *recursive*, and *dynamic*. These are the algorithms that we would use to demonstrate how an algorithm design can determine the intrinsic performance and scalability of a product. We study these algorithms in the next few sections.
- The `checkAddServices` () method. This method is for adding service directory using an external batch job script named `runSd.bat` rather than calling the `adminServer` instance directly in memory. It's for comparison purposes and rarely used.
- The `checkAddSystems ()` method. This method enables adding any number of "`systems`" to leaf nodes of a service directory. It is controlled by the parameter ADD_SYSTEMS specified "`true`" or "`false`" in the `services.properties` file. It can be configured to use multiple threads with the parameter NUM_OF_THREADS specified in the `services.properties` file to test multi-threading performance of a system. Once again, it's rarely used, as the main focus is the most time-consuming part of creating a service directory structure on the client side and then having it displayed on the Service Admin Console, using one of those three algorithms that we discuss next.

Here is the logic flow for those algorithms :

- Each algorithm starts with constructing a service directory tree structure based on the number of levels and number of child nodes for a parent node. This structure is stored in a `Stack` object with the *static* and *recursive* algorithms, but not with the *dynamic* algorithm. The dynamic algorithm sends a tree node as it is created.
- With the static and recursive algorithms, all service nodes stored in a `Stack` object are sent to the Admin Server by calling the `processServiceTree` method, which in turn calls a `writeService` method, which in turn calls the `adminProxy.sendCommand` method to send a command over to the Admin Server.

Next, let us take a look at each of the algorithms mentioned above.

7.2.1 The Static Algorithm

This algorithm is implemented in the `add5LevelServices` method, as is shown in Listing B.7 in Appendix B. It has a fixed level of five and a hard-coded limit of 1000 leaf nodes. Because it is static in nature, it is fastest in performance but also poorest in scalability, because it would not handle larger service directories with more levels and more leaf nodes than hard-coded into it. With real products, sometimes you may hear something like "*this product does not support more than* ... ," which might imply that there are some hard limits hard-coded into it. Supporting more often requires recoding, which is inflexible and undesirable.

7.2.2 The Recursive Algorithm

This algorithm is implemented in the `recur` method, as is shown in Listing B.7 in Appendix B. It creates a service directory tree structure recursively based on the number of levels and number of subservice nodes for an immediate parent node. The service tree structure is stored on a Stack object, which is processed by calling the `processServiceTree` method, which in turn calls the `writeService` method to send the tree structure to the Admin Server.

This algorithm is flexible and there is no hard-limit hard coded into it. Since it involves numerous stack operations, it would be slower than the static method discussed in the previous section. However, this did not turn out to be a problem, as is discussed later.

7.2.3 The Dynamic Algorithm

This algorithm is implemented in the `createServiceDirectory` method, as is shown in Listing B.7 in Appendix B. Since the service directory is a uniform tree structure with a certain number of levels and a certain number of child nodes per parent node, the index of the parent node for a given child node can be calculated *a priori* using a formula. Unlike the static algorithm discussed earlier that uses five for-loops for five levels, this algorithm can be implemented with only two for-loops for an arbitrary number of levels for a service directory tree structure, as demonstrated in the source code shown in Listing B.7. This two for-loop design is intuitive given the fact that a service directory tree structure can be defined with two variables: the number of levels and the number of sub-nodes per parent node. Therefore, it can be implemented with an outer loop looping through all levels and an inner loop looping through all child siblings for a given parent node at a given level.

The next section provides test data to compare these three algorithms quantitatively.

7.3 TEST RESULTS

In this section, we present the test results obtained with a few different test cases, each of which was designed to address a particular performance and scalability concern. Let's start with the first test case next.

7.3.1 Performance Gaps with the Static, Recursive and Dynamic Algorithms

The first test case was designed to compare the time elapsed with each algorithm for creating a service directory tree structure of 5 levels and 8 sub nodes per node. Including the root node, this structure contains 33,479 nodes all together. In order to measure the time spent in each algorithm only, the *ADD_SERVICES* parameter was set to `false` in the `services.properties` file so that the service directory tree structure would not be sent to the Admin Server. The test results are shown in Figure 7.2. It is seen that creating those 33,479 nodes took 46ms, 78ms, and 577ms for the static, recursive, and dynamic algorithms, respectively. It would have been interesting to actually understand the huge performance gaps with those three different algorithms, but my purpose here is to help demonstrate that different algorithmic design decisions may indeed result in drastically different performance for the same function of an application. This is the main purpose of this test case.

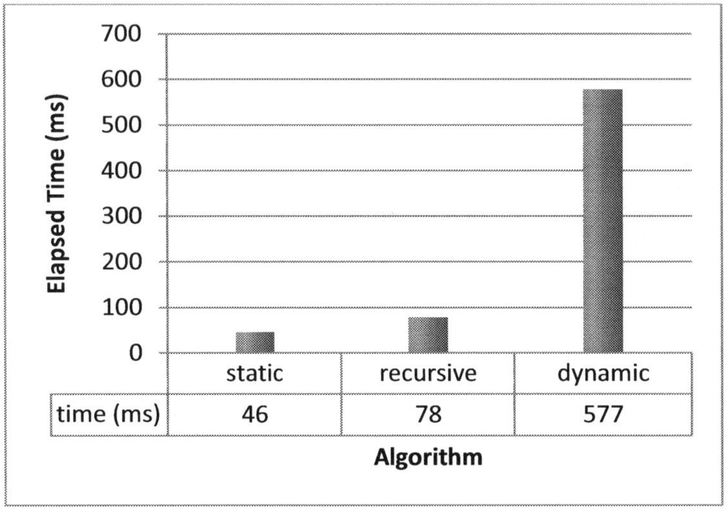

Figure 7.2 Elapsed times associated with creating a service directory tree structure of 33,479 nodes with three different algorithms

Based on these test results, it appears that the recursive algorithm would be the best choice, as it would give orders of magnitude better performance than the dynamic algorithm while avoiding the scalability limitation as associated with the static algorithm. In the meanwhile, did we need to be concerned that the recursive algorithm was 70% slower than the static algorithm? Or did we need to make up many methods using the same static algorithm for different number of tree levels so that if a service directory tree structure has *n* levels then it would be dispatched to a specific method corresponding to that tree level? The next test case helps address this question.

7.3.2 Part versus Whole in Evaluating Performance

With the previous test case, we disabled sending the service directory tree structure to the Admin Server so that only the time spent in an algorithm was measured. It was a valid test case for determining which algorithm would perform best. However, it was not necessarily a complete test case, since this CPUCheck program has two major tasks: one is to create the service directory tree structure on the client side, and the other is to send the tree structure to the Admin Server to be displayed on the Service Admin Console. This is a classical *part versus whole* issue that must be considered in evaluating the performance of a Java application. This notion is re-enforced with the test results shown in Figure 7.3, which compares the total, end-to-end times of creating the same service directory tree structure as with the previous test case, but with the times spent in sending and displaying the tree structure on the Service Admin Console included as well.

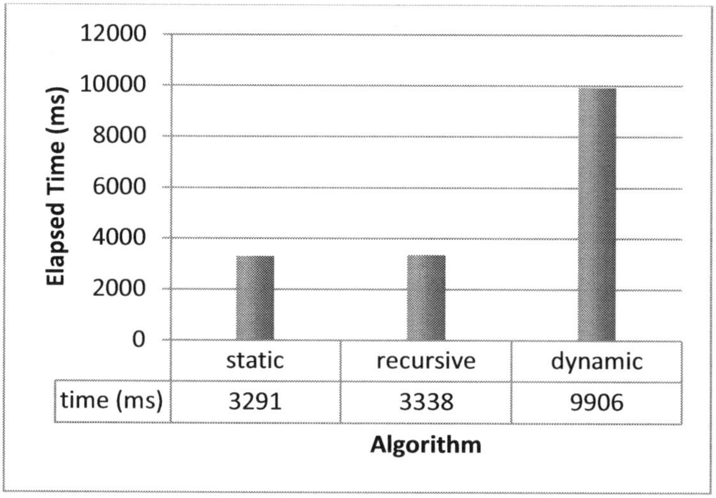

Figure 7.3 Total wall-clock times associated with creating a service directory tree structure of 33,479 nodes using three different algorithms and sending it to the service admin console

I have to mention that for this test case, we essentially re-executed all same runs presented in the previous section with the parameter *ADD_SERVICES* set to *true*, which enabled getting the service directory tree structure created on the client side and displayed on the server side on the Service Admin Console. As is seen, the observation of "*static is faster than recursive and recursive is faster than dynamic*" still holds true, but do we really care that the recursive algorithm was only 47 ms faster than the static algorithm when the total elapsed time was 3.3 seconds? A quick calculation would reveal that in this case the static algorithm was only 1.4% faster than the recursive algorithm instead of 70% faster when it was evaluated with the time spent in each algorithm only. Obviously, this 1.4% difference could be ignored completely.

This test case leads to a very important subject of software performance bottleneck analysis, as is discussed next.

7.4 BOTTLENECK ANALYSIS

Software performance bottleneck analysis is about finding out which resource or resources affect the performance at the *system* level *most*. As mentioned in Chapter 1, I once devised a mathematical formula to help facilitate software performance bottleneck analysis and presented it as *Exercise 4.14* in my other text of *Software Performance and Scalability: An Quantitative Approach* (Wiley, 2009). It is reformulated here as follows:

Suppose we have a computing task that consists of two stages, as shown in Figure 7.4. There are N objects that need to be processed through these two stages. It takes an amount of time ΔT_1 in stage 1 and ΔT_2 in stage 2 sequentially. Accordingly, the throughput for stage 1 and stage 2 can be defined as $X_1 = N/\Delta T_1$ and $X_2 = N/\Delta T_2$, respectively. Similar to two capacitors connected in series in electrical circuits, the total equivalent or system throughput can be expressed as

$$X_0 = \frac{X_1 \times X_2}{X_1 + X_2} \qquad (7.1)$$

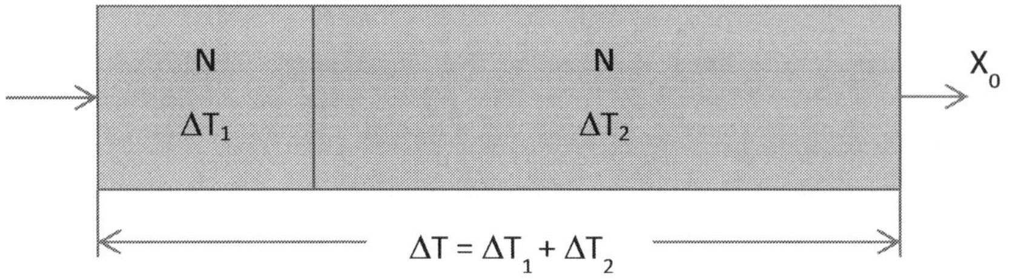

Figure 7.4 A computing task consisting of two sequential stages

Now suppose that stage 1 runs much faster than stage 2, or $\Delta T_1 << \Delta T_2$, which is equivalent to $X_1 >> X_2$, then we have

$$X_0 \cong X_2 \qquad (7.2)$$

which implies that the system performance in terms of throughput is dominated by the throughput of stage 2. In this case, stage 2 is termed the *bottleneck*, which means that one should focus on improving the component performance or throughput in stage 2. This sounds very simple and obvious. However, it reminds me of one of my real experiences with a real product I once worked on. A batch job with that product works exactly like what is shown in Figure 7.4: a large number of objects had to be processed in two sequential stages. It was a database-centric application with the first stage disk read-intensive and second stage disk write-intensive. The first stage was orders of magnitude faster than the second stage. A developer discussed with me on something he was working on, which would significantly speed up the first stage according to his belief. I explained to him using Eqs. (7.1) and (7.2) as discussed above, and tried to help him understand that we really needed to focus on stage 2. However, I don't believe I actually convinced him as I heard him a few days later still telling others excitedly about how much performance improvement on stage 1 he would be able to help make as if I never talked and explained something to him.

So retrospectively, although this CPUCheck program was something I conjured up myself for checking the relative power of one system versus another and also for helping myself explore software performance and scalability best practices, it does seem to bear a lot with what we do in reality. However, we would not just stop here. Now what can we do after we have identified that the second stage of sending a service directory tree structure to the Admin Server and displaying it on the Service Admin Console is the bottleneck.

Actually, for CPU benchmarking purposes, we don't necessarily care which stage is faster, as all we need is a CPU-intensive program that can run on each individual system with the same job and see how they compare with each other relatively. However, I have another objective to fulfill in this chapter, which is to demonstrate how array processing can help enhance the performance and scalability of an application significantly. This CPUCheck program is a perfect choice for this topic, as is discussed in the next section.

7.5 ARRAY PROCESSING TO BOAST PERFORMANCE AND SCALABILITY SIGNIFICANTLY

The CPUCheck program we discussed in the previous sections is a Java RMI-based client/server type of sample application. It creates a service tree structure on the client side in stage 1 and then sends it over to the server as a series of commands for constructing and displaying the entire structure on the Service Admin Console in stage 2. Based on the test data presented in the preceding section, this second stage takes most of the time for an entire run, which constitutes a bottleneck.

So is there anything we can do to help improve stage 2 performance? This actually is a very typical pattern that two components need to communicate with each other and exchange data or the first component needs to send data to the second component torrentially. In this case, a classic technique is to send data in batches rather than one item a time. This is what I call *array processing*, which is also called *batch processing* or *chunking*. Specifically with the CPUCheck program, we can have it send multiple commands a time by setting an externalized parameter named *ARRAY_SIZE*. I actually implemented this technique on the fly while writing this chapter just for demonstrating how effective this technique can be in boasting the performance and scalability of an application, as is discussed next.

Figure 7.5 shows the total execution times using the recursive algorithm with a series of ARRAY_SIZE values of 1, 2, 5, 10, 15, 20, 30, 40, and 50. The tree size was changed to six levels in order to show the efficacy of array processing. The same number of eight sub-nodes per node was used as with all previous runs. Note the following:

- Reduction in total execution time is very significant with the ARRAY_SIZE parameter varied from 1 to 10, an impressive > 5x improvement from over 20 seconds to 4 seconds.
- The improvement begins to level off with ARRAY_SIZE > 30.
- The improvement ends with ARRAY_SIZE = 40, and even a slightly large total execution time resulted with ARRAY_SIZE = 50. We will see this with the dynamic algorithm tests as well, as is discussed next.

Figure 7.6 shows the total execution times using the dynamic algorithm with a series of ARRAY_SIZE values of 1, 10, 20, 30, 40, and 50. The tree size remained the same and the only change was the algorithm, relative to the recursive algorithm runs shown in Figure 7.5. First, note that the dynamic algorithm implementation was orders of magnitude slower than the recursive algorithm implementation. For example, with ARRAY_SIZR = 1 (no array processing), the recursive run took 22 seconds only, while the dynamic run took 605 seconds, a factor of 27 slower. Secondly, the largest gain was obtained with ARRAY_SIZE = 40, representing a 27% improvement relative to the run with ARRAY_SIZE = 1. It's also interesting to see that the run with ARRAY_SIZE = 50 even took slightly longer than the run with ARRAY_SIZE = 40.

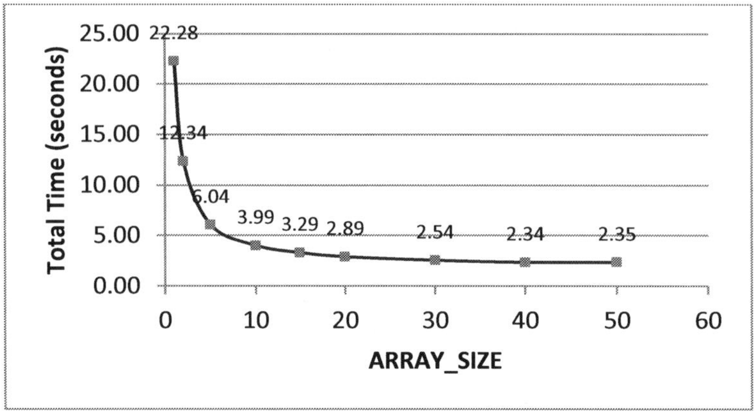

Figure 7.5 Total execution time versus ARRAY_SIZE with array processing applied to the recursive algorithm (tree size: 6 levels x 8 child nodes / per parent node = 299,592 nodes total).

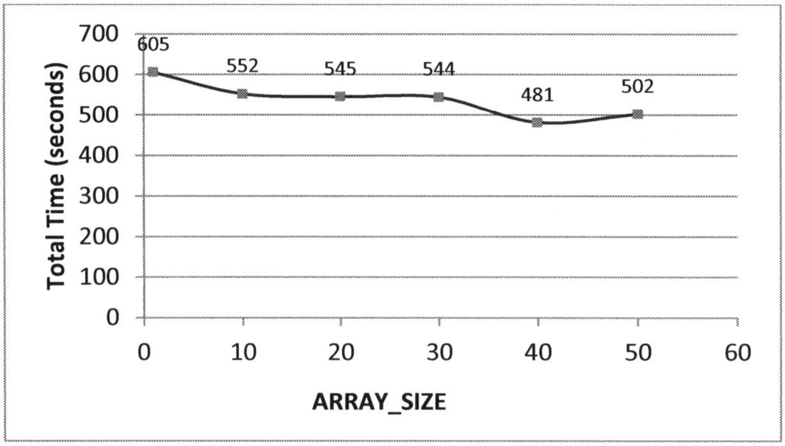

Figure 7.6 Total execution time versus ARRAY_SIZE with array processing applied to the dynamic algorithm for the same tree size of 6x8.

A thoughtful reader may already know exactly why the recursive algorithm got a lot more improvement than the dynamic algorithm with the same array processing technique applied to the recursive and dynamic algorithm implementations. This is reserved as an exercise for a reader to practice profiling with VisualVM and to find the answer to this mystery.

7.6 PERFORMANCE AND SCALABILITY ANTI-PATTERNS

In fact, this CPUCheck program was not totally something I conjured up intentionally. It was actually inspired with my work on a real product. That application also used a similar console to hold services in a tree structure (it is the same application as used for oops exploration presented in chapter 5). For testing purposes, I needed to populate data into the database and had the populated data displayed on the admin console as a tree structure. A major difference was that it did not use a uniform tree structure. I made it a uniform tree structure with the CPUCheck program, because it's much simpler to code with a uniform tree structure.

My inspiration came with a tool used with that product by dev and QA teams, which populates data with a script similar to `runSd.bat` included with this CPUCheck program. It essentially calls a script to execute commands stored in an external text file. Since it was too slow, I developed a Java program to populate service entries for testing the performance and scalability of that application. That Java program I developed was the predecessor of this CPUCheck program we used in this chapter. This CPUCheck program can emulate calling an MS-DOS script to populate a service directory tree structure as well by setting the parameter *USE_PROXY* to `false` in the `services.properties` file.

To see how a script-based approach could perform badly, I conducted one run with the following changes in the `services.properties` file:

- Changed the number of levels for the tree structure from 6 to 5.
- Changed the algorithm to *static*.
- Changed *USE_PROXY* from *true* to *false*.

Not surprisingly, the run took three hours to finish with this script-based approach, while the run with the same tree size using the proxy-based approach and the recursive algorithm took less than 10 seconds. My proxy-based approach is over one thousand times faster than the original script-based approach. This might be a too extreme example of a performance and scalability anti-pattern, but it may happen both in academic research and in reality.

It's tempting to re-use QA-oriented scripts for performing performance and scalability testing. I hope this anti-pattern can also help prove that using QA-oriented scripts for performing performance and scalability testing might be a very inefficient approach. Performance and scalability testing requires all tools to be efficient.

7.7 SUMMARY

In this chapter, we demonstrated the importance of design and implementation in determining the performance and scalability of a Java application using my CPUCheck program. We used three different algorithms implemented in CPUCheck to illustrate quantitatively the huge resultant performance and scalability ramifications associated with them. I also presented a formula that is helpful for bottleneck analysis in order to direct performance and scalability optimization efforts to where they should be spent. It's more likely to see projected performance and scalability enhancements materialized if a quantitative approach is used to analyze bottleneck.

We could have used a much more sophisticated sample application like SOBA I introduced in my other book *Spring 4 for eveloping Enterprise Applications: An End-to-End Approach* to illustrate Java application performance and scalability by design. However, I felt that my CPUCheck program was a better choice as it is more manageable due to its simplicity. In future, I may extend the subject of Java application performance and scalability by design to SOBA when I get a chance to update this text.

EXERCISES

7.1 Run CPUCheck program on a few systems (desktops, laptops and servers if possible) and compare the results obtained with your desktops/laptops/servers. Which class of systems gives better performance numbers? Cross-check your results with relevant PassMark results.

7.2 How do you perform a bottleneck analysis? What would you use as the theoretical foundation for your bottleneck analysis?

7.3 Check with your product to see if the array processing performance pattern is applicable and used. If used, what's the verified optimal array size?

7.4 Does your organization use QA scripts for performance and scalability testing? Is it an effective and efficient approach to use QA scripts for performance and scalability testing?

REFERENCES

H. Liu, Software Performance and Scalability: A Quantitative Approach, Wiley, 2009.

H. Liu, Spring 4 for Developing Enterprise Applications: An End-to-End Approach, 2012.

8 Java Performance and Scalability on Linux

This chapter discusses Java performance and scalability on Linux. Many organizations develop their enterprise software products on Windows and then deploy and test on Linux, as Linux has a large custom base running enterprise software on it. It is not surprising that a large group of developers are more familiar with Windows than with Linux. Therefore, we start with a brief introduction to the origin of Linux as well as some of its major branches popular today to help keep readers stay up-to-date with the current state of Linux. We then focus on optimizing the performance and scalability of enterprise Java applications on Linux using a real product, along with comparisons between Linux and Windows based on the same application and hardware.

In order to trace the origin of Linux, we need to discuss the history of UNIX, which is the subject of the next section.

8.1 THE EVOLUTION OF UNIX

As we know today, UNIX has been a reliable, secure, high-performance, scalable, low maintenance cost operating system (OS) platform for running mission-critical applications for decades. Such unique merits of UNIX are deeply rooted in the simplicity of its design. The UNIX community generally accredited the simplicity of the UNIX design to Ken Thompson and Dennis Ritchie at Bell Labs. With Ken Thompson and Dennis Ritchie as two major contributors, Bell Labs released the first edition of UNIX in 1971. Actually written in assembler, that first edition of UNIX operating system supported running a few application programs written in the B language. Then, from 1971 to 1989, there had been nine more editions released with the tenth edition as the last edition from Bell Labs. In the meanwhile, the B language evolved into the C language in early 1970's, which was later standardized in 1989, resulting in the ANSI Standard X3.159-1989 (C89). The C89 standard was subsequently adopted by the International Standards Organization as ISO/IEC 9899:1900 (C99).

Then UNIX evolved along with the two branches of academic and commercial versions. The academic versions were released as a series of Berkeley Software Distributions (BSDs), starting from the first edition of BSD (1978), which was based on the sixth edition of UNIX from Bell Labs. The subsequent editions include 2BSD (1978), 3BSD (1979), 4BSD (1980), 4.1BSD (1981), 4.2BSD (1982), 4.3BSD

(1986), 4.4BSD (1993), and various flavors of BSD's such as FreeBSD, NetBSD, OpenBSD, and so on. The commercial versions, which still are in business and highly demanded today, include IBM's AIX (latest version 7), HP's HP-UX (latest version 11i v3), and Oracle's Solaris (latest version 11). Apple's Mac OS X also is based on UNIX, with its latest version 10.7 code-named Lion. Various versions of Apple OS are used to power not only Apple computers but also popular consumer products like iPod, iPhone and iPad. Whether academic or commercial editions, it is amazing that the structure of UNIX remains almost intact today after four decades.

So how did Linux come along with the evolution of UNIX? Let us find it out in the next section.

8.2 LINUX AND ITS VARIANTS

As is well-known, it's Linus Torvalds, a CS student at the University of Helsinki, Finland, who developed an operating system kernel in 1991 to satisfy his interests in understanding one of the Intel's earlier processors – 80386, the first x86 microprocessor with a 32-bit instruction set and a paging- and segmentation-based memory management unit (MMU). Linus initially named it "Freax." The name evolved into "Linux" soon afterwards. Prior to that, in 1985, Andrew S. Tanenbaum released a UNIX-like 16-bit operating system named MINIX intended for pedagogical use. Linus actually created his own experimental operating system on MINIX using the GNU C compiler, a key component of the GNU tool suite for developing C-based programs. He actually announced his free operating system kernel to the MINIX user group. However, despite its strong UNIX heritage, Linux is not based on any specific edition or variant of UNIX.

On the other hand, at that time, there were other two free UNIX-like operating systems: one was the GNU kernel called Hurd and the other was the BSD as introduced in the previous section, but the source code of these kernels was not available. Otherwise, according to Linus himself, he might have not created his own.

Retrospectively, one might want to know: 1) why Linux has become a very popular free operating system platform today while others in the similar category have not; 2) the controversy between Linux and MINIX; and 3) how Linux and Microsoft proprietary Windows operating system compete with each other, etc. However, such subjects are beyond the scope of this text. Instead, we focus next on the Linux kernel features evolved from release to release as well as some of its most popular variants as of today. Let us start with the Linux kernel features first in the next section.

8.2.1 Linux Kernel Features

Before we discuss Linux kernel features, we need to clarify on the OS design principle of a *monolithic* kernel versus a *microkernel* or μ-kernel. With a monolithic kernel, the whole OS is compiled into a single binary (*a.out*) file that runs in kernel mode. This binary contains not only the process management and memory management system, but also the file system and so on. With a microkernel, however, most of the OS components or subsystems run as separate processes (or servers) outside the kernel in user space, while the kernel only handles message passing, interrupt handling, low-level process management, and possibly the I/O as well. So the criteria to determine whether a kernel is a monolithic one or a microkernel is to see whether some of the subsystems such as the filesystem, networking system, device drivers, etc., run in the kernel space or user space.

Given the guideline on how to determine whether a kernel is a monolithic kernel or a microkernel as stated above, like many UNIX variants, Linux is a monolithic kernel. Linux supports loadable kernel module (LKM) as many other UNIX variants and Microsoft Windows do, though. An LKM is an object file containing code to extend the functionality of a running kernel, and can be unloaded to free memory if no longer needed. With the concept of an LKM, one does not have to recompile and/or reboot a base kernel every time when new functionality is desired. This to some extent compensates for the inflexibility disadvantage of all monolithic kernels.

As a side note, monolithic kernels seem to have been substantially more ubiquitous and more successful commercially than microkernels, partially maybe because monolithic kernels have more direct access to the underlying hardware and thus better performance. This is understandable given the fact that performance is often one of the most critical factors in marketing a product and no one wants to take the risk of losing the competition against their competitors due to relatively lagging performance of their products.

The next clarification we need to make is what constitutes a Linux system. In general, a Linux system has the following four parts:

- **The kernel**: This is the indispensable, low-level operating system that manages all physical and logical resources on behalf of the users and applications.
- **The shell**: This is a command-line interface, enabling users to execute various computing tasks via scripts written in shells such as the `bash` shell (the default shell), Bourne shell, Korn shell, C shell, and so on.
- **Applications**: These are the programs intended for users, ranging from text editing, multi-media, office applications, networking applications, program development environment, and so on, depending on whether the system is used as a desktop system or a server or something else.
- **X**: This is the graphic user interface (GUI) similar to what you see on a typical Windows PC. It is built on the concept of X windows or X11, which is a system for enabling graphics displaying through a client/server model. GNOME and KDE are two of the most popular X implementations on Linux. They differ by UI looks and menu navigation, etc.

This text is concerned with the Linux kernel only. In fact, we focus on the Linux kernel 2.6.23.n. In this notation, the four numbers separated by periods represent the major, minor, revision, and stable versions. The minor (second) number indicates whether it is a stable (if an even number) or development (if an odd number) version; the last number denotes the build number of a given stable kernel version. Although there are hundreds of contributors, Linus himself oversees the overall development and determines whether a build has reached the stable state for releasing.

Table 8.1 lists the major features of Linux from release to release. It started with version 0.11 in 1991, which was almost fully compatible with UNIX System V. Because it was written from scratch and did not contain code from other UNIX and variants in the kernel, the compiler, the utilities, or the libraries, it could be made available fully free. Initially, it could run only on Intel 386/486 based PCs. The subsequent releases focused on improving existing features and porting to other processor architectures.

Table 8.1 Major Linux features evolved through various releases

Version (year)	Major Features
0.11 (1991)	• Runs in protected mode on 386 and above • Support for extended memory up to 16 MB on 386 and above • Memory paging with copy-on-write • The gnu-born again shell (bash) • Full support for multi-tasking • Most development utilities including ANSI compliant C compiler (gcc) • Demand loading of executables • Page sharing of executables • Supports the real time clock
1.0.0 (1994)	• Supported single-processor only
1.2.0 (1995)	• Ported to Alpha, SPARC, and MIPS architectures
2.0.0 (1996)	• Expanded to support SMP (Symmetric Multi-Processing) and more processor types
2.2.0 (1999)	• Improved SMP support • Expanded to support new file systems including read-only support for Microsoft's NTFS • Expanded to support even more processor architectures • Removed the global spinlock
2.4.0 (2001)	• Expanded to support: o USB, PC Cards, and ISA Plug and Play o Logical Volume Manager (LVM) and RAID o ext3 filesystem o Bluetooth
2.6.0 (2003)	• Expanded to support: o Physical Address Extension (PAE) o Several new lines of CPUs o 64-bit computing o In-kernel preemption o More device types o Up to 2^{32} users and 2^{29} process IDs o File systems of up to 16 TB o Infiniband
3.0 (2011)	"Nothing new." Just for celebrating the 20th anniversary of Linux.

Because of its open source nature, a Linux kernel is freely available to anybody or organization. On the other hand, since a kernel is merely a bare-bone minimal required for an operating system, except for those pure kernel hackers, there must be other supporting packages such as compilers, utilities, libraries, applications, etc., to accompany a kernel to make it a fully usable product with some "out-of-the-box" capabilities for a variety of user bases. This has resulted in over 600 distributions of Linux, with each distribution has its own packaging of a kernel plus everything else on top of the kernel. Therefore, typically, a user has to make a decision on which Linux distribution to choose out of hundreds of selections. In general, one does not have to know all those hundreds of distributions. In the next few sections, we introduce a few most commonly used distributions in case this is an unfamiliar subject to you.

8.2.2 Debian/Ubuntu

Debian GNU/Linux is a community-maintained Linux distribution. It includes the GNU tools and Linux kernel. It provides users with access to twenty nine thousand packages on nine different computer architectures. Its strengths include stability and security. It supports both desktop and server versions.

Ubuntu is a Debian based GNU/Linux distribution. It is named after the Southern African philosophy of Ubuntu that promotes peaceful co-existence among human beings. Ubuntu GNU/Linux is more oriented toward desktops, although server versions exist as well. As Ubuntu's purveyor, a UK-based company called Canonical Ltd. maintains Ubuntu and offers the software for free, but charges for technical support and services. As of this writing, the latest Ubuntu version is 11.04.

8.2.3 Fedora

Fedora GNU/Linux is a community-maintained Linux distribution, with sponsorship by Red Hat. It is an RPM-based distribution that software packages are managed using the RPM package manager (RPM) with which each package is represented as a file with the `.rpm` file format. As of this writing, the latest Fedora version is 15, based on Linux kernel 2.6.38.

8.2.4 Red Hat Enterprise Linux (RHEL)

The RHEL is a commercial, enterprise-class Linux distribution from Red Hat, one of the leading Linux distribution vendors. It is closely tied to Fedora due to the sponsorship of Fedora by Red Hat, with a major difference that one is free and the other is not. However, the development of RHEL is separate from that of Fedora that it has its own set of test phases to make it sufficiently robust for enterprise applications.

The RHEL server editions support x86, x86-64, Itanium, PowerPC and IBM System z, while the desktop editions support x86 and x86-64 only. As of this writing, the latest RHEL version is 6, based on Linux kernel 2.6.32.

8.2.5 OpenSUSE/SUSE Linux Enterprise

Another Linux distribution worth to mention here is OpenSUSE that is a community project sponsored by Novell, acquired from a German company named "*Software und System-Entwicklung*," meaning

"Software and Systems Development." It is meant to be the "world's best Linux distribution." As of this writing, the latest OpenSUSE version is 11.4, based on kernel 2.6.37.

The relationship between OpenSUSE and SUSE Linux Enterprise is similar to Fedora and RHEL as discussed in the previous section. SUSE Linux Enterprise also offers desktop and enterprise server editions. As of this writing, the latest SUSE Linux Enterprise Server (SLES) version is 11, based on Linux kernel 2.6.32.

8.2.6 CentOS

CentOS, or Community Enterprise Operating System, is a free, open-source, enterprise-class, community-supported Linux distribution. It's unique that it's functionally compatible with its upstream source, Red Hat Enterprise Linux (RHEL), which is a commercial enterprise Linux distribution. While RHEL is available only through a paid subscription service that provides access to software updates and varying levels of technical support, CentOS is available free of charge, with tech support primarily provided by the community via official mailing list, web forums, and chat rooms.

CentOS is rooted deeply in Red Hat even at the source code level. CentOS developers use Red Hat's source code to create a final product very similar to RHEL, with Red Hat's branding and logos changed because Red Hat does not allow them to be redistributed.

The latest version of CentOS 7 for x86_64 includes images for the following components:

- **Docker**: An open platform for developers and sysadmins to build, ship, and run distributed applications.
- **Systemd**: A suite of system management daemons, such as *systemd*, *journald*, *logind*, *networkd*, libraries, and utilities, and so on. For many Linux distributions, *systemd* is the first process executed in user space in place of *init* process during Linux startup.
- **XFS**: A high-performance 64-bit journaling filesystem originally created by Silicon Graphics in 1993. It is the default filesystem for CentOS, and supported by most Linux Distributions.

CentOS 7 also supports the following popular open source projects:

- **OpenStack**: A free, open-source cloud computing software platform, primarily as an Infrastructure as a Service (IaaS) solution.
- **Xen 4**: Is free, open-source software that can be used as a hypervisor using a microkernel design, providing services to allow multiple computer operating systems to run on the same computer concurrently.
- **Gluster**: An open-source, distributed filesystem capable of scaling to several petabytes and handling thousands of clients.
- **oVirt**: A virtualization platform with an easy-to-use web interface for managing virtual machines and hosts.

The above open-source projects can be customized directly inside a CentOS project to build a CentOS variant for new workloads on top of the core-CentOS platform. In that sense, a CentOS variant is a special edition of CentOS Linux that starts with the core distribution and replaces or supplements a specific subset of packages, which may include replacing down to the kernel, networking, and other subsystems. Since different open-source projects many need different components to run properly, a CentOS 7 variant allows an open-source project to run on and in CentOS more efficiently.

If you want to select a specific Linux flavor to focus on, I suggest CentOS 7 over others. You can get started with it easily by actually installing a CentOS 7 instance on a physical PC or as a virtual machine on a physical host. I created a CentOS 7 VM on my i5-based Macbook Pro on top of VMware Fusion Pro 7.0.1. It was a very smooth process for me. The next section describes all details.

8.2.7 Installing CentsOS 7 as a VM on VMware Fusion 7

For your reference, here is how I created a CentsOS 7 VM on VMware Fusion 7:

1. Downloaded CentOS-7.0-1406-x86_64-DVD.iso from http://wiki.centos.org/Download.
2. Created a VM by selecting the installation method of *More Options… → Create a custom virtual machine*.
3. Chose Operating System of *Linux > CentOS 64-bit*.
4. Chose a virtual disk option of *Create a new virtual disk*.
5. Before clicking *Finish*, chose Customize Settings: Save As: CentOS7-64bit
6. In the Settings panel, I changed Processors to *2 processor cores*, Memory to 4096 MB, and Hard Disk Disk Size to 50 GB.
7. CD/DVD: Checked the box of *Connect CD/DVD Drive* and selected *Choose a disc or disc image …* for *This CD/DVD drive is configured to use the following*. This step is crucial as it determines from where CentOS 7 will be booted and installed. For your reference, this is how it looks like during my installation (if you click on Show All, it will go back to the All Settings panel.):

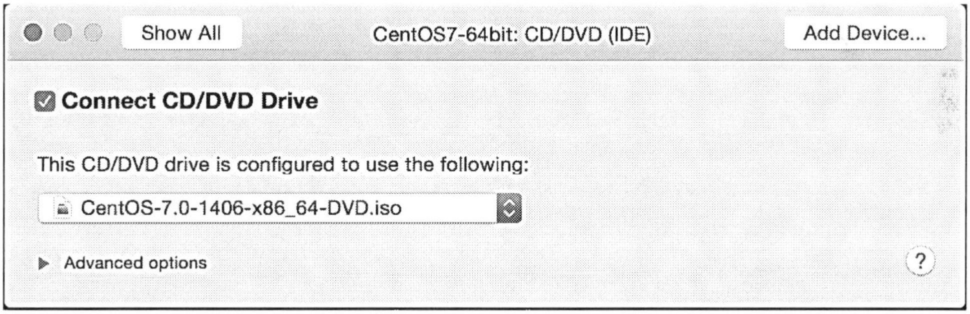

8. Then I right-clicked on the VM's name on Fusion and selected *Start Up*. I then moved to *Install CentOS 7* and hit Return.
9. Then, I set Date & Time and Language.
10. For Software Selection, there are many to choose from. I selected KDE Plasma Workspaces for *Base Environment* and Development Tools for Add-Ons as shown below (once again, I really like CentOS as you see it perhaps is the most *versatile* OS of all):

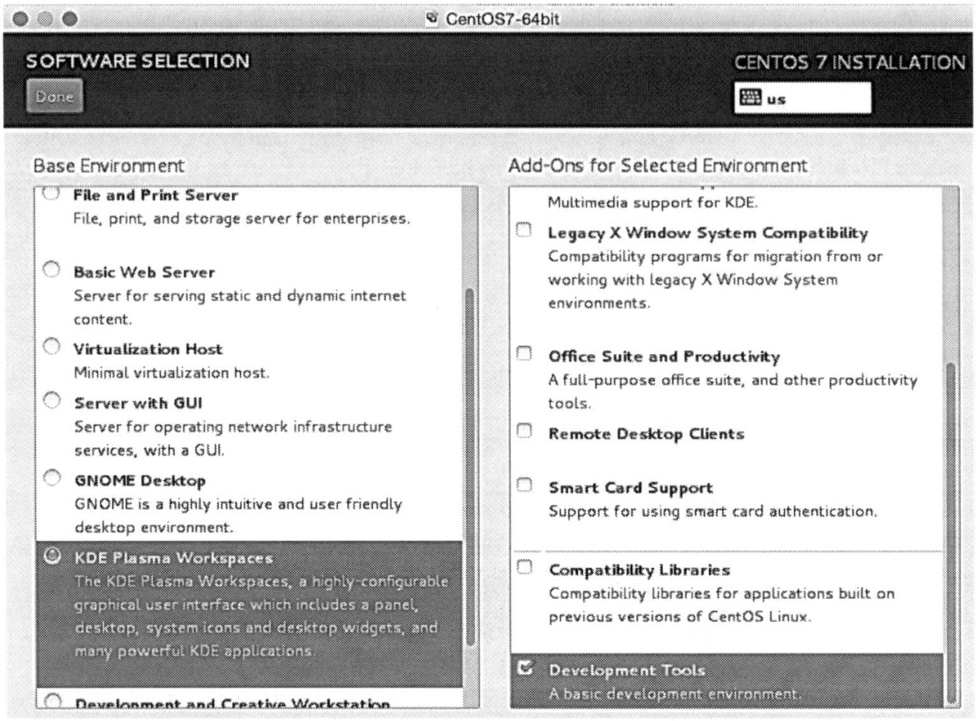

11 For System Installation Destination, I selected Automatic partitioning.
12 Then, I clicked on *Begin Installation* and the installation process began.
13 At this point, there is a User Settings option for setting *ROOT PASSOWRD* and creating a *USER*. I did both. Do not forget check *Make this user administrator*.
14 After completion, I clicked *Reboot*. Then I accepted the license and clicked *FINISH CONFIGURATION*.
15 For Kdump, I did not enable it and clicked *Forward*. I then rebooted the VM again.

I then logged in to my CentOS 7 and I was greeted with a very nice GUI.

There is another option to install CentsOS, which is called *Linux Easy Install* by directly selecting the ISO file at the first step. This option actually took much longer without much customization, so I did not choose that option.

Next, I share some tips about how to configure the CentOS 7 created above.

8.2.8 Configuring CentOS 7

In this section, I share the following CentOS 7 configurations with you:

- How to configure Konsole Workspace Appearance. By right-clicking on the desktop, you can select Konsole to open up a command line terminal. However, the terminal screen has no left edge, which makes it hard to view a terminal when more than one is open. To fix the problem, select System

Settings from the Kickoff Application Launcher located at the left bottom corner, and then select Workspace Appearance > Windows Decorations > Laptop.

- How to configure Internet connection. The other issue is that your Internet connection may not work. You can verify by opening up Firefox from Kickoff Application Launcher > Applications > Internet > Firefox Web Browser. If it doesn't work, select Kickoff Application Launcher > Computer > System Settings > Network Settings > Wired. Click on the Connection (in my case, eno16777736) and then *Edit*. Now check *Connect automatically* as shown below and click *OK*. You should see the State of *Connected* for your connection under the *Wired* tab. Your Firefox should work now.

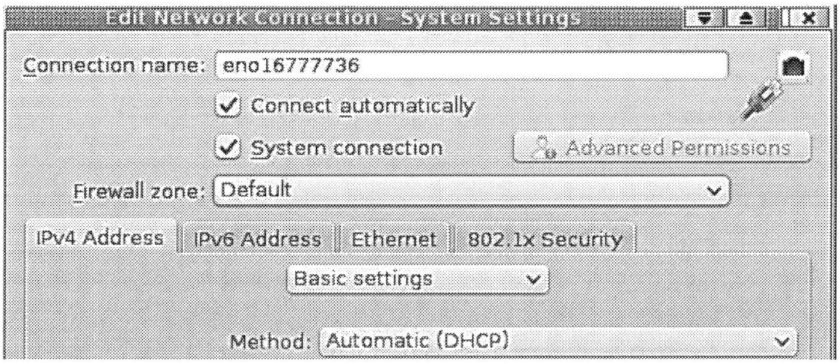

You may also want to install a latest Java 7 JDK. CentOS installs an OpenJDK by default to start with, which can be verified as follows by issuing the highlighted commands at a Konsole command line prompt:

```
[henry@localhost ~]$ java -version
java version "1.7.0_51"
OpenJDK Runtime Environment (rhel-2.4.5.5.el7-x86_64 u51-b31)
OpenJDK 64-Bit Server VM (build 24.51-b03, mixed mode)
[henry@localhost ~]$ which java
/usr/bin/java
[henry@localhost ~]$ ll $(which java)
lrwxrwxrwx. 1 root root 22 Nov 11 12:30 /usr/bin/java -> /etc/alternatives/java
[henry@localhost ~]$ ls -ali /etc/alternatives/java
68880726 lrwxrwxrwx. 1 root root 72 Nov 11 12:30 /etc/alternatives/java ->
 /usr/lib/jvm/java-1.7.0-openjdk-1.7.0.51-2.4.5.5.el7.x86_64/jre/bin/java
[henry@localhost ~]$
```

I installed Oracle JDK 7 by downloading *jdk-7u71-linux-x64.tar.gz* for Linux x64 first. Then, I changed to the *~heny/mspc/myapp* folder, moved the downloaded file to this folder, and issued the following command to untar it to the *myapp* folder:

```
tar xzvf jdk-7u71-linux-x64.tar.gz .
```

Note that CentOS 7 has two default bash script files: *.bashrc* and *.bash_profile*. The former is for global settings, while the latter is for user specific settings. I added the following entries to my *.bash_profile* file so that I can access many tools such as *jvisualvm*, *jstat*, and so on that come with a JDK install:

```
export JAVA_HOME=/home/henry/mspc/myapp/jdk1.7.0_71
```

```
export PATH=$JAVA_HOME/bin:$PATH:$HOME/.local/bin:$HOME/bin
```

Now, a latest Oracle JDK 7 is ready for use. I will use this environment to demonstrate some Linux command line tools later in this chapter.

Having introduced Linux kernel features and a variety of distributions such as Debian/Ubuntu, Fedora/RHEL, OpenSUSE/SUSE Linux Enterprise, and CentOS, let's have a brief overview of Linux kernel architecture from the performance and scalability perspectives next. Unlike Windows, Linux is not a self-tuned platform. It requires some level of understanding of how Linux works in order to optimize and tune Java performance and scalability on Linux.

8.3 LINUX ARCHITECTURE

Let's start with examining the various elements of a typical Linux system for supporting running various types of applications, as shown in Figure 8.1. This would help lay the foundation for understanding Java performance and scalability on Linux.

8.3.1 The Standard C Library

The main purpose of a computer system, be it Linux or something else, is for running applications. Therefore, in Figure 8.1, we see "*Applications*" at the top as the starting point. No matter in what language an application is written, it eventually calls functions in a C library installed on a Linux system to get its application logic executed. Most applications developed on Linux uses the standard C library – the GNU C library called *glibc*, although embedded Linux systems may use other implementations of the standard C library with much-needed smaller memory footprints. If you have access to a Linux system, you can check out the version of the *glibc* on your system by typing "*/lib/libc.so.6*" at a command shell. For example, on one of my Linux servers, I first executed the "*cat /etc/*release**" command to find out what Linux version was running on it and then executed the "*/lib/libc.so.6*" command to find out which version of glibc was installed on:

```
[root@icmn perf_log]# cat /etc/*release*
Red Hat Enterprise Linux Server release 6.0 (Santiago)
cpe:/o:redhat:enterprise_linux:6server:ga:server
[root@icmn perf_log]# /lib/libc.so.6
GNU C Library stable release version 2.12, by Roland McGrath et al.
Copyright (C) 2010 Free Software Foundation, Inc.
......
Compiled by GNU CC version 4.4.4 20100726 (Red Hat 4.4.4-13).
Compiled on a Linux 2.6.32 system on 2011-07-04.
Available extensions:
        The C stubs add-on version 2.1.2.
        crypt add-on version 2.1 by Michael Glad and others
        GNU Libidn by Simon Josefsson
        Native POSIX Threads Library by Ulrich Drepper et al
        BIND-8.2.3-T5B
        RT using linux kernel aio
```

```
libc ABIs: UNIQUE IFUNC
For bug reporting instructions, please see:
<http://www.gnu.org/software/libc/bugs.html>.
[root@icmn perf_log]#
```

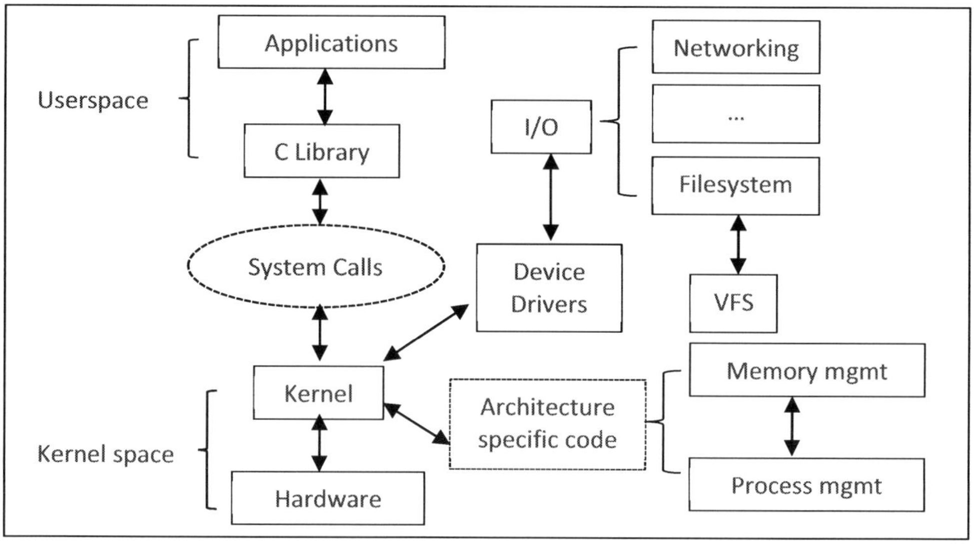

Figure 8.1 The architecture of a typical Linux system

At this point, it's important to keep in mind that many library functions don't initiate system calls, for example, the string manipulation functions. If things were always so simple, however, tuning Java performance and scalability on Linux would have not been so challenging. As is shown in Figure 8.1, C library functions make system calls, which is our subject next.

8.3.2 System Calls

A system call is initiated through a higher-level C-library function on behalf of an application for executing some application logic. For example, when an application needs to open a file, it calls the *fopen ()* library function which in turn makes an *open ()* system call. Another example is the *printf ()* function that everyone is familiar with, which makes a *write ()* system call. As we see, library functions are often made more user-friendly mnemonically than the underlying system calls. To some extent, the C library functions are just *wrappers* of their respective system calls. However, the real question here is why we need system calls. This question can be answered with Figure 8.1 by examining that whenever a system call is made, execution transits from *userspace* to *kernel space*. These two different areas of virtual memory correspond to user mode and kernel mode in which the hardware (or the CPU to be exact) can operate, respectively.

It's important to understand that when running in user mode, the CPU can access only the virtual memory area designated as userspace; when running in kernel mode, on the other hand, the CPU can access both the userspace and the virtual memory area designated as kernel space. Attempts to access kernel space while running in user mode would be met with a hardware exception. Additionally, some operations can be performed only when the CPU is running in kernel mode, for example, stopping the system via executing the halt instruction, initiating device I/O operations, accessing the memory management hardware, and so on. Such isolation is necessary so that many management and controlling responsibilities can be assigned to the kernel, as is discussed next.

8.3.3 Responsibilities of the Kernel

As is seen in Figure 8.1, the Linux kernel interacts with both the hardware CPU and various device drivers (a device driver is a software program that provides the hardware CPU with an interface to interact with the physical device such as a network card, a disk, a mouse, a keyboard, a display monitor, and so on). In addition, the kernel has hardware specific code for memory management and process management. From the Java performance and scalability perspective, we are most concerned with how Linux manages memory and processes. This requires us to understand the concept of virtual memory, which is discussed next.

8.3.4 Virtual Memory

In order to understand how Linux manages memory, we need to start with the concept of *virtual memory*. Virtual memory provides an abstract view between the application and the kernel. It gives an application a perception that it has its own dedicated memory area, but in fact its memory area may overlap with those of other applications. The capacity of virtual memory is quantified with another concept of *virtual address space*. It is called *virtual* because the maximum size of this virtual address space is not tied to the actual amount of physical RAM installed on a system. For example, on a 32-bit system such as IA-32 (where IA stands for Intel Architecture), this maximum size is $2^{32} \cong 4$ GB, as is illustrated in Figure 8.2. The division line is designated with a parameter named *TASK_SIZE*, which equals 3×2^{30} on an IA-32-based Linux system, with the lower 3 GB assigned to the user program and upper 1 GB to the kernel.

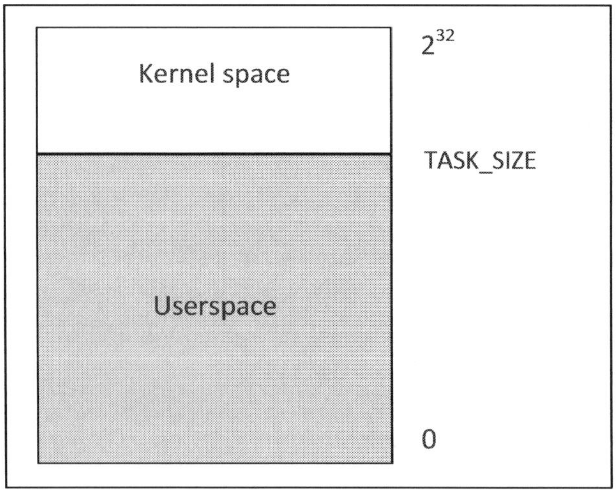

Figure 8.2 Division of a virtual address space between the kernel and a user program on a 32-bit system

The benefits of virtual memory include:

- Multiple programs can run on the system concurrently.
- Programs can be written machine-independent, as the virtual address space is abstract in nature.
- An application can use a larger address space exceeding the actual RAM capacity available on the system.
- An application does not have to have all its code loaded into memory at startup.
- Multiple applications can share a single library image or program.
- Programs are relocatable that they can be placed anywhere in physical memory.

Note that although a user program can have the perception that it owns the entire user address space, in realityy, the kernel has to map this virtual userspace to the underlying physical RAM with the help of the hardware Memory Management Unit (MMU). This is clarified in the next section.

8.3.5 Virtual and Physical Address Spaces

As we stated previously, it is not a programmer's concern about which physical memory areas the program can access. It's the joint responsibility of the kernel and CPU to take care of actual mapping from virtual to physical address space. Figure 8.3 shows a hypothetical example.

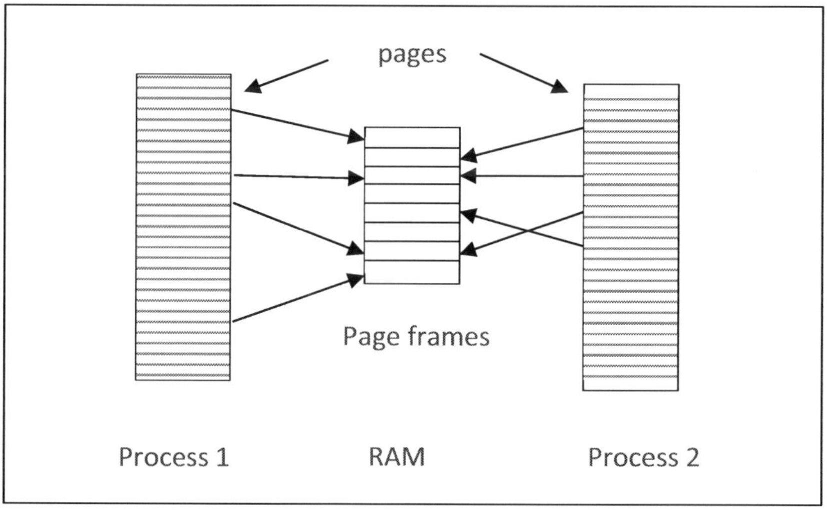

Figure 8.3 Memory mapping from virtual to physical address space

In Figure 8.3, each of the two processes (1 and 2) has its own virtual address space independent of each other. Each virtual address space is divided into portions of equal size, with each portion known as a *page*. The RAM physical address space is also divided into portions of equal size, but each portion is known as a *page frame* to distinguish from a *page* in a virtual address space. Note that a page frame can be mapped to the pages of multiple processes, thanks to the concept of virtual address space.

The next section discusses how mapping of virtual address space to physical address space is implemented with the concept of *page tables*.

8.3.6 Page Tables

Each process maintains a data structure known as a page table to record the mappings from virtual to physical address space. The simplest implementation would be just a single array with the array index representing the page number in the virtual address space and the content of each array element representing the corresponding page frame number in the physical address space. However, a simple back-of-the-envelope type of calculation would immediately reveal that this would be impractical. Let's say we have a 32-bit system and the page size is 4 kB. The total capacity of 4 GB would require to have an array of one million elements. It would be even much worse for a 64-bit system.

To circumvent the above issue, a more efficient implementation would be to use *multilevel paging*. This would not only reduce the size of a page table but also allow unneeded virtual addresses to be ignored. Figure 8.4 shows conceptually how multilevel paging works.

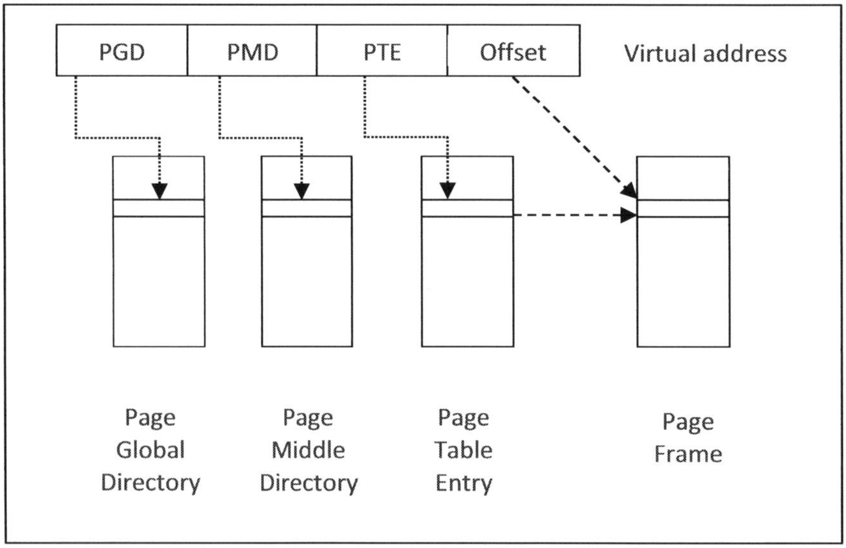

Figure 8.4 Three-level multilevel paging

In Figure 8.4, each level of paging is implemented as an array. The first level paging is implemented as a page global directory (PGD) that each process has an element in it represented by the array index; the content of each PGD array element is a pointer to the second level of paging known as the page middle directory (PMD). A PMD is also represented by an array data structure, which further points to the page table entry (PTE) array data structure. The content of each PTE array element represents the physical page frame that the virtual address is mapped to. Note that the last part of a virtual address is a byte position *offset*, which determines the relative position within the page frame.

The number of levels for multilevel paging is CPU architecture dependent. On a 32-bit system, only two-level paging is implemented without the PMD indirection shown in Figure 8.4, while on 64-bit systems, three-level or even four-level multilevel paging is adopted due to the much larger virtual address space.

To help understand paging further, let's present an example using a 32-bit system. In this case, both PGD and PTE are 10 bits, each of which is capable of addressing 2^{10}=1024 entries; the offset part is 12 bits, which would be capable of addressing 2^{12}=4096 entries. The total number of memory cells that can be addressed would be $1024\times1024\times4096=2^{32}$, as expected. Actually, not all those memory cells are translated from virtual to physical every time. All modern operating systems including Linux have a fast CPU cache called a *Translation Lookaside Buffer* (TLB), which provides immediate page frame information for frequently referenced virtual addresses so that there is no need to go through the multiple-level paging and access the physical memory. Such measures are extremely important for boasting the overall performance of a system.

8.3.7 Swapping and Page Reclaiming

Ideally, all data should be kept in physical memory for all processes so that the kernel and CPU don't have to incur significant latencies when accessing data stored on disk. However, this would limit the number of processes a system can support significantly. To share memory most efficiently, *swapping* is implemented to make space for those processes that need memory more urgently than those which occupy memory but can afford to have their data temporarily written to disk and brought back later when needed. If a page is swapped out to disk, it is tagged in the page table. When it is needed again by its owner process, the CPU issues a page fault that is intercepted by the kernel; the kernel then swaps the data back to RAM. This entire process is transparent to the application.

Linux allows memory and disk caches to grab more and more page frames without releasing them, which is especially true when a Linux system is used as a database server. Sooner or later, all free memory will be assigned to processes and caches, leading to a "low memory condition." This may cause the system to crash if not detected and cured in time. Page reclaiming is a process that checks if the page frames that have their changes already written back to disk can be reclaimed. Typically, pages, including those in disk and memory caches, that are not referenced by any process are reclaimed first. Such pages are called "*harmless*" pages. The Linux page frame reclaiming algorithm (PFRA) actually "instigates" a user process to "steal" page frames from other user processes, so the processes that have been sleeping for a long period may lose more and more page frames.

8.3.8 UMA versus NUMA

As was introduced in §2.3, Intel replaced its bus-based memory access design with the QuickPath Interconnect technology. This fundamentally is an issue of whether adopting the bus-based uniform memory access (UMA) design or network-based non-uniform memory access (NUMA) design for the CPUs to access data in memory. Refer to Figure 2.4 where the left-hand-side diagram shows the UMA scheme whereas the right-hand-side diagram shows the NUMA scheme. To help explain the concepts of UMA and NUMA, Figure 2.4 is re-drawn and shown in Figure 8.5 with some sort of abstraction applied. As you see, with the UMA based design, all CPUs are placed equal distance to the shared memory so that it takes the same amount of time for each CPU to access memory. With the NUMA-based design, however, memory units are attached to CPUs so that it would take longer for a CPU to access another CPU's local memory than its own. Therefore, in the case of NUMA, memory access time is no longer a constant and thus the term of "*non-uniform.*" Note that the concepts of UMA and NUMA apply not only to memory but also to I/O, as you can confirm from Figure 2.4.

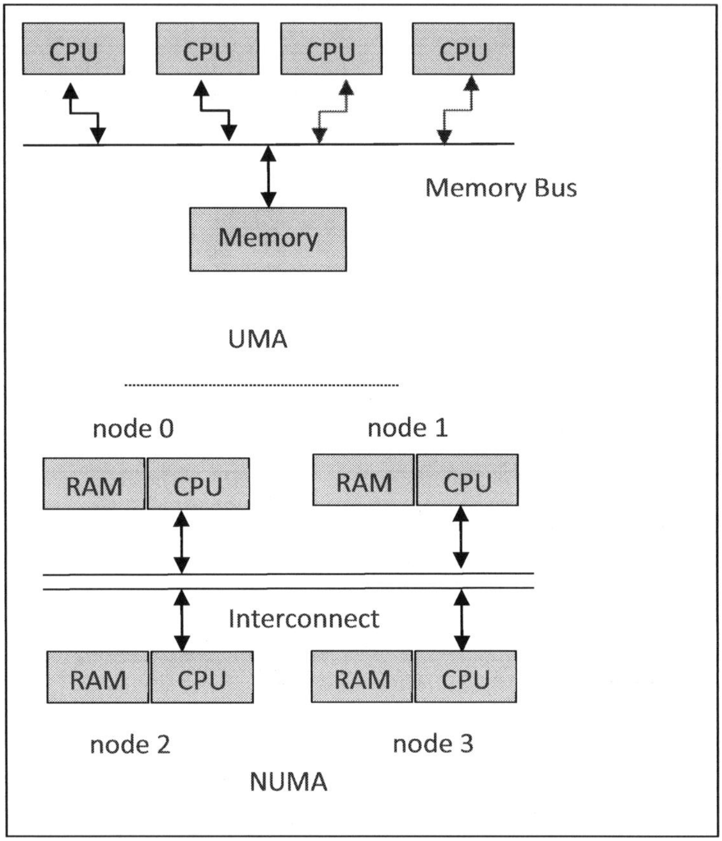

Figure 8.5 Schematic illustrations of UMA (upper) versus NUMA (lower) CPU-RAM paths (note that each CPU-RAM unit is called a *node*)

So why has Intel switched from UMA to NUMA for its latest multiple-core-based processors? It turned out that the traditional UMA design for symmetric multiprocessor (SMP) support did not scale well as the number of CPUs increases, primarily due to increased contentions on the CPU-memory bus. However, with the NUMA design, it places new challenges to the operating system that tasks should be scheduled to run on the CPU where the data is in its local memory. This is a more complicated issue and we would not pursue further. For our purposes here, it's sufficient to understand conceptually what NUMA is about, as we will see the NUMA spec in terms of nodes later when we illustrate how to query the CPU model of a Linux system.

8.3.9 Processes

On UNIX/Linux systems, applications, servers, and other types of user programs are called *processes* from the kernel's point of view. The kernel assigns an address space in the virtual memory of the CPU to each process. All processes are independent of each other and unaware of each other. If the processes need to communicate to each other to exchange data, it must be coordinated through the kernel.

How processes are created on Linux? Linux uses a hierarchical scheme in which each process depends on a parent process. The top most process is created with the *init* program. It then uses the following two mechanisms to create child processes:

- **fork**: Creates an exact copy of the current process with a new process id (PID) assigned to the child process. The same pages are used for both processes until either the parent or child writes to a page, in which case a copy operation is performed. This is a technique known as *copy-on-write*, which apparently is more efficient from both CPU and memory perspectives.
- **exec**: Loads a new program into the existing context and executes it. The memory pages reserved by the old program are flushed, and their contents are replaced with new data.

Since processes are independent of each other, two issues arise. One is how the kernel would coordinate the executions of all processes. This falls into the category of *task switching*. When the kernel needs to switch from one process to another, it performs the following two steps:

- Saving all state information of the process and placing it to the idle state
- Releasing all CPU resources and reassigning them to the new process or task

The other issue is how the kernel decides which process should run next and how long it should run before switching to another process. This falls into the category of *process scheduling*. Linux has evolved through the following four different scheduling schemes:

- **Preemptive multitasking** (prior to version 2.4): With this scheme, each process is allocated a fixed slice of time during which it may execute. Once this period has expired, the kernel switches to another process regardless of the state of the current process (of course, the state information of the current process is saved as stated above so that it can resume its execution when its next turn comes). This scheduling algorithm wastes valuable CPU time as there is no guarantee that every process is actually ready to execute when its turn comes.
- O(**n**) **Scheduler** (version 2.4): This scheduler works based on a multilevel feedback queue in conjunction with priority levels ranging from 0-140, with 0-99 reserved for real-time tasks and 100-140 for *nice* tasks. The time quantum for switching processes was 200 milliseconds for real time tasks and 10 milliseconds for nice tasks, respectively. It also separates processes into categories based on their need for the processor. Besides, a multilevel feedback queue algorithm favors short tasks and I/O bound processes.
- O(**1**) **Scheduler** (version 2.5 – 2.6.22): This scheduler divides CPU time into quanta. Within each quantum, every process can execute up to its share. If a process does not use all of its time slice, then the scheduler carries over and adds the remaining portion of the quantum to its next cycle to allow it to execute longer.
- **Completely Fair Scheduling (CFS)** (version 2.6.23 -): This is a variation of the fair scheduling algorithm that equally distributes CPU time among system users or groups rather than among

processes only. For example, if there are four users in the system, each user would receive an equal portion of 25% of the total CPU time. The CFS algorithm implements a concept called "*sleeper fairness*," which considers sleeping or waiting tasks as well in addition to those on the *runqueue*. The fairness is attempted by tracking the wait time of a sleeping or blocked process so that its *priority* and *timeslice* can be adjusted dynamically (a process that waited longer would receive a higher priority and a longer timeslice). This consideration benefits interactive tasks that spend a significant amount of time waiting for user input or responses from other subsystems.

In the next section, we discuss the concept of a thread in UNIX/Linux context.

8.3.10 Threads

In UNIX/Linux context, the two concepts of processes and threads are similar but not exactly the same. Although both a process and a thread are created by their respective parent processes, they are termed *heavy-weight* and *light-weight* processes, respectively. Perhaps the major difference between a process and a thread is that processes are independent of each other, whereas the threads created by the same parent process are not. For example, a Java program may create multiple threads in its `main` program to execute certain tasks in parallel, in which case, all threads share the same global variables, address space, open files, and so on, and the changes made by one thread are visible to all other threads. Besides, the concept of inter-process communication does not apply to threads. Instead, threads belonging to the same thread group need to be synchronized properly.

In the next section, we summarize how to get to know about your Linux systems quickly.

8.4 KNOWING ABOUT YOUR LINUX SYSTEMS

Diagnosing Linux performance issues should start with knowing about your Linux system from resource configuration perspectives. This includes not only the hardware resource configurations such as CPU, memory, etc., but also system configurations as configured in the */etc/security/limits.conf* file. We summarize the utilities for querying those configuration parameters in this section.

8.4.1 Version of a Linux System

The version information on a Linux system should include both the kernel version and vendor release version. To query the Linux kernel version, use the following command:

```
$uname –r
```

To query the vendor release version, use the following command:

```
$cat /etc/*release*
```

Table 8.2 lists the version information obtained using the above two commands on some of my Linux systems. It's important to get accurate information about the version of the kernel and vendor release, as we learnt in the previous sections that Linux evolves fast that performance and scalability may improve or degrade from one release to another.

Table 8.2 Version information on some latest Linux systems

host	$uname -r	$cat /etc/*release*
mitwo	Red Hat Enterprise Linux Server release 6.0	2.6.32-71.el6.x86_64
pf01	SUSE Linux Enterprise Server 11(x86_64)	2.6.27.19-5-default
icmn	Red Hat Enterprise Linux Server release 6.0	2.6.32-71.40.1.el6.x86_64
w9ms	OpenSUSE 12.1 (Asparagus)	3.1.0-1.2-desktop

8.4.2 CPU model

CPU is one of the most crucial factors in determining the performance and scalability of a Linux system. As have been demonstrated using case studies based on a real enterprise software product in the previous chapters, newer generations of CPUs could perform and scale significantly better than old generations. So it's important to know upfront what kind of CPUs are cranking in your Linux box.

You can use the command

```
$nproc
```

to know the number of CPUs or

```
$ less /proc/cpuinfo
```

to get more detailed information on the CPUs installed in your Linux system. However, there is a command that gives more information than "*nproc*" but much less verbose than "*less /proc/cpuinfo*" that should be used instead, namely, the command of

```
$lscpu
```

For example, Table 8.3 shows the information obtained on the Linux system named "*mitwo*" in Table 8.2. For your convenience, I have converted the output into a table and added some annotations in the last column to help explain what those specs mean. As you see, we know immediately that this Linux server has 2 quad cores without hyper-threading enabled, running at 1.86 GHz. Following Table 8.3, Listings 8.1 – 8.3 show the output obtained on the other Linux systems listed in Table 8.2. Listing 8.2 shows that that Linux system is a hyper-thread enabled system, since it lists 2 threads per core. Note that this command also shows the NUMA configuration associated with a system.

However, the "*lscpu*" command does not give the CPU model name information. If you look up the published CPU benchmarking results, they are often listed by CPU model name. To obtain the CPU model name information on a Linux system, use the following command:

```
$less /proc/cpuinfo | grep "model name"
```

Table 8.4 shows the CPU model name information obtained with the above command on each of the Linux systems listed here. Out of all these CPU models, the Xeon X5550 @ 2.67 GHz is the latest and the most powerful one.

Table 8.3 CPU info obtained with the "lscpu" command on a Linux system (mitwo)

Spec	Info	Comment
Architecture	x86_64	Intel 64-bit
CPU op-mode(s)	32-bit, 64-bit	supports both 32-bit and 64-bit apps
CPU(s)	8	# of CPUs
Thread(s) per core	1	non-hyper-threaded
Core(s) per socket	4	quad-core
CPU socket(s)	2	2 quad-cores
NUMA node(s)	1	
Vendor ID	GenuineIntel	
CPU family	6	
Model	15	
Stepping	7	
CPU MHz	1866.669	CPU @ 1.86 GHz
Virtualization	VT-x	
L1d cache	32K	L1 data cache
L1i cache	32K	L1 instruction cache
L2 cache	4096K	L2 cache
NUMA node0 CPU(s)	0-7	

Listing 8.1 Output from the command of "lscpu" on a Linux VM (pf01)

```
pf01:~ # lscpu
Architecture:          x86_64
CPU(s):                8
Thread(s) per core:    1
Core(s) per socket:    1
CPU socket(s):         8
NUMA node(s):          1
Vendor ID:             GenuineIntel
CPU family:            6
Model:                 15
Stepping:              11
CPU MHz:               2393.890
L1d cache:             32K
L1i cache:             32K
```

```
L2 cache:              3072K
```

Listing 8.2 Output from the command of "lscpu" on a Linux system (physical) (icmn)

```
[root@icmn ~]# lscpu
Architecture:          x86_64
CPU op-mode(s):        32-bit, 64-bit
CPU(s):                16
Thread(s) per core:    2
Core(s) per socket:    4
CPU socket(s):         2
NUMA node(s):          2
Vendor ID:             GenuineIntel
CPU family:            6
Model:                 26
Stepping:              5
CPU MHz:               2659.942
Virtualization:        VT-x
L1d cache:             32K
L1i cache:             32K
L2 cache:              256K
L3 cache:              8192K
NUMA node0 CPU(s):     0,2,4,6,8,10,12,14
NUMA node1 CPU(s):     1,3,5,7,9,11,13,15
```

Listing 8.3 Output from the command of "lscpu" on a Linux desktop system (physical) (w9ms)

```
henry@w9ms:~>lscpu
Architecture:          i686
CPU op-mode(s):        32-bit, 64-bit
Byte Order:            Little Endian
CPU(s):                2
On-line CPU(s) list:   0,1
Thread(s) per core:    1
Core(s) per socket:    2
Socket(s):             1
NUMA node(s):          1
Vendor ID:             GenuineIntel
CPU family:            6
Model:                 23
Stepping:              10
CPU MHz:               800.000
BogoMIPS:              5585.69
Virtualization:        VT-x
L1d cache:             32K
L1i cache:             32K
L2 cache:              6144K
```

NUMA node0 CPU(s): 0,1

Table 8.4 CPU model name information obtained with the command of "less /proc/cpuinfo | grep "model name"" on the four Linux systems discussed here

host	CPU model	
mitwo	Intel® Xeon ® CPU	E5320 @ 1.86 GHz
pf01	Intel® Xeon ® CPU	E7330 @ 2.40 GHz
icmn	Intel® Xeon ® CPU	X5550 @ 2.67 GHz
w9ms	Intel® Core™ 2 Duo CPU	T9600 @ 2.80 GHz

8.4.3 Memory

If you are interested in the information about the memory configuration and other statistical data on your Linux system, there are multiple commands that can be used to query different type of information. The first command I would recommend is the "*cat /proc/meminfo*" command as is shown below. Listing 8.4 shows the output obtained on the Linux machine named *icmn.*

```
$ cat /proc/meminfo
```

This output shows that this system has about 24 GB RAM installed, 13 GB free, 575 MB and 5.5 GB used by buffers and caches, respectively. It also shows a swap file of 25 GB. The *Hugepages_** items with all zeros show that the huge page feature is not used although it has a *hugepagesize* of 2 MB configured (the normal pagesize is 4 kB, and for some applications the large page or huge page feature can help improve performance).

If you are interested in the additional information such as type, speed, manufacturer, etc., use the "*dmidecode --type memory*" command as is shown below. Listing 8.5 shows the output obtained on the same Linux machine named *icmn.*

```
$ dmidecode --type memory
```

If you are interested in a quick look at the general memory usage and the amount of free memory, use the following command instead:

```
$free –m
```

Listing 8.6 shows the output of this command from the same Xeon X5550 Linux system. It is seen that this command shows the *total, used, free, shared, buffers, cached,* and *swap* memory as of the querying. Note the line between "*Mem*" and "*Swap*:" -/+ *buffers/cache*. Since buffers and cache are reclaimable by the kernel, used/free memory was re-calculated by subtracting/adding a (buffers + cache) amount to reflect the fact that the actual used/free memory might be smaller/larger than one might think based on the general notion of used/free memory in Linux. (The difference between buffers and cached is that the former represents temporary storage while the latter contains frequently used data.)

Listing 8.4 Output of the "cat /proc/meminfo" command obtained on a Xeon X5550 Linux system

```
[root@icmn ~]# cat /proc/meminfo
MemTotal:          24597864 kB
MemFree:           13483712 kB
Buffers:           575876 kB
Cached:            5454468 kB
SwapCached:        0 kB
Active:            6556412 kB
Inactive:          3494104 kB
Active(anon):      4020368 kB
Inactive(anon):    1052 kB
Active(file):      2536044 kB
Inactive(file):    3493052 kB
Unevictable:       0 kB
Mlocked:           0 kB
SwapTotal:         25165816 kB
SwapFree:          25165816 kB
Dirty:             1180 kB
Writeback:         0 kB
AnonPages:         4020180 kB
Mapped:            53224 kB
Shmem:             1268 kB
Slab:              930612 kB
SReclaimable:      447412 kB
SUnreclaim:        483200 kB
KernelStack:       11928 kB
PageTables:        20040 kB
NFS_Unstable:      0 kB
Bounce:            0 kB
WritebackTmp:      0 kB
CommitLimit:       37464748 kB
Committed_AS:      4959096 kB
VmallocTotal:      34359738367 kB
VmallocUsed:       336512 kB
VmallocChunk:      34346245832 kB
HardwareCorrupted: 0 kB
AnonHugePages:     3858432 kB
HugePages_Total:   0
HugePages_Free:    0
HugePages_Rsvd:    0
HugePages_Surp:    0
Hugepagesize:      2048 kB
DirectMap4k:       6628 kB
DirectMap2M:       25149440 kB
[root@icmn ~]#
```

Listing 8.5 Output of the "dmidecode --type memory" command obtained on the same Xeon X5550 Linux system

```
[root@icmn ~]# dmidecode --type memory
# dmidecode 2.11
SMBIOS 2.6 present.

Handle 0x1000, DMI type 16, 15 bytes
Physical Memory Array
        Location: System Board Or Motherboard
        Use: System Memory
        Error Correction Type: Multi-bit ECC
        Maximum Capacity: 192 GB
        Error Information Handle: Not Provided
        Number Of Devices: 18

Handle 0x1100, DMI type 17, 28 bytes
Memory Device
        Array Handle: 0x1000
        Error Information Handle: Not Provided
        Total Width: 72 bits
        Data Width: 64 bits
        Size: 4096 MB
        Form Factor: DIMM
        Set: 1
        Locator: DIMM_A1
        Bank Locator: Not Specified
        Type: DDR3
        Type Detail: Synchronous Registered (Buffered)
        Speed: 1333 MHz
        Manufacturer: 00AD009780AD
        Serial Number: 35109699
        Asset Tag: 0110151D
        Part Number: HMT151R7BFR4C-H9
        Rank: 2
...
```

Listing 8.6 Output of the "free –m" command from the same Xeon X5550 Linux system

```
[root@icmn ~]# free -m
             total     used      free     shared   buffers    cached
Mem:         24021     10854     13166         0       562      5326
-/+ buffers/cache:      4965     19055
Swap:        24575         0     24575
```

8.4.4 Disk

To query about the filesystems provisioned by the kernel on your Linux machine, use the following command:

```
$df –m
```

where the "*-m*" option denotes that the unit of MB should be used. If you specify "*-k*" in place of "*-m*", the unit of kB will be used. Listing 8.7 shows an example output obtained on the same *icmn* Linux machine using the "*df –m*" command. If any directory's usage is getting close to 100%, you need to free up some space before continuing.

Listing 8.7 Output of the "df –m" command on Linux

```
[root@icmn ~]# df -m
Filesystem                      1M-blocks   Used Available Use% Mounted on
/dev/mapper/vg_icmn-LogVol00    19686       909  17778     5%  /
tmpfs                           12011       1    12011     1%  /dev/shm
/dev/sda1                       1008        81   876       9%  /boot
/dev/mapper/vg_icmn-LogVol05    195070      4374 180787    3%  /data1
/dev/mapper/vg_icmn-LogVol03    4922        445  4227      10% /opt
/dev/mapper/vg_icmn-LogVol01    4922        140  4532      3%  /tmp
/dev/mapper/vg_icmn-LogVol02    24608       5047 18311     22% /usr
```

8.4.5 Network

On Windows, we use the "*ipconfig*" command to look up the IP address of a system. On Linux, we use the "*ifconfig*" command to look up the IP address of a Linux system as follows:

```
$ ifconfig
```

There is another command that I use very often to check if a specific port is already in use, which is:

```
$ netstat
```

For example, Listing 8.8 shows the output of executing this command on the Linux machine named "*icmn*," piped with the *grep* command to filter for the entries containing the word "ESTABLISHED." As is seen, this command displays the *network protocol*, *Receiving and Sending queues*, *local* and *remote addresses*, and the *state* of the connection. Since *icmn* was used as a Java application server and *mitwo* a database server, each entry shown in Listing 8.8 implies an established connection from the Java application server to the database server. To find out the number of connections established, pipe the above command with the "*wc -l*" command, which gave a number of 440 in this case, meaning that there were 440 connections established between the Java application server and the database server at the time when the command was executed.

Of course, don't forget the *ping* command that applies to both Windows and UNIX/Linux.

Listing 8.8 Output of the netstat command executed on a Linux machine named "icmn"

```
[root@icmn ~]# netstat | grep "ESTABLISHED"
Active Internet connections (w/o servers)
Proto Recv-Q Send-Q Local Address Foreign Address       State
tcp        0      0 icmn:35460    mitwo:ncube-lm  ESTABLISHED
```

```
tcp    0    0 icmn:58051        mitwo:ncube-lm  ESTABLISHED
tcp    0    0 icmn:46385        mitwo:ncube-lm  ESTABLISHED
......
```

To check a particular port, use the following *netstat* command:

```
netstat -ano | grep <port>
```

8.4.6 Checking and Configuring Kernel Parameters

In general, Windows is a self-tuned platform whereas Linux is not. It means that it's very likely that Windows would outperform Linux, given exactly the same hardware configurations and workload. However, after applying tunings, it's very possible that Linux could outperform Windows with exactly the same hardware configurations and application. We will show such a case study later, but now let's focus on understanding some key Linux kernel parameters that can have significant impacts on how a Java application performs and scales on Linux.

In order for a Java application or any application to perform and function properly on a Linux system, certain sizing guidelines must be followed so that the Linux system would have the required resources in terms of CPU, RAM, network interfaces and storage, etc., to support the projected workload. However, it's insufficient just to have the right hardware configurations. The kernel parameters must be configured properly based on the requirements derived from rigorous, internal performance and scalability testing or production operational analysis. In this section, we first explain what those kernel parameters are and how to configure them. In a later section, we demonstrate the impacts of some of the kernel parameters on the performance and scalability of a real enterprise Java application.

Linux kernel parameters can be classified into the following categories:

1 **Semaphores**: Semaphores are used in Linux to control accesses to shared resources. A semaphore is like a spin lock that it does not allow a kernel control path to proceed unless the lock is open. A semaphore is represented as a counter to indicate whether the resource it represents is available or not. If a semaphore has a larger than zero count value, then it means that this resource is available; otherwise, the resource is not available and the requester has to wait until it becomes available. Note that semaphores can only be changed by the kernel. User programs do not have the privilege to modify semaphores. See Table 8.6 for semaphores and their meanings on Linux.

2 **Shared Memory**: This is a mechanism for implementing inter-process communications (IPC), which supplements the semaphore and message queue mechanisms. It provides a single chunk of memory that two or more processes can use to communicate with each other. See Table 8.7 for the shared memory parameters we are concerned with from the enterprise Java application performance and scalability perspective.

3 **File Handle and IP Port Range**: This category includes the parameters related to the number of file handles and the range of IP port numbers. See Table 8.8 for how these parameters are defined and their meanings.

Tables 8.9 – 8.11 illustrate some typical values for those kernel parameters set on the four Linux systems mentioned in the previous sections. You can set these parameters in the */etc/sysctl.conf* file. For example, the *mitwo* Linux machine was used as an Oracle 11g database server, and those parameters were set in its

/etc/sysctl.conf file as shown in Listing 8.9. Note that if it's the first time you set these parameters, you need to reboot your Linux server for them to take effect.

Table 8.6 Semaphores on a Linux system (defined in /proc/sys/kernel/sem file)

Semaphore	**Meaning**
sem**msl**	Maximum number of semaphores per ID
sem**mns**	Maximum number of semaphores in the system (must be equal or greater than semmni * semopm)
sem**opm**	Maximum number of operations per semaphore call
sem**mni**	Maximum number of semaphore identifiers

Table 8.7 Shared memory parameters on a Linux system (defined in /proc/sys/kernel/(shmall, shmmax, shmmni) files)

Shared memory paramneter	**Meaning**
shmall	Maximum number of shared memory pages system-wide
shmmax	Maximum size of a shared memory segment. This also sets the maximum size of the Oracle SGA if the Linux machine is used as an Oracle database server.
shmmni	Maximum number of shared memory segments system-wide

Table 8.8 File handle and IP port range parameters on a Linux system (defined in /proc/sys/fs/file-max and /proc/sys/net/ipv4/ip_local_port_range files)

Semaphore	**Meaning**
file-max	Maximum number of file handles that Linux allocates
ip_local_port_range	The range of IP port numbers, which determines how many outgoing connections can be made

Table 8.9 Semaphore parameter values queried on four Linux systems (cat /proc/sys/kernel/sem)

host	**Semmsl / semmns / semopm / semmni**	**Vendor**
icmn	250 / 32000 / 32 /128	Red Hat Enterprise 6
mitwo	250 / 32000 / 100 / 128	Red Hat Enterprise 6
pf02	250 / 32000 / 100 / 128	Red Hat Enterprise 6
pf01	1250 / 32000 / 100 / 256	SuSE Enterprise 11

Table 8.10 Shared memory parameter values queried on four Linux systems (cat /proc/sys/kernel/<parameter>)

host	shmall / shmmax / shmmni	Vendor
icmn	2,097,152 / 33,554,432 / 4,096	Red Hat Enterprise 6
mitwo	2,097,152 / 536,870,912 / 4,096	Red Hat Enterprise 6
pf02	4,294,967,296 / 68,719,476,736 / 4,096	Red Hat Enterprise 6
pf01	2,097,152 / 3,294,967,298/4,096	SuSE Enterprise 11

Table 8.11 File handle and IP port range parameter values queried on four Linux systems (cat /proc/sys/fs/file-max and /proc/sys/net/ipv4/ip_local_port_range>)

host	File-max / ip_local_port_range	Vendor
icmn	2,398,614/32,768 - 61,000	Red Hat Enterprise 6
mitwo	6,815,744/9,000 - 65,500	Red Hat Enterprise 6
pf02	6,5533,600/9,000 - 65,500	Red Hat Enterprise 6
pf01	131,072/1,024 - 65,000	SuSE Enterprise 11

Listing 8.9 Setting kernel parameters on a Linux machine used as an Oracle 11g database server (portion of the /etc/sysctl.conf file)

```
# oracle 11g r2 for linux
fs.suid_dumpable = 1
fs.aio-max-nr = 1048576
fs.file-max = 6815744
kernel.shmall = 2097152
kernel.shmmax = 536870912
kernel.shmmni = 4096
# semaphores: semmsl, semmns, semopm, semmni
kernel.sem = 250 32000 100 128
net.ipv4.ip_local_port_range = 9000 65500
net.core.rmem_default=4194304
net.core.rmem_max=4194304
net.core.wmem_default=262144
net.core.wmem_max=1048586
```

8.4.7 Configuring Shell Limits for a User

Configuring the kernel parameters described in the previous section is only the first step to customize a Linux system for your application. The next step is to set user specific shell limits. Typically, at least your need to set two parameters: one is *nofile* and the other is *nproc*. The *nofile* parameter sets the number of open files a user shell login session can have, whereas the *nproc* parameter sets the number of processes a user login session can have. They both have *soft* and *hard* limits, with the *soft* limit for *per-session* and *hard* limit for all sessions from the same user.

These parameters are set in the */etc/security/limits.conf* file. For example, Listings 8.10 and 8.11 show how these parameters were set on my Oracle and Java application servers, respectively. It's necessary to log out and in after these parameters were set the first time.

To check the values of these parameters on a Linux machine, you can "*cat*" the */etc/security/limits.conf* file or use the *ulimit* command. Keep in mind that this command displays the resource limits for the user currently logged-in (you need to make sure that you login with the user you intend to use). With this *ulimit* command, you can simply issue the following command to get a glimpse of all parameters:

```
$ ulimit –a
```

Listings 8.12 and 8.13 show the output of the above command on the Oracle server and Java application server, respectively. Note the following about the use of this command:

- The "*ulimit –a*" command is equivalent to "*ulimit –a –S*," which displays the *soft* values. To display the *hard* values, use the "*ulimit –a –H*" command, instead.
- You can query an individual parameter by using the option designated in the parenthesis for each parameter. For example, you can use the following commands to query the settings for the number of open files and number of processes:

```
$ulimit –n (this is the same as ulimit –Sn)
$ulimit –Hn
$ulimit –u
$ulimit –Hu
```

To avoid confusion, I'd like to mention that there is an *nproc* command, which displays the number of CPUs and has nothing to do with the *nproc* parameter set in the */etc/security/limits.conf* file. Similarly, the *nofile* parameter is not the same as the *file-max* parameter discussed previously: the former *is per-user* while the latter is *system-wide*.

Listing 8.10 Shell limits set for the oracle user on the Oracle server (mitwo) in /etc/security/limits.conf

```
# oracle 11g r2 for linux
oracle          soft   nproc   2047
oracle          hard   nproc   16384
oracle          soft   nofile  4096
oracle          hard   nofile  65536
oracle          soft   stack   10240
```

Listing 8.11 Shell limits set for the root user on the Java application server (icmn) in /etc/security/limits.conf

```
root soft nofile 5600
```

root hard nofile 16800
root soft nproc 7000
root hard nproc 21000

Listing 8.12 output of the command "ulimit –a" executed on the Oracle server (mitwo)

```
[root@mitwo backup]# ulimit -a
core file size          (blocks, -c) 0
data seg size           (kbytes, -d) unlimited
scheduling priority     (-e) 0
file size               (blocks, -f) unlimited
pending signals         (-i) 127499
max locked memory       (kbytes, -l) 64
max memory size         (kbytes, -m) unlimited
open files              (-n) 1024
pipe size               (512 bytes, -p) 8
POSIX message queues    (bytes, -q) 819200
real-time priority      (-r) 0
stack size              (kbytes, -s) 10240
cpu time                (seconds, -t) unlimited
max user processes      (-u) 1024
virtual memory          (kbytes, -v) unlimited
file locks              (-x) unlimited
```

Listing 8.13 output of the command "ulimit –a" executed on the Java application server (icmn)

```
[root@icmn ~]# ulimit -a
core file size          (blocks, -c) 0
data seg size           (kbytes, -d) unlimited
scheduling priority     (-e) 0
file size               (blocks, -f) unlimited
pending signals         (-i) 192056
max locked memory       (kbytes, -l) 64
max memory size         (kbytes, -m) unlimited
open files              (-n) 5600
pipe size               (512 bytes, -p) 8
POSIX message queues    (bytes, -q) 819200
real-time priority      (-r) 0
stack size              (kbytes, -s) 10240
cpu time                (seconds, -t) unlimited
max user processes      (-u) 7000
virtual memory          (kbytes, -v) unlimited
file locks              (-x) unlimited
```

8.4.8 Linux Performance Diagnostic Utilities

In this section, we introduce a few very useful utilities for diagnosing performance issues on Linux. We start with the *top* utility first.

#1 top

The *top* utility is an interactive tool that displays various metrics in real-time. To start up *top*, simply type "*top*" and hit "*Enter*" at a command prompt (to quit, press '*q*'). Figure 8.6 shows what a typical *top* session looks like. From the top summary section, you can learn immediately the current state of the Linux machine as follows:

- Line 1: How long the machine has been running; how many users are running, and load average for the last one, five and fifteen minutes.
- Line 2: Tasks: total, running, sleeping, stopped and zombie.
- Line 3: Current CPU usage breakdowns such as %*us* (user), %*sy* (kernel), %wa (IO waiting), and so on.
- Line 4: Current memory usage (total, used, free, buffers).
- Line 5: Swap (total, used, free, cached).

Then, the current state of each process is displayed, sorted by CPU usage by default. Here, some of the columns are explained as follows:

- PID: Process ID
- VIRT: Virtual image size in kB
- RES: Resident size in KB (or the actual physical memory used by the process)
- SHR: Shared memory size
- S: State (R for running and S for sleeping)
- Time+: Accumulative CPU Time since the last start/restart of the process

So, from a top session, you can get a quick glimpse of which processes are busy and how much memory each of them is using.

There are many options you can use with the *top* utility. To see all startup options, you can run "*top –h*" at a command prompt. For example, on one of my Linux machines, I got the following output with the "*top –h*" command:

```
[root@icmn ~]# top -h
usage: top -hv | -bcisSHM -d delay -n iterations [-u user | -U user] -p pid [,pid ...]
```

As is shown, you can use the '-u user' or '-p pid0,pid1,..." option to display the information for a specific user or a few targeted processes.

```
top - 22:47:37 up 15 days, 16:48,  6 users,  load average: 0.14, 0.06, 0.04
Tasks: 380 total,   1 running, 379 sleeping,   0 stopped,   0 zombie
Cpu(s):  0.0%us,  0.0%sy,  0.0%ni,100.0%id,  0.0%wa,  0.0%hi,  0.0%si,  0.0%st
Mem:  24597864k total, 11140172k used, 13457692k free,   583844k buffers
Swap: 25165816k total,        0k used, 25165816k free,  5454856k cached

  PID USER      PR  NI  VIRT  RES  SHR S %CPU %MEM    TIME+  COMMAND
 7344 root      20   0 15184 1412  900 R  0.3  0.0   0:00.15 top
18774 root      20   0 12.8g 3.8g  16m S  0.3 16.1 656:17.46 java
    1 root      20   0 19236 1464 1176 S  0.0  0.0   0:01.39 init
    2 root      20   0     0    0    0 S  0.0  0.0   0:00.04 kthreadd
    3 root      RT   0     0    0    0 S  0.0  0.0   0:00.00 migration/0
    4 root      20   0     0    0    0 S  0.0  0.0   0:01.21 ksoftirqd/0
    5 root      RT   0     0    0    0 S  0.0  0.0   0:00.00 watchdog/0
    6 root      RT   0     0    0    0 S  0.0  0.0   0:02.75 migration/1
```

Figure 8.6 A typical top session

On the other hand, when a top session is running, you can press 'h' to start up the help screen as shown in Figure 8.7.

```
Help for Interactive Commands - procps-ng version 3.3.9
Window 1:Def: Cumulative mode Off.  System: Delay 3.0 secs; Secure mode Off.

  Z,B,E,e   Global: 'Z' colors; 'B' bold; 'E'/'e' summary/task memory scale
  l,t,m     Toggle Summary: 'l' load avg; 't' task/cpu stats; 'm' memory info
  0,1,2,3,I Toggle: '0' zeros; '1/2/3' cpus or numa node views; 'I' Irix mode
  f,F,X     Fields: 'f'/'F' add/remove/order/sort; 'X' increase fixed-width

  L,&,<,> . Locate: 'L'/'&' find/again; Move sort column: '<'/'>' left/right
  R,H,V,J . Toggle: 'R' Sort; 'H' Threads; 'V' Forest view; 'J' Num justify
  c,i,S,j . Toggle: 'c' Cmd name/line; 'i' Idle; 'S' Time; 'j' Str justify
  x,y     . Toggle highlights: 'x' sort field; 'y' running tasks
  z,b     . Toggle: 'z' color/mono; 'b' bold/reverse (only if 'x' or 'y')
  u,U,o,O . Filter by: 'u'/'U' effective/any user; 'o'/'O' other criteria
  n,#,^O  . Set: 'n'/'#' max tasks displayed; Show: Ctrl+'O' other filter(s)
  C,...   . Toggle scroll coordinates msg for: up,down,left,right,home,end

  k,r       Manipulate tasks: 'k' kill; 'r' renice
  d or s    Set update interval
  W,Y       Write configuration file 'W'; Inspect other output 'Y'
  q         Quit
          ( commands shown with '.' require a visible task display window )
Press 'h' or '?' for help with Windows,
Type 'q' or <Esc> to continue
```

Figure 8.7 Select options when top is running (taken from a CentOS 7 Linux)

For example:

- When a top session is running, you can press letter 'M' to sort by memory. To sort by a different field, first, press 'F' and then select the field; then, press 's' and "esc" to quit. You can toggle the sort order by pressing 'R'. Some other sort options include:
    - A – by age

    - P - by CPU
    - N – by pid
    - T – by time/cumulative time

- You can press letter 'I' to turn off/on Irix mode. The default mode is Irix on, which reports total CPU usage from all CPUs; when Irix mode is off, however, the %CPU column reports the CPU usage averaged across all CPUs with 100% as the maximum.
- To change the update interval, press letter 'd' and enter a new value and then press Enter.
- To add another column to top, press 'f' and then move to the desired column, for example, PPID; then press 'dq' to get back. To move a column, press 'f' and use '↓' or '↑' key to move to desired column; use the '→' key to select it, and press 'dq' to save and exit.

For real applications, very often you might want to see the complete command used to start up a process. You can achieve this by starting up *top* with "-c" appended as follows:

```
$top -c
```

You can also collect metrics for particular processes using the following top command:

```
$top –d 1 –b –n 10 –p 17250,18852
```

Here, "–d 1" means "*delay one second,*" "–b" means *batch mode*, "–n 10" means "*10 samples,*" and "–p 17250,18852" means "*processes with pid's of 17250 and 18852.*" You can adjust delay, # of samples, and pid's and direct the output to a text file to suit your particular needs. Note that the %cpu metric is cumulative by default, namely, the max would be 200% for a 2-cpu machine. A Java program named *TopIt*, included in the download for this book, helps post-process the data collected using the above command.

#2 vmstat

Of all Linux performance diagnostics utilities, *vmstat* is my favorite. The *vmstat* utility gives a lot more information than the *top* utility. Besides, you can redirect the output to a text file and analyze the data at your leisure afterwards. I often use this utility as follows:

```
$vmstat –t –n 10 420 –SM >tags_timestamp_run_number.txt
```

in which the '-t' option is for including timestamp, '-n' for displaying the header only once rather than periodically, '10' for the update interval in seconds, '420' for the total number of intervals (in this case 70 minutes total), '-SM' for the unit of MB, and the last part for scooping the output to a text file. Figure 8.8 shows what one would get with this utility. See Table 8.12 for the notations of the counters for each category.

However, not all Linux vendors support the '-t' and '-SM' options with the *vmstat* utility. (For some Linux variant, -SM should have a space between S and M like '-S M'.) You can try the following command instead by pipelining an *awk* command:

```
vmstat -n 10 420 -S M | awk '{now=strftime("%Y-%m-%d %T "); print now $0}'
```

```
procs -----------memory---------- ---swap-- -----io---- --system-- -----cpu------
 r  b   swpd   free   buff  cache   si   so    bi    bo   in   cs us sy id wa st
 1  0      0    678    276  12266    0    0     1    10    0    3  1  0 99  0  0
 0  0      0    685    276  12266    0    0     0    14  637  648  1  0 99  0  0
```

Figure 8.8 The *vmstat* utility output showing all metrics it collects

Table 8.12 Category and counters for the *vmstat* utility

Category	Counters
procs	**r**: The number of processes waiting for run time. **b**: The number of processes in uninterruptible sleep.
memory	**swpd**: the amount of virtual memory used. **free**: the amount of idle memory. **buff**: the amount of memory used as buffers. **cache**: the amount of memory used as cache.
swap	**si**: Amount of memory swapped in from disk (/s). **so**: Amount of memory swapped to disk (/s).
io	**bi**: Blocks received from a block device (blocks/s). **bo**: Blocks sent to a block device (blocks/s).
system	**in**: The number of interrupts per second, including the clock. **cs**: The number of context switches per second.
cpu	These are percentages of total CPU time. **us**: Time spent running non-kernel code. (user time, including nice time) **sy**: Time spent running kernel code. (system time) **id**: Time spent idle. Prior to Linux 2.5.41, this includes IO-wait time. **wa**: Time spent waiting for IO. Prior to Linux 2.5.41, included in idle. **st**: Time stolen from a virtual machine. Prior to Linux 2.6.11, unknown.

#3 sar

The *sar* utility is a very versatile utility that it can almost display counters in every category on a Linux system. It is typically invoked with the following command:

$ sar -<option> n m

in which *<option>* is a single letter to indicate the category, and *n* and *m* are the update interval in seconds and the number of updates, respectively. Table 8.13 lists some of the options that can be used with the *sar* command. Out of all these options, my favorites are the –u and –r options, which display the CPU and memory utilizations since the last midnight with a 10-minute interval by default (you can specify a start time like 8:00:01 by adding –s 8:00:01 at the end of the command), respectively. You can decide which option or options you want to use based on your needs for your application.

Table 8.13 Options for the sar command

option	comment
-u	Cumulative real-time CPU utilizations
-P ALL	Statistics for all individual cores
-r	Memory statistics
-b	I/O statistics
-d	Activities for each block device
-w	Reports total # of processes per second and total # of context switches per second.
-q	Reports the run queue size and load average for the last 1, 5, and 15 minutes.
-n	Network statistics

Here are some example *sar* commands that you might want to try out:

```
sar 5 10 ( 10 samples of every 5 seconds for cpu)
sar -r 5 10 ( 10 samples of every 5 seconds for ram)
sar -d -p 5 10 ( 10 samples of every 5 seconds for dev)
```

#4 ps

The *ps* utility can be used to find out what processes are running on a Linux system as follows:

```
$ ps -ef
```

Some of the common options for the ps command include:

-e → all processes

-f → full listing

-C→ by command name

-p → by pid

-o → user specified

However, I found out that it's more convenient to use a script named *ps_mon.sh* as shown in Listing 8.14 to log all data associated with a process into a text file and then perform post-analysis afterwards. As you see, this is a *bash* script. You need to specify how often you want to sample (*sleepTime*) and enter a string (*pattern*) that uniquely identifies your process. Then you extract the *processId* of that process. Using that *processId*, you keep polling in an infinite loop for the counters you want to record. With this script, three counters of *vsz*, *rss*, and *pcpu* are logged for the virtual memory size, resident memory size and CPU usage associated with that process. The counters *vsz* and *rss* are equivalent to the virtual bytes and private bytes counters of *perfmon* on Windows, respectively. These counters are very useful for monitoring memory growth associated with a process. However, they are *accumulative* since the startup of the process, namely, each data point does not represent the value of the counter when it's reported.

To execute this script, change to the bash shell environment and issue the following command:

```
$ ./ps_mon.sh > filename.txt &
```

The output is directed to a text file that you can analyze later. The text file is formatted with comma, so you can import it into an Excel spreadsheet to draw whatever charts you are interested in. Remember that this is an infinite loop, so you need to bring it to the foreground using the *fg* command and stop it after you are done.

If you cannot run this script, you might need to execute "*chmod +x ps_mon.sh*" to set proper permissions.

Listing 8.14 A bash script (ps_mon.sh) for monitoring a process on a Linux system

```
#!/bin/bash
sleepTime=60
pattern="yourPattern"
x=0
procId=$(ps -eo pid,pcpu,time,args | grep $pattern | grep -v grep | awk '{print $1}')
echo "procId="$procId
while [ $x -ge 0 ]
do
  date=$(date)
  ps0=$(ps -o vsz,rss,pcpu -p $procId )
  x=$((x+1))
  echo $x $date $ps0 | awk '{print $1, $3, $4, $5, $8, \
       $11/1000.0, $9, $12/1000.0, $10, $13, $14}'
sleep $sleepTime
done
```

In addition, the *ps* command can be used for the following purposes:

- Display process by user: *ps -f -u <user>*. For example, *ps -f -u henry* on one of my Linux machines.
- Show processes by command: *ps –f -C <command>*. For example, *ps –f -C java* to list all java processes on a Linux machine.
- Show processes by process-id: *ps -f -p <pid0>,<pid1>*.
- Sort processes by cpu or memory: *ps aux --sort=-pcpu,-pmem* (Note that "-" means descending order while "+" means ascending order.)
- Display process hierarchy in a tree style: pstree –s –p <pid>
- Display parent ID and full launching command for a process: *ps -f --forest –C <command>*.
- Display parent and child processes: *ps -o ppid,pid,pcpu,pmem,uname,comm,args -C <command>*, or *ps -f --ppid <ppid>* to display all child processes of a parent process.
- Display threads of a process: *ps -p <pid> -L*. You can find the number of threads by piping it with " | grep "<pattern>" | wc –l."

One particularly useful command with *ps* is for displaying the full command used to launch a process. The command "*top –c*" can also do this, but the command text may be chopped off for many applications. In such cases, use the following *ps* command with a *pid* you can find using *top*:

ps –fwwp <pid>

Finally, be aware that the *ps* command is different from the *top* command that the *ps* command always reports the metrics averaged over the period since the process was started, while the *top* command reports real-time metrics except the first output. Therefore, the above *ps*-based script is okay only if the CPU and memory metrics of the process being monitored stay constant without going up and down regularly, which typically is the case with really CPU-intensive processes.

8.5 CASE STUDY: JAVA PERFORMANCE AND SCALABILITY ON LINUX

This case study uses the same Java application as detailed in Chapter 6. It was first tested on Windows. In this section, we present the performance and scalability test results on Linux with the same Java application server converted from Windows to Linux.

Note that the entire setup consists of three separately installed servers: an Oracle 11g R2 database server, an authentication server, and a Java enterprise application server. The authentication server was on Windows 2008 R2, while both the database server and the Java application server were on two separate Red Hat Enterprise Linux server 6 machines. Our focus here is on the Java enterprise application server, as this was where the application's performance and scalability were bottlenecked on.

In this section, we present this case study by starting with the Linux system activity monitoring procedure used for running the performance and scalability tests associated with this enterprise application. We then present the test results illustrating the performance and scalability of this enterprise Java application on the Linux machine tested. The post-analysis section summarizes all relevant resource consumptions for this application. The last section compares the results obtained on this Linux machine with those obtained earlier on Windows 2008 R2 with exactly the same hardware configuration.

8.5.1 The Linux System Activity Monitoring Procedure

We would use the same performance testing tool named SilkPerformer as we used previously on Windows to drive the performance and scalability testing for this enterprise Java application on Linux. As you may recall, the workload consists of five scripts to simulate about 50 actions for each virtual user. Out of those 50 actions, fourteen most representative actions were selected to calculate the average response time in seconds, which would be used as the single metric to evaluate the performance and scalability of this enterprise Java application with different number of concurrent users. Although customers might be more interested in the actual average response time of each representative action, this single metric of the average response time out of the fourteen selected representative actions is sufficient for our purpose of demonstrating Java performance and scalability on Linux here.

For your reference, the following Linux system activity monitoring procedure was followed after starting up the Java application server but prior to launching a test run:

- Launch the *top* utility and then press letter 'c' to look up the command for starting up the Java application to be tested. Identify a unique string from the command as a "*pattern*" for identifying this process and put it into the *ps_mon.sh* script as illustrated in Listing 8.14. This is a one-time effort for configuring the *ps_mon.sh* script to monitor the application to be tested.
- Start up the *ps_mon.sh* script by executing the following command (your output text file should have a more mnemonic name to identify the test run to be monitored):

  $./ps_mon.sh > output_file.txt &

- Start up the *vmstat* utility as introduced in the previous section as follows (once again, your output text file should have a more mnemonic name to identify the test run to be monitored):

  $vmstat –t –n 10 420 –SM >output_file.txt

- Start up the *visualvm* tool by executing the following command (note it's necessary to set up X11 per instructions given in Appendix D):

  $<jdk_path>/bin/jvisualvm

- Launch the SilkPerformer run with the intended number of concurrent users.

After a test run is complete as indicated on the SilkPerformer Workbench, perform the following tasks:

1 Take a screenshot of the Monitor View from the VisualVM GUI.
2 Take a screenshot of the GC View from the VisualVM GUI.
3 Take an application snapshot of the application monitored from the VisualVM GUI (note that this was not always possible as sometimes the options displayed after right-clicking on the process dimmed out immediately).
4 Bring the *ps_mon.sh* process to the foreground by executing the command of "*fg*" and terminate it by pressing Ctrl-C.

The next section presents the test results on the performance and scalability of this enterprise Java application on Linux.

8.5.2 Test Results

The Linux machine used for the Java application server for this enterprise Java application was named "*icmn*" and you can look up all of its specs from the listings given in the previous section. Here is a quick re-cap of some of its specs:

- OS: Red Hat Enterprise Linux Server 6.0 with Linux kernel 2.6.32-71.40.1.e16.x86_64.
- CPU: Intel Xeon X5550 two quad-cores @ 2.67 GHz with hyper-threading enabled for a total of 16 logical CPUs.
- RAM: 24 GB.
- JDK: 1.6.0_31 (64-bit)

Since the application was an enterprise Java application and had been thoroughly tested on Windows 2008 R2 on the same hardware, the same deployment directory on Windows was copied to the Linux machine. After installing the Oracle 11g R2 client software, the application was started up successfully with no issues at all. Since it had been established that the same application on the same hardware could support up to 700 concurrent users on Windows 2008 R2 prior to this system was reimaged to Linux, the first test run was launched with 700 concurrent users as well to see if we would get the comparable test results between Windows and Linux.

However, the above test run failed with massive errors of "*too many open files* ...." Since this is a well-known symptom that is caused by setting "*nofile*" too low, the same test was launched again after setting it from the default setting of 1024 for both *soft* and *hard* limits to 5600 for *soft* and 16800 for *hard* limits, respectively, as described in §8.4.7. This time, all errors of "too many open files ..." disappeared, but the test run still ended up with too many errors reported by the SilkPerformer.

After some deliberation, I suspected that it was due to insufficient number of processes configured for the *root* user, which was used to login onto the Linux machine and run the application. This corresponds to the *nproc* parameter as discussed in §8.4.7. By default, it was set to 1024 for the *soft* limit and 192056 for the *hard* limit. I also looked up my previous 200 concurrent user run on a Windows 2008 R2 VM and found that a maximum number of 1306 threads were created. I scaled and rounded up that number to 7000 processes for 700 concurrent users on this Linux machine (the *Threads* counter was not logged on the previous Windows 2008 R2 run of 700 concurrent users on the same hardware so I had to derive from a different Windows 2008 R2 run as stated).

Then, I added those two *nproc* lines as shown in Listing 8.11, together with those two *nofile* lines as stated above, logged off, logged in again, and re-launched the same 700 concurrent user run. This time, the test run completed successfully. Then, another two runs were conducted, one with 800 concurrent users to see if this Linux machine could support up to that many concurrent users, and the other with 500 concurrent users just to have one more data point for evaluating the scalability of this application. Based on those three test runs as stated above, Figure 8.9 shows the test results in terms of the average response times in seconds for 500, 700, and 800 concurrent users.

It seems that an increase of 40% more concurrent users from 500 to 700 resulted in a 46% larger average response time from 0.98 seconds to 1.43 seconds, whereas an increase of 14% more concurrent users from 700 to 800 resulted in a 35% larger average response time from 1.43 seconds to 1.93 seconds. This indicates that the system seemed to have reached its maximum capacity with 800 concurrent users. The next section analyzes the system resource consumptions associated with those test runs, which would give a more accurate evaluation of the system state regarding whether a load intensity of 800 concurrent users was indeed the maximum number of concurrent users that this Linux machine can support with this enterprise Java application.

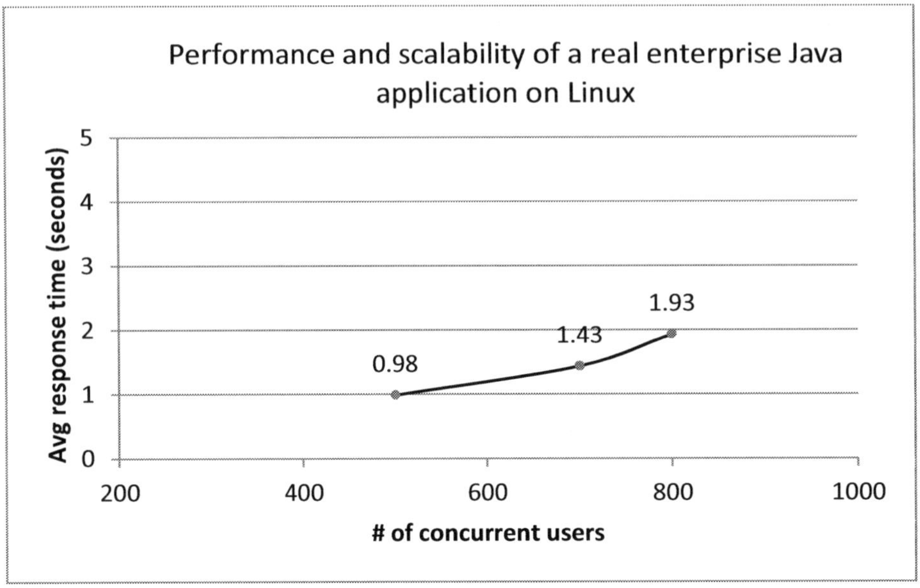

Figure 8.9 Performance and scalability of a real enterprise Java application on Linux

8.5.3 Post-Analysis

In this section, we present some post-analysis based on the system activity data gathered during those test runs. First, we give a full analysis based on all data collected with the 500 concurrent user run, which will help us understand better about those Linux system activity monitoring utilities we introduced in the previous sections. We then compare how the CPU utilization level had increased with the number of concurrent users increased from 500 to 700 and 800. We start with the "top" analysis first.

#1 "top" analysis

We collected three "top" screenshots at the intervals of 24 minutes, 28 minutes, and 55 minutes since the 500 concurrent user run started. See Figure 8.10 for those three screenshots. We are particularly interested in the following metrics:

- **Load average**: This category summarizes the system load average in the last three intervals of 1 minute, 5-minutes and 15-minutes, respectively. They can also be read from the */proc/loadavg* file. You might wonder what it means by "load average." The metric "load" measures the number of processes either using or waiting for CPU. There is a difference between UNIX and Linux that UNIX does not count those processes waiting on I/O while Linux does (in my opinion, processes waiting for I/O should be counted because they are active processes). The other factor is how we count the number of CPUs – whether we should include logical CPUs such as hyper-threaded logical CPUs. For instance, the Intel Xeon 5550 processors we used here were hyper-threaded that although the OS may display "16 CPUs," there were actually eight physical cores or CPUs. This is an important issue as we need to know how many CPUs are installed on a Linux system when we look at the load average numbers reported by the *top* utility. For example, in screenshot (a) shown in Figure 8.10, the first load average number was 1.88, which would be equivalent to (1.88/8) 100 = 23.5% CPU busy if we consider only the physical cores, while the same number would mean (1.88/16)/100 = 11.75% CPU busy if we consider all hyper-threaded logical CPUs as well. Actually, in this case, notice that 76.3% idle CPU reported? It implies that the system was (100 – 76.3) = 23.7% busy, which is very close to the 23.5% CPU usage number derived based on the first load average number of 1.88. My recommendation is to look at all three load average numbers to help get an idea on whether the CPU utilization has been steady during the last fifteen minutes. However, it's more reliable to count on the CPU *%idle* number to evaluate how busy the system is. Finally, note the 366.7% number under the %CPU column, which is a sum out of all. Dividing it by 16 (CPUs) would yield a number of 22.9%, which is the %us number reported in the top Cpu(s) section as well.

- **Cpu(s)**: This category breaks CPU utilization down to several sub-categories such as *us* for user, *sy* for system or kernel, *ni* for nice, *id* for idle, and so on. In addition to the absolute number for the *%us* metric, I pay particular attention to the ratio of the *%sy* metric to the *%us* metric. My experience is that an application stops scaling to more users when the system overhead represented by the *%sy* metric starts to become significant..

```
top - 11:32:19 up 18 days,  5:33,  6 users,  load average: 1.88, 1.89, 1.26
Tasks: 390 total,   1 running, 389 sleeping,   0 stopped,   0 zombie
Cpu(s): 22.9%us,  0.5%sy,  0.0%ni, 76.3%id,  0.0%wa,  0.0%hi,  0.2%si,  0.0%st
Mem:  24597864k total, 10923320k used, 13674544k free,   591444k buffers
Swap: 25165816k total,        0k used, 25165816k free,  5454716k cached

  PID USER      PR  NI  VIRT  RES  SHR S %CPU %MEM    TIME+  COMMAND
22426 root      20   0 12.3g 3.4g  16m S 366.7 14.6  66:03.93 /data1/app/jdk6/jdk1.6.0_31/
24101 root      20   0 3689m 145m  12m S  4.0  0.6   1:02.92 /data1/app/jdk6/jdk1.6.0_31/b
   21 root      RT   0     0    0    0 S  0.3  0.0   0:02.60 [migration/6]
30714 root      20   0 15204 1424  900 R  0.3  0.0   0:00.64 top
    1 root      20   0 19236 1464 1176 S  0.0  0.0   0:01.39 /sbin/init
```

(a) The top screenshot taken 24 minutes after the test was launched

```
top - 11:34:02 up 18 days,  5:34,  6 users,  load average: 2.30, 1.92, 1.33
Tasks: 389 total,   1 running, 388 sleeping,   0 stopped,   0 zombie
Cpu(s): 25.0%us,  0.7%sy,  0.0%ni, 73.9%id,  0.0%wa,  0.0%hi,  0.3%si,  0.0%st
Mem:  24597864k total, 10934048k used, 13663816k free,   591444k buffers
Swap: 25165816k total,        0k used, 25165816k free,  5453540k cached

  PID USER      PR  NI  VIRT  RES  SHR S %CPU %MEM    TIME+  COMMAND
22426 root      20   0 12.3g 3.4g  16m S 407.4 14.6  72:35.34 /data1/app/jdk6/jdk1.6.0_31
24101 root      20   0 3689m 145m  12m S  4.0  0.6   1:07.69 /data1/app/jdk6/jdk1.6.0_31/
23976 root      20   0  103m 1228 1060 S  0.3  0.0   0:00.02 /bin/bash ./ps_mon.sh
23990 root      20   0  6168  652  564 S  0.3  0.0   0:00.12 vmstat -t -n 10 400 -SM
30714 root      20   0 15204 1424  900 R  0.3  0.0   0:01.01 top
    1 root      20   0 19236 1464 1176 S  0.0  0.0   0:01.39 /sbin/init
    2 root      20   0     0    0    0 S  0.0  0.0   0:00.04 [kthreadd]
```

(b) The top screenshot taken 28 minutes after the test was launched

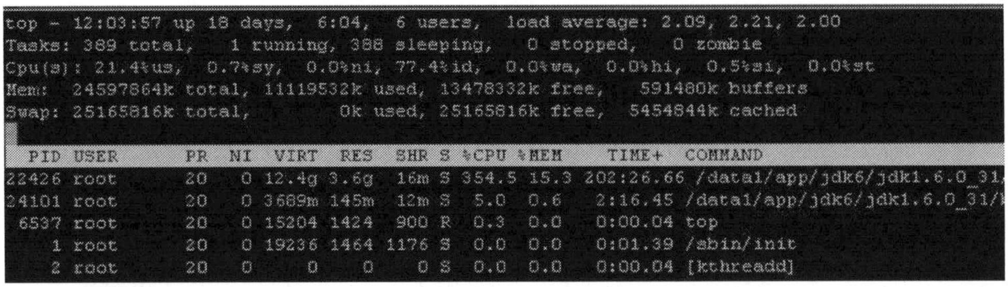

```
top - 12:03:57 up 18 days,  6:04,  6 users,  load average: 2.09, 2.21, 2.00
Tasks: 389 total,   1 running, 388 sleeping,   0 stopped,   0 zombie
Cpu(s): 21.4%us,  0.7%sy,  0.0%ni, 77.4%id,  0.0%wa,  0.0%hi,  0.5%si,  0.0%st
Mem:  24597864k total, 11119532k used, 13478332k free,   591480k buffers
Swap: 25165816k total,        0k used, 25165816k free,  5454844k cached

  PID USER      PR  NI  VIRT  RES  SHR S %CPU %MEM    TIME+  COMMAND
22426 root      20   0 12.4g 3.6g  16m S 354.5 15.3 202:26.66 /data1/app/jdk6/jdk1.6.0_31
24101 root      20   0 3689m 145m  12m S  5.0  0.6   2:16.45 /data1/app/jdk6/jdk1.6.0_31/
 6537 root      20   0 15204 1424  900 R  0.3  0.0   0:00.04 top
    1 root      20   0 19236 1464 1176 S  0.0  0.0   0:01.39 /sbin/init
    2 root      20   0     0    0    0 S  0.0  0.0   0:00.04 [kthreadd]
```

(c) The top screenshot taken 55 minutes after the test was launched

Figure 8.10 Three "top" screenshots taken at the intervals of 24 minutes, 28 minutes, and 55 minutes since the 500 concurrent user run started.

#2 "vmstat" analysis

Listing 8.15 shows a portion of the *vmstat* data gathered during the 500 concurrent user run. This portion was selected around the maximum number of run queue size of 18 as highlighted (note that the test was started around 11:11:00 AM). The general rule of thumb is that the run queue size should be smaller than twice the number of CPUs before the CPU becomes the bottleneck. The *vmstat* log data gives this kind of information. We'll use the *vmstat* data to compare the three runs with 500, 700, and 800 concurrent users later, so let's move on to the *sar* utility next.

Listing 8.15 Portion of the vmstat data gathered during the 500 concurrent user run

```
procs -----------memory---------- ---swap-- -----io---- --system-- -----cpu------ ---timestamp-
 r  b   swpd   free   buff  cache   si   so    bi    bo   in   cs us sy id wa st
.....
 1  0      0  13156    577   5327    0    0     0   346 30075 20534 27  1 72  0  0   11:55:22
 5  0      0  13158    577   5327    0    0     0   231 20154 13323 20  1 79  0  0   11:55:32
 7  0      0  13158    577   5327    0    0     0   239 33057 21768 32  2 66  0  0   11:55:42
 2  0      0  13157    577   5327    0    0     0   404 26018 19184 29  1 70  0  0   11:55:52
 6  0      0  13157    577   5328    0    0     0   198 25527 17481 26  1 73  0  0   11:56:02
10  0      0  13158    577   5326    0    0     0   254 25704 16565 24  1 74  0  0   11:56:12
 4  0      0  13157    577   5326    0    0     0  5788 35593 24213 34  3 63  0  0   11:56:22
 8  0      0  13157    577   5326    0    0     0   306 28743 20456 29  1 70  0  0   11:56:32
 3  0      0  13151    577   5326    0    0     0   165 25182 17041 32  1 67  0  0   11:56:42
 4  0      0  13152    577   5327    0    0     0   222 35185 24424 36  2 62  0  0   11:56:52
 4  0      0  13153    577   5327    0    0     0   217 26182 17993 27  1 72  0  0   11:57:02
 3  0      0  13153    577   5327    0    0     0   152 20890 13711 21  1 78  0  0   11:57:12
18  0      0  13153    577   5327    0    0     0   322 35751 22762 33  2 65  0  0   11:57:22
 3  0      0  13148    577   5327    0    0     0   135 24223 15709 24  1 75  0  0   11:57:32
 3  0      0  13144    577   5328    0    0     0   157 21657 14233 20  1 79  0  0   11:57:42
 5  0      0  13144    577   5327    0    0     0   354 21142 14199 19  1 80  0  0   11:57:52
 4  0      0  13144    577   5328    0    0     0   242 27932 17411 27  1 72  0  0   11:58:02
 7  0      0  13139    577   5326    0    0     0   235 23077 15758 20  1 79  0  0   11:58:12
```

```
2 0    0 13139   577  5326   0  0    0  342 22655 15205 23  1 76  0  0     11:58:22
...
```

#3 "sar" analysis

Here, we present five sets of data gathered with the *sar* utility as follows:

1 **From the "sar –u –s 11:11:01" command**: This set of data was retrieved after the test run completed. Note the use of "-s" option in Listing 8.16 (a) for setting the start point for the data since the test was launched. Also, note the interval of every 10 minutes. This command is most useful for trouble-shooting performance issues in production, since it gives a historical view of the CPU activities that occurred on the system. Once again, pay attention to the portion of the system overhead as indicated by the *%system* metric.

2 **From the "sar –r –s 11:11:01" command**: This set of data was also retrieved after the test run completed. Note the use of "-s" option in Listing 8.16 (b) for setting the start point for the data since the test was launched. Also, note the interval of every 10 minutes. This command is most useful for trouble-shooting performance issues in production, since it gives a historical view of the memory activities that occurred on the system. If you see large fluctuations in the *kbmemfree* metric accompanied with intermittent high *%system* metric values, you might want to consider tuning your Linux system with *HugePages*. The HugePages feature allows an application to use 4 MB pages in place of the 4 kB pages to reduce the page tables size significantly and thus reducing CPU activities on paging/swapping, as huge pages cannot be paged out. This is especially true with databases such as Oracle on Linux, but it was not an issue in our case since the Oracle database was not the bottleneck.

3 **From the "sar –q 5 10" command**: This set of data was gathered about 44 minutes later after the test run started. As is shown in Listing 8.16 (c), it displays the *runq*-sz (run queue length – the number of tasks waiting for run time), *plist-sz* (number of tasks in the task list), and load averages during the last 1, 5, and 15 minutes, respectively. Note that this arguably is a better alternative than "top" as it gives similar information in time series rather than instant numbers jumping around.

4 **From the "sar –w 5 10" command**: This set of data was gathered about 43 minutes later after the test run started. As is shown in Listing 8.16 (d), it displays two metrics: *proc/s* (total number of tasks created per second) and *cswch/s* (total number of context switches per second). The context switch data is very useful for estimating lock contentions.

Listing 8.16 (a) Output from the "sar –u –s 11:11:01" command

```
Linux 2.6.32-71.40.1.el6.x86_64 (icmn)  12/03/2012   _x86_64_  (16 CPU)

11:00:01 AM   CPU    %user   %nice  %system  %iowait   %steal    %idle
11:10:01 AM   all     0.30    0.00     0.15     0.02     0.00    99.52
11:20:01 AM   all    11.66    0.00     0.66     0.03     0.00    87.65
11:30:01 AM   all    21.60    0.00     1.13     0.03     0.00    77.24
11:40:01 AM   all    23.30    0.00     1.16     0.02     0.00    75.52
11:50:01 AM   all    26.73    0.00     1.32     0.02     0.00    71.92
12:00:01 PM   all    28.11    0.00     1.33     0.02     0.00    70.54
12:10:01 PM   all    26.41    0.00     1.30     0.02     0.00    72.26
```

```
Average:        all    19.76    0.00    1.01    0.02    0.00    79.21
```

Listing 8.16 (b) Output from the "sar –r –s 11:11:01" command

```
Linux 2.6.32-71.40.1.el6.x86_64 (icmn)  12/03/2012  _x86_64_  (16 CPU)

11:00:01 AM kbmemfree kbmemused  %memused kbbuffers  kbcached  kbcommit   %commit
11:10:01 AM  15314740   9283124     37.74    591368   5454540   4175936      8.39
11:20:01 AM  14667332   9930532     40.37    591408   5454008   4639660      9.32
11:30:01 AM  13699276  10898588     44.31    591444   5454564   4654268      9.35
11:40:01 AM  13627876  10969988     44.60    591448   5455456   4650008      9.34
11:50:01 AM  13528368  11069496     45.00    591456   5455072   4695836      9.44
12:00:01 PM  13461376  11136488     45.27    591480   5454536   4656404      9.36
12:10:01 PM  13483172  11114692     45.19    591484   5454088   4753976      9.55
Average:     13968877  10628987     43.21    591441   5454609   4603727      9.25
```

Listing 8.16 (c) Output from the "sar –q 5 10" command

```
Linux 2.6.32-71.40.1.el6.x86_64 (icmn)  12/03/2012  _x86_64_  (16 CPU)

11:55:32 AM   runq-sz  plist-sz   ldavg-1   ldavg-5  ldavg-15
11:55:37 AM         7      1084      1.74      2.01      1.83
11:55:42 AM         7      1084      1.76      2.01      1.83
11:55:47 AM         5      1084      1.62      1.98      1.82
11:55:52 AM         9      1086      1.49      1.94      1.81
11:55:57 AM         4      1084      1.61      1.96      1.81
11:56:02 AM         3      1084      1.64      1.96      1.81
11:56:07 AM         6      1086      1.75      1.98      1.82
11:56:12 AM         7      1084      1.85      2.00      1.83
11:56:17 AM        10      1085      1.78      1.98      1.82
11:56:22 AM         1      1083      2.12      2.05      1.84

Average:            6      1084      1.74      1.99      1.82
```

Listing 8.16 (d) Output from the "sar –w 5 10" command

```
Linux 2.6.32-71.40.1.el6.x86_64 (icmn)  12/03/2012  _x86_64_  (16 CPU)

11:54:32 AM    proc/s   cswch/s
11:54:37 AM    371.09  16527.92
11:54:42 AM    455.47  17526.84
11:54:47 AM    570.69  23185.15
11:54:52 AM    403.60  12528.40
11:54:57 AM    393.66  18247.52
11:55:02 AM    512.33  21444.33
11:55:07 AM    519.28  19540.36
11:55:12 AM    520.28  19337.97
```

```
11:55:17 AM    533.67  16983.07
11:55:22 AM    581.24  23904.99

Average:       486.08  18925.35
```

#4 "ps_mon.sh" data

Listing 8.17 shows the data collected with the *ps_mon.sh* script as shown in Listing 8.14 during the 500 concurrent user run (to save space, the middle portion of the data was omitted). This set of data is particularly useful for diagnosing CPU bottleneck and memory leaks for a given process, since other utilities provide system-wide data. Figure 8.11 shows the resident size evolution as represented by the RSS metric, which is more indicative than the data in tabular form.

Listing 8.17 Data collected using the ps_mon.sh script during the 500 concurrent user run.

```
procId=22426
1 Dec 3 11:08:00 VSZ 12493.4 RSS 1933.7 %CPU 6.7
2 Dec 3 11:09:00 VSZ 12499.6 RSS 1935.35 %CPU 6.6
3 Dec 3 11:10:00 VSZ 12519.4 RSS 1947.96 %CPU 6.9
4 Dec 3 11:11:00 VSZ 12677.7 RSS 1994.48 %CPU 8.0
5 Dec 3 11:12:00 VSZ 12729.4 RSS 2017.24 %CPU 10.1
6 Dec 3 11:13:00 VSZ 12842.5 RSS 2039.4 %CPU 13.9
7 Dec 3 11:14:00 VSZ 12857.9 RSS 2056.62 %CPU 18.3
8 Dec 3 11:15:00 VSZ 12882.1 RSS 2090.12 %CPU 23.0
9 Dec 3 11:16:00 VSZ 12888.4 RSS 2097.94 %CPU 28.3
10 Dec 3 11:17:00 VSZ 12888.4 RSS 2120.51 %CPU 33.2
11 Dec 3 11:18:00 VSZ 12888.4 RSS 2290.2 %CPU 38.6
12 Dec 3 11:19:00 VSZ 12903.2 RSS 2454.6 %CPU 44.9
13 Dec 3 11:20:00 VSZ 12933 RSS 2605.02 %CPU 51.7
14 Dec 3 11:21:00 VSZ 12934 RSS 2698.05 %CPU 58.3
15 Dec 3 11:22:00 VSZ 12938.2 RSS 2877.95 %CPU 65.2
16 Dec 3 11:23:00 VSZ 12940.2 RSS 3032.2 %CPU 70.9
17 Dec 3 11:24:00 VSZ 12940.2 RSS 3168.92 %CPU 76.2
18 Dec 3 11:25:00 VSZ 12941.2 RSS 3532.96 %CPU 82.7
19 Dec 3 11:26:00 VSZ 12941.2 RSS 3537.86 %CPU 88.4
20 Dec 3 11:27:00 VSZ 12941.2 RSS 3549.92 %CPU 93.9
......
50 Dec 3 11:57:01 VSZ 12965.1 RSS 3787.96 %CPU 222
51 Dec 3 11:58:01 VSZ 12965.1 RSS 3796.02 %CPU 224
52 Dec 3 11:59:01 VSZ 12965.1 RSS 3798.84 %CPU 226
53 Dec 3 12:00:01 VSZ 12965.1 RSS 3792.71 %CPU 229
54 Dec 3 12:01:01 VSZ 12965.1 RSS 3784.19 %CPU 232
55 Dec 3 12:02:01 VSZ 12965.1 RSS 3779.63 %CPU 234
56 Dec 3 12:03:01 VSZ 12965.1 RSS 3783.3 %CPU 237
57 Dec 3 12:04:01 VSZ 12965.1 RSS 3773.56 %CPU 239
58 Dec 3 12:05:01 VSZ 12965.1 RSS 3771.31 %CPU 240
59 Dec 3 12:06:01 VSZ 12965.1 RSS 3767.06 %CPU 242
60 Dec 3 12:07:01 VSZ 12965.1 RSS 3778.26 %CPU 244
```

61 Dec 3 12:08:01 VSZ 12965.1 RSS 3768.42 %CPU 246
62 Dec 3 12:09:01 VSZ 12965.1 RSS 3755.77 %CPU 250
63 Dec 3 12:10:01 VSZ 13065.9 RSS 3763.48 %CPU 252
64 Dec 3 12:11:01 VSZ 13075.1 RSS 3766.99 %CPU 254
65 Dec 3 12:12:01 VSZ 13075.1 RSS 3781.54 %CPU 251
66 Dec 3 12:13:01 VSZ 13074.1 RSS 3779.09 %CPU 249

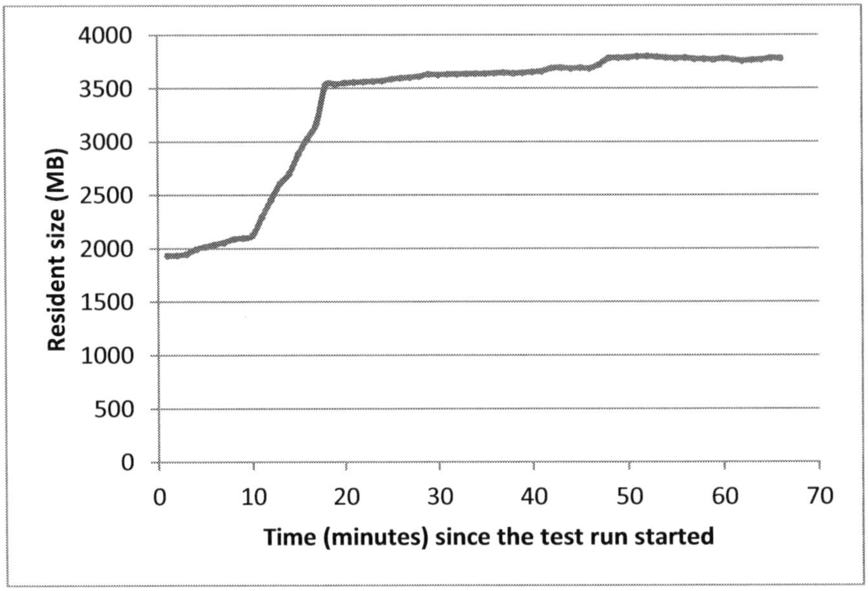

Figure 8.11 Resident size evolution of the enterprise Java application under test with 500 concurrent users

Scalability Analysis

Figure 8.9 shows that the average response time essentially doubled from 0.98 seconds to 1.93 seconds when the number of concurrent users increased from 500 to 800, which calls for a scalability analysis. For this purpose, we analyze the CPU activities associated with those three runs with 500, 700, and 800 concurrent users, respectively. During those runs, we gathered *vmstat* data using the *vmstat* utility as we described previously. This utility gives most comprehensive information on various types of activities on a Linux system, including CPU usage breakdowns and run queue lengths, etc. It is an ideal tool for monitoring CPU activities on a Linux system.

Figure 8.12 shows the user CPU activities for those three runs of 500, 700 and 800 concurrent users. The x-axis represents the time in seconds since the test run started, while the y-axis represents the average total CPU usage in user mode in percentage. Table 8.14 further shows the breakdowns of CPU activities in user mode and kernel mode based on the flat part of each curve starting at $t = 1000$ seconds. Note that it's important to pay attention to both average and peak CPU utilizations, as high peak CPU utilization levels may result in large response times, which may potentially lead to customer escalations.

Table 8.15 shows the average and peak CPU run queue lengths associated with each of those three test runs, obtained from the same *vmstat* data files. It is seen that the peak CPU run queue length had reached 33 with 800 concurrent users, indicating that this was approximately the capacity that this Linux machine can support for this enterprise application.

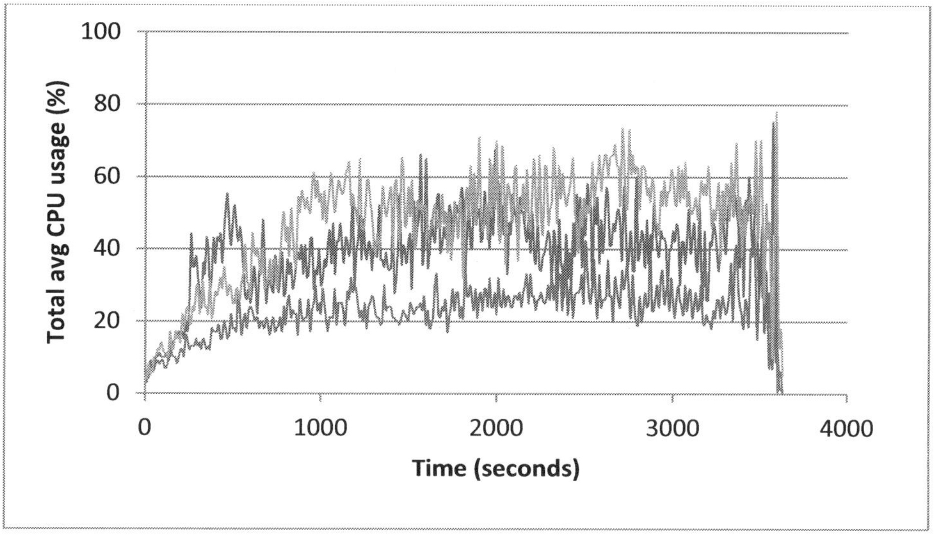

Figure 8.12 CPU utilizations with 500 (lower curve), 700 (middle curve), and 800 (upper curve) concurrent users (this chart was made by importing *vmstat* data into Excel, which required replacing the first space at the beginning of each line of the *vmstat* data files by applying ":1,$s/^ //g" in the *vi* editor)

Table 8.14 Total average/peak CPU utilizations in user mode and kernel mode with 500, 700 and 800 concurrent users

# of concurrent users	Total avg/peak CPU usage in user mode	Total avg/peak CPU usage in kernel mode
500	26/59	1.2/3
700	42/75	2/4
800	53/78	2/7

Table 8.15 CPU queue lengths with 500, 700 and 800 concurrent users

# of concurrent users	Avg CPU queue length	Peak CPU queue length
500	4.3	19
700	7.4	29
800	9.1	33

8.5.4 Linux versus Windows

As is known, Java applications are portable and platform-neutral. In fact, the enterprise Java application under test runs on both Windows and Linux. Therefore, it would be interesting to see how its performance compares with each other when deployed on the two different OS platforms. This kind of information is helpful for customers to make informed choices.

Figure 8.13 shows the performance comparison with the same workload of 700 concurrent users tested on the same hardware with everything else the same. Table 8.16 shows the # of transactions out of the same five user groups (or scripts) completed in each case. It is seen that the average response times on Linux and Windows are very close to each other, with the Linux number only 4% better than the Windows number. However, as is shown in Table 8.16, about 1.6% more transactions were carried out on Windows than on Linux. Therefore, we conclude that the performance numbers on both platforms are comparable to each other.

For your reference, Figure 8.14 shows the CPU traces on both platforms using the *vmstat* data on Linux and *perfmon* data on Windows. It is seen that Windows incurred more CPU activities than Linux. Table 8.17 further shows the differences between the two platforms in terms of the average/peak user CPU usage, average/peak kernel CPU usage, and average/peak kernel CPU queue length. However, keep in mind that comparable performance was achieved on Linux as a result of applying the *nofile* and *nproc* tunings as described in the previous section. If those tunings were not applied, Linux would have not been able to support 800 or even 700 concurrent users. Windows is a self-tuned platform, which in general outperforms Linux out of the box. The bottom line is that proper tunings are required on Linux so that it can actually deliver comparable performance achievable on Windows.

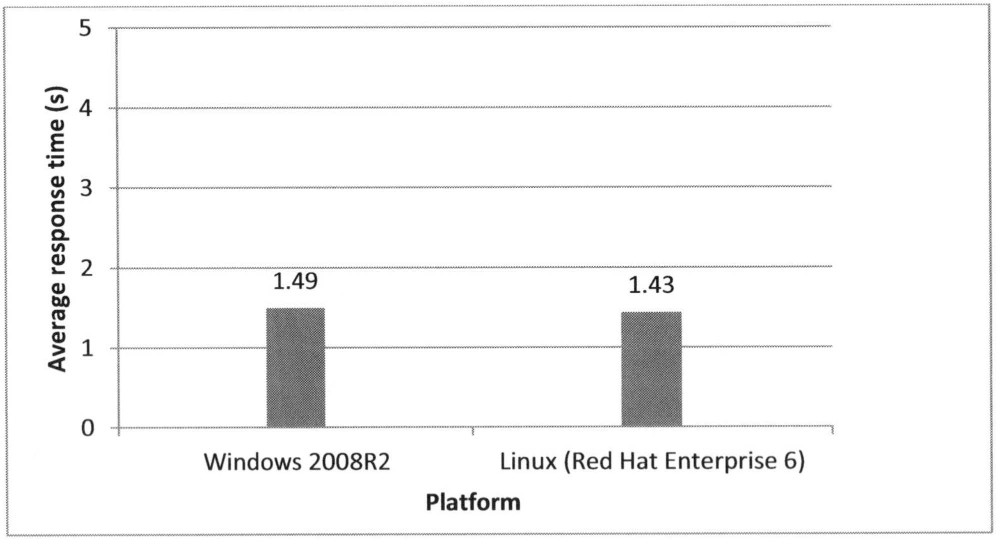

Figure 8.13 Performance comparison between Windows and Linux using a same enterprise Java application with 700 concurrent users

Table 8.16 # of transactions completed with the same workload of 700 concurrent users on Windows and Linux

User group	Windows	Linux
1	482	481
2	2,057	2,021
3	587	570
4	118	118
5	376	373
total	3,620	3,563

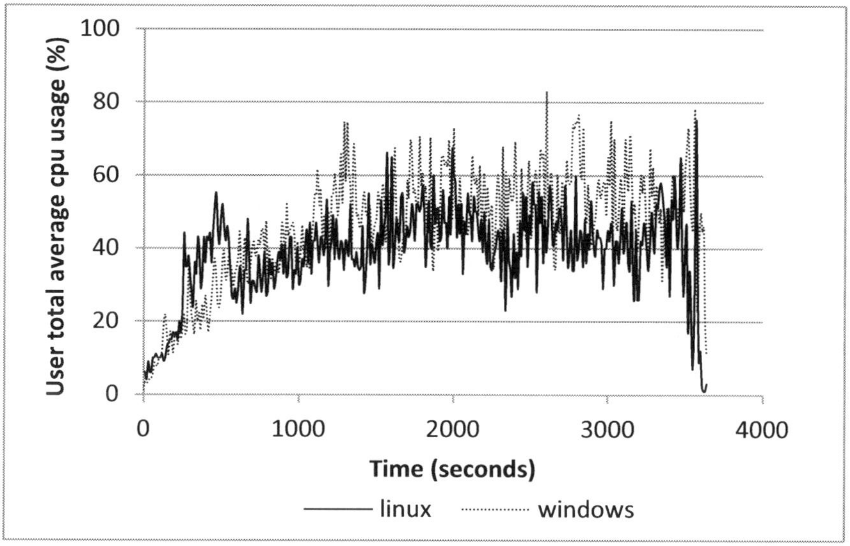

Figure 8.14 User CPU trace comparison between Windows (lighter, dotted curve) and Linux (darker, solid curve)

Table 8.17 CPU activity comparison between Windows and Linux for the same 700 concurrent user runs

Metric	Windows	Linux
Avg/peak user cpu (%)	53/83	42/75
Avg/peak sys cpu (%)	5/9	2/4
Avg/peak cpu queue length	1/12	7.4/29

It's also interesting to compare the GC statistics on Linux and Windows with the same 700 concurrent user runs. Table 8.18 gives such information on each platform in terms of average compile time, average class load time, average GC time, average Eden GC time and average OldGen GC time. The calculations were based on the VisualVM GC screenshots taken at the end of each run. Each average number was obtained by dividing the total time by the total count for each given metric. Once again, the GC statistical numbers are comparable between the two platforms as well. Figures 8.15 and 8.16 show the VisualVM Monitor views for the Linux and Windows runs, respectively. These screenshots provide additional information about the CPU and GC activities as well as class loading and thread creation that occurred on each platform.

Table 8.18 GC activity comparison between Windows and Linux for the same 700 concurrent user runs in terms of the average time calculated by dividing the total time by the total count (time/count => average time in milliseconds)

Metric	Windows	Linux
Avg compile time	86/6570 => 13 ms	94/6582 => 15 ms
Avg class load time	16/21317 => 0.75 ms	13/21269 => 0.62 ms
Avg GC time	287/3743 => 77 ms	355/3756 => 95 ms
Avg Eden time	238/3660 => 65 ms	291/3671 => 79 ms
Avg OldGen time	49/83 => 590 ms	64/85 => 753 ms

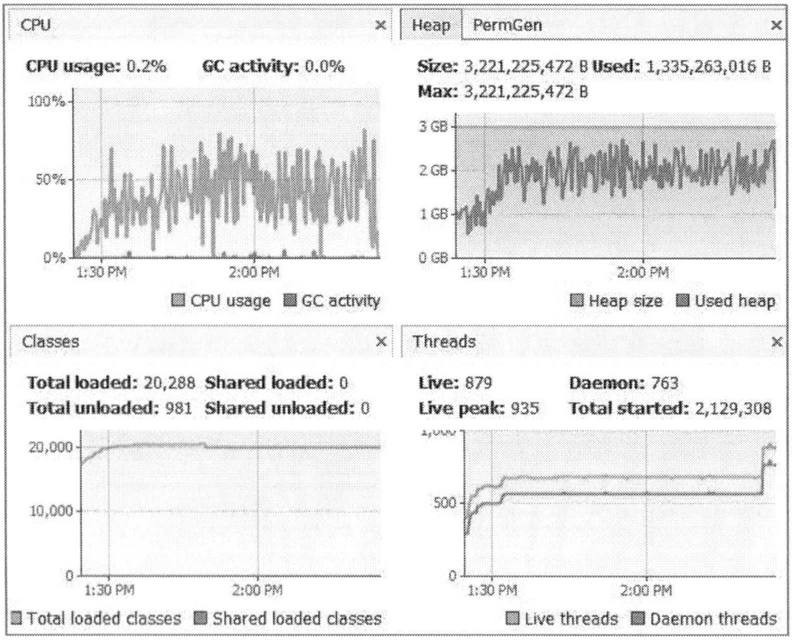

Figure 8.15 VisualVM CPU and GC activity screenshot for the Linux run

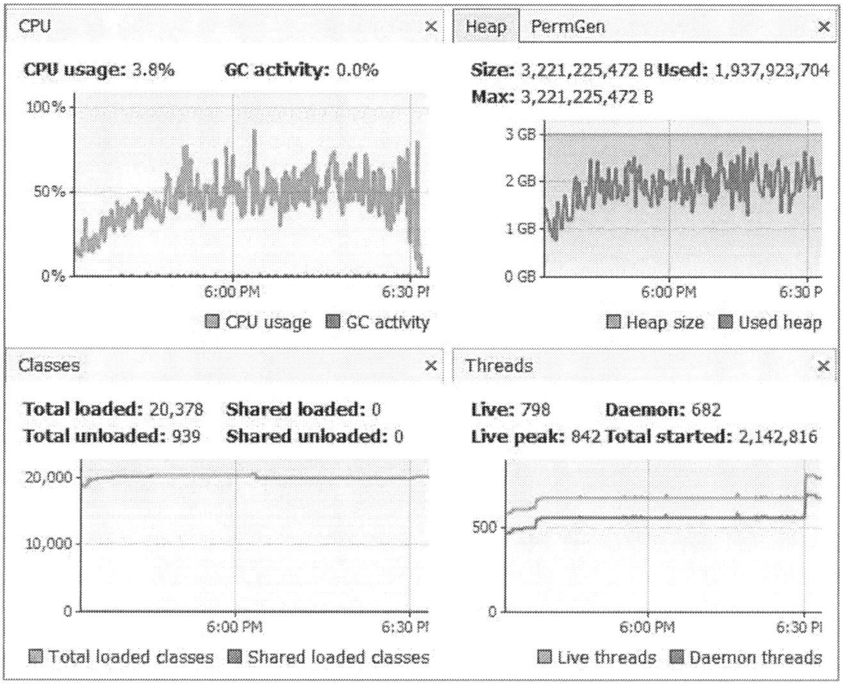

Figure 8.16 VisualVM CPU and GC activity screenshot for the Windows run

8.6 SUMMARY

In this chapter, we focused on understanding the Linux platform from the perspective of optimizing Java performance and scalability on Linux. We introduced not only the core concepts associated with the Linux kernel but also utilities for monitoring system activities. We also covered the following important topics:

- How to get to know about your Linux machine quickly from the system performance and scalability perspectives.
- How to check and configure Linux kernel parameters from the application performance and scalability perspectives.
- How to check and configure user shell limits for the user who launches the application.

Finally, we used a case study based on a real product to help illustrate the above concepts and procedures. We also compared the performance and scalability of the same enterprise application on the same hardware by running the tests first on Windows and then reimaging the same hardware into a Linux machine and re-running the same tests as on Windows. Perhaps the most important walk-away from this chapter is that out-of-the-box, Windows outperforms Linux since Windows is more self-tuned than Linux, but by applying proper tunings, Linux can deliver comparable performance as on Windows, given the same application and same hardware.

EXERCISES

8.1 Describe the various parts that a typical Linux system has.

8.2 What are the two major Linux offerings for enterprise computing?

8.3 Describe the architecture of a typical Linux system.

8.4 What is the role of system calls on a Linux system?

8.5 What are the benefits of virtual memory? Is the size of virtual memory tied to the amount of RAM installed on a Linux system?

8.6 What's the difference between a page and a page frame?

8.7 Explain the concept of page tables.

8.8 Explain the difference between UMA and NUMA. Which one favors system scalability over the other?

8.9 What's the difference between a process and a thread in UNIX/Linux?

8.10 Explain how Linux scheduling works.

8.11 What commands would you use to quickly look up the CPU information on a Linux machine?

8.12 What are the first two steps for preparing a Linux machine for maximum application performance and scalability?

8.13 How would you know if your application may benefit from the *HugePages* feature?

REFERENCES

The following Linux texts are helpful for understanding Linux architecture and concepts:

W. Mauerer, *Professional Linux Kernel Architecture*, Wrox, 2008.

D. Bovet & M. Cesati, *Understanding the Linux Kernel*, O'Reilly, 2006.

M. Kerrisk, *The Linux Programming Interface*, 2010.

Appendix A A Case Study with the Intel Turbo Boost Technology on Linux

In this appendix, I'd like to share a real-product based case study about how the Intel Turbo Boost technology can affect the performance and scalability of an enterprise Java application drastically, depending on whether it's configured properly. This may have a huge impact if you have a larger number of systems that the Intel Turbo Boost feature is relevant. The purposes of this appendix include:

- Raising your awareness of this issue whether you have a small number of systems in a R&D environment or in a large production environment
- Share some performance numbers I obtained with my testing using a real product so that you can gauge whether it is a big deal or not for your environment
- Sharing with you a procedure about how to check if this issue potentially exists in your environment and what you can do to get it right if it does.

Although the product I worked on was coded in Java, the best practices shared here apply to any applications coded in any languages. Let us start with an introduction to the Intel Turbo Boost technology next.

A.1 INTRODUCTION

Intel Turbo Boost Technology is a new feature that is built into Intel's latest generations of processors. It allows processor cores to run faster than the base operating frequency if the cores are operating below power, current, and temperature limits. It enables dynamically increasing the performance of an application when more CPU power is needed. It is meant for saving power while providing adequate performance. However, it's a double-edge weapon that it can either severely hurt or enhance the performance and scalability of an application, depending on how it is configured.

Next, we start with describing the dynamic power management feature built into latest systems that utilize Intel's new Core i7/Xeon processors. We then discuss briefly how CPU overclocking works, which depends on both power scaling and CPU frequency scaling. A case study using a real product is then presented to demonstrate quantitatively the efficacy of configuring the Intel Turbo Boost feature on a Linux system. Finally, I share with you my recommendations on how to go about this issue if you decide to check it out and/or pursue it on your systems.

Let us start with Intel Core i7/Xeon dynamic power management next.

A.2 INTEL CORE I7/XEON DYNAMIC POWER MANAGEMENT

Power management is an important issue for all kinds of electronic computing devices such as smart phones, laptops, desktops, and servers. To increase compatibility, a standard named the Advanced Configuration and Power Interface (ACPI) has been established for power management for microprocessors and computer systems, which defines platform-independent interfaces for hardware discovery, configuration, power management and monitoring.

Intel has incorporated the ACPI in their microprocessors since their Pentium III product line. With the introduction of the Nehalem microarchitecture, further improvements have been made at all levels such as the transistor level, the circuit level, the microarchitecture level, and so on. Various OS platforms such as Windows and Linux have provided corresponding support accordingly.

The central concept around power management is the so-called *state* that spans multiple physical and logical layers as shown in Table A.1.

Table A.1 Intel power management states

State	Description
S-State	System sleep states
T-State	Microprocessor thermal or throttle states
C-State	Microprocessor and package idle states
P-State	Microprocessor performance states

When a system is booted up, initially it is placed in state S0, which is considered an "ON" state. The subsequent states are S1, S2, S3, S4 and S5, with S5 considered an "OFF" state. Here is a more detailed description about what each state is meant for:

- **State S0**: This is the active state of the system to indicate that the system is completely operational and is keeping track of its architectural state precisely. When a system is in this state, the processor can be in any other states like T state, C state, and P state as described in Table A.1.
- **State S1**: This is the minimal wake-up time state that all microprocessor and hardware state is maintained. The system can be waked up with interrupts such as keystrokes or mouse movements.
- **State S2**: This is the second minimal wake-up time state that the microprocessor actually loses power, causing all microprocessor state and cache contents to be lost. However, the system can still be waked up with interrupts such as keystrokes or mouse movements.

- **State S3**: This is the third minimal wake-up time state that not only the microprocessor and hardware context but also the chipset context would be lost. Nevertheless, the system can still be waked up with interrupts such as keystrokes or mouse movements.
- **State S4**: This state is mostly called *Hibernate*, which almost completely shuts off the system. The system can still be waked up with interrupts such as keystrokes or mouse movements, upon which the architectural state is restored from the hard disk and the system is brought back to the S0 state.
- **State S5**: This is the *Shutdown* state but it is different from unplugging the power cord. For example, an unexpected power outage may shut the system off, but when the power resumes, the system may be powered back automatically without having to manually push the power button.

If you are on Windows, you can see some of these states when you press CTRL+ALT+DELETE, such as *Lock this computer*, *Switch User*, *Log Off*, or *Sleep*, *Hibernate*, *Shutdown*, etc. I believe "*Lock this computer*" may correspond to S1, "*Switch User*" and "*Log Off*" may correspond to S2, "*Sleep*" S3, "*Hibernate*" S4, and "*Shutdown*" S5. Incidentally, if you just want to lock up your system to prevent others from accessing it while you still want your running jobs to continue to run, select the "*Lock this computer*" option. If you select the "*Log Off*" option, all your running jobs will be forced to stop.

The next set of states we are concerned with are the *C-states*, which could be at the thread level, physical core level, or package level. These states are called *idle states*. Similar to the S states that we discussed above, the C0 state is the active state or normal operational state. The C1 state is defined as the HALT state that no instructions are being executed. At the C1 state, the core clock is turned off, but the core still is considered an active core. Other states ranging from C2 to Cn where n could be as large as 7 are optional, so not of them are implemented or supported. In addition to taking longer and longer to be waked up than a core at state C1, cores at states C2 – Cn are considered *inactive* with their core caches flushed to the Last Level Cache (LLC). Listing A.1 shows the output of the command "`cpupower idle-info`" executed on a Red Hat 6 Linux system with Intel's Xeon CPU E5-4650 @ 2.70 GHz. It is seen that in addition to the C0 state, this system also supports C1, C3, C6 and C7 states with longer and longer latencies of 80, 104 and 107 milliseconds, respectively, which are significantly longer than the 1 millisecond latency for the C1 state.

Listing A.1 Output of the command *cpupower idle-info* executed on a Red Hat Linux system with Intel(R) Xeon(R) CPU E5-4650 @ 2.70GHz

```
[root@perf01 ~]# cpupower idle-info
CPUidle driver: intel_idle
CPUidle governor: menu

Analyzing CPU 0:
Number of idle states: 5
Available idle states: C0 SNB-C1 SNB-C3 SNB-C6 SNB-C7
C0:
Flags/Description: CPUIDLE CORE POLL IDLE
Latency: 0
Usage: 11637
Duration: 111103632
SNB-C1:
```

Flags/Description: MWAIT 0x00
Latency: 1
Usage: 14818666
Duration: 4245332845
SNB-C3:
Flags/Description: MWAIT 0x10
Latency: 80
Usage: 2064274
Duration: 749220123
SNB-C6:
Flags/Description: MWAIT 0x20
Latency: 104
Usage: 32176
Duration: 45059311
SNB-C7:
Flags/Description: MWAIT 0x30
Latency: 109
Usage: 52230017
Duration: 1113531590988

A.3 CPU OVERCLOCKING

In the previous section, we focused on understanding the power management feature built into the latest generations of Intel processors since the Nehalem microarchitecture. In this section, we briefly discuss CPU overclocking, as this is the ultimate goal we would like to pursue for adequate performance with given CPUs that support overclocking.

CPU overclocking is actually a very complicated technology. However, let's start with a simple formula showing the CPU frequency as the product of the *BaseClockFrequency* and *CPU Multiplier* as follows:

CPU Frequency = BaseClockFrequency × CPU_Multiplier

Here, *BaseClockFrequency* is the base clock frequency, which is similar to that of the previous front-side-bus (FSB) technology but not exactly the same. (Base clock is also termed *bclock* or *bclk* in other texts). The CPU_Multiplier is a multiplier that determines the ultimate CPU frequency together with the base clock frequency. For example, if the base clock frequency is 133 MHz and the multiplier is 20, then the CPU frequency would be 133 × 20 = 2660 MHz. Furthermore, if the base clock frequency is set to 200, and a multiplier of 22 is supported with your CPU cores, the cores could essentially run at 200×22 = 4400 MHz. However, overclocking may result in system stability issues, so I would not recommend overdoing it. (My recommendation is that your CPUs should operate within the range as defined by the base frequency and max Turbo frequency – more about this later.) If you have a production environment, applying overclocking with caution for obvious reasons.

On Intel-architecture based systems, CPU overclocking has a lot to do with Intel's SpeedStep technology. Typically, CPU frequency scaling would involve various voltage scaling up or down, but it's particularly noteworthy that with Intel's Enhanced Intel SpeedStep® Technology (EIST), frequency scaling and voltage scaling are allowed to proceed separately, which has greatly simplified CPU overclocking. (Visit this URL for more details http://software.intel.com/en-us/articles/enhanced-intel-speedstepr-technology-and-demand-based-switching-on-linux/).

In addition to the concept of base clock frequency, there are also two other related concepts of QPI frequency and uncore frequency as explained as follows:

- **QPI frequency**: First, QPI stands for QuickPath Interface, which is Intel's newly-introduced distributed shared memory architecture in place of the previous FSB technology. QPI speeds are a function of base clocks, which will also increase with increasing base clock frequencies. Thus, overclocking CPU frequency will also help increase QPI speed and bandwidth, thus further increasing system performance overall.
- **Uncore frequency**: First, an *uncore* is a microprocessor aside from the regular computing task oriented cores. It helps enhance the performance of computing cores by interacting with QPI controllers, L3 cache, on-die memory controller, etc. Like CPU clock, DRAM, QPI, the frequency of an uncore is a multiple of the base clock frequency. In general, it's recommended that a frequency ratio of 2:1 be maintained between the DRAM and an uncore.

With the basic concepts of CPU power management and CPU overclocking as introduced above, we are ready to look at a case study out of my own real experience next.

A.4 A CASE STUDY WITH INTEL'S TURBO BOOST TECHNOLOGY

This case study was about testing the performance and scalability of an enterprise software product on a RedHat 6 Linux system. The CPU model with that Linux machine was Intel's Xeon E5-4650. It had eight quad-cores with HyperThreading on, resulting in 64 CPUs. From http://ark.intel.com/products/64622/, I quickly learnt that its base CPU frequency is 2700 MHz, and its max Turbo frequency is 3.3 GHz. (I would recommend that whenever you get a new system to work on, first, check out its CPU specs and do some CPU benchmarking on it so that you would get an idea of what performance you should expect out of it).

In the meanwhile, I had another Windows 7 Enterprise system with a single quad-core Core i7-3820QM @ 2.7 GHz with HyperThreading enabled. The same workload was run on both the Linux and this Windows system with the # of threads varied from 1 to 10, 20, 30, 40, 50 and 60. As you see from Figure A.1, clearly, something looked suspicious on the Linux system: The average elapsed time out of five sampled requests went up exponentially. I also put up jvisualvm and observed severe contention on the Linux machine and almost no contention on the Windows machine with the test case of 30 threads.

I suspected that it was a Turbo Boost issue on Linux based on the output from the "lscpu" command executed on that Linux box. As shown in Figure A.2, the base frequency for a CPU on that Linux box was 1200 MHz instead of 2700 MHz as it should have been. Secondly, I checked the *scaling_gonvernor* setting, which was set to "*userspace*" instead of "*performance*," as shown in Figure A.3.

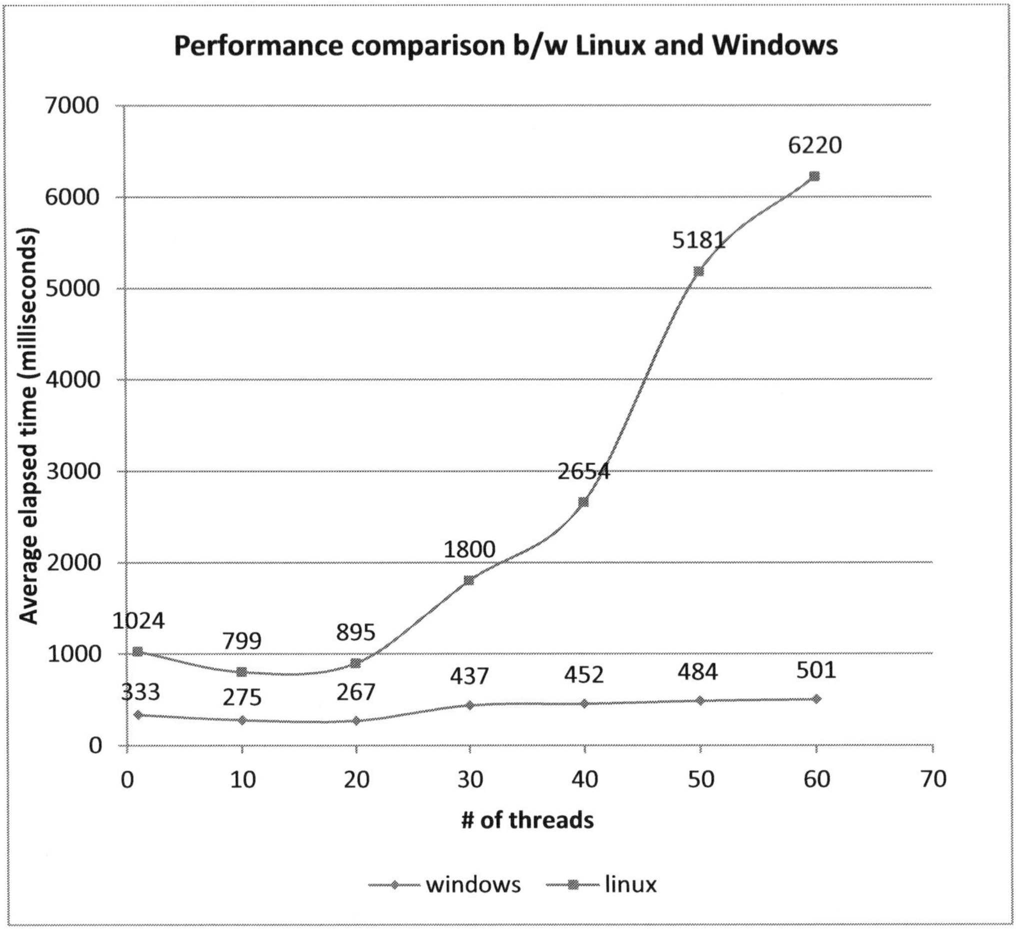

Figure A.1 Performance comparison between Windows (lower) and Linux (upper) when the Turbo Boost feature was not configured properly on Linux

```
-bash-4.1$ lscpu
Architecture:          x86_64
CPU op-mode(s):        32-bit, 64-bit
Byte Order:            Little Endian
CPU(s):                64
On-line CPU(s) list:   0-63
Thread(s) per core:    2
Core(s) per socket:    8
CPU socket(s):         4
NUMA node(s):          4
Vendor ID:             GenuineIntel
CPU family:            6
Model:                 45
Stepping:              7
CPU MHz:               1200.000
BogoMIPS:              5386.33
```

Figure A.2 Output of the "lscpu" command on the Linux box

```
-bash-4.1$ cat /sys/devices/system/cpu/cpu0/cpufreq/scaling_governor
userspace
-bash-4.1$ cat /sys/devices/system/cpu/cpu0/cpufreq/scaling_available_governors
userspace performance
-bash-4.1$
```

Figure A.3 Initial setting of *the cpufreq scaling_governor* on the Linux box (the first command shows the effective scaling governor out of the two available settings of *userspace* and *performance* as shown by the second command)

These were enough evidences for me to suspect that the issue might be related to the Turbo Boost feature on that Linux box. After installing the *cpupower* utility on that Linux box, I checked the frequencies of the CPUs while having a 30-thread test running. Surprisingly, CPUs were running at approximately 1200 MHz as shown in Figure A.4. At that point, I was more sure that the CPU frequency was the issue.

```
[root@psrlq01 ~]# cpupower -c 0-3 monitor
              |Nehalem                   || SandyBridge          || Mperf              || Idle_Stats
PKG |CORE|CPU | C3   | C6   | PC3  | PC6  || C7   | PC2  | PC7  || C0   | Cx   | Freq || C0   | C1   | C3   | C6   | C7
   0|   0|   0|  0.00|  0.00|  0.00| 88.20|| 100.1| 10.24|  0.00||  0.35| 99.65|  1195||  0.00|  0.00|  0.00|  0.00| 99.93
   0|   1|   1|  0.00|  0.00|  0.00| 88.20|| 100.2| 10.24|  0.00||  0.31| 99.69|  1196||  0.00|  0.00|  0.00|  0.00| 99.96
   0|   2|   2|  0.00|  0.00|  0.00| 88.20|| 100.2| 10.24|  0.00||  0.31| 99.69|  1196||  0.00|  0.00|  0.00|  0.00| 99.96
   0|   3|   3|  0.00|  0.00|  0.00| 88.20|| 100.2| 10.24|  0.00||  0.32| 99.68|  1195||  0.00|  0.00|  0.00|  0.00| 99.95
[root@psrlq01 ~]#
```

```
[root@psrlq01 ~]# cpupower -c 0-3 monitor
              |Nehalem                   || SandyBridge          |
PKG |CORE|CPU | C3   | C6   | PC3  | PC6  || C7   | PC2  | PC7  |
   0|   0|   0|  0.00|  0.00|  0.00| 88.20|| 100.1| 10.24|  0.00|
   0|   1|   1|  0.00|  0.00|  0.00| 88.20|| 100.2| 10.24|  0.00|
   0|   2|   2|  0.00|  0.00|  0.00| 88.20|| 100.2| 10.24|  0.00|
   0|   3|   3|  0.00|  0.00|  0.00| 88.20|| 100.2| 10.24|  0.00|
[root@psrlq01 ~]#
```

```
| Mperf                  || Idle_Stats
| C0     | Cx     | Freq || C0     | C1     | C3     | C6     | C7
|   0.35| 99.65|  1195||  0.00|  0.00|  0.00|  0.00| 99.93
|   0.31| 99.69|  1196||  0.00|  0.00|  0.00|  0.00| 99.96
|   0.31| 99.69|  1196||  0.00|  0.00|  0.00|  0.00| 99.96
|   0.32| 99.68|  1195||  0.00|  0.00|  0.00|  0.00| 99.95
```

Figure A.4 Output of the command "cpupower –c 0-3 monitor" on that Linux box (in case you cannot see clearly the upper most screenshot, I have chopped it into two segments as shown by the middle and bottom screenshots)

Then after studying a Red Hat Linux guide, I made two changes one after another. First, I had the power management setting set to "OS control" at the BIOS level when the system was being rebooted together with the scaling governor altered from *userspace* to *performance*. After this change, the average elapsed time with 30 threads came down from 1800 ms to 1403 ms. While the test was running, I monitored the CPU frequency, which was captured and is shown in Figure A.5 (a). However, after the test was finished and the system was pretty much idle, the CPU frequency dropped back to 1200 MHz. Then, I had the base CPU frequency increased from 1200 MHz to 2700 MHz which was the base frequency marked by Intel, and re-ran the same 30 thread test. Then, the average elapsed time with 30 threads came down further from 1403 ms to 491 ms. During that run, I monitored the running CPU frequency again, which was captured and is shown in Figure A.5 (b). As is seen, some of the cores were running above 3 GHz. Figure D.6 illustrates the effects of these settings.

```
| Mperf                  ||
| C0     | Cx     | Freq ||
|  11.12| 88.88|  1243||
|  14.67| 85.33|  2063||
|   0.39| 99.61|  1821||
|   9.95| 90.05|  2422||

| Mperf                  ||
| C0     | Cx     | Freq ||
|  16.20| 83.80|  2246||
|  69.54| 30.46|  2546||
|   0.28| 99.72|  2520||
|   0.31| 99.69|  2499||
```

(a)

```
|| Mperf                  ||
|| C0     | Cx     | Freq ||
||   4.20| 95.80|  3172||
||   0.31| 99.69|  2620||
||   0.31| 99.69|  2593||
||   0.30| 99.70|  2619||

|| Mperf                  ||
|| C0     | Cx     | Freq ||
||   3.06| 96.94|  3052||
||   2.34| 97.66|  3056||
||   0.34| 99.66|  2414||
||   0.23| 99.77|  2624||
```

(b)

Figure A.5 (a) Left: Core running frequencies after setting power management to "OS-Control" at the BIOS level when the system was being rebooted; (b) Right: Core running frequencies after increasing the base CPU frequency from 1200 MHz to the marked base frequency of 2700 MHz.

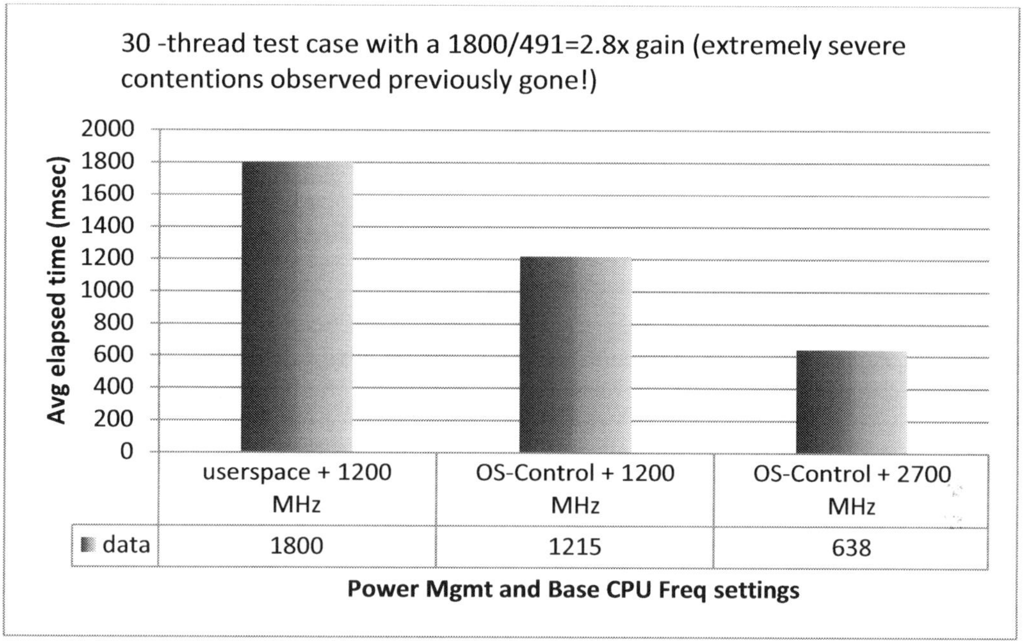

Figure A.6 Effects of the Turbo Boost settings on the average elapsed time in milliseconds of the application tested with 30 threads

A.4 RECOMMENDATIONS

First, I have to mention that I tried the same 30 thread test case on that Windows system by changing the power scheme from *Balanced (Recommended)* to *Maximum Performanc*e, and observed severe contentions, which led to significantly degraded performance. Therefore, if you decide to explore this feature on Windows, test it thoroughly before you decide to configure your systems to use the *Maximum Performance* power scheme.

However, the settings I applied on that Linux system as described in the previous section have not caused any side effects up to now for several months. These settings had been verified with other types of applications, which had all led to significant performance gains. Therefore, I feel comfortable to share the tunings with you as follows if this is relevant to your systems as well:

1 Set the power management setting to "OS-Control" while the system is being rebooted
2 For each CPU, change the default flag of *ondemand* to *performance* to get the marked base frequency in the following file (where <cpunum> should be replaced with cpu0, cpu1, …, etc.):

   /sys/devices/system/cpu/<cpunum>/cpufreq/scaling_governor

3 Add the following line to the */etc/rc.local* file to persist the above settings so that they would survive future reboots (this is where you can put all your own stuff to be executed after all other init scripts) have been executed):

/usr/bin/cpupower frequency-set --governor performance

See Figure A.7 on the contents of the /sys/devices/systems/cpu folder and Figure A.8 on the scaling_governor of *performance* for cpu0 after carrying out step 2.

Of course, you should first execute the "*lscpu*" command to look up the CPU frequency configured on your system. Then execute the command "*cat /proc/cpuinfo*" to look up the exact CPU model. You can further look up the published base frequency and the max Turbo frequency for the CPU model in question. If the CPU frequency shown from the "*lscpu*" command is below the published base frequency of your CPU model, then, you can consider to have your system administrator to apply the settings suggested above.

After applying the proper settings, install a monitoring tool such as the "*cpupower*" on Red Hat, put some load on your system so that you can observe the actual frequency running real-time. If it is configured properly, you should not see your CPUs running below the minimum frequency you configured. You can also check the frequencies set after carrying out step 3 using the following command:

cpupower frequency-info

Listing A.2 shows the output on my Linux system for your reference.

This concludes our case study with the Intel Turbo Boost technology on Linux.

```
-bash-4.1$ ls /sys/devices/system/cpu
cpu0   cpu20  cpu32  cpu44  cpu56    cpuidle
cpu1   cpu21  cpu33  cpu45  cpu57    kernel_max
cpu10  cpu22  cpu34  cpu46  cpu58    offline
cpu11  cpu23  cpu35  cpu47  cpu59    online
cpu12  cpu24  cpu36  cpu48  cpu6     possible
cpu13  cpu25  cpu37  cpu49  cpu60    present
cpu14  cpu26  cpu38  cpu5   cpu61    sched_mc_power_savings
cpu15  cpu27  cpu39  cpu50  cpu62    sched_smt_power_savings
cpu16  cpu28  cpu4   cpu51  cpu63
cpu17  cpu29  cpu40  cpu52  cpu7
cpu18  cpu3   cpu41  cpu53  cpu8
cpu19  cpu30  cpu42  cpu54  cpu9
cpu2   cpu31  cpu43  cpu55  cpufreq
-bash-4.1$
```

Figure A.7 The contents of the /sys/devices/systems/cpu folder

```
-bash-4.1$ cat /sys/devices/system/cpu/cpu0/cpufreq/scaling_governor
performance
-bash-4.1$
```

Figure A.8 The scaling governor for cpu0 after carrying out step 2

Listing A.2 Frequencies after carrying out step 3

```
analyzing CPU 0:
  driver: acpi-cpufreq
  CPUs which run at the same hardware frequency: 0
  CPUs which need to have their frequency coordinated by software: 0
  maximum transition latency: 10.0 us.
  hardware limits: 1.20 GHz - 2.70 GHz
  available frequency steps: 2.70 GHz, 2.70 GHz, 2.60 GHz, 2.50 GHz,
2.40 GHz, 2.30 GHz, 2.20 GHz, 2.10 GHz, 1.90 GHz, 1.80 GHz, 1.70 GHz,
1.60 GHz, 1.50 GHz, 1.40 GHz, 1.30 GHz, 1.20 GHz
  available cpufreq governors: userspace, performance
  current policy: frequency should be within 1.20 GHz and 2.70 GHz.
The governor "performance" may decide which speed to use within this
range.
  current CPU frequency is 2.70 GHz.
  cpufreq stats: 2.70 GHz:100.00%, 2.70 GHz:0.00%, 2.60 GHz:0.00%,
2.50 GHz:0.00%, 2.40 GHz:0.00%, 2.30 GHz:0.00%, 2.20 GHz:0.00%, 2.10
GHz:0.00%, 1.90 GHz:0.00%, 1.80 GHz:0.00%, 1.70 GHz:0.00%, 1.60
GHz:0.00%, 1.50 GHz:0.00%, 1.40 GHz:0.00%, 1.30 GHz:0.00%, 1.20
GHz:0.00%  (1)
  boost state support:
    Supported: yes
    Active: yes
    25500 MHz max turbo 4 active cores
    25500 MHz max turbo 3 active cores
    25500 MHz max turbo 2 active cores
    25500 MHz max turbo 1 active cores
```

Appendix B CPUCheck: An Client/Server Java Program for Benchmarking CPUs

In this appendix, I'd like to share an RMI-based client/server Java program named *CPUCheck* I developed several years ago. It emulates a service admin console application. You can download it from this book's web site at http://www.perfmath.com/download.htm. It can be used both for benchmarking CPUs and for demonstrating Java performance and scalability by design, as we did in Chapter 7. Because it's so simple, it typically takes no more than five minutes to get a quick assessment on the power of the CPUs of a system. Computer hardware architecture evolves constantly and I need an objective method of my own to know how much faster if I have system X versus system Y with different CPU configurations. Marketing propagandas are vague and unreliable.

This program has two parts: the server part and the client part. It essentially mimics what a service admin console does in general by building a service directory tree structure on a console GUI. The next few sections describe how to get each part up and running and how to run it on a system. I'll also provide some representative CPU bench-marking results obtained on many of the systems I had access to.

At this point, if you are not interested in how this program works and you just want to run the program to get the benchmarking number for your system, follow the procedure given in the next section.

B.1 How to Run CPUCheck

To run the CPUCheck program on your system, follow the below procedure:

- Download and unzip the ServiceAdmin-1.0 program into a folder on your system. The pre-compiled classes are ready to go.
- Make sure you have a 1.6 JDK or newer installed on your system to be tested.

- To start up the Admin Server, cd to the `CPUCheck-1.0` folder and run the command "`runServer <yourJDKPath>`" by replacing `<yourJDKPath>` properly with something like C:\jdk1.6.0_31_64 up to the `bin` directory of your JDK install.
- To start up the client, open up another MS-DOS command prompt, cd to the `CPUCheck-1.0` folder, run the command "`runClient <yourJDKPath>`" and press *Enter*. It may take up to a few minutes to complete, depending on the CPU power of your system. At the end, look for the "`total execution time = ...`" at your client command console, which is the CPU benchmarking number as a yardstick to measure the relative power of your system. Refer to Figure B.1 for an example output on one of my systems. At this point, you can compare your system under test with those I tested as shown in Table B.1. You can also check out the service directory created and displayed on the service admin console as shown in Figure B.2.

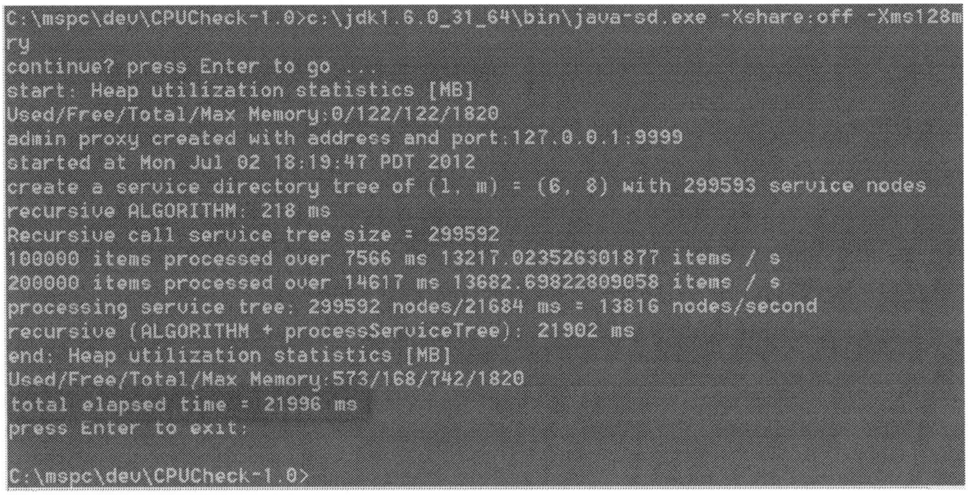

```
C:\mspc\dev\CPUCheck-1.0>c:\jdk1.6.0_31_64\bin\java-sd.exe -Xshare:off -Xms128m
ry
continue? press Enter to go ...
start: Heap utilization statistics [MB]
Used/Free/Total/Max Memory:0/122/122/1820
admin proxy created with address and port:127.0.0.1:9999
started at Mon Jul 02 18:19:47 PDT 2012
create a service directory tree of (l, m) = (6, 8) with 299593 service nodes
recursive ALGORITHM: 218 ms
Recursive call service tree size = 299592
100000 items processed over 7566 ms 13217.02352630187 items / s
200000 items processed over 14617 ms 13682.69822809058 items / s
processing service tree: 299592 nodes/21684 ms = 13816 nodes/second
recursive (ALGORITHM + processServiceTree): 21902 ms
end: Heap utilization statistics [MB]
Used/Free/Total/Max Memory:573/168/742/1820
total elapsed time = 21996 ms
press Enter to exit:

C:\mspc\dev\CPUCheck-1.0>
```

Figure B.1 An example output of running CPUCheck on the client console

Table B.1 Total execution times (T.E.T in seconds) on a list of representative systems I tested with CPUCheck program

CPU/OS Configuration	CPUCheck	PassMark	JDK 1.6.0
Core i7-2600 (a quad core @ 3.4 GHz with HT enabled)/Win7 Prof.	22	8889	u31 (64-bit)
Core 2 Duo (E8500@3.16 GHz, 2 CPUs)/Win XP	33	2371	u18 (32-bit)
Phenom II X4 830 (a quad-core @2.8 GHz w/o HT)/ Win 7	32	3480	u31(64-bit)
E5320 (2 quad-core@1.86 GHz with HT disabled)/Win2k8R2	86	2270	u21 (64-bit)
E5620 (2 quad-core @ 2.39 GHz with HT enabled)/Win2k8R2	51	4696	u21 (64-bit)

X5650 (2 6-core @ 2.67 GHz with HT enabled)/Win2k8R2	50	7954	U21 (64-bit)
X5550 (2 quad cores @2.67GHz With HT enabled)/Win2k8SP2	31	5170	u31(64-bit)

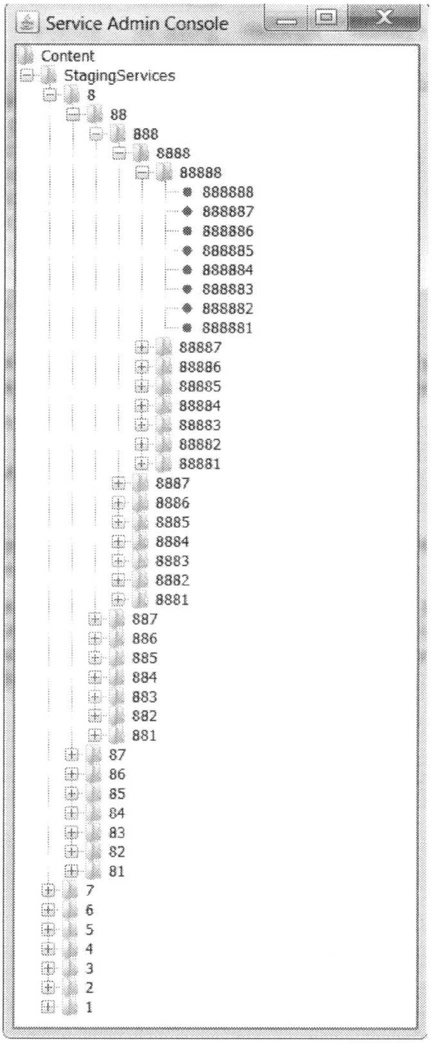

Figure B.2 A service directory tree structure of 6 levels deep with 8 sub-nodes per node

B.2 MORE ABOUT CPUCHECK

This section provides enough information about how to recompile CPUCheck and how it is run, in case you want to explore more about it beyond a quick check on the relative power of your system. You should also refer to Chapter 7 for a more thorough coverage on CPUCheck, especially its various algorithms and the definitions of the parameters contained in a `services.properties` file, which is the configuration file for running CPUCheck.

B.2.1The Admin Server

The admin server consists of three Java classes: `AdminInterface.java`, `AdminServer.java`, and `AdminConsole.java`. The `AdminInterface` class has only one method: `processCommand (String cmd)`. The class `AdminServer` implements the `AdminInterface` and extends `java.rmi.server.UnicastRemoteObject`. The `AdminConsole` class creates a tree structure for holding a service directory.

With Java RMI, it's necessary to create a surrogate object called a *stub*, which should reside on the client side. The client calls remote methods on the server via the stub, which typically involves parameter marshaling/unmarshalling and packaging, etc. The specific details about how RMI works are less important, so let's get to how to make it work next.

If you want to recompile, execute the script named `compileServer.bat` as follows:

```
cmd>compileServer <yourJDKPath>
```

Note that you need to specify the path to your JDK install, e.g., c:\jdk1.6.0_31_64 on one of my systems. See Listing B.1for the contents of the script `compileServer.bat`.

Listing B.1 compileServer.bat

```
set jdk_path=%~1\bin
%jdk_path%\javac AdminInterface.java AdminConsole.java AdminServer.java
%jdk_path%\rmic AdminServer
```

Then, before starting up the service admin server, execute the script named `copyBinary.bat` as follows:

```
cmd>copyBinary <yourJDKPath>
```

Once again, you need to specify the path to your JDK install. As you see from Listing B.2, the script `copyBinary.bat` creates two new JVM executables, one named `java-sd.exe` for running the client, and the other named `java-as.exe` for running the server. Note that if you want to run the client and server on two separate systems, you need to create the JVM executables for the client and server separately.

Listing B.2 copyBinary.bat

```
set jdk_path=%~1\bin
copy %jdk_path%\java.exe %jdk_path%\java-sd.exe
copy %jdk_path%\java.exe %jdk_path%\java-as.exe
```

Then, execute the following command to start up the admin server for receiving commands from the client (See Listing B.3 for the contents of the script `runServer.bat`):

```
cmd>runServer <yourJDKPath>
```

Listing B.3 runServer.bat

```
set jdk_path=%~1\bin
%jdk_path%\java-as.exe -server -Xms128m -Xmx1024m AdminServer
```

At this point, you should see an output message about the name, IP address and TCP port of 9999 for the server. In addition, you should see an empty service admin console as shown in Figure B.3. The next step is to run the client to have this empty console filled with a specified service directory tree structure, which is explained next.

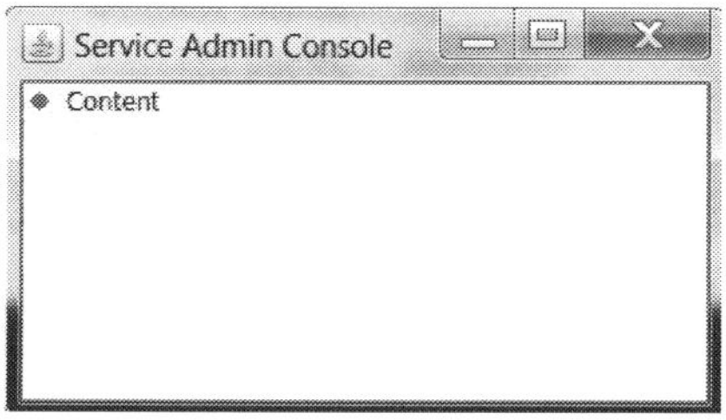

Figure B.3 Initial empty service admin console

B.2.2 The Client

The client side consists of three Java classes as well: `AdminProxy.java`, `ServiceDirectory.java`, and `AdminClient.java`. The `AdminProxy` class has a constructor for setting up a connection to the Admin Server with a given server name or IP and a TCP port. It has only one method: `sendCommand (String command)`, which calls the `processCommand` method on the Admin Server. The class `ServiceDirectory` constructs a service directory tree structure based on a properties file named `services.properties`, and sends this service directory structure to the Admin Server. Then the service directory tree structure is displayed on the service admin console.

In order to understand this entire process better, let us take a look at each step one at a time.

First, if you want to recompile, execute the script named `compileClient.bat` as follows:

```
cmd>compileClient <yourJDKPath>
```

Note that you need to specify the path to your JDK install, e.g., c:\jdk1.6.0_31_64 on one of my systems. See Listing B.4 for the contents of the script `compileClient.bat`.

Listing B.4 compileClient.bat

```
set jdk_path=%~1\bin
%jdk_path%\javac ServiceDirectory.java AdminProxy.java AdminClient.java
```

At this step, if you have not made a *java-sd.exe* executable for running the client, make one by following the procedure given in the preceding section. Then, edit the contents of the file `services.properties`, if you want to have a different service tree structure than the one specified in this file as shown in Listing B.5 (replace the parameter SERVER_ADDRESS with its actual IP if the client is installed separately on a remote system). By default, it creates a service tree structure of 6 levels deep with 8 child nodes per node. Unless you want to explore more, these settings are adequate for benchmarking the CPUs of your systems in general.

Listing B.5 services.properties

```
SERVICE_NAME_PREFIX=system_
SYSTEM_START_INDEX=0
SYSTEM_END_INDEX=799
TOP_SERVICE_NAME=StagingServices
SERVICE_NAME_PREFIX=
NUM_OF_LEVELS=6
SUBSERVICES_PER_NODE=8
NUM_OF_THREADS=1
ADD_SERVICES=true
ADD_SYSTEMS=false
#ALGORITHM=static
ALGORITHM=recursive
#ALGORITHM=dynamic
ARRAY_SIZE=1
SERVER_ADDRESS=127.0.0.1
SERVER_PORT=9999
USE_PROXY=true
CLEAR_SERVICE_TREE=true
HEART_BEAT=100000
DEBUG=false
TRACING=false
```

Finally, execute the following command to start sending a service directory tree structure to the Admin Server (See Listing B.6 for the contents of the script `runClient.bat`):

```
cmd>runClient <yourJDKPath>
```

Listing B.6 runClient.bat

```
set jdk_path=%~1\bin
%jdk_path%\java-sd.exe -Xms128m -Xmx1024m -DparameterFile=services.properties ServiceDirectory
```

The remaining part is the same as we described in section B.1.

B.2.3 ServiceDirectory.java

The `ServiceDirectory.java` program is listed in Listing B.7 in case you are interested in taking a closer look at it. This is the core part of CPUCheck program that would take more time to understand.

Listing B.7 ServiceDirectory.java

```
import java.io.*;
```

```
import java.lang.management.ManagementFactory;
import java.lang.management.ThreadInfo;
import java.lang.management.ThreadMXBean;
import java.util.*;
import java.rmi.*;

public class ServiceDirectory {
    static boolean ADD_SERVICES;
    static String SERVICE_NAME_PREFIX;
    static String TOP_SERVICE_NAME;
    public static int THREAD_COUNT_DOWN;
    public static int NUM_OF_SYSTEMS;
    public static String SERVER_ADDRESS;
    public static String SERVER_PORT;
    public static boolean USE_PROXY;
    public static AdminProxy adminProxy;
    public static int SUBSERVICES_PER_NODE;
    public static int NUM_OF_LEVELS;
    public static int NUM_OF_THREADS;
    public static int SYSTEM_START_INDEX;
    public static int SYSTEM_END_INDEX;
    public static int HEART_BEAT;
    public static int ARRAY_SIZE;
    public static int LAST_BUCKET;
    public static String ALGORITHM;
    public static boolean ADD_SYSTEMS;
    public static boolean DEBUG;
    public static boolean TRACING;
    public static String SYSTEM_NAME_PREFIX;
    public static String[] commandBuffer;
    public static PrintWriter logWriter;
    public static PrintWriter commandWriter;
    public static String commandFileName;

    public static void main(String args[]) {
        delayStart();
        long startTime = System.currentTimeMillis();
        init();
        ArrayList leafSubServiceNames = dispatch();
        checkAddServices();
        checkAddSystems(leafSubServiceNames);
        // wait to exit (for having extra time to examine memory usage ...)
        checkMemory("end:");
        String printString = "total elapsed time = "
                + (System.currentTimeMillis() - startTime) + " ms";
        System.out.println(printString);
        logWriter.println(printString);
```

```
        if (TRACING)
            printStackTrace();
        Console console = System.console();
        String exit = console.readLine("press Enter to exit: ");
        logWriter.close();
    }

    public static void delayStart() {
        Console con = System.console();
        String input = con.readLine("continue? press Enter to go ...");
        if (input.length() >= 1)
            System.exit(0);
    }

    // initialize
    public static void init() {
        checkMemory("start:");
        String parameterFile = System.getProperty("parameterFile");
        InputStream propsFile;
        Properties props = new Properties();
        try {
            propsFile = new FileInputStream(parameterFile);
            props.load(propsFile);
        } catch (IOException io) {
            System.out.println("Failed to read " + "properties file ... "
                    + io.getMessage());
            System.exit(-1);
        }
        String SYSTEM_NAME_PREFIX =
            props.getProperty("SYSTEM_NAME_PREFIX",
                "sys");
        SYSTEM_START_INDEX = Integer.parseInt(props
                .getProperty("SYSTEM_START_INDEX"));
        SYSTEM_END_INDEX = Integer.parseInt(props
                .getProperty("SYSTEM_END_INDEX"));
        NUM_OF_SYSTEMS = SYSTEM_END_INDEX –
            SYSTEM_START_INDEX;
        NUM_OF_LEVELS =
    Integer.parseInt(props.getProperty("NUM_OF_LEVELS"));

        SUBSERVICES_PER_NODE = Integer.parseInt(props
                .getProperty("SUBSERVICES_PER_NODE"));

        SERVICE_NAME_PREFIX =
            props.getProperty("SERVICE_NAME_PREFIX", "s");
        TOP_SERVICE_NAME = props.getProperty("TOP_SERVICE_NAME",
                "\"Staging Services\"").trim();
```

```
NUM_OF_THREADS =
    Integer.parseInt(props.getProperty("NUM_OF_THREADS",
        "2"));
HEART_BEAT = Integer
        .parseInt(props.getProperty("HEART_BEAT", "100000"));
NUM_OF_THREADS =
    Integer.parseInt(props.getProperty("NUM_OF_THREADS",
        "2"));
ARRAY_SIZE = Integer.parseInt(props.getProperty("ARRAY_SIZE", "1"));
commandBuffer = new String[ARRAY_SIZE];
LAST_BUCKET = 0;
initCommandBuffer();
THREAD_COUNT_DOWN = NUM_OF_THREADS;
ADD_SERVICES =
    Boolean.parseBoolean(props.getProperty("ADD_SERVICES",
        "false"));
ADD_SYSTEMS =
    Boolean.parseBoolean(props.getProperty("ADD_SYSTEMS",
        "false"));
DEBUG = Boolean.parseBoolean(props.getProperty("DEBUG", "false"));
TRACING = Boolean.parseBoolean(props.getProperty("TRACING", "false"));
ALGORITHM = props.getProperty("ALGORITHM", "dynamic");
// added on 2/10/2009
SERVER_ADDRESS = props.getProperty("SERVER_ADDRESS",
    "192.168.1.100");
SERVER_PORT = props.getProperty("SERVER_PORT", "9999");
USE_PROXY = Boolean
        .parseBoolean(props.getProperty("USE_PROXY", "true"));
boolean CLEAR_SERVICE_TREE = Boolean.parseBoolean(props.getProperty(
        "CLEAR_SERVICE_TREE", "true"));
if (USE_PROXY) {
    adminProxy = new AdminProxy(SERVER_ADDRESS, SERVER_PORT);
    System.out.println("admin proxy created with address and port:"
            + SERVER_ADDRESS + ":" + SERVER_PORT);
    if (CLEAR_SERVICE_TREE) {
        adminProxy.sendCommand("removeAll");
    }
} else {
    commandFileName = "commandFile_" + getFileNameSuffix();
    commandWriter = createWriter(commandFileName);
}
if (ADD_SYSTEMS) {
    createSystemFile(SYSTEM_NAME_PREFIX, SYSTEM_START_INDEX,
            SYSTEM_END_INDEX);
}
// calculate total # of services to create with given level and base
System.out.println("started at " + (new Date()).toString());
```

```
    System.out.println("create a service directory tree of (l, m) = " + "("
            + NUM_OF_LEVELS + ", " + SUBSERVICES_PER_NODE + ")
    with " + +(1 + findEndIndex(NUM_OF_LEVELS - 1,
        SUBSERVICES_PER_NODE))
            + " service nodes ");
    String logFileName = "ServiceDirectory_" + getFileNameSuffix();
    logWriter = createWriter(logFileName);
    logWriter.println("SYSTEM_NAME_PREFIX=" +
        SYSTEM_NAME_PREFIX);
    logWriter.println("SYSTEM_START_INDEX=" +
        SYSTEM_START_INDEX);
    logWriter.println("SYSTEM_END_INDEX=" + SYSTEM_END_INDEX);
    logWriter.println("TOP_SERVICE_NAME=" + TOP_SERVICE_NAME);
    logWriter.println("SERVICE_NAME_PREFIX=" +
        SERVICE_NAME_PREFIX);
    logWriter.println("NUM_OF_LEVELS=" + NUM_OF_LEVELS);
    logWriter.println("SUBSERVICES_PER_NODE" +
        SUBSERVICES_PER_NODE);
    logWriter.println("NUM_OF_THREADS=" + NUM_OF_THREADS);
    logWriter.println("ARRAY_SIZE=" + ARRAY_SIZE);
    logWriter.println("ADD_SERVICES=" + ADD_SERVICES);
    logWriter.println("ADD_SYSTEMS=" + ADD_SYSTEMS);
    logWriter.println("DEBUG=" + DEBUG);
    logWriter.println("ALGORITHM=" + ALGORITHM);
    logWriter.println("SERVER_ADDRESS=" + SERVER_ADDRESS);
    logWriter.println("SERVER_PORT=" + SERVER_PORT);
    logWriter.println("USE_PROXY=" + USE_PROXY);
    logWriter.println("clearServiceTree=" + CLEAR_SERVICE_TREE);
    logWriter.println("HEART_BEAT=" + HEART_BEAT);
}

public static ArrayList dispatch() {
    // add a service directory in a single thread and return names of all
    // leaf sub Services
    ArrayList leafSubServiceNames = new ArrayList(1000);
    long startTime = System.currentTimeMillis();
    if (ALGORITHM.equals("static")) {
        add5LevelServices(NUM_OF_LEVELS, SUBSERVICES_PER_NODE,
                SERVICE_NAME_PREFIX);
        System.out.println("static (total): "
                + (System.currentTimeMillis() - startTime) + " ms");
    } else if (ALGORITHM.equals("recursive")) {
        Stack services = new Stack();
        Stack trace = new Stack();
        recur(0, NUM_OF_LEVELS, SERVICE_NAME_PREFIX,
        SUBSERVICES_PER_NODE,
                services, trace, leafSubServiceNames);
```

```
            String printString1 = "recursive ALGORITHM: "
                    + (System.currentTimeMillis() - startTime) + " ms";
            String printString2 = "Recursive call service tree size = "
                    + services.size();
            System.out.println(printString1 + '\n' + printString2);
            logWriter.println(printString1 + '\n' + printString2);
            processServiceTree(services, SUBSERVICES_PER_NODE);
            String printString3 = "recursive (ALGORITHM + processServiceTree): "
                    + (System.currentTimeMillis() - startTime) + " ms";
            System.out.println(printString3);
            logWriter.println(printString3);

        } else if (ALGORITHM.equals("dynamic")) {
            leafSubServiceNames = createServiceDirectory(NUM_OF_LEVELS,
                    SUBSERVICES_PER_NODE, SERVICE_NAME_PREFIX);
            System.out.println("dynamic: "
                    + (System.currentTimeMillis() - startTime) + " ms");
        } else {
            System.out.println("ALGORITHM " + ALGORITHM + " doesn't exist");
            System.exit(0);
        }
        return leafSubServiceNames;
    }

    public static void checkAddServices() {
        if (ADD_SERVICES && !USE_PROXY) {
            System.out.println("adding service directory ...");
            long startTime = System.currentTimeMillis();
            executeCommand();
            System.out.println("Adding service directory: "
                    + (System.currentTimeMillis() - startTime) + " ms");
        }
    }

    public static void checkAddSystems(ArrayList leafSubServiceNames) {
        if (ADD_SYSTEMS) {
            System.out.println("adding systems to "
                    + leafSubServiceNames.size() + " leaf node services ...");
            int ServiceStartIndex = 0;
            int ServiceEndIndex = leafSubServiceNames.size() - 1;

            int systemsPerThread = (int) ((SYSTEM_END_INDEX
                    - SYSTEM_START_INDEX + 1 + 0.5 * NUM_OF_THREADS) /
                    NUM_OF_THREADS);
            int ServicesPerThread = (int) ((ServiceEndIndex - ServiceStartIndex
                    + 1 + 0.5 * NUM_OF_THREADS) / NUM_OF_THREADS);
            if (systemsPerThread < 1) {
```

```
        System.out
                .println("# of systems per thread must be larger than one");
        System.exit(0);
    }
    if (ServicesPerThread < 1) {
        System.out
                .println("# of Services per thread must be larger than one");
        System.exit(0);
    }
    // use multi-threading to add systems to existing Services
    PrintWriter[] writer = new PrintWriter[20];
    long startTime = System.currentTimeMillis();
    AdminProxy[] proxies = new AdminProxy[NUM_OF_THREADS];
    if (USE_PROXY) {
        for (int i = 0; i < NUM_OF_THREADS; i++) {
            if (USE_PROXY) {
                proxies[i] = new AdminProxy(SERVER_ADDRESS,
                    SERVER_PORT);
            } else {
                proxies[i] = null;
            }
        }
    }
    for (int i = 0; i < NUM_OF_THREADS; i++) {
        int systemStart = SYSTEM_START_INDEX + i * systemsPerThread;
        int systemEnd = SYSTEM_START_INDEX + (i + 1) *
            systemsPerThread - 1;
        int ServiceStart = ServiceStartIndex + i * ServicesPerThread;
        int ServiceEnd = ServiceStartIndex + (i + 1)
                * ServicesPerThread - 1;
        if (i == (NUM_OF_THREADS - 1)) {
            systemEnd = SYSTEM_END_INDEX;
            ServiceEnd = ServiceEndIndex;
        }
        String threadFileName = "Thread_" + i + "_"
                + getFileNameSuffix();
        writer[i] = createWriter(threadFileName);
        ServiceThread deviceThread = new ServiceThread(proxies[i],
                SYSTEM_NAME_PREFIX, systemStart, systemEnd,
                ServiceStart, ServiceEnd, ADD_SYSTEMS, threadFileName,
                writer[i], leafSubServiceNames, "Thread_" + i);
        deviceThread.start();
        System.out.println("Thread " + i
                + " started with leaf node services " + ServiceStart
                + "-" + ServiceEnd + " and systems " + systemStart
                + "-" + systemEnd);
        try {
```

```
                Thread.sleep(1000);
            } catch (InterruptedException ie) {
                System.out.println(ie.toString());
            }
        }
    }
}

// create directory by calculating path
public static ArrayList createServiceDirectory(int levelMax, int base,
        String SERVICE_NAME_PREFIX) {
    long startTime = System.currentTimeMillis();
    int count = 0;
    ArrayList leafSubServiceNames = new ArrayList(1000);
    int level = levelMax; // change to zero-based indexing
    int numOfServices = (int) Math.pow(base, level);
    System.out.println("number of leaf node sub Services to be created = "
            + " at level " + level + " (0-based) : " + numOfServices);
    String containerServiceName = "";
    String serviceName = "";
    int beginIndex = 0;
    int endIndex = 0;
    // exclude level 0
    for (int i = level; i > 0; i--) {
        beginIndex = findBeginIndex(i - 1, base);
        endIndex = beginIndex + (int) Math.pow(base, i) - 1;
        for (int j = endIndex; j >= beginIndex; j--) {
            containerServiceName = getContainerServiceName(j, base);
            serviceName = getServiceName(containerServiceName, j, base);
            String path = findPath(j, base);
            if (i == level) {
                // leafSubServiceNames.add ("/" + path + serviceName);
                leafSubServiceNames.add(serviceName);
                if (ADD_SERVICES)
                    writeService(" addNode " + serviceName);
                // count++;
                // checkHeartBeat (count, startTime);
            }
            if ((j % base) == 0) {
                if (ADD_SERVICES)
                    writeService(" addContainer " + containerServiceName
                            + " " + serviceName);
            } else {
                if (ADD_SERVICES)
                    writeService(" addContainee " + containerServiceName
                            + " " + serviceName);
            }
```

```
                count++;
                checkHeartBeat(count, startTime);
                // writeNode (i, base, j , containerServiceName, serviceName);
            }
        }
        String printString = "dynamic total: " + count + " nodes/"
                + (System.currentTimeMillis() - startTime) + " ms = "
                + (count * 1000 / (System.currentTimeMillis() - startTime))
                + " nodes/second";
        System.out.println(printString);
        logWriter.println(printString);
        return leafSubServiceNames;
    }

    public static void writeNode(int level, int base, int j,
            String containerServiceName, String serviceName) {
        int index = (j - 1) % base;
        if (index == 0) {
            System.out.println(" | <f" + index + "> " + serviceName + " \"];");
            int parentIndex = findParentIndex(j, base);
            parentIndex = base * ((parentIndex + base - 1) / base);
            System.out.println(" \"node_" + (level - 1) + "_" + parentIndex
                    + "\":f1 -> " + " \"node_" + level + "_" + (j + base - 1)
                    + "\":f1;");
        } else if (index == (base - 1)) {
            System.out.print(" node_" + level + "_" + j + " [label = \"<f"
                    + index + "> " + serviceName);
        } else {
            System.out.print(" | <f" + index + "> " + serviceName);
        }
    }

    public static int findLevel(int m0, int base) {
        int level = 0;
        int m = 0;
        while (m < m0) {
            level++;
            m = m + (int) Math.pow(base, level);
        }
        return level;
    }

    public static int findParentIndex(int m, int base) {
        int blockNumber = findBlockNumber(m, base);
        int level = findLevel(m, base) - 1;
        int parentIndex = findBeginIndex(level - 1, base) + (blockNumber - 1);
        return parentIndex;
```

```
}

public static String getContainerServiceName(int m, int base) {
    String containerServiceName = "";
    if (m > base) {
        containerServiceName = SERVICE_NAME_PREFIX
                + findParentIndexChain(m, base);
    } else if (m == 0) {
        containerServiceName = "";
    } else {
        containerServiceName = TOP_SERVICE_NAME;
    }
    // System.out.println ("m = " + m + " container = " +
    // containerServiceName + " service = " + serviceName);
    return containerServiceName;
}

public static String getServiceName(String containerServiceName, int m,
        int base) {
    String serviceName = "";
    serviceName = containerServiceName + (((m - 1) % base) + 1); // base = 3
    if (m > 0 && m <= base) {
        serviceName = SERVICE_NAME_PREFIX + m;
    }
    return serviceName;
}

public static String findParentIndexChain(int index, int base) {
    // given current index
    int i = index;
    String name = "";
    while (i > base) {
        i = findParentIndex(i, base);
        if (i > base) {
            name = (((i - 1) % base) + 1) + name;
        } else {
            name = i + name;
        }
        // System.out.println ("index = " + index + " i = " + i + " name = "
        // + name);
    }

    return name;
}

public static String findPath(int m, int base) {
    // given current index m
```

```
        int n = m;
        String path = "";
        String containerServiceName = "Test";
        while (!(containerServiceName = getContainerServiceName(n, base))
                .equals("")) {
            path = containerServiceName + "/" + path;
            n = findParentIndex(n, base);
        }
        return path;
    }

    public static int findBlockNumber(int m, int base) {
        int level = findLevel(m, base) - 1;
        int beginIndex = findBeginIndex(level, base);
        int blockNumber = (m - beginIndex) / base + 1;
        return blockNumber;
    }

    public static int findBeginIndex(int level, int base) {
        int beginIndex = 0;
        for (int i = 0; i <= level; i++) {
            beginIndex = beginIndex + (int) Math.pow(base, i);
        }

        return beginIndex;
    }

    public static int findEndIndex(int level, int base) {
        int endIndex = findBeginIndex(level, base)
                + (int) Math.pow(base, level + 1) - 1;
        return endIndex;
    }

    public static String converter(int m0, int base) {
        int ak = m0 % base;
        int m = m0;
        String result = "" + ak;
        String temp = "";
        while (m > 0) {
            ak = (m / base) % base;
            if (m >= base) {
                temp = ak + temp;
            }
            m = m / base;
        }
        result = temp + result;
        return result;
```

```
}

public static void recur(int level, int levelMax,
        String SERVICE_NAME_PREFIX, int SUBSERVICES_PER_NODE,
        Stack services, Stack trace, ArrayList leafSubServiceNames) {
    String serviceName = "";
    String parentService = "";
    String path = "";
    level++;
    if (level >= levelMax) {
        path = getPath(trace, level);
        parentService = getParentService(path);
        String prefix = path + "/" + parentService;
        for (int j = 1; j <= SUBSERVICES_PER_NODE; j++) {
            serviceName = SERVICE_NAME_PREFIX + prefix + j;
            writeDot(parentService, parentService + j);
            leafSubServiceNames.add("" + j);
            services.push(serviceName);
        }
        trace.pop();
        return;
    } else {
        // System.out.println (" ++level = " + level + " serviceName = " +
        // serviceName);
        for (int i = 1; i <= SUBSERVICES_PER_NODE; i++) {
            path = getPath(trace, level);
            parentService = getParentService(path);
            if (level == 1) {
                parentService = SERVICE_NAME_PREFIX + "0";
                serviceName = SERVICE_NAME_PREFIX + i;
                writeDot(parentService, serviceName);
            } else {
                serviceName = path + "/" + parentService + i;
                writeDot(parentService, parentService + i);
            }
            services.push(serviceName);
            trace.push(serviceName);
            recur(level, levelMax, SERVICE_NAME_PREFIX,
                    SUBSERVICES_PER_NODE, services, trace,
                    leafSubServiceNames);
        }
        return;
    }
}

public static void writeDot(String parent, String child) {
    // System.out.println (parent + " -> " + child + ";");
```

```
}

public static String getPath(Stack p, int level) {
    while (p.size() >= level) {
        p.pop();
    }
    if (p.size() == 0) {
        return "";
    } else {
        return p.peek().toString();
    }
}

public static String getParentService(String path) {
    if (path.contains("/")) {
        return path.substring(path.lastIndexOf("/") + 1);
    } else {
        return path;
    }
}

public static void processServiceTree(Stack serviceTree,
        int SUBSERVICES_PER_NODE) {
    String currentService = "";
    int currentLevel = 1;
    int previousLevel = 0;
    String serviceName = "";
    String parentServiceName = "";
    Hashtable parentIdTable = new Hashtable();
    long startTime = System.currentTimeMillis();
    long keepTime = System.currentTimeMillis();
    int count = 0;
    String commandArray = "";
    while (!serviceTree.empty()) {
        currentService = serviceTree.peek().toString();
        currentLevel = getServiceLevel(currentService);
        if (currentLevel < previousLevel) { // parent
            serviceName = getServiceName(serviceTree.pop().toString());
            parentServiceName = getParentServiceName(currentService);
            String COMMAND_DIRective = checkParentNameTable(parentIdTable,
                    parentServiceName);
            writeService(COMMAND_DIRective + parentServiceName + " "
                    + serviceName);
            count++;
            checkHeartBeat(count, startTime);
            previousLevel = currentLevel;
        } else {
```

```
                // process all sibling child services
                currentService = serviceTree.pop().toString();
                serviceName = getServiceName(currentService);
                parentServiceName = getParentServiceName(currentService);

                writeService(" addNode " + serviceName);
                writeService(" addContainer " + parentServiceName + " "
                        + serviceName);
                count += 1;
                checkHeartBeat(count, startTime);
                for (int i = 1; i < SUBSERVICES_PER_NODE; i++) {
                    currentService = serviceTree.pop().toString();

                    writeService(" addNode " + getServiceName(currentService));
                    writeService(" addContainee " + parentServiceName + " "
                            + getServiceName(currentService));
                    count += 1;
                    checkHeartBeat(count, startTime);
                }
                previousLevel = getServiceLevel(currentService);
            }

        }
        // need to flush for batch processing
        if (USE_PROXY) {
            writeService("");
            adminProxy.sendCommand("reload");
        }
        String printString = "processing service tree: " + count + " nodes/"
                + (System.currentTimeMillis() - startTime) + " ms = "
                + (count * 1000 / (System.currentTimeMillis() - startTime))
                + " nodes/second";
        System.out.println(printString);
        logWriter.println(printString);
    }

    public static void checkHeartBeat(int count, long startTime) {
        if ((count % HEART_BEAT) == 0) {
            long currentTime = System.currentTimeMillis();
            System.out.println(count + " items processed over "
                    + (currentTime - startTime) + " ms "
                    + (count * 1000.0 / (currentTime - startTime))
                    + " items / s");
        }
    }

    public static String checkParentNameTable(Hashtable ht, String name) {
```

```
        if (!ht.containsKey(name)) {
            ht.put(name, new Integer(0));
            return " addContainer ";
        } else {
            int value = ((Integer) ht.get(name)).intValue() + 1;
            ht.put(name, new Integer(value));
            return " addContainee ";
        }
    }

    public static String getServiceName(String path) {
        StringTokenizer st = new StringTokenizer(path, "/");
        String name = path;
        while (st.hasMoreTokens()) {
            name = st.nextToken();
        }
        return name;
    }

    public static String getParentServiceName(String path) {
        StringTokenizer st = new StringTokenizer(path, "/");
        String name = TOP_SERVICE_NAME;
        int count = st.countTokens();
        int index = 1;
        while (index < count) {
            name = st.nextToken();
            index++;
        }
        return name;
    }

    public static int getServiceLevel(String path) {
        StringTokenizer st = new StringTokenizer(path, "/");
        return st.countTokens();
    }

    public static void writeService(String command) {
        if (TRACING)
            printStackTrace();
        if (LAST_BUCKET == (ARRAY_SIZE - 1) || command.equals("")) {
            commandBuffer[LAST_BUCKET] = command;
            if (ADD_SERVICES && USE_PROXY) {
                adminProxy.sendCommand(commandBuffer);
            } else {
                command = ".\\sd.bat " + command;
                commandWriter.println(command);
            }
```

```
            LAST_BUCKET = 0;
            initCommandBuffer();
        } else {
            commandBuffer[LAST_BUCKET] = command;
            LAST_BUCKET++;
        }
    }

    public static void initCommandBuffer() {
        for (int i = 0; i < ARRAY_SIZE; i++) {
            commandBuffer[i] = "";
        }
    }

    public static void executeCommand() {
        commandWriter.close(); // must be closed otherwise system cannot find
                               // the file
        String s = null;
        String command = "./runSd.bat ./output/" + commandFileName;
        try {
            Process p = Runtime.getRuntime().exec(command);
            BufferedReader stdInput = new BufferedReader(new InputStreamReader(
                    p.getInputStream()));
            BufferedReader stdError = new BufferedReader(new InputStreamReader(
                    p.getErrorStream()));
            while ((s = stdInput.readLine()) != null) {
                if (!s.trim().startsWith("Warning"))
                    System.out.println(s);
            }
            while ((s = stdError.readLine()) != null) {
                System.out.println(s);
            }
            p.destroy();
        } catch (IOException e) {
            System.out.println("exception happened with reading " + command
                    + " - here's what I know: ");
            System.out.println("exception happened - here's what I know: ");
            e.printStackTrace();
            System.exit(-1);
        }
    }

    public static String getFileNameSuffix() {
        String fileNameSuffix = (new Date().toString()).replace(' ', '_');
        fileNameSuffix = fileNameSuffix.replace(':', '_') + ".txt";
        return fileNameSuffix;
    }
```

```
public static PrintWriter createWriter(String fileName) {
    PrintWriter Writer = null;
    File file = new File("output");
    if (!file.exists()) {
        String logsDir = "output";
        boolean success = (new File(logsDir)).mkdir();
        if (success)
            System.out.println("folder output has been created");
    }
    try {
        Writer = new PrintWriter(new FileWriter("./output/" + fileName),
                true);
    } catch (IOException ioe) {
        System.out.println("Error in creating writer with " + fileName);
    }
    return Writer;
}

public static void createSystemFile(String SYSTEM_NAME_PREFIX,
        int SYSTEM_START_INDEX, int SYSTEM_END_INDEX) {
    String fileName = "system_" + getFileNameSuffix();
    PrintWriter writer = createWriter(fileName);
    for (int i = SYSTEM_START_INDEX; i <= SYSTEM_END_INDEX; i++) {
        writer.println(SYSTEM_NAME_PREFIX + i);
    }
    writer.close();
}

// for verifying recursive algorithm
public static ArrayList add5LevelServices(int level,
        int SUBSERVICES_PER_NODE, String SERVICE_NAME_PREFIX) {
    ArrayList leafSubServiceNames = new ArrayList(1000);
    int numOfServices = (int) Math.pow(SUBSERVICES_PER_NODE, level);
    System.out.println("number of leaf node sub Services to be created = "
            + numOfServices);
    long startTime = System.currentTimeMillis();
    Stack services = new Stack();
    for (int i1 = 1; i1 <= SUBSERVICES_PER_NODE; i1++) {
        String s1 = SERVICE_NAME_PREFIX + i1;
        services.push(s1);
        for (int i2 = 1; i2 <= SUBSERVICES_PER_NODE; i2++) {
            String s2 = s1 + i2;
            services.push(s1 + "/" + s2);
            for (int i3 = 1; i3 <= SUBSERVICES_PER_NODE; i3++) {
                String s3 = s2 + i3;
                services.push(s1 + "/" + s2 + "/" + s3);
```

```
                for (int i4 = 1; i4 <= SUBSERVICES_PER_NODE; i4++) {
                    String s4 = s3 + i4;
                    services.push(s1 + "/" + s2 + "/" + s3 + "/" + s4);
                    // leafSubServiceNames.add(s4);
                    for (int i5 = 1; i5 <= SUBSERVICES_PER_NODE; i5++) {
                        String s5 = s4 + i5;
                        services.push(s1 + "/" + s2 + "/" + s3 + "/" + s4
                                + "/" + s5);
                        leafSubServiceNames.add(s5);
                    }
                }
            }
        }
    }
    System.out.println("totalNumOfServices =" + services.size());
    System.out.println("totalNumOfLeafServices ="
            + leafSubServiceNames.size());
    System.out.println("static (ALGORITHM): "
            + (System.currentTimeMillis() - startTime) + " ms");
    processServiceTree(services, SUBSERVICES_PER_NODE);
    return leafSubServiceNames;
}

public static void checkMemory(String comment) {
    int mb = 1024 * 1024;
    Runtime runtime = Runtime.getRuntime();
    String printString1 = comment + " Heap utilization statistics [MB]";
    // UsedFree/Total/Max memory
    String printString2 = "Used/Free/Total/Max Memory:"
            + (runtime.totalMemory() - runtime.freeMemory()) / mb + "/"
            + runtime.freeMemory() / mb + "/" + runtime.totalMemory() / mb
            + "/" + runtime.maxMemory() / mb;
    System.out.println(printString1 + '\n' + printString2);
    if (logWriter != null) {
        logWriter.println(printString1 + '\n' + printString2);
    }
}

public static void printStackTrace() {
    ThreadMXBean bean = ManagementFactory.getThreadMXBean();
    ThreadInfo[] threads = bean.dumpAllThreads(true, true);
    logWriter.println(System.currentTimeMillis() + ",bean,"
            + bean.getCurrentThreadCpuTime() + ","
            + bean.getCurrentThreadUserTime() + bean.toString());
    for (ThreadInfo thread : threads) {
        logWriter.println(System.currentTimeMillis() + ",thread,"
                + thread.getThreadId() + "," + thread.getThreadName() + ","
```

```
                    + thread.getThreadState() + "," + thread.toString());
            StackTraceElement[] elements = thread.getStackTrace();
            for (StackTraceElement ste : elements) {
                logWriter.println(System.currentTimeMillis() + ",trace,"
                        + ste.getClassName() + ',' + ste.getMethodName() + ','
                        + ste.toString());
            }
        }
    }
}

class ServiceThread extends Thread {
    AdminProxy adminProxy;
    int SYSTEM_START_INDEX;
    int SYSTEM_END_INDEX;
    int serviceStartIndex;
    int serviceEndIndex;
    String SYSTEM_NAME_PREFIX;
    String fileName;
    PrintWriter writer;
    String name;
    boolean ADD_SYSTEMS;
    ArrayList leafSubServiceNames;

    public ServiceThread(AdminProxy proxy, String SYSTEM_NAME_PREFIX,
            int SYSTEM_START_INDEX, int SYSTEM_END_INDEX,
            int ServiceStartIndex, int ServiceEndIndex, boolean ADD_SYSTEMS,
            String FileName, PrintWriter Writer, ArrayList LeafSubServiceNames,
            String Name) {
        adminProxy = proxy;
        SYSTEM_START_INDEX = SYSTEM_START_INDEX;
        SYSTEM_END_INDEX = SYSTEM_END_INDEX;
        serviceStartIndex = ServiceStartIndex;
        serviceEndIndex = ServiceEndIndex;
        SYSTEM_NAME_PREFIX = SYSTEM_NAME_PREFIX;
        leafSubServiceNames = LeafSubServiceNames;
        fileName = FileName;
        writer = Writer;
        name = Name;
        ADD_SYSTEMS = ADD_SYSTEMS;
    }

    public void run() {
        long startTime = System.currentTimeMillis();
        addSystemToServices();
        writer.close();
        if (ADD_SYSTEMS && adminProxy == null) {
```

```
            executeAllCommands();
        }
        long endTime = System.currentTimeMillis();
        ServiceDirectory.THREAD_COUNT_DOWN--;
        double throughput = 1000.0
                * (SYSTEM_END_INDEX - SYSTEM_START_INDEX + 1)
                / (endTime - startTime);
        System.out.println(getThreadName() + " adding "
                + (SYSTEM_END_INDEX - SYSTEM_START_INDEX + 1)
                + " systems: "
                + (endTime - startTime) + " ms " + " (" + throughput
                + " systems / sec)");
        if (ServiceDirectory.THREAD_COUNT_DOWN < 1) {
            System.out.println(new Date().toString() + ": system throughput = "
                    + (1000 * ServiceDirectory.NUM_OF_SYSTEMS)
                    / (endTime - startTime) + " systems / sec ("
                    + ServiceDirectory.NUM_OF_SYSTEMS + " systems / "
                    + (endTime - startTime) + " ms)");
        }
    }

    public void addSystemToServices() {

        int numOfServices = serviceEndIndex - serviceStartIndex + 1;
        int numberOfsystemsPerService = (int) ((SYSTEM_END_INDEX
                - SYSTEM_START_INDEX + 1 + 0.5 * numOfServices) /
                    numOfServices);
        // for each subService add assigned systems with random system type
        for (int i = serviceStartIndex; i <= serviceEndIndex; i++) {
            int systemStart = SYSTEM_START_INDEX + (i - serviceStartIndex)
                    * numberOfsystemsPerService;
            int systemEnd = SYSTEM_START_INDEX + (i - serviceStartIndex + 1)
                    * numberOfsystemsPerService - 1;
            if ((i == serviceEndIndex)) {
                systemEnd = SYSTEM_END_INDEX;
            }
            for (int j = systemStart; j <= systemEnd; j++) {
                String addSystemCommand = "addEntry "
                        + leafSubServiceNames.get(i).toString() + " "
                        + SYSTEM_NAME_PREFIX + j;
                if (adminProxy != null) {
                    adminProxy.sendCommand(addSystemCommand);
                } else {
                    addSystemCommand = ".\\sd.bat addEntry "
                            + leafSubServiceNames.get(i).toString() + " "
                            + SYSTEM_NAME_PREFIX + j;
                    writer.println(addSystemCommand);
```

```
                }
            }
        }
    }

    public void executeAllCommands() {
        String s = null;
        System.out.println(name + " adding systems ... from file " + fileName);
        try {
            String command = ".\\runSd.bat .\\output\\" + fileName;
            Process p = Runtime.getRuntime().exec(command);
            BufferedReader stdInput = new BufferedReader(new InputStreamReader(
                    p.getInputStream()));
            BufferedReader stdError = new BufferedReader(new InputStreamReader(
                    p.getErrorStream()));

            while ((s = stdInput.readLine()) != null) {
                if (!s.trim().startsWith("Warning"))
                    System.out.println(s);
            }
            while ((s = stdError.readLine()) != null) {
                System.out.println(s);
            }
            p.destroy();
        } catch (IOException e) {
            System.out.println("exception happened - here's what I know: ");
            e.printStackTrace();
            System.exit(-1);
        }
    }

    public String getThreadName() {
        return name;
    }
}
```

Appendix C The DiskCheck Program for Benchmarking IO

DiskCheck is another simple tool I developed long time ago that I can use to quickly check the IO subsystem performance on a drive or drives to be used to store database files. To use this tool, follow the below procedure:

- Download DiskCheck from my website at http://www.perfmath.com.
- Unzip it to the drive on which you intend to run and check its IO performance in terms of throughput.
- Run the tool with the command

  cmd>java –classpath . DiskCheck ioTest1.txt

- Look for the read and write throughput numbers at the end of the output console. Figure C.1 is an example output out of a DiskCheck run on my Intel i7-2600 based Windows 7 PC. You can see that with a 58 MB input data file, the total time was 2 seconds only. That 2 second run gave me information immediately on the disk read throughput of 178 MB/s and write throughput of 25 MB/second. This is what I call a *quick disk IO performance check*.

```
c:\mspc\dev\DiskCheck-1.0>java -classpath . DiskCheck ioTest1.txt
test data file size = 58.06 MB
total time = 2 seconds
# of reads = # of writes = 772484
total read time (ms) = 327
average time (ms)/read = 4.2330974E-4
total write time (ms) = 2324
average time (ms)/write = 0.0030084765
read is 7 times faster than write
Read throughput on this drive: 177.56 MB/second
Write throughput on this drive: 24.98 MB/second

c:\mspc\dev\DiskCheck-1.0>
```

Figure C.1 An example DiskCheck run output on an i7-2600 based Windows PC

Table C.1 lists some sample disk IO throughput numbers I obtained using this DiskCheck program on a number of systems that I had access to. Note that the X5550-base system and the i7-based system had the best IO performance. I have to mention that this tool is not intended for benchmarking IO performance characteristically and elaborately. It's intended for a quick check only. Also, if the size of the included file is not what you want, you can substitute it with a different one. This `ioTest1.txt` file was actually the log file created with the CPUCheck program introduced in this text with the `services.properties` file as shown in Listing C.1 with TRACING turned on. You can re-run it with the tree size increased to make it larger.

Table C.1 Some sample IO throughput numbers in MB/second obtained with DiskCheck on a number of systems

IO Subsystem	OS	CPU Model	JDK version (1.6.0, 64-bit)	Throughput (MB/s)	
				Read	Write
RAID 0	Wind2k8R2	Xeon E5320	Update 21	70	6
RAID 0	Linux 2.6.32	Xeon E5320	Update 17	88	15
Local	Win2k8R2	Xeon E5320	Update 18	78	5
RAID 10	Win2k8	Xeon X5550	Update 31	196	14
Local	Win2k8	Xeon E5620	Update 31	138	10
Local	Windows 7	I7-2600	Update 31	178	25
Local	Windows 7	Phenom II X4	u18 (32-bit)	80	9

Listing C.1 The services.properties file used with CPUCheck for generating the ioTest1.txt file

```
SERVICE_NAME_PREFIX=system_
SYSTEM_START_INDEX=0
SYSTEM_END_INDEX=799
TOP_SERVICE_NAME=StagingServices
SERVICE_NAME_PREFIX=
NUM_OF_LEVELS=5
SUBSERVICES_PER_NODE=8
NUM_OF_THREADS=1
ADD_SERVICES=true
ADD_SYSTEMS=false
#ALGORITHM=static
ALGORITHM=recursive
#ALGORITHM=dynamic
ARRAY_SIZE=1
SERVER_ADDRESS=127.0.0.1
SERVER_PORT=9999
USE_PROXY=true
```

```
CLEAR_SERVICE_TREE=true
HEART_BEAT=100000
DEBUG=false
TRACING=true
```

In case you are interested in how this DiskCheck program works behind the scene, Listing C.2 shows its source code.

Listing C.2 DiskCheck.java

```
//usage: need a file in the same directory
//java -classpath . DiskCheck ioTest1.txt
import java.io.BufferedReader;
import java.io.File;
import java.io.FileReader;
import java.io.FileWriter;
import java.io.IOException;
import java.io.PrintWriter;
import java.math.BigDecimal;
import java.util.Date;

public class DiskCheck {
    public static void main(String[] args) {
        String fileName = args[0];
        readWriteTest("./" + fileName);
    }

    public static void readWriteTest(String fileName) {
        BufferedReader reader = null;
        PrintWriter writer = null;
        long totalReadTime = 0;
        long totalWriteTime = 0;

        try {
            reader = new BufferedReader(new FileReader(fileName));
            String date = (new Date().toString()).replace(' ', '_');
            String writeFileName = "writeTest_" + date.replace(':', '_')
                    + ".txt";

            writer = new PrintWriter(new FileWriter(writeFileName), true);
        } catch (IOException ioe) {
            System.out.println(fileName + " not found");
        }

        String line = null;
        int count = 0;
        long startTime = System.currentTimeMillis();
```

```
    do {
        try {
            long time0 = System.currentTimeMillis();
            line = reader.readLine();
            long time1 = System.currentTimeMillis();
            totalReadTime = totalReadTime + (time1 - time0);
            time0 = System.currentTimeMillis();
            writer.println(line);
            time1 = System.currentTimeMillis();
            totalWriteTime = totalWriteTime + (time1 - time0);
            count++;

        } catch (IOException io) {
            System.out.println("Error reading or writing with " + fileName);
        }

    } while (line != null);
    long fileSize = (new File(fileName)).length();
    System.out.println("test data file size = "
            + format(fileSize * 0.000001) + " MB");
    System.out.println("total time = "
            + (System.currentTimeMillis() - startTime) / 1000 + " seconds");
    System.out.println("# of reads = # of writes = " + count);
    System.out.println("total read time (ms) = " + totalReadTime);
    System.out.println("average time (ms)/read = " + totalReadTime
            / (float) count);
    System.out.println("total write time (ms) = " + totalWriteTime);
    System.out.println("average time (ms)/write = " + totalWriteTime
            / (float) count);
    System.out.println("read is " + totalWriteTime / totalReadTime
            + " times faster than write");
    System.out.println("Read throughput on this drive: "
            + format(0.001 * fileSize / totalReadTime) + " MB/second");
    System.out.println("Write throughput on this drive: "
            + format(0.001 * fileSize / totalWriteTime) + " MB/second");
}

public static double format(double d) {
    return ((new BigDecimal(d)).setScale(2, BigDecimal.ROUND_HALF_UP))
            .doubleValue();
}
```

Appendix D Setting up X11 for Linux

When you work on a Linux server that does not have a console attached to directly, you need to have X11 configured properly so that graphics based applications such as the VisualVM can be initiated. This appendix describes how to perform this task so that you don't have to experiment with it yourself.

This procedure consists of two parts: one is to install an SSH client program like Putty and an X11 server like Xming on a Windows machine, and the other is to enable X11 on the Linux machine. We describe how each part is done next.

First, on your Windows machine, perform the following steps:

- Download and install putty.
- Download and install Xming (For your reference, I downloaded and installed Xming-6-9-0-31.exe on my Windows machine using all default settings).
- Go to Start / All Programs / Xming and click on XLaunch. This step configures Display Settings, Session Type, and Additional Parameters, etc. Keep clicking on Next until you finish using all default settings.
- Now in the notification area at the lower right corner of your Windows task bar, make sure you see the "X" icon. Double click on it and a pop-up window as shown in Figure D.1 should appear, which means that your X11 server is running. Click on Cancel to exit this dialog box.
- Now start up Putty and configure a session for you to access your Linux server by following the below instructions:
    - Enter the host name of your Linux server under Host Name (or IP address).
    - Expand the tabs of Connection / SSH and click on X11.
    - Check the box of "*Enable X11 forwarding*". Then, enter *:0.0* in the "*X display location*".
- Go back to "*Session*" at the top under *Category*, type a session name (or just your Linux server name) under the tab "*Saved Sessions*" and click on *Save*. Each time when you start up *Putty*, click on the item corresponding to your saved session name and click *Load*. This will bring up the saved session for your Linux server. You can just click on *Open* and log into your Linux server with all the X11 settings as described above activated.
- Now you need to go one extra step on your Windows machine, that is, enter the host name or IP of your Linux server in the file of *X0.hosts* located in *C:\Program Files (x86)\Xming* (I entered both the host name and IP of my Linux server). To be sure, stop/start X11 server by clicking on the Exit

button as is shown in Figure D.1 and then the Xming icon from *Start* (note that you don't have to click on *XLaunch* again since that is for configuring X11 server only, which is a one-time task).

The next step is to configure your Linux server, which is as simple as to make sure that:

- The following two lines are uncommented out in the */etc/ssh/sshd_config* file:
  - X11Forwading yes
  - X11UseLocalhost yes
- Stop/start/check the status of your SSH daemon as follows (choose only one from start|stop|status in the following command):

  $service sshd start | stop | status
- Type *xclock* and hit *Enter*. You should see a digital clock popped up as shown in Figure D.2. Now you can run any graphics based applications on your Linux server with the graphics actually displayed on your Windows.

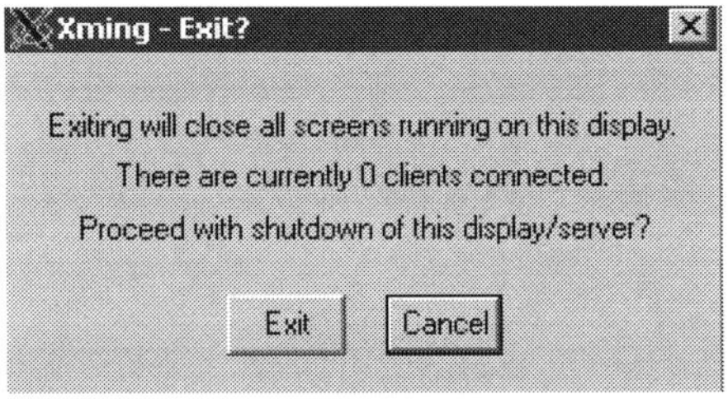

Figure D.1 Status of the Xming server on Windows

Figure D.2 The *xclock* program for verifying that X11 has been set up properly between Linux and Windows

Appendix E Linux System and Performance Utilities

This appendix summarizes common system and performance utilities available on a Linux machine. Linux professionals use these utilities to check their Linux system configurations and monitor/diagnose performance issues on their Linux systems. We already introduced them in the main text, and summarizing them here is just for more convenience.

E.1 LINUX SYSTEM UTILITIES

Table E.1 summarizes common Linux system utilities. You can use this list of utilities to get a good understanding of the *raw* performance from your Linux system.

Table E.1 Common Linux system utilities

<table>
<tr><th>Utility</th><th>Description</th></tr>
<tr><td>cat /etc/*release*</td><td>Check vendor release version</td></tr>
<tr><td>uname -r</td><td>Check Linux kernel version</td></tr>
<tr><td>nproc</td><td>Check # of CPUs</td></tr>
<tr><td>less /proc/cpuinfo</td><td>CPU specs</td></tr>
<tr><td>lscpu</td><td>Less verbose CPU specs</td></tr>
<tr><td>cat /proc/meminfo</td><td>Detailed memory usage</td></tr>
<tr><td>free -m</td><td>Check memory utilizations</td></tr>
<tr><td>df -m</td><td>Check disk utilizations</td></tr>
<tr><td>ifconfig</td><td>Basic statistics about network interfaces</td></tr>
<tr><td>netstat</td><td>Check port status. Add –ano | grep “<port>” to check a particular port</td></tr>
<tr><td>ulimit -a</td><td>Check kernel settings</td></tr>
</table>

E.2 Linux Performance Diagnosing/Monitoring Utilities

Table E.2 summarizes the usage of the Linux utilities for diagnosing/monitoring the performance of a particular Linux system. The utilities are mentioned for how to identify:

- Whether the system is lightly or heavily loaded overall
- Whether the system is bottlenecked on CPU or IO
- Which processes are particularly *hot*

With the `vmstat` utility, note the following:

- The first output always displays average values since the last reboot.
- You can add pipe " `| awk '{now=strftime("%Y -%m -%d %T "); print now $0}'` " to precede each output line with a timestamp to be used with a graphing tool.

Table E.2 Common Linux performance utilities

<table>
<tr><th>Category</th><th>Utilities</th></tr>
<tr><td>Overall</td><td>Use <code>top</code> to get a quick assessment of whether the system is lightly or heavily loaded. The important columns include pid, RES, R|S, %CPU, %MEM, TIME+, and so on. Keep in mind that by default, <code>top</code> sorts by %CPU, but you can toggle sorting with Shift+M for %MEM, Shift+T for TIME+, and Shift+P for %CPU. Shift+I also allows you to turn Irix mode off so that the %CPU column would display total average rather than cumulative CPU utilizations.</td></tr>
<tr><td>CPU or IO bottlenecks</td><td>Run the <code>vmstat -n <interval> <count> -S M</code> command and:
■ If the r column is high, it means CPU is the bottleneck, as r means the # of processes in the run queue, waiting for a free CPU slot.
■ If the b column is high, it means IO (disk or network) is the bottleneck, as b means the # of processes waiting for a resource other than a CPU.
■ You can also use <code>sar</code> utility with the <code>-d</code> option as described in the next section or <code>iostat</code> utility to help identify IO bottlenecks. The "<code>sar -d</code>" option outputs wait time, service time and disk utilizations, where <code>iostat</code> gives a detailed breakdown of the average CPU usage as well as IO throughput in terms of the # of blocks read/written per second.</td></tr>
<tr><td>Hot processes</td><td>Run <code>top -c</code> to identify hot processes that have high %CPU, high %MEM, and high TIME+. Use sort-by as described above to toggle the top processes. To learn how a (hot) process is launched, run the <code>ps -fwwp <pid></code> command, where <code><pid></code> can be found with the <code>top -c</code> command. You can also run the <code>top -d <interval> -b -n <count> -p <pid1>,<pid2>,...</code>command to obtain samples for the identified hot processes. Use the <code>pstree</code> command to find out the ancestor processes of a hot process, all the way to <code>init</code> or <code>systemd</code>.</td></tr>
</table>

E.3 THE SAR UTILITY

Linux has a very versatile utility called `sar`. This utility requires the `sysstat` package, which may not be installed by default. However, it's easy to install it. For example, on openSUSE, use the below procedure to get `sar` working:

1 Run `zypper in sysstat` to install `sysstat`.
2 Run `/etc/init.d/boot.sysstat start` to start the `sadc` daemon to enable collecting data automatically. This will add a link to `/etc/cron.d/` that calls `sadc` with the following default configurations:

- All available data will be collected in `/var/log/sa/saDD`, where `DD` stands for the current day. If a file already exists, it will be archived.
- The summary report is written to `/var/log/sa/sarDD`.
- Data is collected every 10 minutes, and a summary report is generated every 6 hours. Of course, these settings are customizable.

The `sar` utility can be run on the fly with the following form:

```
sar <option> <interval> <count>
```

, where <option> can be:

- –**u**: CPU
- –**r**: RAM (memory)
- –**B**: paging, with high `majflt/s` (major faults per second) indicating insufficient main memory
- –**d**: disk, with the following specially interesting columns:
  - `avgque-sz`: average queue length
  - `await`: service time + latency in milliseconds
  - `svctm`: service time in milliseconds
  - `%util`: percent utilization
- –**n** ALL: network
- –**q**: run-queue (# of tasks waiting), plist (# of tasks in the task list), and load average
- –**w**: proc/s and cswch/s

In addition, you can add `–s hh:mm:ss` to query past data since the specified start time. At last, don't forget adding the `–p` option for pretty print, for example:

```
sar –d –p 5 10
```

Keep using these utilities all the time!

Appendix F The Harp Utility for Optimizing UI Performance

This appendix introduces the Harp utility I developed for facilitating optimizing UI performance. This has turned out to be an extremely powerful tool for facilitating optimizing UI performance. I have had many very successful use cases with using this tool for my projects, which motivates me to share this tool with you.

My Harp tool is a Java-based tool developed for offline post-analyzing HTTP traffic captured with Chrome Dev Tool (CDT) or FireBug with FireFox. Based on the HAR files saved with the CDT or FireBug, it parses the given input file in Har format, calculates some important metrics such as the server time, client time, network latency, as well as some other metrics such as the # of HTTP requests, page weight, maximum # of connections issued *concurrently* from the browser, and so on. At the end, it generates an HTML5-based file that can be opened with any browser for a timeline chart that illustrates the HTTP requests issued from the client to the server with all timings displayed on the chart. It's a very useful tool for accurately assessing where majority of the time spent (whether on client or server side) and which parts contribute most to the end-to-end response time of a page, etc.

The article at https://developer.chrome.com/devtools/docs/network#resource-network-timing explains more about CDT and the Har format. As an example, an HTTP response may return a timings element as follows:

```
"timings": {
        "blocked": 1.52799999341369,
        "dns": -1,
        "connect": -1,
        "send": 0.3029999788850499,
        "wait": 3586.530999979001,
        "receive": 9.739000117409432,
        "ssl": -1
      },
      "connection": "353",
      "pageref": "page_2"
    },
```

On the HTTP traffic chart, the above timings element would manifest as shown in Figure F.1, which shows a waiting of 3.59s (TTFB - time-to-first-byte). If you click on *Explanation* visible on the mouse-over popup shown in Figure F.1, you would get an explanation as shown in Figure F.2.

The CDT/Harp combination is a useful tool, as each large wait time displayed on the HTTP traffic timeline chart, whether online through CDT or offline through Harp, is a potential UI response time optimization opportunity. By the way, the Harp tool is preferred as you can save each Harp profile for comparisons over time.

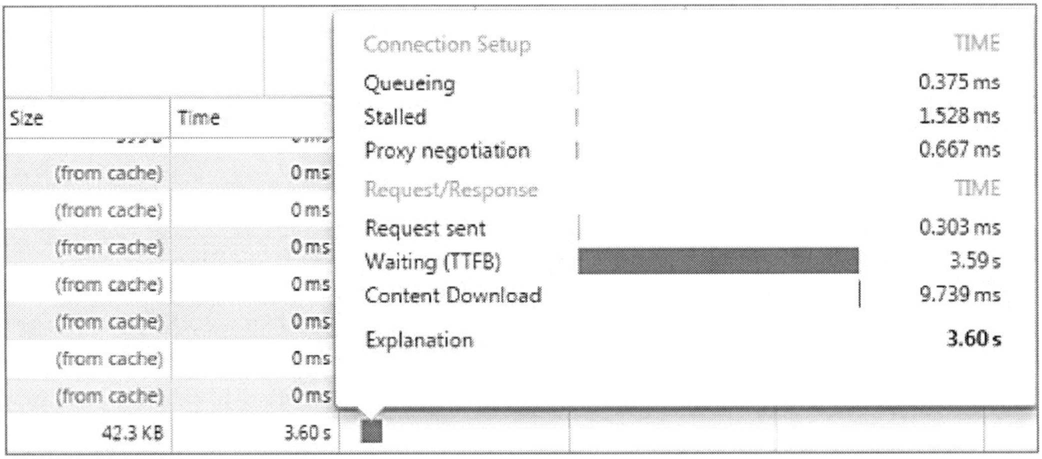

Figure F.1 An HTTP request/response displayed on CDT

F.1 SETTING UP A JDK FOR RUNNING THE HARP TOOL

Steps to get started with using Harp:

1 Since Harp processes Har files, it's very helpful to spend some time understanding the Har (HTTP archive) format. Although it's not required to fully understand the Har format, it's highly recommended to have a cursory look at the introduction to HAR posted online at https://dvcs.w3.org/hg/webperf/raw-file/tip/specs/HAR/Overview.html so that you would know immediately what you are dealing with.
2 The next step is to download the Harp tool. You can download it from this book's website at http://www.perfmath.com.
3 Make sure you have a JDK 7 installed on the machine you intend to run the tool. It may not work with Java 6 or earlier versions of JDKs. If you encounter any issues, please send me an email using my email address provided in this book.

Next, we describe how to save a Har file with CDT.

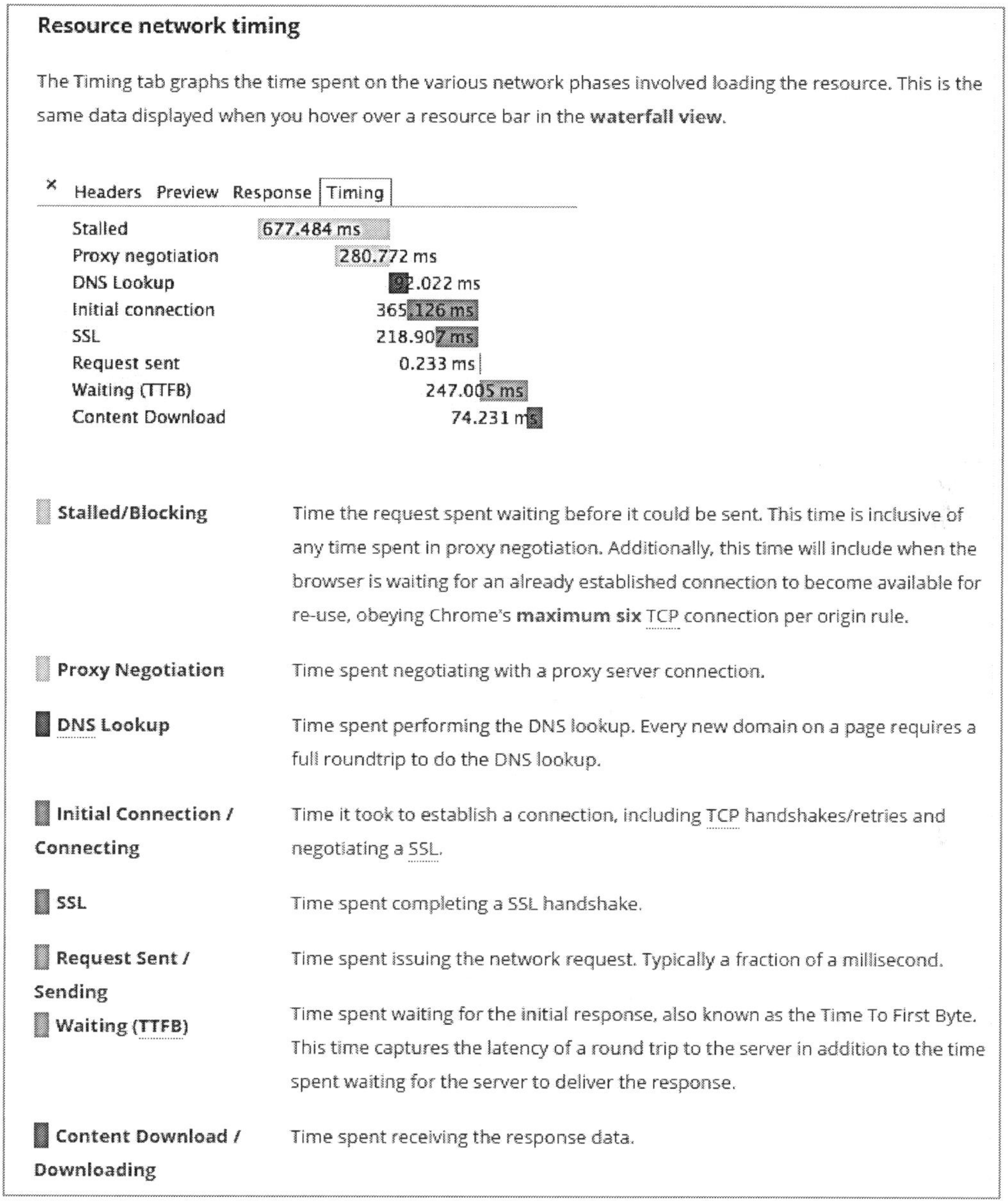

Resource network timing

The Timing tab graphs the time spent on the various network phases involved loading the resource. This is the same data displayed when you hover over a resource bar in the **waterfall view**.

× Headers Preview Response Timing

Stalled	677.484 ms
Proxy negotiation	280.772 ms
DNS Lookup	92.022 ms
Initial connection	365.126 ms
SSL	218.907 ms
Request sent	0.233 ms
Waiting (TTFB)	247.005 ms
Content Download	74.231 ms

Stalled/Blocking	Time the request spent waiting before it could be sent. This time is inclusive of any time spent in proxy negotiation. Additionally, this time will include when the browser is waiting for an already established connection to become available for re-use, obeying Chrome's **maximum six** TCP connection per origin rule.
Proxy Negotiation	Time spent negotiating with a proxy server connection.
DNS Lookup	Time spent performing the DNS lookup. Every new domain on a page requires a full roundtrip to do the DNS lookup.
Initial Connection / Connecting	Time it took to establish a connection, including TCP handshakes/retries and negotiating a SSL.
SSL	Time spent completing a SSL handshake.
Request Sent / Sending	Time spent issuing the network request. Typically a fraction of a millisecond.
Waiting (TTFB)	Time spent waiting for the initial response, also known as the Time To First Byte. This time captures the latency of a round trip to the server in addition to the time spent waiting for the server to deliver the response.
Content Download / Downloading	Time spent receiving the response data.

Figure F.2 Explanations on resource network timing

F.2 HOW TO SAVE NETWORK TRAFFIC CAPTURED WITH CDT IN HAR FORMAT

Of course, you are interested in this tool because you want to use it to help you analyze your own Har profiles. It's very important that you create your own Har files properly by following the below procedure:

1 After opening up your Chrome browser, press Ctrl+Shift+I to start up the CDT. Figure F.3 shows how CDT looks like with the Google home page opened with Chrome.
2 Verify that the *Network* tab is selected.
3 The left most solid dot icon controls starting/stopping recording. When it's red, it means "recording is active." Otherwise, it means "recording is inactive."
4 Make sure *Disable cache* is checked. I recommend disabling cache for repeatable results unless you are investigating effects of caching the page you are testing at the browser level.
5 You can simulate different network bandwidth by choosing a desired throttling setting as shown in Figure F.4. In general, I choose *No throttling* with my projects.
6 When you initiate an action on a UI, for example, entering the URL of a website or clicking a tab on a page, etc., you'll start seeing network traffic recorded in the content pane of CDT. After a page is completed, right click anywhere in the content pane and select "*Save as HAR with content*" as shown in Figure F.4. This is how a Har file is saved, and the Harp tool processes such Har files as described next.

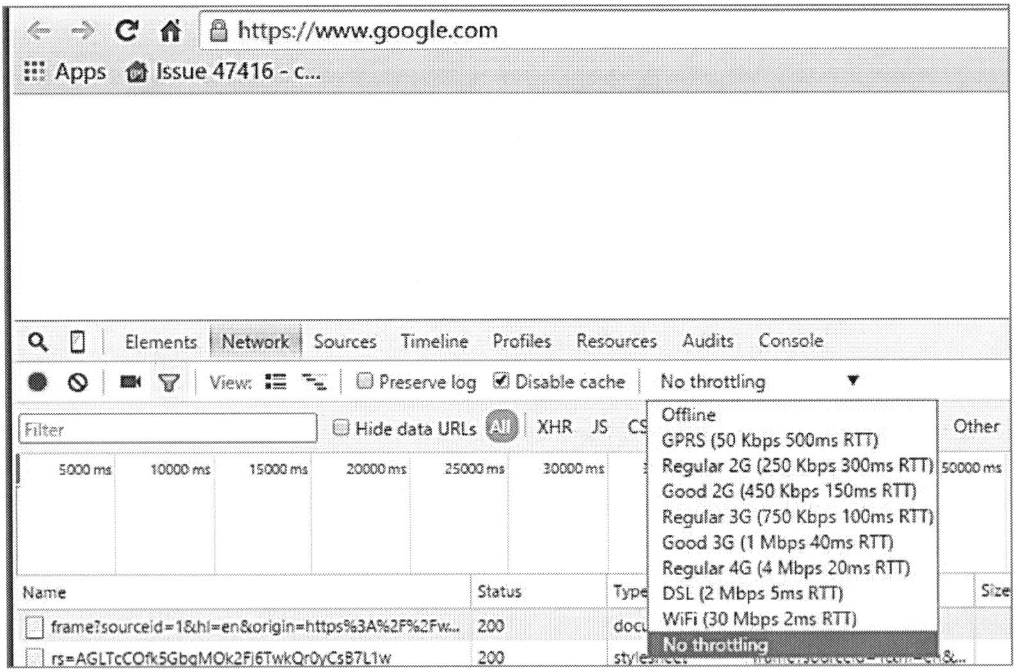

Figure F.3 CDT with Chrome

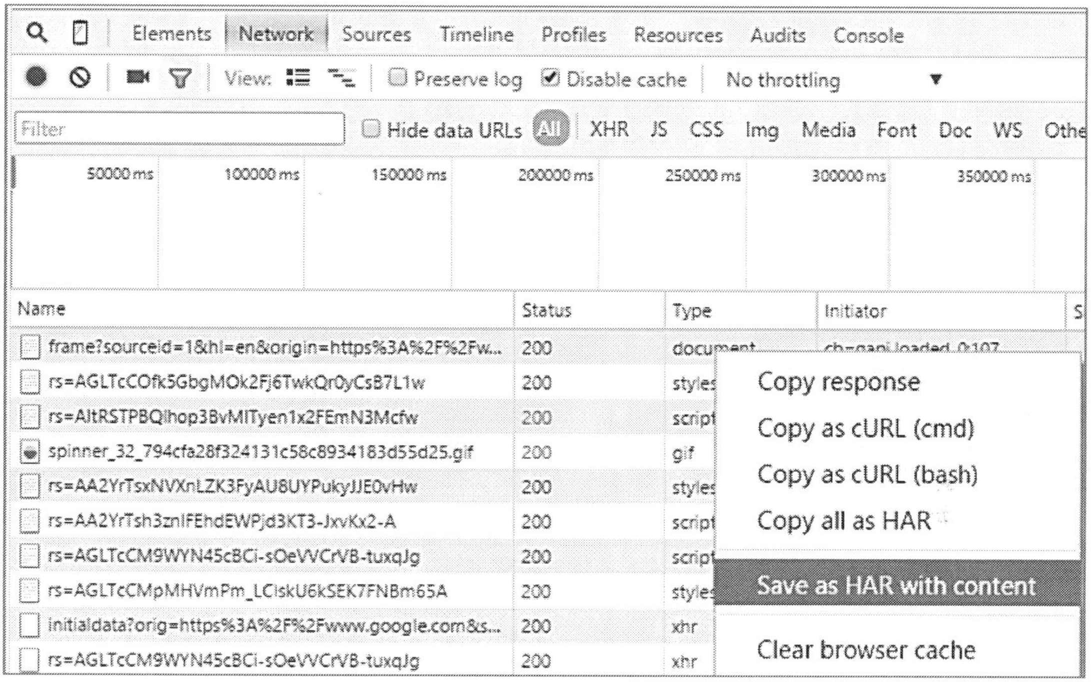

Figure F.4 Save As HAR with content option with CDT

F.3 HOW TO RUN THE HARP TOOL

After downloading the tool, setting up your JDK, and saving a Har file, use the following procedure to run my Harp tool against your Har file:

1. Change to the folder where your Har file resides.
2. Put the following content in a .bat script in you are on Windows, for example, a file named `run-harp.bat`:

   ```
   java -jar Harp2-1.0-SNAPSHOT-jar-with-dependencies.jar %1 %2 %3
   ```

3. Then issue the command "`run-harp <your-har-file>`" to process the designated Har file. The remaining two parameters are for `clickInterval` and `requestLimit`, which are for special cases. For example, if the total # of HTTP requests were 50, and the last request was not a part of the UI rendering (e.g., a log request), you can run the Harp tool with "`run-harp <your-har-file> 10000 49`" to prevent the last request from being counted into the total end-to-end time. Here, 10000 means 10000 milliseconds for distinguishing multiple clicks, but this is still an experimental feature and not used very often even by myself.

After conducting the above run, you should see an HTML file in the folder that is named the same as your Har file without the `.har` extension. Open up that HTML file in a browser, and you should see a chart similar to what was displayed on CDT, except that you will also see timing and data breakdowns, etc. There are also some auxiliary files in that folder that can be used to get details about the HTTP requests/responses processed by the Harp tool.

In case you encounter any errors, please contact me, as the Harp tool may not deal with some Har files out of ordinary properly.

F.4 FEEDBACK

Your feedback is very important for me to improve this tool over time. Please feel free to send me emails. Whatever feedback you give, it will be taken seriously.

F.5 BEST PRACTICES WITH USING THE HARP TOOL

This section summarizes some known best practices with using this tool:

1 Always save a Har file per user transaction, which simply is a single click. The tool is developed for analyzing each individual user action, so recording multiple user transactions into one Har file may complicate the analysis of those user transactions.

2 As soon as you see a user transaction is completed, for example, you notice that the spinner has just stopped spinning, put down the # of requests displayed at the lower left corner of CDT and then save as fast as you can, as it's very likely that the browser may continue to record additional HTTP traffic that is not supposed to be part of the traffic initiated by a user action. You may want to stop recording before saving the network traffic into a Har file to avoid including un-related HTTP requests, such as some spurious alerts or logging requests.

3 If you noticed that some extra, spurious HTTP requests had been recorded at the end of a user action, you can instruct the program to exclude such requests, as described in §F.3 (step 3), by giving one extra command-line argument to specify exactly how many requests should be processed. The Harp tool actually ignores some known types of spurious HTTP traffic.

4 If you did not stop recording after saving your Har file, click the "Clear" icon (second from the left) before starting a new recording. This will give you a fresh new start for the next user action. This action is not required if you stopped and restarted recording, which automatically clears the previously recorded HTTP traffic.

5 If you see gaps between adjacent requests, most likely, caching is not implemented properly on the server side. With one of my projects, large gaps were observed with some user actions, and those large gaps disappeared after extension IDs of plug-ins on the server side were cached properly. You should conduct such gap analysis constantly with the UI pages you optimize.

6 If you observe that the same CSS files are downloaded multiple times from the server and each download gets longer and longer, it might be due to some gadgets having no sharing implemented, which can be re-considered to enhance sharing. With one of my projects, a UI page's end-to-end response time was reduced from 12 seconds to about 3 seconds after an issue like this was identified with Harp and cured with the above resolution.

Please share your experience in using Harp with me so that it can be improved over time.

Index

32-bit computing, 28-29, 123
64-bit computing 32, 106-107, 204

A

AccessController, 134-136, 140-143
Active cores, 37, 263
Adaptive optimization, 65-66
Address space 29, 31, 106
Addressing modes, 29, 46
AGP, 32, 35
Algorithm
  dynamic 192-195, 197-198, 270
  recursive 97, 192-195, 197-199
  static 192-195, 199, 270-271
AMD64 106-108, 110, 123
Analysis
  database activity, 162, 166
  JVM activity, 162, 164
  thread pool, 162, 165-166
Application architecture, 126
Application profiling, 80, 130
Architecture
  accumulator, 51, 106
  instruction set 29, 31-32, 41
  load-store, 49
  microarchitecture 29-33, 35-37, 41
  processor hardware, 29, 31
  register-memory, 49, 51
  register-oriented, 49-50
  register-register, 49, 51
  stack-oriented, 49, 63
Array processing 10, 196-198, 200
Array size, 77, 158
Arrival rate, 5, 8-9
Artifact, 3, 45
Authentication Server 10-12, 155, 161-162
AVX, 32
AWR 156, 161-162, 166
AWT, 65, 184

B

B language, 201
Baseline 92, 137, 144
Batch jobs, 16, 154
Bell Labs, 201
Bottleneck analysis 8, 195, 199-200
BSD, 201-202
Bus interface unit, 33, 35
Byte index, 50
Bytecode, 43-51, 65-66

C

C/C++ 47, 52, 66
Cache 22, 24, 30-35
  L1 30-32, 38, 110
  L2 30-33, 35, 38
  L3 32-33, 38, 221
Caching 24, 38, 304
Cat 97-99, 210, 219
CentOS 95, 206-210, 232
CFS, 217-218
Circuit 3-5, 24-25, 254

Class 44, 46-48, 50
Class libraries, 44
Class sharing, 88
Classloader, 46, 165
Closed model, 9
CMS 66, 68, 70-73
Code
  native 43, 66, 109
Code prefetch unit, 33
Cold start-up, 66
Command line options
  developer, 74
  HotSpot JVM, 74, 77
  standard, 74
Compatible 32, 106-107, 203
Completely fair scheduling. See CFS
Concurrency 11, 48, 65
Concurrent 4-6, 11-12, 16-19
Concurrent users 4-6, 11-12, 16-19
Constant pool, 48
Context switching, 66
Core i7 12-13, 32-33, 35-40
CPU benchmarking 28, 39, 41
CPU usage 1, 13-14, 18
CPU-bound, 153
CPU-intensive 12, 126-127, 196
CPUCheck 40-41, 78-79, 82-83
  E5320 versus Core 2 Duo E8500, 40
  NUM_OF_LEVELS 92, 270-271, 275
  runClient 92, 266, 270
  runServer 92, 266, 268-269
  service directory tree structure 92, 194, 196
  services.properties 92, 97-98, 190
  SUBSERVICES_PER_NODE 92, 270-271, 275
Cpuinfo 219, 262, 297
Cyclic reference, 53-55

D

Data type 29, 45, 47
Denominator, 27-28
Df, 225, 297
Disk 1, 19-20, 22
DiskCheck, 126, 291-293
DMI, 36, 224
Dmidecode, 222, 224
Drop_caches, 24

E

E5320 12-13, 40, 222
E5620 12-13, 16, 21
E7330, 12, 222
Echo, 24, 236
EM64T, 106-108, 123
EnableAudit, 127
Equilibrium condition 5, 9, 155
Exception handling, 29
Exec, 217
Execution unit, 33-35

F

Feedback 8-9, 217, 306
File handle, 226-228
File-max, 227-229
Finalizing, 47
Fork, 217
Fragmentation 59-60, 71, 73
Frame 48, 60, 79
Free 22, 53, 59-61
FSB, 35-37, 256-257

G

G1 66, 73, 162
Garbage collection
  CMS 68, 70, 76
  full 61-62, 89, 101
  live object copying, 89
  MarkSweep, 79
  minor 62, 89, 145
  minor GC, 89
  monitoring 65, 77, 100
  Old Generation 62, 75, 79
  ParallelGC, 70, 79
  patterns, 89

pause 53, 69-70, 75
premature promotion, 89
promotion failure, 89
Survivor spaces overflowing, 89
throughput 68-70, 75-76, 79
tuning 44, 74-77, 100
Young Generation 62, 68, 70
Garbage collection algorithm 51-54, 63, 65
reference counting, 52-54
tracing, 54
vectorial, 54
Garbage collector
CMS 66, 68, 73
compacting 59, 78, 100
concurrent 66, 68, 73
copying 59, 68-69, 78
footprint, 43-44, 69
frequency, 69
G1 66, 73, 175-176
metrics, 68-69
non-compacting, 59
parallel 59, 66, 69
parallelOld, 100
pause 66, 69, 73
promptness, 69
serial 59, 69, 78
throughput 68-69, 73, 75-76
Garbage collector. See GC
Garbage object 52-53, 55, 57-59
GC strategy
compacting, 59-61
concurrent, 61-62
copying, 59-62, 69
generational, 62-63, 69
incremental, 62-63
non-compacting, 59-61
parallel 59, 61, 69
serial 59, 61, 69
stop-and-copy, 61-62
Gcutil, 96, 99
Generation
Eden 68-69, 79, 89
old 62, 75, 79-81
permanent, 68, 109
survivor 68, 75, 79
tenured 68-73, 75, 78
young 62, 68-70, 72-73
GNOME, 203

H

Har, 301-306
Hard 14-15, 33, 55
Hardware specs, 126-127
Harp, 301-306
Heap 46-48, 52-53, 55
Code Cache 79, 113-114, 116-117
Compile Time 89, 145, 164
current utilization, 89
currentCapacity, 89, 145
Eden 68-69, 76, 79
Eden space 89, 98, 111
GC Time 89, 95-96, 145
maxCapacity, 89, 145
memory usage, 79, 111
Old 75, 79, 89
Old Gen 75, 79, 89
old generation 75, 79, 89
Perform GC, 79, 83
Perm 68-69, 74, 76
Perm Gen 79, 89, 145
PermGen 76, 83, 109
S0 89, 96, 145
S1 69, 89, 96
sizing, 74-76, 101
survivor 68, 75-76, 79
tenured 68-69, 73, 75-76
tenured space 73, 111, 113-114
tuning 74-77, 131, 145
used space, 111, 114
young generation 68, 75, 78-79
Hosking, 64, 101
HotSpot JVM 2, 51, 63
HTML 162, 301, 305
Hunt 60, 64, 89
Hyper-thread, 32, 219
Hyper-threaded 12, 14, 18
Hyper-threading 14, 24-25, 32

I

I7 12-14, 21, 32-33
I7-2600 12-13, 39-40, 78
IA64, 107-108
Iadd, 49-51
IBM 43, 45, 205
Idiv, 49
Ifconfig, 225, 297
Iload, 49-51
Imul, 49
Inclusive shared L3 cache, 38
Input/Output Hub. See IOH
Instruction decoder unit, 33
Instruction set 29, 31-32, 41
  0-operand, 51
  1-operand, 51
  2-operand, 51
  n-operand, 50
Instruction set architecture 29, 32, 41
Instructions 29, 31-33, 47
Integer 30, 49-51, 71
Intel processors
  4004, 28
Intel Processors
  history, 28
Intel processors
  multicore, 28
  Netburst, 32
  x86, 32
  x86-64, 32
Interface 20, 29, 33-36
Interrupt 22, 29, 202
IO-bound, 22
IP port range, 226-228
Istore, 49-51
Isub, 49
Itanium, 106-108, 205

J

Java
  ergonomics 70, 74, 101
  language specification, 46
  reference type, 47, 109
Java APIs, 44
Java Enterprise Application Server. See JEAS
Java performance and scalability on Linux 103, 201, 203
Java quick starter, 66-68
Java Virtual Machine Profiler Interface. See JVM PI
Java Web Start, 66
Java2D, 66
JConsole 43, 65, 77-82
JDBC tuning
  max-pool-size, 158
  min-pool-size, 157-158
JDBC tunings, 153, 157-158
JDK 43, 45, 65
JEE Application Server 10-13, 16, 18-19
JIT, 43-44, 65-66
JNDIBasedSecurityManagement, 127
Jones, 63-64, 101
JProfiler, 132
JRE 43-44, 46, 77
JRockit, 45, 66
JSP, 76
JVM 2, 12, 44-49
  64-bit 12, 46, 48-49
  activity analysis, 162, 164
  exit, 47, 97
  implementation 45-46, 48, 63
  initializing, 46
  linking, 46, 48
  loading, 46, 164
  specification 45-47, 51, 64
  start-up 46, 51, 65-66
  statistics 97, 148, 153
JVM options
  ParallelGCThreads, 77
  UseCompressedOops, 77
JVM Tuning 143, 148, 151

K

KDE, 203, 207

Kernel 23, 134, 202-206
Kernel parameters 226, 228, 251

L

Latency 35, 71, 80
Limits.conf, 218, 229
Linear addresses, 35
Linear scalability, 18
Linux 2-3, 11, 15
  Debian, 205, 210
  Fedora, 205-206, 210
  file system caching, 24
  OpenSUSE 205-206, 210, 219
  RHEL, 205-206, 210
  Ubuntu, 205, 210
Linux versus Windows, 248
List
  singly-linked, 53
LKM, 203
Load average 231, 235, 240-241
Load testing, 127, 154
Locality, 60
Lock contention 5, 85, 166
Logical addresses, 35
Long 3, 22, 24
LP6, 107-108
Lscpu 219-221, 262, 297

M

Marking 55-58, 70-71, 96
MBean
  dynamic, 134
  standard, 134
Meminfo, 222-223, 297
Memory 1, 3, 19
  resident 24, 231, 235
  virtual 19, 22, 24
Memory bloat 105, 107-108, 123
Memory leak 43, 76, 245
Memory management 33, 43-44, 48
Memory Management Unit. See MMU
Memory structure, 29
Memory-bound, 22, 153
Method area, 48
Microarchitecture
  Core 31-33, 35-37, 138
  Nehalem 31-32, 35-37, 138
  Netburst, 30-32
  Sandy Bridge, 31-32
Microkernel, 202-203, 206
Minix, 202
MMU, 34, 213
Moss, 64, 101
MQMS, 7-8
Multicore 25, 28, 31
Mutator, 57

N

Nehalem 31-32, 35-37, 138
Netstat, 225-226, 297
NIO, 65-67
Node 9-10, 53-55, 82
Nofile 228-230, 239, 248
Notation
  infix, 49
  postfix, 49
  prefix, 49
Nproc 219, 228-230, 239
NUMA 35, 215-216, 219-222
NumberOfCores, 14
Numerator, 27-28

O

Object 1, 8, 19
  allocation 53, 59, 61
  de-allocation, 53, 109
  dead, 52
  garbage 43-44, 47-48, 52-55
  live 52, 57-58, 60-62
  reachable 54-55, 57, 59-62
  root 54-55, 57-58, 70
OLTP 6, 70, 114
OOME, 46
Oops 109-119, 122-123, 148

compressed 109, 113-114, 116-117
uncompressed 113, 116, 118-119
Opcode, 32, 47-51
Open model, 9
OpenJDK 45, 98, 209
Operator, 109
Opteron, 110
OutOfMemoryErrors 76, 101, 118

P

Page directory, 35
Page frames, 213, 215
Page reclaiming, 215
Page table entries, 35
Page tables 214, 243, 252
Pages 76, 213, 215
Paging unit, 35
Parallelism, 31, 73
Passing
by reference, 47
by value, 47
PassMark 39-41, 138-139, 200
Pattern
CPU 131, 145, 157
heap GC, 163-164
Pause 53, 66, 69-70
PCI, 32
PCI-X, 32, 35
PCIe, 32, 35-37
Pcpu, 24, 235-236
Perfmon 19, 21, 162
Performance and scalability
anti-pattern, 198-199
Performance and scalability issues 2, 5, 11
Performance and scalability metrics, 3
Performance counters 1, 3, 19-22
Performance law 6-8, 10, 27
Performance monitor snap-in, 20
PGD, 214-215
PMD, 214-215
Pointer 43, 47-49, 52
managed, 48, 109
unmanaged
Pointers 43, 47, 49
Power consumption, 37
Preemptive multitasking, 217
Processes 22, 33, 78
Profile
execution 66, 92, 135
Profiling
self time, 86, 93
Ps 22, 79, 235-238
PSI-Probe 159-162, 165-166, 178-180
PTE, 214-215

Q

QPI 36, 139, 257
Quantifying performance and scalability issues, 126
Queuing node, 9
Queuing theory 2, 5-6, 10
Queuing workload model, 127, 155
QuickPath Interconnect 32, 36, 139
QuickPath Interconnect. See QPI

R

RAID 0, 110, 292
Reachability, 57
Reference 25, 39, 41-42
cyclic, 53-55
Register 29, 31-32, 34
Registers
AX, 106
BP, 106
BX, 106
control, 33-34, 105
CX, 106
DI, 106
DX, 29, 106
eax, 51, 107
ebp, 107
ebx, 107
ecx, 51, 107
edi, 107
edx, 51, 107

esi, 107
esp, 107
floating point, 105
integer 49, 51, 105-107
r10, 107
r11, 107
r12, 107
r13, 107
r14, 107
r15, 107
r8, 107
r9, 107
rax, 107
rbp, 107
rbx, 107
rcx, 107
rdi, 107
rdx, 107
rsi, 107
SI, 106
SP, 106
Residence time, 9-10
Resolution
late, 46
lazy, 46
static, 46
Resource utilization 5-6, 9-10, 19
Response time 4-7, 9-10, 12-13
Response time performance laws, 6-7
RMI 54, 182, 197
Root 54-58, 70, 125
Root set, 57-58
Rss 24, 235-236, 245-246
Runtime 41, 43-44, 46-48
Runtime data area, 47-48, 51

S

Sar 22, 234-235, 242-243
Scalability 25, 27-28, 30
Scalability analysis, 246
Scalability testing 3, 18, 25
Scaling-out, 7
Scaling-up, 7-8
See loadable kernel module. See LKM
Segment descriptor cache, 35
Segmentation unit, 35
Semaphore, 226-227
Semmni, 227-228
Semmns, 227-228
Semmsl, 227-228
Semopm, 227-228
Service demand, 9-10, 24
Service time 6-7, 9-10, 24
ServiceDirectory 78, 82-83, 93
Shared memory 36, 215, 226-228
Shell limits, 228-229, 251
Shmall, 227-228
Shmmax, 227-228
Shmmni, 227-228
Silk Performer 11, 127, 133-134
Single core, 28, 36
Sipush, 50
Sizing guidelines, 126, 226
Sizing thread pools, 153, 159
Soft, 229-230, 239
Solaris 68, 101, 108
SQMS, 7-8
SQSS, 7-8
Stack 44, 47-51, 63
Stack trace 100, 274, 281
StackOverFlowError, 48
Standard C library, 210
StandardMBean, 134-135, 140-141
Start
cold, 66-68
warm, 66-68
Stop-the-world 53, 61-63, 70-71
Swapping, 215, 243
Sweeping 55-56, 71-72, 96
Swing 65, 183, 185
Symbol table, 48
Sync, 24
System
physical 12-14, 18, 20
virtual 2, 14, 19
System call, 211, 252

T

Task Manager 14-15, 21, 24
TASK_SIZE, 212
Test environment 10-11, 126-127, 130
Threads 32, 37, 48
Throughput 4-6, 8, 16
Throughput performance law, 8
Time range, 21
TLB, 215
Top 24, 51, 57
Translation lookaside buffer, 34-35, 215
Tuning
  AggressiveOpts 74, 162, 170-171
  DoEscapeAnalysis 162, 170-171, 173
  JDBC connection pool 157-159, 161-162, 167
Turbo Boost Technology 37, 253, 255
Turbo clock rate, 37
Type
  array 47, 197, 224
  class 46-48, 52, 86
  interface 20, 29, 46-48
  numerical, 47
  primitive, 47
  reference 25, 41, 46-48
  returnAddress, 47

U

Ulimit, 229-230, 297
UMA versus NUMA, 215
Uname 218-219, 236, 297
UNIX 44-45, 48, 201-203
Unloading, 47
Use cases 126, 153, 301
UseCompressedOops 77-78, 98, 105

V

Variable table, 50
Virtual memory 22, 24, 68
Visual VM
  snapshot, 82
VisualGC 89, 92, 100-101
  Graphs, 89
  Histogram, 89
  Spaces 89, 145, 149
VisualVM 43, 65, 77
  Back Traces, 135, 143
  Call Tree, 93-94
  Classes 80, 83, 86
  Combined, 93
  CPU 80, 83, 85-87
  CPU profiling 86-87, 92, 94
  CPU sampling 86, 92-93, 132
  Heap 77, 83, 89
  heap dump, 83
  Hot Spots, 93-94
  instrumenting, 86
  invocation, 86
  jconsole 43, 65, 77
  jinfo, 82
  jstack, 82
  jstat, 82, 209
  Memory profiling 86, 88, 92
  memory sampling, 86-87, 92
  monitor 77, 82-84, 90
  offline analysis 77, 93, 162
  overhead 88, 90, 92-93
  overview 80, 82-84, 93
  Pause live results, 86
  perform GC, 83
  plugins, 89
  Profiler 83, 86, 88
  Sampler 83, 85-87, 92-93
  sampling 86-87, 92-93, 100
  self time 86, 93, 135
  settings 86, 92-93, 131
  snapshot 82, 86, 88
  Threads 80, 83-85, 93
  Time 43, 65, 77
  Update live results, 86
  VisualGC 89, 92, 100
VM slice, 12
Vmstat 22-24, 162, 233-234
Vsz 24, 235-236, 245-246

W

Web Server 8, 10, 16
Windows 2-3, 11, 14
Wmic, 14
Word, 47
Working set 19, 57-58, 69
Workload 12, 73, 76

X

X86 29, 31-32, 51
Xeon
  5550, 240
  E5620 12-13, 16, 39-40

Other texts by the same author, available on Amazon:

46093307R00195

Made in the USA
Lexington, KY
22 October 2015